English G 21

B2
für Realschulen

English G 21 • Band B 2

Im Auftrag des Verlages herausgegeben von
Prof. Hellmut Schwarz, Mannheim

Erarbeitet von
Barbara Derkow Disselbeck, Köln
Allen J. Woppert, Berlin
sowie Susan Abbey, Nenagh, Irland
Laurence Harger, Wellington, Neuseeland

unter Mitarbeit von
Wolfgang Biederstädt, Köln
Joachim Blombach, Herford
Helmut Dengler, Limbach
Jennifer Seidl, München
Andrea Ulrich, Bonn

in Zusammenarbeit mit der Englischredaktion
Kirsten Bleck (Projektleitung);
Klaus G. Unger (verantwortlicher Redakteur); Susanne Bennetreu (Bildredaktion); Dr. Philip Devlin; Bonnie S. Glänzer; Uwe Tröger *sowie* Nathalie Schwering

Beratende Mitwirkung
Uwe Chormann, Einselthum; Matthew George, Frankfurt (Main); Prof. Dr. Liesel Hermes, Karlsruhe; Bernhard Hunger, Dettingen; Gabriele Künstler, Altlußheim; Anja Bersch, Waldstetten; Sibille Renz-Noll, Schorndorf; Tobias Schumacher, Kleinfischlingen; Michael Semmler, Lünen; Karl Starkebaum, Diekholzen; Elke Storz, Freiburg i. Br.

Illustrationen
Graham-Cameron Illustration, UK: Fliss Cary, Grafikerin *sowie* Roland Beier, Berlin

Fotos
Rob Cousins, Bristol

Layoutkonzept und technische Umsetzung
Aksinia Raphael; Korinna Wilkes

Umschlaggestaltung
Klein & Halm Grafikdesign, Berlin

Für die freundliche Unterstützung danken wir der Cotham School, Bristol.

www.cornelsen.de
www.EnglishG.de

Die Links zu externen Webseiten Dritter, die in diesem Lehrwerk angegeben sind, wurden vor Drucklegung sorgfältig auf ihre Aktualität geprüft. Der Verlag übernimmt keine Gewähr für die Aktualität und den Inhalt dieser Seiten oder solcher, die mit ihnen verlinkt sind.

Dieses Werk berücksichtigt die Regeln der reformierten Rechtschreibung und Zeichensetzung.

1. Auflage, 6. Druck 2012

Alle Drucke dieser Auflage sind inhaltlich unverändert und können im Unterricht nebeneinander verwendet werden.

© 2007 Cornelsen Verlag, Berlin

Das Werk und seine Teile sind urheberrechtlich geschützt. Jede Nutzung in anderen als den gesetzlich zugelassenen Fällen bedarf der vorherigen schriftlichen Einwilligung des Verlages.
Hinweis zu den §§ 46, 52 a UrhG: Weder das Werk noch seine Teile dürfen ohne eine solche Einwilligung eingescannt und in ein Netzwerk eingestellt oder sonst öffentlich zugänglich gemacht werden. Dies gilt auch für Intranets von Schulen und sonstigen Bildungseinrichtungen.

Druck: Mohn Media Mohndruck, Gütersloh

ISBN 978-3-06-031311-2 – broschiert
ISBN 978-3-06-031361-7 – gebunden

 Inhalt gedruckt auf säurefreiem Papier aus nachhaltiger Forstwirtschaft.

Dein Englischbuch enthält folgende Teile:

Welcome back	Einstieg in das Buch – hier triffst du die Lehrwerkskinder wieder
Units	die sechs Kapitel des Buches
Topics	besondere Themen – z.B. die Geschichte von Robinson Crusoe
Skills File (SF)	Beschreibung wichtiger Lern- und Arbeitstechniken
Grammar File (GF)	Zusammenfassung der Grammatik jeder Unit
Vocabulary	Wörterverzeichnis zum Lernen der neuen Wörter jeder Unit
Dictionary	alphabetische Wörterverzeichnisse zum Nachschlagen

Die Units bestehen aus diesen Teilen:

Lead-in	Einstieg in das neue Thema
A-Section	neuer Lernstoff mit vielen Aktivitäten
Practice	Übungen
Text	eine spannende oder lustige Geschichte

In den Units findest du diese Überschriften und Symbole:

Looking at language	Hier sammelst du Beispiele und entdeckst Regeln.
STUDY SKILLS	Einführung in Lern- und Arbeitstechniken
DOSSIER	Schöne und wichtige Arbeiten kannst du in einer Mappe sammeln.
Background File	Hier findest du interessante Informationen über Land und Leute.
GAME	Spiele für zwei oder für eine Gruppe – natürlich auf Englisch
GETTING BY IN ENGLISH	Alltagssituationen üben
MEDIATION	Hier vermittelst du zwischen zwei Sprachen.
LISTENING	Aufgaben zu Hörtexten auf der CD
Now you	Hier sprichst und schreibst du über dich selbst.
POEM / SONG	Gedichte/Lieder zum Anhören und Singen
PRONUNCIATION	Ausspracheübungen
REVISION	Übungen zur Wiederholung
WORDS	Übungen zu Wortfamilien, Wortfeldern und Wortverbindungen
Checkpoint	Im Workbook kannst du dein Wissen überprüfen.
Extra	Zusätzliche Aktivitäten und Übungen
	Partnerarbeit/Gruppenarbeit
	nur auf CD / auf CD und im Schülerbuch
>	Textaufgaben

Inhalt

Seite	Unit	Sprechabsichten	Sprachliche Mittel: • grammatische Strukturen • Wortfelder	STUDY SKILLS DOSSIER
6	**Welcome back** Die Lehrwerkskinder in den Sommerferien	Über die Ferien berichten; über das Wetter sprechen	• Reisen, Verkehrsmittel, Urlaubsorte, Urlaubsaktivitäten zu Hause und unterwegs; Landschaft; Wetter	**STUDY SKILLS** Mind maps **DOSSIER** My holiday
10	**Unit 1** **Back to school** Das neue Schuljahr hat begonnen; die Lehrwerkskinder lernen eine neue Mitschülerin kennen	Bilder beschreiben; sagen, wo sich etwas befindet; über den Schulalltag sprechen; über Vergangenes berichten; neu in der Schule: sich gegenseitig vorstellen; Gefühle ausdrücken	• REVISION simple past: positive statements • simple past: negative statements, questions • Bildbeschreibung; Ortsangaben; Zeitangaben; Schule und schulische Aktivitäten; Freizeit- und häusliche Aktivitäten	**STUDY SKILLS** Describing pictures Linking words **DOSSIER** An exciting day on the beach
24	**EXTRA Topic 1** **A trip to Jamaica**	Mr. Kingsley berichtet über seinen Urlaub auf Jamaica und erzählt eine Legende aus der Karibik		
26	**Unit 2** **What money can buy** Taschengeld und andere Geldfragen; ein Schulprojekt zum Thema „Kleidung"	Sagen, wofür man sein Taschengeld ausgibt oder ob man spart; über einen schrecklichen Tag sprechen; Dinge und Personen miteinander vergleichen; etwas vorschlagen; sagen, was man besser findet	• comparison of adjectives (-er/-est, more/most) • possessive pronouns (mine, yours, ...) • REVISION some / any • Taschengeld, Kleidung, Mode, Kaufhaus; make/do; much/many–more–most	**STUDY SKILLS** Learning words Mediation **DOSSIER** A different point of view A special day in my family
40	**EXTRA Topic 2** **Special days around the world**	Besondere Feste in der englischsprachigen Welt: Guy Fawkes Day in Großbritannien • Weihnachten in Neuseeland • Holi in Indien • Independence Day in den USA		
42	**Unit 3** **Animals in the city** Eine Fernsehsendung über Tiere in der Stadt; wie Ananda das Leben von Igelbabys rettet	Über Lieblingssendungen im Fernsehen sprechen; über Zukünftiges sprechen; sagen, was unter einer bestimmten Bedingung passieren wird; sagen, wie man bestimmte Dinge macht; über den Umgang mit Tieren sprechen	• will-future • conditional sentences (1) • adverbs of manner • REVISION comparison of adjectives • EXTRA comparison of adverbs • Fernsehsendungen, Haustiere, frei lebende Tiere in der Stadt, Zootiere; Adverbien der Art und Weise	**STUDY SKILLS** Listening Scanning Multiple-choice exercises **DOSSIER** Animals Pet of the day
56	**EXTRA Topic 3** **Animal songs and poems**	Lieder und Gedichte über Tiere		

Inhalt

Seite	Unit	Sprechabsichten	Sprachliche Mittel: • grammatische Strukturen • Wortfelder	STUDY SKILLS DOSSIER
58	**Unit 4** **A weekend in Wales** Dan und Jo sind zu Besuch bei den Großeltern; Dan wird krank und nicht alles läuft wie geplant.	Stadt/Land beschreiben, über Unterschiede sprechen; sagen, was man gerade/schon/noch nicht gemacht hat; sagen, dass man sich nicht wohl fühlt/was einem fehlt; sich nach dem Befinden anderer erkundigen; über ein Ereignis berichten	• REVISION word order (S–V–O) • word order *place – time* • present perfect • REVISION conditional sentences (1) • Stadt, Land, Reisen; Sehenswürdigkeiten; Körperteile, Krankheiten; technische Anweisungen (Computer); Verkehrsunfall	**STUDY SKILLS** Topic sentence **DOSSIER** A special place
73	**EXTRA Topic 4** **The red dragon and the white dragon**	Die Sage von Merlin und warum der walisische Drachen rot ist		
74	**Unit 5** **Teamwork** Wie gut kennen die Lehrwerkskinder Bristol? Sie nehmen an einem Bristol-Quiz teil und erstellen eine Broschüre.	Ein Brettspiel spielen; sagen, was man zu tun beabsichtigt, über (Zukunfts-)Pläne sprechen; im Café/in der Eisdiele etwas bestellen; sagen und begründen, warum man etwas gut/nicht gut findet	• *going to*-future • REVISION present perfect; adverbs of manner • EXTRA question tags with *be* • Spielewortschatz; Aktivitäten in der Stadt; Pläne	**STUDY SKILLS** Marking up a text Structuring a text **DOSSIER** Lesley's diary
89	**EXTRA Topic 5** **Robinson Crusoe**	Die Abenteuer von Robinson Crusoe und seinem treuen Gefährten Freitag		
92	**Unit 6** **A trip to Bath** Die Klasse 8PK macht einen Ausflug ins benachbarte Bath und besucht historische Sehenswürdigkeiten.	Sagen, wie man etwas empfunden hat; Gespräche führen; nach dem Weg fragen und den Weg beschreiben; sagen, was man zu einem bestimmten Zeitpunkt in der Vergangenheit gemacht hat	• REVISION *going to*-future; present progressive • past progressive • Schulausflug; Fahrradtour; Wegbeschreibung; *mustn't/needn't*	**STUDY SKILLS** Talking to people Correcting mistakes **DOSSIER** A school trip
106	**EXTRA Topic 6** **Dan and Jo's summer holidays in New Zealand**	Dan und Jo planen einen Besuch bei ihrer Mutter in Neuseeland		

108 Partner B
112 Skills File
124 Grammar File (Lösungen auf S. 139)
140 Grammatical terms
141 Vocabulary

168 Dictionary (English – German)
189 Dictionary (German – English)
205 English Sounds / The English alphabet
206 Names / Countries and continents
208 Irregular verbs
210 Classroom English
211 Arbeitsanweisungen

Welcome back – After the holidays

1 🎧

15th August

Dear Jack
We travelled to Cornwall on Saturday. There were no holiday flats, so we're in a caravan by the sea.
On Monday it was cold and windy and rainy, but yesterday it was hot and sunny. We went swimming and met a nice girl on the beach!

Dan Jo

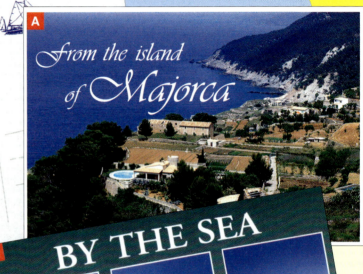

A – from the island of Majorca

B – BY THE SEA

2 🎧

Dear Sophie

We're staying at home this summer, but here's a funny postcard for you anyway! Last week it was warm and sunny, so I went into town and watched some street theatre. It was great. I took lots of photos. There's a nice French family here this week. Yesterday it was cool but sunny, so I went for a walk in the country with the French boy.
It was fun – really! Call me when you get back.

Jack

3 🎧

Dear Danandjo!

This city is so great! This was the view from the plane as we flew in on Monday. We went on a boat trip yesterday – all round Manhattan. We saw a lot! It was cloudy, but that was good: it's very very hot when the sun shines!

See you soon.
Ananda

To:
From:
Sent:

4

Dear Ananda

It's great here. The weather is fantastic – blue sky and hot sun every day. And we've got a house and our own pool! On Sunday we were in the mountains. We went there by car. Yesterday we rode our bikes to the beach because Emily wanted to see 'something new' (boys of course!).
But I think it's more fun at our pool, so that's where I am today!
Lots of love
Sophie

1 The cards

a) Read the cards. Match the messages to the pictures. Give reasons for your choice.
Dan and Jo write about the sea and a beach in Cornwall. Card B shows a beach. I think card B is from Dan and Jo.

b) Collect holiday words and phrases from the cards.

places	weather	how they travelled
by the sea	cold	by car

c) Extra   Add more words and phrases.

▶ SF Learning words – Step 1 (p. 113) • WB 1–2 (p. 1)

2 Your holidays – at home or away?

Make appointments with three students.
Ask each other about the summer holidays.

1 Where were you?
2 Was it nice?
3 What was the weather like?
4 Were you in a hotel/ holiday flat/house/caravan?

My appointments
1 o'clock   Marek
2 o'clock   ...
3 o'clock   ...

We were in a village ...

Yes, it was very nice.

We were in a house.

It was sunny and ...

8 Welcome back

3 What's the weather like in ...?

a) Go to the maps of Britain and Europe on the inside covers. Find the countries in the box below.

> Belgium • Denmark • England • France • Germany • Italy • Poland • Scotland • Spain • The Netherlands • Wales

b) Partner B: Ask questions about the weather in these countries.
Partner A: Look at the weather map. Answer Partner B's questions. Swap after five questions.

B: What's the weather like in Spain?
A: It's 29 degrees and sunny in Spain.

sunny
foggy
windy
cloudy
stormy
rainy
temperature

4 Holiday weather

a) The Millers are on their summer holidays. Listen to the CD. Use a copy of the chart. Tick who wants to do what.

	mum	Barry	Laura
day in the country			
day in town			
day on the beach			

b) Listen. Take notes on the weather for today and tomorrow. What plans can the three make for today? And for tomorrow?

today	tomorrow
cloudy start	...
...	

▶ WB 3–4 (p. 2)

5 Extra ACTIVITY

Make a weather calendar for your classroom. You can change it every day.

Welcome back

6 A holiday diary 🎧

Dear Diary
It's holiday time and the house is empty. My family isn't here. They went abroad, but I had to stay at home alone. It rained last night and it's cold and cloudy today. And it's very boring.
Well, it isn't boring all the time …
On Friday I played in every room and nobody grumbled. That was fun!
On Saturday I spoke to Uncle Henry. Then we played tennis – in the afternoon. That was fun too. Yesterday I listened to all Emily's CDs and then I threw them on the floor. Then I tried on all Emily's clothes and put them in the fridge. And then I read all Emily's magazines and put them in Toby's room.
Yesterday was great! Hee, hee, hee.

> Who is writing the diary? Where does she live? What did she do in the holidays? Find at least four things.

7 Now you

a) Collect ideas for a diary entry about your holiday. The ideas can be about a real holiday or a dream holiday.

b) Use your mind map and write one page about your (dream) holiday. You can add pictures or maps.

STUDY SKILLS Mind maps

Denk daran: **Mind maps** können dir helfen, Ideen zu sammeln und zu ordnen.

▶ SF Mind maps (p. 114) • WB 5 (p. 3)

DOSSIER My holiday

I went on holiday to Italy. My family and I went by car. We were by a little lake in the mountains and stayed in a big flat. It was hot and sunny, so I went swimming every day. And I ate lots of spaghetti! I met a nice girl from Holland – we often played tennis. Here is a picture of the lake. It's very beautiful.

DOSSIER My dream holiday
I flew to Mars. It was very hot and the people were very interesting: they were green, and their eyes …

Unit 1

Welcome to Cotham School

1

2

4

5

© Cotham School
All Rights Reserved.

Back to school

1 👥 Talking about school
a) *What do you remember about Cotham School?*
A: At Cotham they've got a Dance Club.
B: Yes, and they've got a Junior Band. ...

b) **Extra** *Compare Cotham School with your school. What's different?*

2 Describing pictures 🎧

STUDY SKILLS | **Describing pictures**

Um ein Bild zu beschreiben, musst du sagen können, wo sich etwas genau befindet. Am besten gehst du dabei in einer bestimmten Reihenfolge vor, z.B. von unten nach oben oder von vorne nach hinten.

3

6

👥 *Listen to the photo descriptions. There are two mistakes in each description. What are they?*
Photo 1: The man says the teacher is helping a girl. But she's helping a boy. And ...

3 Find the red balls
Say where the red balls are in the photos. You can use the words in the box and the words from **2**.
In photo 1 there's a red ball ...

behind • between • in front of • next to • under

▶ SF Describing pictures (p. 115) • P 1–4 (pp. 16–17) • WB 1–4 (pp. 4–6)

1 Friends meet again 🎧

Jack	Tell me about New York, Ananda.
Ananda	Oh, Jack, it was so fantastic. We stayed with my aunt and uncle – they were really great, the weather was great, …
Jack	You were there with Dilip, right?
Ananda	Well, we flew there together, but he came back a week before me.
Jack	Was the flight OK?
Ananda	Well, it was my first time on a plane, so I was a bit nervous. But it wasn't scary. Not like the subway – that was scary!
Jack	Yeah, I heard that the underground is dangerous.
Ananda	No, not dangerous – just very fast.
Jack	Oh look, there's Sophie.

Sophie	Hi, you two. So, what was the best thing about New York, Ananda?
Ananda	The Empire State Building! We took the elevator – oops, that was American English again. We took the lift to the top. It's amazing! You can see for miles and …

▷ Why is Ananda so excited? What two American English words does Ananda use?

▶ P 5–6 (p. 18) • WB 5–9 (pp. 6–8)

Extra Background File

The Empire State Building
The building is 443.2 metres high and has got 102 floors, 73 lifts, 1,860 steps and 6,500 windows.
The fastest lift in the building travels over 7 metres in one second.
From the observatory on the 86th floor, you can see over 120 kilometres on a clear day.
Every year there's a run up to the observatory. The best runners can do it in 10 minutes.
To find out more, visit the building's website at www.esbnyc.com.

Looking at language

Revision
Ananda talks about what happened in the past.
– Find the **simple past** forms of *(to) be* in **1**.
– Find the **simple past** of *(to) stay*. How do you make the **simple past** form of regular verbs?
– Look at the irregular simple past forms (*flew, came, heard, took*). What are the infinitives?

▶ GF 1: Simple past, positive statements (pp. 125–126)

2 A new girl 🎧

When they got to their classroom, the friends saw a girl at the back of the room.

Sophie   Hi! I'm Sophie and this is Ananda. Are you new?
Lesley   Of course I'm new.
Ananda   What's your name?
Lesley   Lesley.
Sophie   Hi, Lesley. Where are you from?
Lesley   Mind your own business. I didn't want to come here, you know.
Sophie   I don't come from Bristol, Lesley, and I didn't want to come here. But I really like it here now.
Lesley   Oh, just go away!

Ananda and Sophie went back to the group.

Ananda   She doesn't like us, Sophie.
Jo   Why? What happened?
Sophie   Well, she didn't say much.
Ananda   And after she said 'Mind your own business' we didn't ask her much!
Jack   Wow! That was rude of her!
Dan   Maybe she was nervous or …
Jo   Yeah, yeah.
Jack   Hey, here comes Mr Kingsley.

▸ What can you say about the new girl?

Looking at language

Find all the negative sentences in **2**. Make two lists, one for the **simple present**, one for the **simple past**. How do you make the negative form of the **simple past**?

▸ GF 2: Negative statements (p. 126) • P 7–9 (p. 19) • WB 10–13 (pp. 9–11)

3 Now you

a) How is school time different from your holidays? Make sentences like these: *I usually get up early. In the holidays I didn't get up early.* Here are some more ideas:

> do my homework • eat a big lunch •
> go to bed at 9 o'clock • go to school •
> only watch TV for an hour •
> work in the afternoons

b) 👥 Tell a partner.

4 Lunch break 🎧

Dan	The food is better this year.
Jack	Do you really think so?
Dan	Yes, I do. This veggie burger is very good.
Sophie	It's fish, Dan.
Dan	Oh ... Hey, I don't see that new girl.
Jo	Well, she's right behind you.
Dan	Maybe she'd like to eat with us.
All	No way!
Dan	Come on, she's new. Try to be nice!
Jo	Did she try to be nice to Sophie and Ananda this morning? No, she didn't. Did she talk to them? No, she didn't.
Dan	Did *you* talk to *her*, Jo? No, you didn't. Or, when we were on holiday, did *you* help when Jody was in trouble? No, you didn't. But you wanted to be the big hero anyway.
Jack	Hey Dan, calm down.
Dan	I don't want to calm down. I'm going outside.
Sophie	Why did Dan get so angry?
Jack	Yeah, and who's Jody?
Jo	Oh, it's nothing. Let's eat.

Looking at language

'Do you really think so?' is a question in the **simple present**. Look at **4**. Find questions in the **simple past**. How do you make them?

5 Now you

a) What did you do on your last birthday? Write down five things.

b) 👥 Ask different partners what they did on their last birthday. Find somebody who did three of the same things as you.

▶ GF 3: Questions (p. 126) • P 10–14 (pp. 20–21) • WB 14–18 (p. 11–13)

6 A role play 🎧

a) *How can you complete the dialogue? Think of ideas.*
A: Hi, my name is … Are you new here?
B: Yes, I am. My name is …
A: Well, welcome to … School.
B: Thanks. What are the teachers like?
A: Most of them are OK/nice/…
What school did you go to last year?
B: I went to … School.
A: And where do you live?
B: We've got a flat/… in … What about you?
A: I live in a … in …
B: I really like football/shopping/… Have you got any hobbies?
A: Yes, I have. I like …
B: Great. Maybe we can … together.
A: Good idea.

b) **Extra** *Listen to the dialogues.*
Which dialogue did you like best? Why?
I liked the first/… dialogue best.
It was easy/funny/…
The students had lots of good ideas.
It was very fast/…

c) 👥 *Prepare the dialogue in a) with a partner. Act it out for your class.*

▶ P 15 (p. 21) • WB 19 (p. 13)

7 Extra SONG Hooray for friends! 🎧

Sophie is my friend,
We laugh and play and run.
Sophie is my friend,
She's clever and she's fun!

Chorus
Hooray, hooray for friends!
Friends are really great!
Hooray, hooray for friends!
There's nothing like a mate!

Caspar is my friend,
We laugh and play and run.
Caspar is my mate,
He's clever and he's fun!

Chorus
…

Maria/Tobias/… is my friend,
…

Chorus
…

16 1 Practice

1 WORDS School

a) Make lists like these. Choose words and phrases from the box.

Things in my school bag	Things in the classroom	School subjects	What I do at school	Sports
book	CD player…	Art	answer questions	basketball
…		…	…	…

answer questions • Art • basketball • Biology • book • CD player • chair • computer • cupboard • desk • do an exercise • do a project • Drama • English • exercise book • felt tip • football • French • Geography • German • History • hockey • listen to the CD • look at the board • Maths • Music • paint pictures • PE • pen • pencil • pencil case • pencil sharpener • play with my classmates • practise pronunciation • RE • read • rubber • ruler • Science • sing songs • spell • swimming • talk to my friend • talk to the teacher • tennis • timetable • volleyball • work with a partner

b) Extra Write about one of these topics. You can use words and phrases from your lists.

A day in the life of my school bag   or   _A day at school_
I'm Pia's school bag. In the morning, Pia puts lots   A: Hi Ben. How was school today?
of books in me. Her mother gives me a sandwich box.   B: Oh, we had a really easy day. First, we had PE.
Then we take the bus to school. The first lesson …   And then we …

2 WORDS Where's the black cat?

a) Say where the black cat is. For each picture, decide which answer is correct.

1 behind the orange cat
2 in front of the orange cat

3 next to the cupboard
4 near the cupboard

5 between the armchairs
6 under an armchair

7 in the middle
8 on the right

9 inside
10 outside

11 at the top of the tree
12 at the bottom of the tree

b) Say where the orange cat is – and where the mouse is.

3 LISTENING Aliens at school 🎧

*You're playing a computer game with your friend – 'Aliens at school'.
You have to find all the aliens in the classroom.*

a) Look at the picture. Say where you see aliens.
There are two aliens on … There's one alien in front of …

b) Your friend knows where there are more aliens. Listen to him on the CD and look.

c) Listen again. Draw the other aliens on a copy of the picture.

d) **Extra** 👥 Check with a partner. Don't show your picture. Say: There's an alien in front of the …

4 👥 SKILLS Describing pictures

Partner B: Go to p. 108.

a) Partner A: Draw a picture with a house, two people, two trees and a ball. (There are two examples on the right.)

b) Describe your picture to your partner. (Don't show him/her your picture!)
There's a house in the middle. On the right, there are …
Your partner draws the picture.
Then compare the two pictures.

c) Now your partner describes his/her picture and you draw it. Then compare.

5 PRONUNCIATION (Vowel sounds)

a) Say these words. Look at the sound balls. Match the balls to the goals.

bird ...	fair ...	hear ...
heard ...	their ...	here ...
hurt ...	where ...	year ...

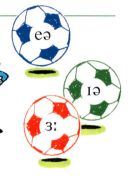

b) Make a copy of the word lists. Add these words to the correct list:
hair, dear, ear, girl, first, her, near, share, they're

c) Listen and check.

d) **Extra** Give your partner a word. He or she must give you a rhyming word for it.

6 WRITING Linking words

a) Copy the flow chart. Put the verbs in brackets in the simple past and complete the story.

 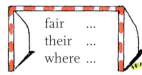 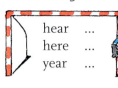 

| **After breakfast** Ms Travelot *rode* (ride) her ... to her ... | **At 10 o'clock** she ... (go) to Dover by ... | She ... (get on) a ... there and ... (take) it to Dover station. | She ... (be) late, so she ... (run) to the train. |

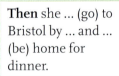   

| **Then** she ... (go) to Bristol by ... and ... (be) home for dinner. | **An hour later** she ... (get on) a ... and ... (fly) to Leeds. | **After that** she ... (take) the ... | She ... (take) the ... to London and ... (get off) there. |

b) Make a flow chart with 8 boxes. Use linking words to write what you did last Saturday. If you need ideas, look at the green box.

help my mother • listen to music • make a model • call Eva • play basketball • meet my friends • ride my bike • go swimming

STUDY SKILLS Linking words

Wenn du beschreiben willst, in welcher Reihenfolge etwas passiert ist, helfen dir Zeitangaben (Englisch: **time phrases**) wie
after breakfast/lunch/..., *at 10 o'clock*, *after that*, *an hour later*, *then* usw.

▶ SF Linking words (p. 121)

Practice **1** 19

7 Extra REVISION **The Grumbles** (Simple present: negative statements)

a) Greg, Griselda, Graham and Grandma Grumble are very negative: everything is wrong for them.
Write down their sentences.

1 Greg: The sun ☹ shine when we go out.
The sun doesn't shine when we ...
2 Griselda: My friends ☹ call me.
3 Grandma: Griselda ☹ listen to nice music on the radio.
4 Graham: Dad ☹ take me to school when I ask him.
5 Greg: No, Graham, but you ☹ say 'please' or 'thank you'.
6 Grandma: The neighbours ☹ talk to us.
7 Griselda: Well, they ☹ like us, Grandma!

b) And the Grumbles grumble when they go on holiday too.
What do you think they say? Make four more sentences. Here are some ideas:
friend's dog – like me   people at the shop – talk English   bus – stop near our hotel

8 Grandma Grumble is grumbling (Simple past: positive and negative statements)

a) Grandma Grumble was away in London yesterday.
Before she went, she made a list of nine jobs.
Listen. Which three jobs did Graham, Greg and
Griselda do? Write them down.

b) Say what the Grumbles did – and what they
didn't do.
Graham tidied the living room. But he didn't ...

c) Extra Make two short lists.

What I did last week	What I didn't do last week
I helped my dad in the garden. ...	I didn't go shopping. ...

9 Are you a good detective? (Simple past: positive and negative statements)

Are you a good detective? Find out what's wrong. You can check on pp. 12–13.

1 Ananda went to London in her holidays.
Ananda didn't go to London – she went to New York.
2 She went there by boat.
3 She stayed with her grandparents.
4 Dilip went to Germany in his holidays.
5 Sophie and Ananda talked to the new boy.
6 Lesley said 'Hi!'
7 Sophie and Ananda stayed with Lesley.
8 Mr Kingsley went out.

10 REVISION Is your partner a music person? (Simple present: yes/no questions)

a) What do you think: Is your partner a music person? Fill in a copy of the chart.
Does he/she …

1. … do his/her homework with music on?
2. … sometimes sing in the shower?
3. … read about pop stars in magazines?
4. … often take an MP3 player to school?
5. … play the piano or sing in a choir?
6. … sometimes listen to live music?

	I think	Partner's answer
1	Yes	…
2	…	
3		
4		
5		
6		

I'm a music person.

b) Now ask your partner the questions.
Fill in his/her answers in the chart.
A: Do you do your homework with music on?
B: Yes, I do. / No, I don't.
Were you right or wrong?

11 Did you or didn't you? (Simple past: yes/no questions)

Use the chart and ask a partner at least six questions. He/She gives short answers.

Did	you your father your mother your parents your pet your … …	watch … play … listen to … call … eat … wear … read … go to … …	yesterday? two days ago? last Saturday? in the holidays?

A: Did you watch TV yesterday?
B: Yes, I did. / No I didn't. /
   I don't remember.
B: Did your grandparents do sport last week?
A: Yes, they did. / No, they didn't. /
   I don't know.

12 Find somebody who … (Simple past: yes/no questions)

a) Copy these questions. Write three more.

1 Did you stay at home in the holidays?
2 Did you go abroad?
3 Did you go to the mountains?
4 Did you do something new?
5 Did you play basketball?

b) Find somebody who did number **1**. Write down his/her name. Now find somebody who did numbers **2**, **3**, etc.

c) Report to your partner.
Oliver stayed at home.
Anna went abroad in the holidays. She was …

13 Questions, questions, questions! (Simple past: wh-questions)

Ask questions with question words (*what, where, when, why*).
1 Mum: *What did* you *do* (do) at school today?
  Tom: Not much.
2 *What* subjects ... you ... (have)?
  – Well, we had French, Maths, History and Geography this morning.
3 And ... you ... (do) in the afternoon?
  – We went to the library.
4 ... the trip ... (finish)?
  – At 3 o'clock.
5 And ... you ... (go) after that?
  – I went into town with some friends.
6 ... you ... (buy)?
  – A goldfish.
7 ... you ... (buy) a goldfish?
  – Because the piranhas were too expensive.

14 👥 Yesterday afternoon (Simple past: wh-questions)

a) Partner B: Go to p. 108. Partner A: Ask your partner about the gaps in your chart. Fill in a copy of the chart. Then answer your partner's questions.

	Where did ... go?	How ... go?	What ... do?	When ... go to bed?
Ananda		by bike	help her mum + watch TV	
Dan and Jo	the Downs	by bike		9.30
Jack				9.30
Sophie	the library		read a book	
You				
Your partner				

b) Fill in the answers for 'you' in your chart. Ask your partner and add his/her answers.

c) Write about your partner or one of the Bristol kids. Then swap and check.

15 GETTING BY IN ENGLISH At school today

a) Can you say these things in English?
1 Das geht dich nichts an. (p. 13)
2 Das war unverschämt! (p. 13)
3 Wieso? Was ist passiert? (p. 13)
4 Auf keinen Fall! (p. 14)
5 Beruhige dich. (p. 14)
6 Warum ist Dan so böse geworden? (p. 14)

b) 👥 Prepare the dialogue. Act it out. The colours show you where you can use phrases from a).

Partner A

Erzähl B, dass es in eurer Klasse einen neuen Jungen gibt. Er ist nicht sehr nett.

Du hast ihn nach seinem Namen gefragt. Er sagte: „Das geht dich nichts an."

Du wurdest auch böse. Aber dann hast du dich beruhigt. Vielleicht würde der Junge gerne mit euch spielen.

Partner B

Frag A, was passiert ist.

Das war wirklich unverschämt, findest du.

Das willst du auf keinen Fall!

Saved! 🎧

▶ *Look at the pictures. Where and when do you think the story takes place?*

The sun came through the window of the caravan. Dan opened his eyes and looked round. His dad was still asleep. From the top bunk Dan could hear the 'bleep bleep' of
5   a gameboy.
'Hi, Jo,' he whispered.
'Hi, Dan!' Jo said. 'Breakfast?'
'Good idea!' said Dan.
Dan made the tea and some toast, Jo went and
10 got milk.
'Mmm, is that breakfast?' Mr Shaw said.
'Morning, Dad. Can we pull out the table?'
'Yes, please!'

After breakfast they went to Hayle Beach.
15 'Do you want to go swimming, boys?' Mr Shaw asked.
'Yeah!' Jo said.
'Come on, then! Let's go before the tide starts to go out – it's much too dangerous then.'

20 As they came out of the water, Dan saw Jody. He and Jo sometimes talked to her when they met her on the beach.
'Hi, Jody!' Dan called.
'Who's that?' Mr Shaw asked.
25 'That's Jody. She's really nice, Dad,' Dan said.
'She's staying in the village with her aunt,' Jo said. 'What about a game of football, Jody?' he called.
'Maybe, but I want to go swimming first. See
30 you!' She ran into the sea.

Jo went to get the football. Soon lots of other people came to play with the Shaws.
'Dan!' his dad shouted. But it was too late: the ball flew past Dan and one of the others had it.

'Oh, Dan!' Jo grumbled.   35
'It's Jody,' Dan said. 'Look, she's so far away. And the tide is going out too.'
'Don't worry! She's a good swimmer.' Jo went back to the game. But Dan looked out to sea again. Suddenly, Jody started to wave.   40
'Oh, no! She's in trouble. Dad! Dad!' Dan shouted.
'Dan, the ball!' It was Jo, but Dan didn't hear him.
'Dad,' Dan shouted, 'we have to do something.   45
Look!'
Mr Shaw looked out to sea. Other people looked out to sea too. One man had binoculars.
'The boy's right. That swimmer is in trouble,' he said.   50
'Dad, where's your mobile? We have to call the lifeboat,' Dan said.
'Right,' Mr Shaw said. He called 999.
'Lifeboat, please,' he said.

55 A few minutes later the man with the binoculars shouted, 'There's the lifeboat! It's coming from St Ives, I can see it.'
'But where's Jody? I can't see Jody!' Dan was really scared.

ST IVES TIMES

Bristol twins save girl

Photo: R. Cousins

On Tuesday, 21st August the St Ives lifeboat went out to save a young swimmer, Jody Brooks, 14, from London. 'I'm a good swimmer,' the teenager said, 'But I didn't know about the tides.'
'I saw her swim out,' said Jo Shaw, 13, from Bristol. 'And then I saw her wave. "She's in trouble because the tide is going out!" I said to my dad. So he called the lifeboat.'
The story had a happy ending: the lifeboat got to Jody in time.
'The lifeboatmen saved my life,' Jody said, 'And the twins!'

60 'It's all right,' the man said. 'I can see her. But she isn't waving now. Maybe she's too tired. Now the lifeboat is almost there ... it's there. Oh, I can't see her ... Wait ... they've got her, now they're pulling her out, but ...'
65 'Dad, do you think Jody's OK?' asked Dan. 'Can we drive to St Ives and see her? Please, Dad.'
'Come on then,' said Mr Shaw.

Working with the text

The story

a) Correct this report on the text. Write it down.
Dan and Jo Shaw and their class were at a caravan park. After lunch they went to Duckpool Beach. They met Jody Brooks, 12, from Chester. Jody went surfing and the twins started to play volleyball. Then Jo saw Jody on her surfboard in the water. She was in big trouble. The teacher called 110. Twenty minutes later the police pulled the girl out of the water.

b) There are differences between the story and the newspaper report. Find examples. These questions can help you:
– What does Dan do? What does Jo say?
– Who worries about Jody? Who doesn't?

DOSSIER An exciting day on the beach

Write a short text about an exciting day on the beach. Before you start, make a list of your ideas. Then look back at the Skills box on p. 18. Remember that you can use time phrases to link your sentences.

▶ SF Linking words (p. 121) • WB 20 (p. 14)
▶ SF Stop – check – go (p. 112)   **Checkpoint 1**   ▶ WB (p. 15)

Extra A trip to Jamaica

1 Mr Kingsley's talk
Mr Kingsley is telling Form 8PK about his trip to Jamaica in the Caribbean.

a) Write down these questions about Jamaica:
What sort of place is it? What's the weather like? What can you see there?
Now listen to the CD. Take notes about Mr Kingsley's talk. Use the questions as headings.

b) 👥 Compare your notes with a partner.

Topic **1** 25

**2 Anansi and the calabash of wisdom –
an Afro-Caribbean legend** 🎧

a) *Look at the pictures. Describe what Anansi the
spider is doing. You can use words from the box.*

| sitting • green and yellow calabash • asking •
climbing • front • talking • back • throwing |

b) *Now listen to the CD.*

c) *Now retell the story in your own words.
The pictures can help you.*

Unit 2
What money can buy

Where does your pocket money go?

Last month we asked our readers:
1. How do you spend your pocket money?
2. Do you save any of your pocket money?

Lots of readers answered our questions. Here are the results of the survey.

1 Our readers spend their money on …

Food and drink

Clothes

Free-time activities

42 Hi! • September

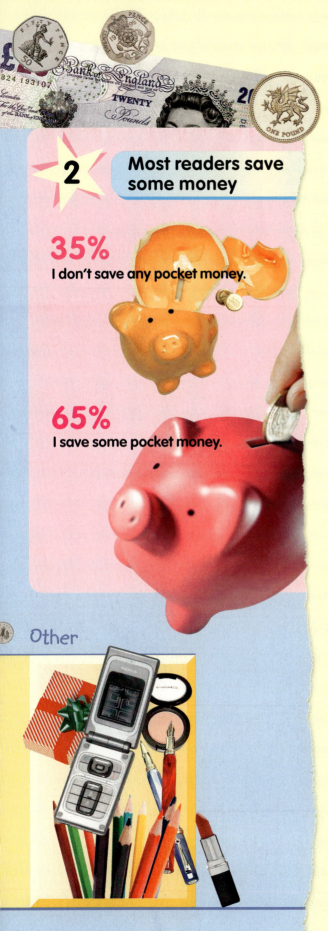

2 Most readers save some money

35% I don't save any pocket money.

65% I save some pocket money.

Other

1 Talking about shopping

a) *Talk about what you bought last week.*
A: What did you buy last week?
B: Well, I bought … And what did you buy?

b) *Look at the magazine page. Then put the words from the box in these groups: food and drinks, free-time activities, clothes, other. Add more words to the groups.*

blouse • cap • chips • cinema ticket • comic • crisps • dress • jacket • magazine • make-up • pens and pencils • present • pullover • shirt • skirt • sports gear • sweets • (pair of) trainers • (pair of) trousers

STUDY SKILLS | **Learning words – Step 2**

*Vokabeln kannst du dir besser merken, wenn du sie in **Wortfeldern** lernst. Um ein Wortfeld zusammenzustellen, brauchst du erst einen Oberbegriff **(group word)**.*
Bei cousin, aunt *und* married *zum Beispiel ist der Oberbegriff* **family**.

▶ SF Learning words – Step 2 (p. 113) • P 1 (p. 32) • WB 1 (p. 16)

2 Extra GAME

Choose something from the box in 1b). Describe where it is in the picture. Can your partner find it?
A: What is it? It's under 'clothes', near the top, on the right. It's orange.
B: The dress! What is it? It's …

3 Where does *your* pocket money go?

a) *Ask your partner questions.*
– What do you buy with your pocket money?
– Who goes shopping with you?
– What do your parents buy for you?
– Do you save any of your pocket money?

b) *Tell the class about your partner.*
Maria usually buys … with her pocket money.
She saves … every week.
…

▶ P2 (p. 32) • WB 2–3 (pp. 16–17)

1 Who needs money? 🎧

Prunella   What's the matter, Sophie?
Sophie   I had an awful day!
Prunella   Mine was awful too.
Sophie   Oh – tell me about it.
Prunella   No, tell me about yours first.
Sophie   Well, everybody was fed up. Jack's mum lost her job yesterday. So he was really fed up. And then Ananda and Dilip argued about lunch money …
Prunella   Whose lunch money – his or hers?
Sophie   Hers.
Prunella   So, why did they argue?
Sophie   It disappeared. 'You lost your lunch money!' he shouted. 'No, somebody took it!' she shouted.
Prunella   Just like you and Emily! Hee hee hee!
Sophie   It isn't funny, Prunella!
Prunella   Why not?
Sophie   My parents have lots of money – theirs don't, OK?
Prunella   OK, OK. So who needs money? I don't!
Sophie   Well, I do! I want to buy a new book on Saturday.

▷ Why was Sophie's day awful?

2 👥 SONG Chair rap 🎧
Make groups of four. Do the rap with one partner.

This chair is yours, that chair is mine.
Yeah, that's fine, yeah, that's fine!
This chair is hers, that chair is his.
Yes, it is, yes, it is!
These chairs are ours, those chairs are theirs.
Make new pairs, make new pairs!

Go on with a different partner.
This bag/… is yours, that bag is …

▶ P 3–5 (pp. 32–33) • WB 4–7 (pp. 17–19)

3 👥 Now you
Make notes about a bad day at school.
Then write a short dialogue with your partner.
Act it out.

- Why? What happened?
- Tell me about your day.
- I lost …
- I argued with …
- Somebody took …
- We had a Maths test …
- I had an awful day.

4 Money problems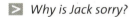

'Can I have some money, Mum?' Jack asked. Mrs Hanson looked up from her newspaper. 'What for, Jack?' she asked.
Jack was quiet for a moment. 'Well, I need a new pair of trainers. They can be cheap. But my old ones are too small. I'm sorry, Mum.'
'Don't be sorry, dear,' his mum said. 'Kids grow.'
'But I know we haven't got much money right now,' Jack said.
'Yes, we had more money when I had a job. But we've still got more than lots of other people. And there's enough for most things.'
'Do you think you can find a new job, Mum?' Jack pointed to the newspaper.
'Well, there aren't many jobs in the paper for me at the moment,' his mum said.
'But I'm sure I can find something soon.'

> Why is Jack sorry?

▶ P 6–8 (pp. 33–34) • WB 8–11 (pp. 19–21)

5 Extra How much can you buy for £10?

> What do 'Q' and 'A' mean?

6 Now you
a) *Think:* What do you buy every week? Write everything down.

b) *Pair:* Compare lists with your partner. Agree on a shopping list for €10. How can you save?

c) *Share:* Compare your shopping list with another pair. Who can buy more for €10?

7 ACTIVITY A shopping diary
a) Keep a diary about what you buy next week. Write down how much you pay for everything.

b) Compare your diaries at the end of the week.

8 Ananda's letter to her grandma 🎧

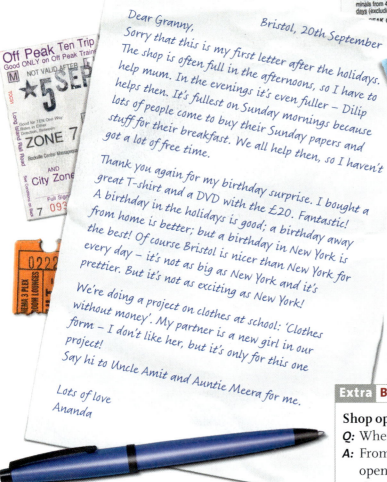

Bristol, 20th September

Dear Granny,

Sorry that this is my first letter after the holidays. The shop is often full in the afternoons, so I have to help mum. In the evenings it's even fuller – Dilip helps then. It's fullest on Sunday mornings because lots of people come to buy their Sunday papers and stuff for their breakfast. We all help then, so I haven't got a lot of free time.

Thank you again for my birthday surprise. I bought a great T-shirt and a DVD with the £20. Fantastic! A birthday in the holidays is good; a birthday away from home is better; but a birthday in New York is the best! Of course Bristol is nicer than New York for every day – it's not as big as New York and it's prettier. But it's not as exciting as New York!

We're doing a project on clothes at school: 'Clothes without money'. My partner is a new girl in our form – I don't like her, but it's only for this one project!

Say hi to Uncle Amit and Auntie Meera for me.

Lots of love
Ananda

> What was Granny's birthday surprise?
> Who is Ananda's partner for the clothes project?

Extra Background File

Shop opening hours in Britain

Q: When are the shops open in Britain?
A: From Mondays to Saturdays, shops can open when they want. On Sundays, big shops can open for six hours.
Q: What about smaller shops?
A: They can open when they want.
Q: Can I go shopping late at night?
A: Most big shops close at 7 or 8 pm, but corner shops are often open till 11 pm.

Looking at language

How do you say 'Bristol ist schöner als New York' und 'Es ist nicht so groß wie New York'?

Copy and complete.

full	fuller	fullest
...	...	nicest
pretty	...	...
good	...	...

▶ GF 4a, 4c, 4d: Comparison of adjecsstives (pp. 127–128) • P 9–11 (p. 35) • WB 12–13 (pp. 21–22)

9 GAME

In groups of three make comparisons.

dog/cat/... • bike • book • essay • hair • school bag • T-shirt	big • fast • full • good • long • new • old • pretty • small

A: My cat is fast.
B: My rabbit is faster.
C: But my dog is the fastest. My turn. My ...

10 Project ideas 🎧

Ananda — What can you do with clothes? You put them on, you wear them, you take them off. Not very interesting.
Lesley — No.
Ananda — Why don't we do a report on poor people and their clothes?
Lesley — Boring.
Ananda — Then what about a poster?
Lesley — That's even more boring.
Ananda — Maybe we can write about clothes at a charity shop.
Lesley — I thought your other ideas were boring. But that one's the most boring.
Ananda — OK, so what ideas have you got?
Lesley — Recycling.
Ananda — What about it?
Lesley — You are slow. Clothes with recycled stuff.
Ananda — Like a dress from old newspapers?
Lesley — Maybe.
Ananda — Mmm, I like that.
Lesley — So let's do it.

▷ Who has got more ideas for the project?
Who has got the best idea?

11 👥 Now you

Think about these questions:
– What's the most boring subject at school?
– What's the most exciting TV show?
– What's the most terrible football team?
Say what you think. Talk about it in your group.
You can use the phrases in the box.

> I think • I agree with you • I don't agree •
> I think … is more boring/… than …

▶ GF 4b–d: Comparison of adjectives (more/most) (pp. 127–128) •
P 12–15 (pp. 36–37) • WB 14–19 (pp. 22–25)

12 Extra POEM Why is it? 🎧

Why is it some mornings
Your clothes just don't fit?
Your pants are too short
To bend over or sit,
Your sleeves are too long
And your hat is too tight –
Why is it some mornings
Your clothes don't feel right?

by Shel Silverstein

2 Practice

1 STUDY SKILLS Wortfelder

a) *Find the group word*
1 red • blue • colour • green
2 dance • hobby • models • music
3 Art • Geography • PE • subject
4 dog • hamster • pet • parrot
5 apple • fruit • banana • orange
6 fish • food • fruit • meat
7 clothes • jeans • shoes • socks
8 milk • drink • juice • lemonade

b) *Find the group word*
1 form, break, teacher, project, learn
   form, break, teacher, project, learn: school
2 sister, son, uncle, mum, divorced
3 kitchen, bathroom, living room, bedroom
4 tennis ball, win, player, football, match
5 go swimming, beach, by the sea, hotel, caravan
6 rainy, sun, cloud, hot, shine, cool

2 WORDS Clothes

a) *Read the sentences and find the right words. The pictures can help you.*
1 You wear them on your feet when you play football.
2 Girls wear them in the summer – and sometimes to parties.
3 Boys and girls wear them when it's hot or when they do sport.
4 Every boy and girl has got a pair of these – usually they're blue.
5 When it's cold you can wear this over a shirt or blouse.
6 Some kids wear shoes, but most kids wear these all the time.

b) **Extra** *Copy and complete the mind map.*

my favourite clothes
I want
my favourite colours
Clothes and me
I need
a new pair of jeans
I don't like

c) **Extra** 👥 *Make appointments with three different partners.*
Tell them about your favourite clothes. (You can use your mind map from b).
Find out about their favourite clothes.

3 A Geography lesson (Possessive pronouns)

In a Geography lesson the children are talking about where their clothes and things are from.
Complete the sentences. Use **mine** *(3x),* **yours** *(3x),* **his, hers, ours, theirs.**
1 Ananda   My new T-shirt is from China. Where's ... from, Sophie?
2 Sophie   ... is from China too. What about ..., Dan and Jo?
3 Dan and Jo   Oh, ... are from Thailand. And our MP3 players are from Japan. ... too, Tom?
4 Tom   No, ... is from the USA. But my new mobile is from Japan.
5 Derek   My brother has got a new mobile too. But ... is from Taiwan.
6 Jack   My parents have got a new mobile too. ... is from Finland.
7 Sophie   Emily and I have got new trainers. ... are from Korea, but I don't know
               where ... are from.

4 REVISION OK, but ... (Simple past)

Use the correct forms of the simple past.

1 What (the children/find) in the kitchen?
   – They (find) the dog, but they (not/find) their lunch.

2 What (your Maths teacher/say) about your homework?
   – Oh, she (like) my answers. But she (not/like) your answers, Dad.

3 (you/have) a good trip to Italy?
   – Yes, we (see) a lot and (have) a very good trip. But all our bags (go) to Spain.

4 (you/like) the food in Italy?
   – Yes, I (eat) lots of spaghetti. I (not/know) that it was so difficult to eat.

5 WORDS 'make' or 'do'?

a) *Fill in the right form of 'make' or 'do'.*
1 I often ... my bed before I go to school.
2 My brother ... judo on Mondays.
3 We both ... our homework in the kitchen.
4 My mother says we always ... a mess.
5 Yesterday my brother ... a model.
6 Last month we ... a project on pocket money.

b) **Extra** *Do the words in the box go with make or with do? Write four sentences with these words.*

> a joke • a mistake •
> an exercise • a sandwich •
> dinner • sport • tricks

6 Extra REVISION On the beach (some and any)

Complete the sentences with some or any.
1 Jack, is there *any* bread? We need *some* for the sandwiches.
2 I don't want ... sweets, but I'd like ... apples, please.
3 Please, don't make ... noise. The baby needs ... sleep.
4 I want to buy an ice cream, but I haven't got ... money with me.
5 Sorry I didn't give you ... money yesterday. But I can give you ... now.
6 I haven't got ... soap for the shower. – No problem, I can give you ...
7 Did you make ... phone calls when we were in the water? – No, but I have to make ... now.
8 Can I have ... juice, please? – I'm sorry, there isn't ...

7 PRONUNCIATION The big red and black bag (Consonants at the end of words)

I like the big red and black bag! But I hate the white jacket.

a) What sound do you hear at the end of each word? Hold up a red or a blue pen:

[b] or [p]   [g] or [k]   [d] or [t]

b) Say the words from the box. Write down: Are they 'red' or 'blue' words? Listen and check.

> add • back • bag • bed • big • clock • club •
> date • dog • heard • hurt • job • plate • played •
> ride • right • sport • step • stop • web

c) `Extra` There are four pairs in the box. Can you find them?

d) Try to say these tongue-twisters. Be careful with the ends of the words.
– Bob's pet is in his bed.
– I like legs but I don't feed feet.
– We like the big bird, but we hate the mad dog.
Listen and check.

8 How many computer games, how much time? (much/many – more – most)

a) Partner B: Look at p. 109. Partner A: Read the information about Lennart. Then ask your partner about Christine. Write the answers in a copy of the chart. Now answer your partner's questions about Lennart.

	Lennart	Christine	You	Your partner
computer games – know	10			
time – need for homework	60 minutes			
TV – watch every day	2 hours			
money – spend on sweets	€ 3 every week			
comics – buy every week	1			
books – read	one every month			

A: How many computer games does Christine know?
B: She knows ... computer games.
A: How much time does she ...?

b) Fill in the answers for 'You' in your chart. Ask your partner and add his/her answers.

c) `Extra` Report to the class. Make comparisons. Use *more* and *most*.
My partner knows more computer games than Lennart. I know more computer games than my partner. But Christine knows the most.

9 Mr Bean is funnier than ... (Comparison of adjectives)

a) Look at the pictures. What do you think? Compare. *b)* Compare your answers.

1 I think Mr Bean is funnier than a clown.
   But Prunella is the funniest.

1 funny

2 big

3 easy

4 pretty

5 nice

6 fast

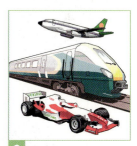
7 cold

8 loud

10 About as big as ... (Comparison of adjectives)

Two things are about the same. Write sentences.

1	big	Denmark, the USA, the Netherlands,	5	cold	Rome, Oslo, Stockholm
		Denmark is about as big as the Netherlands.	6	long	a poem, a song, a book
2	sunny	England, Turkey, Germany	7	small	a mouse, a hamster, an elephant
3	sweet	chocolate, banana, ice cream	8	warm	April, August, October
4	old	my mum, my dad, my grandpa	9	scary	classmate, pirate, bank robber

11 LISTENING Quiz show

a) Make two teams. One student from each team goes to the front. Listen to the first question. Do you know the answer? Then buzz. Who can buzz first? You've got 10 seconds for your answer.
– What can you wear? Say three things.
– Buzz! – Shoes, trousers and caps.
– That's right. One point for Team A. / That's wrong. One point for Team B. Next pair please!

b) Extra Make more questions for your own quiz show.

12 Jumble sale (Comparison of adjectives)

a) Look at Rebecca's table and Ronnie's table at the village jumble sale:

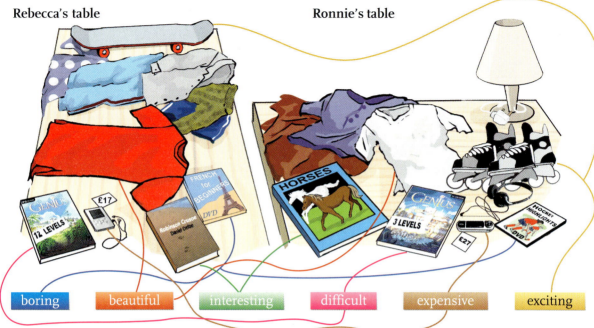

Compare the things on the two tables.
Rebecca's computer game is more difficult than Ronnie's game.
Ronnie's MP3 player is more ...

b) Which table do you think is better? Why?

c) **Extra** What is the most beautiful thing at the sale? The most exciting? And the most boring? Why?
The T-shirt on Rebecca's table is the most beautiful thing there. Red is my favourite colour.

13 What do you think? (Comparison of adjectives)

a) **Think:** *Make questions for a group survey. Then write down your answers.*
1. difficult – Maths / English
   What do you think is more difficult – Maths or English?
2. good – a pet rabbit / a pet dog
   What do you think is better – ...
3. exciting – a computer game / a football match
4. interesting – a holiday by the sea / a holiday in the mountains
5. nice – a red pullover / a blue pullover
6. boring – three hours in the car / three hours shopping
7. funny – Bart Simpson / Donald Duck
8. dangerous – to travel by car / to travel by plane

b) **Pair:** *Compare and discuss your answers.*

c) **Share:** *Make a group of four.*
Compare your results and then prepare a report for your class.
We all think Maths is more difficult than English. Two of us think a pet dog is better ...

14 MEDIATION London shopping

a) *Imagine you're shopping with your little brother in London. He needs your help. Tell him what the assistant says.*

Assistant	Hi! Can I help you?
You	Yes, please. My brother wants to buy some souvenirs for his best friend and for himself.
Assistant	Well, we've got T-shirts or baseball caps in the sports department on the second floor. There's a special offer at the moment. Most of them are only £3.99 now.
You	…
Your brother	T-shirts sind langweilig. Ich brauche was Besonderes für David.
You	My brother would like something really special for his friend.
Assistant	Hm … let me see … What about a model? We've got great models of Big Ben for example. Your brother's friend can put it together at home.
You	…

> **STUDY SKILLS Mediation**
>
> *Manchmal musst du zwischen zwei Sprachen vermitteln. Versuche, nicht alles wörtlich zu übersetzen. Gib nur das Wesentliche weiter.*
>
> ▶ SF Mediation (p. 123)

b) *Now listen to the rest of the dialogue. Tell your little brother what the assistant says.*

c) **Extra** *Act out the dialogue. Your teacher can give you a copy of the text.*

15 GETTING BY IN ENGLISH Shopping for a present

a) *Can you say these things in English?*
1 Wir haben im Moment nicht viel Geld. (p. 29)
2 Ich kann ganz bestimmt etwas finden. (p. 29)
3 Bristol ist im Alltag schöner als New York. (p. 30)
4 Was kann man mit Kleidern schon anfangen? (p. 31)
5 Wollen wir einen Bericht machen? (p. 31)
6 Hm, das finde ich gut. (p. 31)

b) *You and your partner want to buy a birthday present for your friend Emma. Prepare a dialogue.*

Partner A

Du schlägst vor, Emma einen Fußball zu kaufen, denn sie mag Sport.

Den Vorschlag findest du gut. Du hast gerade aber nicht so viel Geld.

Du kennst einen Second-Hand-Laden. Du schlägst vor, dahin zu gehen.

Partner B

Was kann Emma damit schon anfangen? Du findest, eine Tasche ist ein besseres Geschenk – die kann sie jeden Tag benutzen.

Du bist sicher, dass ihr etwas finden könnt.

Du bist einverstanden.

The Clothes Project 🎧

Part 1 At Sophie's house

> Sophie and Jack are working on 8PK's 'Clothes Project'. Who is with them?

It was Tuesday afternoon, after school. Jack was at Sophie's house. They wanted to work on their clothes project.
'Clothes without money. What can we do?'
5 Jack asked as he took another biscuit.
'I've got an idea,' Sophie said.
'Good!' Jack said. 'I've got ideas about lots of things, but not about clothes. Clothes are really boring!'
10 'No, they aren't!'
'Yes, they are!'
'Do you want to hear my idea?' Sophie asked.
'Oh, all right,' Jack answered.
'Well,' Sophie said, 'Rachel and Tom want to do
15 a fashion show. And Ananda and Lesley want to join them and I thought we ...'
'What?!' Jack said. 'Me in a fashion show? No way!'
'Not you. Me. You can be the presenter,'
20 Sophie said.
'Oh – OK. So what's your idea?'
'Come up to the attic and see,' Sophie said.
Prunella floated over to Sophie: 'Oh good! We're going up to the attic!' she said.
25 'No, we aren't!' Sophie whispered.
'You're staying here.'
'What did you say?' Jack asked.
'Nothing,' Sophie said. 'Come on!'
Prunella was the first in the attic.
30 She went to the shelf with Grandma's plates.
'I love plates!' Prunella said. She took one.
Sophie and Jack came into the attic.
'Wow!' said Jack.
'Careful!' whispered Sophie.
35 'Oops!' said Prunella and dropped the plate. Crash!
'What was that?' Jack said.
'Er ... nothing,' Sophie said. 'Come here and look.' She opened a wardrobe and took
40 out a beautiful, long, blue dress.

'Isn't this beautiful? It was my grandma's dress. She designed it. And she made it too. And here's a hat ... It's all very old, but still beautiful. What do you think?'
45 'An outfit from grandma's wardrobe? That's a nice idea. We can say a bit about when she lived and ...'
Suddenly Prunella took the hat from Sophie and floated over to the mirror. She tried the hat
50 on. Of course Jack couldn't see Prunella – he only saw the hat. He stood there with his mouth open.
'No! I don't like it!' Prunella said and dropped the hat on the floor.
55 'Ooops! The wind in here!' Sophie said as she went and got the hat. 'Come on, Jack. Let's take the stuff down and start work.' She hurried to the door.
'What about shoes?' asked Prunella.
60 'Oh, no!' said Sophie.
Crash! A pair of black shoes landed at Jack's feet. Bang! A pair of red shoes. Wallop! A pair of blue shoes.

'I don't understand,' Jack said. 'Hey, Sophie,
65 maybe you've got a poltergeist? Maybe …'
'You and your mad ideas, Jack!' Sophie
laughed. 'Now hurry up. We have to prepare
our presentation. It has to be ready tomorrow.'
'Hee! Hee! Hee!' Prunella laughed as Sophie
70 took a very puzzled Jack downstairs.

▷ Jack asks: 'Maybe you've got a poltergeist?'
Why does he think so?
Find three reasons in the text.

Part 2 The fashion show 🎧

a) Now listen to the end of the story. There are two parts.
1 The ball dress
2 An outfit from the bin

b) Look at the pictures. Listen again and spot the mistakes.

Working with the text

1 Heads and tails

a) Match the heads and tails of these four sentences.

– Ananda was the model	… Prunella tried on the hat.
– When Sophie showed Jack the dress	… when she wore Grandma's dress.
– Jack liked Sophie's idea	… but Lesley designed the outfit.
– Sophie looked lovely at the fashion show	… but he didn't want to be in a fashion show.

b) Write the sentences in the right order.

DOSSIER **A different point of view**

Describe the scene in the attic (ll. 29–70) from Jack's point of view.
*I went up to the attic with Sophie.
It was great. There were lots of …*

▶ WB 20 (p. 26)

---

2 Extra ACTIVITY A fashion show 🎧

a) Collect clothes words (for example *skirt*) and useful adjectives (for example *long/short*/…).

b) 👥 Prepare your show:
– collect clothes
– choose music
– decide who can be the model/presenter
– write the presentation
Here are some ideas. Listen again for more ideas.

Our topic is …   We want to show you …
He's/She's wearing …
                  We found this dress/… in …
We made this hat/… out of …

c) 👥 First rehearse, then put your show on for your class.

▶ SF Giving a presentation (p. 116)
Checkpoint 2 ▶ WB (pp. 27–29) • Activity page 1

Extra: Special days around the world

1 Special days

a) Work in groups of four. Each group reads one text, answers the questions and fills in a copy of the chart.
– What is the special day?
– What country is the text about?
– When do people celebrate the special day?
– How do they celebrate it?

Special day	Where?	When?	How?
Guy Fawkes Day	England	5 Nov	

b) Make a new group. Each student must know a different text. Use your chart to tell the others about the special day in your text.

▶ SF Understanding new words (p. 114)
▶ SF Working with a dictionary (p. 115)

A

■ Fawkes, Guy (1570–1606)

Fawkes and his men were Catholics, and they did not want a Protestant king. In the night of 5 November 1605, they put 20 barrels of gunpowder under the parliament building. The king and his ministers wanted to meet there the next day. But the king's men found out about the plan, killed Guy Fawkes and saved the king.

Every year the English celebrate 'Guy Fawkes Night' on 5 November: they burn a 'Guy' on big bonfires and have fireworks.

Guy Fawkes, or 'Bonfire Night', is very popular in England.

B

YOU HAVE RECEIVED AN E-CARD FROM CATHERINE THOMPSON SHAW

Dan and Jo
Merry Christmas from Down Under

To:
From:
Sent:

The card shows the 'New Zealand Christmas tree'.
It's really the pohutukawa tree, and it gets flowers at Christmas – summertime here. So we aren't planning to celebrate at home – we're going to the beach for a Christmas barbecue! Father Christmas comes on a surfboard every year. That reminds me – did you get my parcel in time?

Lots of love – from Pat too!

Topic **2** 41

C 🎧

My dear Ananda

Thank you for your last letter. It's always nice to hear from my granddaughter.

The city seems so quiet now after a week of Holi. Do you celebrate Holi in Bristol? Here in India, the young people have so much fun! They go out in the morning in white clothes, and then the fun starts. They throw gulal and kumkum (coloured water and powders) till everybody looks like the flowers of spring.

At night there's singing and dancing in the streets. It's very pretty to see the people dance with the colours everywhere. That's what Holi is: the Festival of Colour.

I'm sending a photo of your cousin Sandhya at Holi. She's

D 🎧

★ Queens Star Chronicle ★ July 5

Queens celebrates on a beautiful day

The people of Queens, New York, celebrated Independence Day yesterday with all the traditions: a morning parade, an afternoon barbecue, and evening fireworks.

"It was perfect Fourth of July weather," said Mike Wu of the National Weather Service.

The traditional parade started with a band from Cardozo High School. Next were two trucks full of red, white and blue flowers, one with a giant Statue of Liberty. Two open cars followed. They were full of tall young men – Cardozo's champion basketball team, including team captain Jay Gupta.

More on p. 3

Photo: Cardozo High School band at the Fourth of July Parade

2 Who sent the e-card?

Who sent the e-card? And the newspaper article? Who sent the letter? How do you know?
I think ... sent the e-card.
She's got the same name as ..., and she lives ...
So it must be from her.

▶ WB Activity page 4

3 Now you

a) *Write about a special day in your family. You can add pictures and put it in your dossier.*

Our special day is ... / ...
We eat/drink/make ...
I like it because ...

b) *Make a poster about your special day. Use the poster to tell the class about it.*

Unit 3
Animals in the city

Thursday 18 November

TV • Thursday

7.00 BBC 1
Animals in the City
The fox

A new series of five programmes about wild animals in the city, from the BBC's Natural History Unit in Bristol.

Tonight's programme:
The fox and how it survives in our cities.
With this new series, the BBC again shows that it is the top channel for fine animal programmes.

BBC 1		BBC 2		ITV 1	
3.30	**Pitt and Kantrop** Cartoon	3.30	**FILM The man on the train** (2002) Film about a bank robber and an old teacher	3.50	**Art Attack** Art ideas for young Picassos
4.15	**Best of Friends** Things to do with friends			4.00	**Tricks on TV** Card tricks
4.00	**Batman** Cartoon	4.30	**Ready, Steady, Cook** Great food for parties	4.30	**My Parents Are Aliens** Series Mel and Josh argue
5.00	**Blue Peter** The team visits Japan and shows how to do origami	5.15	**Art School** More lessons in art	5.00	**The Paul O'Grady Show**
		6.00	**Clever Heads** Quiz show	6.00	**Around the West Country**
5.35	**Neighbours** Series				
6.00	**BBC News**				
6.30	**Spotlight** News, sport and weather				
7.00	**Animals in the City**				

1 Talking about animals

a) Name as many animals as you can.

b) `Extra` Choose two animals and make a mind map about each of them.

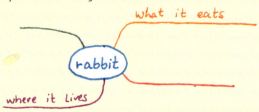

c) `Extra` 👥 Tell your partner about them.

2 Now you

a) Which English TV programme would you like to watch? Why?
I'd like to watch 'Batman' on BBC 1 because I like cartoons.

b) `Extra` 👥 Tell your partner about your favourite programmes on German TV. Does he/she like them too?
I like 'Sportschau' because it's exciting.
– I like that too. / Oh, I don't think it's exciting. It's boring. I like …

Deer

Woodpecker

Grey squirrel

Mole

Hedgehog

Frog

3 A BBC radio interview
Listen to the radio interview with the presenter of 'Animals in the city'. Which animals does he name? What's their order in the series?

Programme	Animal
1	foxes
2	...

▶ P 1 (p. 48) • WB 1 (p. 30)

STUDY SKILLS Listening

Vielleicht fällt es dir manchmal schwer, einen Hörtext zu verstehen. So kannst du dir helfen:
– Lies dir die Aufgabe gut durch, um dich einzustimmen. Worum geht es in dem Hörtext? Was genau sollst du herausfinden?
– Bereite deine Notizen vor. In Aufgabe 3 links z.B. kannst du die Tabelle schon vorschreiben. Weitere Tipps findest du auf S.117.

▶ SF Listening (p. 117)

1 Hello hedgehogs!

Ananda opened the back door, walked over to the dustbin and put the rubbish in. Suddenly she saw two baby hedgehogs. 'You poor little things. Where's your mum? You'll be very cold tonight without her.' She looked round the yard. Their mother wasn't there. Ananda went inside. 'Sophie knows all about animals', she thought. So she called her.

'You'll have to wait,' Sophie said. 'Maybe their mother will come later.'
'But maybe she won't come back tonight', Ananda said. 'Then what? Will they need milk?'
'No, they won't need milk. It's bad for them. But they'll want water.'
'OK. What about food: will they be hungry?'
'No, they probably won't. But I'm not sure.'
'Sophie, will they survive without their mum?'
'Yes, I think they will. You know what? Mail that TV programme Animals in the City. Their Animal Hotline will help.'
So Ananda sat down at her computer and wrote an e-mail to the Animal Hotline.

▶ *Write Ananda's e-mail to the Animal Hotline. You can use these ideas.*

| Thanks for your help. | Will they need … |
| Will they be cold outside? |
| What about food? | Dear Animal Hotline |
| I found two baby hedgehogs in our yard. |

2 Now you

a) *Write sentences. Use ideas from the box.*
In 20 years I'll probably … / I probably won't …

> be a pop star • be married • have a family • have a horse • like the same music • live abroad • live at home • travel to the moon

b) *Compare with a partner.*

Looking at language

Sophie and Ananda are talking about the future. Collect sentences with **'ll, will, won't.**
'You'll be very cold tonight …'
'Maybe their mother will …'
'Maybe she won't …'

3 Extra A tongue-twister

The happy hedgehog hopped into the hat, so the not-so-happy hamster hopped out.

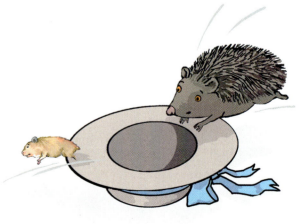

▶ GF 5: will-future (p. 129) • P 2–4 (pp. 48–49) • WB 2–4 (pp. 31–32)

4 The Animal Hotline 🎧

To: anandakap@yahoo.co.uk Subject: Re: Hedgehog babies

Hi Ananda!

Thanks very much for your e-mail about hedgehog babies.
They'll need food and water. If you give them food for young dogs or cats, they'll be happy. Don't give them milk and bread! They'll get very ill if you do that. If you pick up the hedgehogs, you'll have to be very careful. But the most important thing is to keep the babies warm. If you put a hot-water bottle in their box, they'll be fine.
You'll find more help if you visit our website. The babies will have a better chance of survival if you take them to the animal clinic at the Bristol RSPCA as soon as you can.

Good luck!
Susan at Animal Hotline

> What will happen if ...
... Ananda gives the hedgehogs cat food?
... she puts a hot water bottle in their box?
... she takes them to the RSPCA?

5 Now you

a) Make notes. What will you do if ...

> you get a '1' for your next English test •
> you're late for school •
> you can't understand your Maths homework •
> your teacher says there's no homework

b) 👥 Find out what your partner will do.
A: What will you do if you get a '1' for your next English test?
B: I'll have a big party and invite all my friends.

Extra | Background File

Royal Society for the Prevention of Cruelty to Animals (RSPCA)

Most people in Britain love animals – but it wasn't always like that. In 1824, a small group of people wanted to stop cruelty to animals. So they started the Society for the Prevention of Cruelty to Animals.

Today the RSPCA is a big organization. If somebody in Britain is cruel to an animal, the RSPCA will soon be there.

For more information, visit their website at:
www.rspca.org.uk.

▶ GF 6: Conditional sentences (1) (p. 130) • P 5–8 (pp. 50–51) • WB 5–9 (pp. 32–34)

6 Dilip killed my hedgehogs 🎧

'... so,' Ananda explained, 'I took the box with the hedgehogs slowly and carefully back down to the yard. Then, this morning, I went out very quietly with some water and ... the yard was empty.'

'Empty?' asked Sophie.
'Yes,' Ananda said angrily, 'Dilip put all the old boxes out for the rubbish collection. He killed my hedgehogs!'
'That's terrible!' said Jack.
'I'm sure there's an explanation,' said Dan.
'Hey, people, guess what?!' Jo sat down at the table.
'What?' asked Jack.
'Simon's new pen disappeared at break. And ...,' Jo said slowly, '... guess who was in the classroom at break?'
'Who?' asked Ananda.
'Lesley, of course! Do you know what I think ...'
Just then Sophie jumped up. 'Look, there's Dilip,' she said. She walked over to him quickly.
'You horrible person: you killed Ananda's hedgehogs,' she shouted angrily.
'No, I didn't!' said Dilip. 'I put them in the garage. They're warm and safe.'

Looking at language

a) How do people do or say things? Write down phrases from 6 like 'I took the box with the hedgehogs slowly ...' What word describes **how** somebody does something? Underline it.

b) Where do the words with '-ly' at the end come from? Write down pairs like this:

slowly   slow
carefully   ...
...   ...

▶ GF 7a–b: Adverbs of manner (p. 131) • P 9–10 (p. 51) • WB 10–12 (pp. 35–36)

7 GAME Act the adverbs

a) Each group writes eight activities on blue cards and eight adverbs on orange cards. Here are some ideas:

b) Put all the cards together. One person takes a blue card and an orange card and mimes what is on them. The others guess what he/she is doing.

feed the dog	write an e-mail	slowly	quickly
sing	laugh	angrily	happily
clean the board	eat a sandwich	nervously	quietly
walk	put jeans on	madly	dangerously

"I think you're cleaning the board madly."

"Yes, that's right. Your turn. / No, that's wrong. Try again."

8 Goodbye hedgehogs 🎧

'You did a good job with the hedgehogs,' said the woman at the RSPCA Animal Clinic.
'Really?' Ananda asked.
'The babies will be fine – you did well. So, would you like to see the clinic? Steve, one of our volunteers, can show you everything.'
Steve showed Ananda the small animals: 'This rabbit came with a broken leg last week. She still can't run quickly, but she's running more quickly now. Soon she'll be back in the woods again.'
'I'd like to help animals too,' Ananda said. 'Is it hard work?'
'Well yes, I work hard,' Steve answered. 'But it's fun too. I'm afraid you have to be 16 to be a volunteer. But you can collect money for the RSPCA. We have fun runs every year.'
'Fun runs?' Ananda asked. 'I'm quite fast.'
Steve laughed. 'You don't have to run fast for a fun run. People give you money for each mile. Then you give the money to the RSPCA.'
'Oh, that's a good idea,' Ananda said.

> What is a fun run? Are there fun runs where you live? Who gets the money?

9 More about animals
Complete the chart. You can scan these websites for the missing information:
www.EnglishG.de/B2/fox
www.EnglishG.de/B2/squirrel
www.EnglishG.de/B2/hedgehog

	foxes	squirrels	hedgehogs
food			
number of babies			
enemies			

Looking at language

You did a <u>good</u> job. – You did <u>well</u>.
Which word is an adjective, which is an adverb?

▶ GF 7c–d: Adverbs of manner – irregular forms (pp. 131–132) • P 11 (p. 52) • WB 13–14 (pp. 36–37)

▶ **Extra** GF 7e: Comparison of adverbs (p. 132)

DOSSIER Animals

Extra *Write a short report on one of the animals. The phrases below can help you. You can put your report in your dossier.*
They eat …
They have one/two/… babies in the spring/…
They have no/a few/… enemies.
Their biggest enemies are …

STUDY SKILLS Scanning

Wenn du bei einem langen Text nur bestimmte Informationen suchst, musst du ihn nicht von vorn bis hinten genau lesen. Such stattdessen nach Schlüsselwörtern und lies nur dort genauer, wo du sie findest.

▶ SF Scanning (p. 118) • P 12–16 (pp. 52–53) • WB 15–17 (pp. 38–39)

48   3 Practice

1 WORDS Animals

a) Put the animals in two groups: pets and wild animals. Can any animals go in both groups?

budgies • cats • deer • dogs • foxes • frogs •
guinea pigs • hamsters • hedgehogs • horses •
mice • moles • parrots • rabbits • squirrels •
tortoises • woodpeckers

b) Which adjectives go with which animals? Match them.

big • boring • clever • fast •
loud • pretty • quiet • slow • small • sweet

Polly is a pretty bird!

c) Compare your results.
A: Budgies: I think they are small and sweet.
B: Well, I think they're small, but I don't think they're sweet. – My turn. Cats: I think cats are ...

2 In 2050 (will-future)

a) Write a caption for each picture with **will** or **won't**.

1 live – on Mars

2 not use – computers

3 not live – in hotels

4 be warm – in winter

5 fly – to work

6 not read – e-books

7 not need – shops

8 live – under the sea

In 2050 people will probably live on Mars. In 2050 babies probably won't ...

b) **Extra** Do you and your partner agree with the captions?
A: Caption 1 says: 'In 2050 people will probably live on Mars'. I think that's wrong.
B: I agree/don't agree with you. I think people will live on Mars then. What about caption 2?

Practice **3**   49

3 Fifi the fortune-teller (will-future)

a) *Prunella goes to Fifi the fortune-teller. Fill in the correct forms of the* **will**-*future.*

1 P: … Sophie … (be) a doctor, like her mum?
  F: No, she … (not be) a doctor. Maybe she … (be) a teacher.
  Will Sophie be a doctor, like her mum?
  – No, she …
2 P: … she … (have) children?
  F: Oh, yes. She … (have) at least three children.
3 P: Where … she (live)? … she still … (live) in my house in 20 years?
  F: I don't know where she … (live), but she … (not be) in your house.
4 P: When … she … (go)?
  F: She … (go) when she's twenty.
5 P: Oh! But … Sophie … (remember) me?
  F: Yes, she … always … (remember) you.

b) *Your partner is a fortune-teller.*
Ask him/her about your future. Swap after five questions.

4 READING   A book: No Small Thing

Read about the book. Then answer the questions.
1 No Small Thing is a book for …
  A young people.   B old people.
  C boys only.   D girls only.

2 Life isn't easy for Nathaniel and his sisters because their …
  A father isn't there.   B mother went away.
  C parents have no jobs.   D father is dead.

3 The children see that somebody wants to …
  A sell a horse.   B buy a horse.
  C give away a horse. D kill a horse.

4 When the children tell their mother about the horse she says that …
  A she's not sure.   B she doesn't like horses.
  C she wants a dog.   D they can have it.

5 The horse's name is …
  A Natale.   B Smokey.
  C Cid.   D Queenie.

6 When there's a fire in Smokey's barn …
  A somebody wants to buy Smokey.
  B Smokey runs away.
  C the fire kills Smokey.
  D Smokey survives.

▶ SF Multiple-choice exercises (p. 116)

STUDY SKILLS | Multiple-choice exercises

Lies bei **Multiple-choice**-Aufgaben erst alle Lösungen durch, bevor du dich entscheidest.

No Small Thing ♦ by Natale Ghent
10–14 years, 256 pages

Life isn't easy for Nathaniel and his two sisters, Queenie and Cid. Their father went away and now they live with their mother. They all want something to make them happy again. One day, the children see an ad in the newspaper for a horse. And the great thing is – it's free! First they don't tell their mother about it. They're sure she will say no. But, when they tell her, she says yes. The children are happy again. They ride Smokey, take care of him, and share many happy hours together. Then one day there's a fire in Smokey's barn. Luckily Smokey survives. But things get worse when the family has to sell their house and somebody wants to buy Smokey. **No Small Thing** is a great book about a horse. It is warm and funny. You have to read it!

5 If you find a baby hedgehog ... (Conditional sentences)

Match and complete.

1 If you find a baby hedgehog,
2 If you pick the hedgehog up,
3 If you take the hedgehog to an animal clinic,
4 If you give the baby hedgehog milk,
5 If you don't give the baby hedgehog water,
6 If you ask your Biology teacher,
7 If you visit the Animal Hotline website,

you / he/she / it

'll / won't

have to be very careful.
find more help.
get very ill.
have to keep it warm.
survive.
have a better chance of survival.
tell you more about hedgehogs.

If you find a baby hedgehog, you'll have to keep it warm.

6 What will they do if ...? (Conditional sentences)

a) Partner B: Look at p. 109.
Partner A: Ask your partner for the missing information.
Then answer his or her questions.
A: What will Maike do if she finds a baby squirrel?
B: She'll ...

	find a baby squirrel	get a 5 in English	need a new mobile
Maike		practise every day	
Jan	put it in a box		buy one with his pocket money
Christoph	ask the Biology teacher for help	talk to his English teacher	
You			
Your partner			

b) **Extra** Write three sentences: one about one of the people, one about your partner and one about you.
*If Maike finds a baby squirrel, she'll take it to an animal clinic.
If my partner Finn finds a baby squirrel, he'll ... If I ...*

7 WORDS Fourth word

Find the fourth word.

1 bird – birds
  deer – ?
2 deer – run
  birds – ?
3 invite – invitation
  survive – ?
4 Maths – subject
  apple – ?
5 small – smaller
  big – ?
6 do – don't
  will – ?
7 left – right
  background – ?
8 meet – met
  hear – ?
9 mouse – mice
  fox – ?

8 WRITING Pet of the day (Linking ideas)

Link the sentences with the words in brackets.
Together, they make an e-mail to the website www.petoftheday.com.

1 Hi! Rosie is a 7-month-old cat. I love her very much. (and)
   Hi! Rosie is a 7-month-old cat and I love her very much.
2 I get up in the mornings. She wants to play. (after)
   After I get up in the mornings, she ...
3 She follows me round the house. She wants to play. (because)
4 I feed her. She wants to sit with me. (after)
5 Sometimes I want to play. I can't find her. (but)
6 I call her. She doesn't usually come. (when)
7 The window is usually open for her. She often goes outside. (so)
8 Sometimes cats are mad. That's OK. I love Rosie very much. (but, because)

DOSSIER Pet of the day

Write an e-mail to 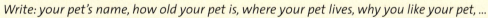 pet@petoftheday.com
about your pet (or a friend's pet).
Add a photo. Put it in your dossier.
Write: your pet's name, how old your pet is, where your pet lives, why you like your pet, ...

9 Poor little dog (Adverbs of manner)

Complete the sentences. Use the adverb forms of the words in brackets.

Jack and Ananda were out together. 'I love the Downs,' Jack said (happy). 'Me too,' Ananda said. 'Tell me about your hockey match,' Jack said. 'Well, we didn't win. But we played (bad), so it wasn't really a surprise.'
Suddenly she stopped. 'Can you hear that noise?' Jack listened (careful). 'You're right,' he said (slow). 'It sounds like a dog. I think it needs help.' They ran (quick). Soon they could hear the dog (clear). Then they saw a man. 'Don't hit the dog!' Ananda said. 'Mind your own business,' the man answered (rude).

'Stop that!' Jack shouted (angry). The man ran away. 'Poor little dog,' Ananda said, 'we'll take you to the RSPCA.'

10 PRONUNCIATION [f] – [v] – [w]

a) Listen. What sound do you hear at the beginning of each word? Is the first letter *f*, *v* or *w*?
Write the correct words into your exercise book.

_ery • _eek • _illage • _ind • _eed • _ater • _isit •
_ord • _ith • _iew • _irst • _alk • _ace • _oman •
_olleyball • _hite • _ood • _ind • _oodpecker

b) Say the words from a).

c) **Extra** Now try these tongue-twisters:
Willy Walter won't wear white in winter, will he?
Fiona's got a very funny visitor from Valencia.
Where's the village with the very wild view?
Val fell on the floor when Vinny phoned Will.

11 LISTENING She's talking loudly (Adverbs of manner)

a) Write down the adverb forms of these adjectives:

angry • careful • fast • happy • loud • quiet • slow

b) Listen. Write down how the people are talking.
1 The first person is talking ...
2 The second person is talking ...

12 STUDY SKILLS Scanning

Scan the magazine page and answer the questions below.

BBC 2	ITV 1	C4
3.30 **FILM** The man on the train (2002) Film about a bank robber and an old teacher	3.50 **Art Attack** Art ideas for young Picassos	3.15 **Countdown** Quiz show
	4.00 **Tricks on TV** Card tricks	4.00 **Back in the day** Comedy
4.30 **Ready, Steady, Cook** Great food for parties	4.30 **My Parents Are Aliens** Series Mel and Josh argue	4.30 **Richard & Judy** Talk show with guests
5.15 **Art School** More lessons in art	5.00 **The Paul O'Grady Show**	5.35 **All about Big brother**
6.00 **Clever Heads** Quiz show	6.00 **Around the West Country** Local news	6.00 **The Simpsons** The children are trapped in the school

1 Which programme will be about art?
2 Which programme is about cooking?
3 When and where can you see tricks on TV?
4 When and where can you see the Simpsons?
5 When and where can you see news?
6 How many series are there?

13 MEDIATION Longleat Safari Park

Imagine you want to go to Longleat Safari Park with your parents. They don't understand English, so tell them in German:

– what animals you can see in the park
– how much it costs for you and your parents
– what you have to do in Tiger Territory
– what animals you may feed

Welcome to Longleat

East Africa Reserve
Like in Africa, our giraffes and zebras live happily together in this **25**-hectare reserve. Also look out for the camels.

Monkey Jungle
Monkey Jungle is great fun because monkeys are great entertainers.

Tiger Territory
The tigers are one of the biggest attractions at Longleat. Your car windows must be closed. Tigers can be very dangerous!

Deer Park
We first brought deer to Longleat in **1540**. This is the only reserve where you may feed the animals.

Open 10 am, last entry at **4** pm (**5** pm weekends)

Prices £10 / **£7** child (**3–14** yrs)

14 WORDS Word building

a) Make nouns from the verbs.

+ er	+ r	+ ner / + mer	+ or
work	dance	run	act
sing	explore	swim	collect
listen	write	win	visit
paint			

b) Complete the sentences with words from a).
1 Ashton Kutcher is my favourite ... I try to see all his films.
2 Sophie is one of the best ...s in the Dance Club at Cotham School.
3 If I see a book by Stephen King, I'll buy it. He's a really scary ...
4 There were more than 100 ... in the fun run.
5 You're a fantastic ...! Why aren't you in the choir?

c) **Extra** 👥 Choose three more words from a) and make sentences like the ones in b).
Swap. Can your partner find the missing words?

15 REVISION Three cities

There was a survey on British cities. Here are the results for London (**L**), Bristol (**B**) and Manchester (**M**).
Read them and make three statements on each.
Manchester isn't as pretty as London or Bristol. London is prettier than ... Bristol is the prettiest.

1 Is ... pretty?

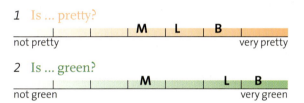

2 Is ... green?

3 Is ... exciting?

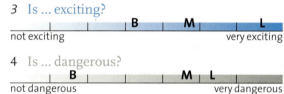

4 Is ... dangerous?

16 GETTING BY IN ENGLISH The Maths test

a) Can you say these things in English?
1 Vielen Dank für deine E-Mail. (p. 45)
2 Viel Glück! (p. 45)
3 Du bekommst eine 1 in der nächsten Englischarbeit. (p. 45)
4 Ich bin sicher, es gibt eine Erklärung. (p. 46)
5 Ratet mal, wer ... (p. 46)
6 Das hast du gut gemacht. (p. 47)
7 Ich arbeite hart. (p. 47)
8 Du musst leider 16 sein, um ... (p. 47)

b) 👥 Complete the dialogue with a partner. Then act it out.

Partner A

| Du hast Neuigkeiten. B soll raten, was passiert ist. |
| Du hast in einem Mathetest eine 1 bekommen. |
| Bedanke dich für B's Hilfe. Frag, ob er/sie dir wieder helfen kann. |
| Du wirst dann wieder hart arbeiten müssen. |

Partner B

| Du bist sicher, es ist etwas Tolles. |
| Du findest, dass A das gut gemacht hat. |
| Du hast leider keine Zeit, A zu helfen. |
| Du wünschst A viel Glück. |

El's best friend

> Look at the pictures and scan the text. Who is El's 'best friend'?
> ▶ SF Scanning (p. 118)

Everybody called the four girls the Black Angels. They looked dangerous, but they weren't – they were OK. El was the youngest in the group. She was 12, but she looked older.

At their school in London, the Black Angels were always together – nobody bullied them! 'And if somebody tries to bully one of the little kids,' they said, 'we'll be there to help them.' At home El's best friend was her dog Scruffy. When her parents argued (and they argued a lot) she went to her room with Scruffy, and told him all her problems.

One day El came home from school and found two big suitcases in the hall. When she went to her bedroom her mother was there with a third suitcase.
'Quick, pack your things,' her mum said.
'We're leaving.'
'Leaving?' El didn't understand.

'Yes, I'm leaving your father! We'll go and stay with my friend Milly in Bristol. We'll find a flat there and a new school.'
'But what about my friends? What about Scruffy ... and Dad?'
'You'll find lots of new friends, dear. And Scruffy can come when we've got our own place.'
'I don't want new friends, I want my old friends,' El said angrily. 'And I don't want to ...'
'Just get your things, El. The train leaves in an hour.'
Her mum left the room. El sat down on the bed. Scruffy jumped up and sat next to her. She looked at him sadly.
'Oh, Scruffy, I'll miss you so much. But I'll come and get you, I promise.'

Tuesday, 27th November

Dear Dad

I hate the new school – it's full of boring kids – all neat and tidy in their school uniforms. I really want Scruffy – I need Scruffy! Please, please bring him to us.

Love

El

Hi, sweetheart!
I had to move out of our flat. I've got a nice room, but I'm afraid I can't have a pet. So I had to take Scruffy to Battersea Dogs Home. I'm sure he'll be OK there. Sorry, sweetheart. I'll write again soon.
Love
Dad

'Battersea Dogs Home?' thought El. 'But that's where people go when they want to give a dog a new home. Maybe somebody will want to give Scruffy a new home – and then I'll never see him again! I have to call Dad!'

It was 5.30 in the morning. El's mum and her friend Milly were still asleep. But El had plans. 'I have to get to London – today!' she thought as
45 she came quietly down the stairs. 'I have to save Scruffy.'
'Money!' She counted: 'I'll need £8.25 for the return ticket to London, £3.60 for a return ticket on the underground ... Oh dear! I've only
50 got £11.'
El searched through her jacket ... another 45p ... and in her jeans pocket she found another 50p. She left the house and closed the door very quietly behind her.

55 On the trip back to Bristol, Scruffy was very good. He sat quietly at El's feet. When they got out at the bus station, he was really happy. 'Come on, Scruffy,' said El. 'I haven't got any more money, so we'll have to walk home.'
60 And so they started the long walk. After about 45 minutes they were near Milly's house. Suddenly El heard somebody call.
'Hey, Lesley!'
El turned. It was Jack from her new school.
65 He came towards them. 'So you're a dog person, Lesley. I didn't know that.'
She smiled at Jack.
'Yes, I love dogs. This is my dog Scruffy.'
'Hello Scruffy,' said Jack. 'That's a nice name.'
70 El said shyly: 'In London all my friends called me El.'
'That's nice too. Can I call you El?' asked Jack.
'OK,' said Lesley.

Working with the text

1 The story in two sentences
Which sentences summarize the first part of the story (ll.1–36) best?
A When El and her mum came to Bristol, El tried to find new friends. She left her dog Scruffy with the Black Angels.
B El's mum and dad argued a lot, so El and her mum moved to Bristol. She was sad because she had to leave her dog Scruffy in London.
C El and her mum moved to Bristol. El hated it and went back to London to live with her dad and Scruffy.

2 The story in parts
a) Match the titles to the parts of the story:
a ll. 1–8   El and the new school
b ll. 9–12   Scruffy at the dogs' home
c ll. 13–31   The Black Angels
d ll. 32–36   Scruffy, El's best friend
e letter 1   Leaving El's dad
f letter 2   Goodbye Scruffy

b) **Extra** *Find titles for these parts of the story. ll. 37–41; ll. 42–54; ll. 55–61; ll. 62–73*

3 How El felt
Find at least one part of the story when El felt:

afraid • angry • happy • sad

I think El felt afraid when she ... *sadly*

4 That evening
What will happen when El gets back to her mum? Do either a) or b).
a) *Write a short dialogue.*
Mum ─── *Where were you?*
El ─── *In London, Mum. I'm sorry.*

b) *Write Lesley's diary entry for the day.*

▶ WB 18 (p.40)
Checkpoint 3 ▶ WB (p.41)

Extra Animal songs and poems

Read, listen to and enjoy these animal songs and poems. Then choose one task.

1 SONG I know an old lady who swallowed a fly 🎧

I know an old lady who swallowed a fly.
I don't know why she swallowed the fly –
Perhaps she'll die.

I know an old lady who swallowed a spider
That wriggled and jiggled and tickled inside her.
She swallowed the spider to catch the fly.
But I don't know why she swallowed the fly –
Perhaps she'll die.

I know an old lady who swallowed a bird.
How absurd – to swallow a bird.
She swallowed the bird to catch the spider
That wriggled and jiggled and tickled inside her.
She swallowed the spider to catch the fly.
But I don't know why she swallowed the fly –
Perhaps she'll die.

I know an old lady who swallowed a cat.
Imagine that. She swallowed a cat.
She swallowed the cat to catch the bird.
She swallowed the bird to catch the spider
That wriggled and jiggled and tickled inside her.
She swallowed the spider to catch the fly.
But I don't know why she swallowed the fly –
Perhaps she'll die.

I know an old lady who swallowed a dog.
What a hog! To swallow a dog!
She swallowed the dog to catch the cat.
She swallowed the cat to catch the bird.
…

I know an old lady who swallowed a goat.
Opened her throat and down went the goat!
She swallowed the goat to catch the dog.
She swallowed the dog to catch the cat.
…

I know an old lady who swallowed a horse –
She's dead of course!

by Rosemary Bedeau, Alan Mills

> The old lady in the song swallowed the spider to catch the fly. Write one more verse for the song with a new animal.

…who swallowed a duck   … a fox

… a mouse   … a mole

Oh how yuck, she swallowed a duck!

… she went in the house

… she opened a box

… she looked in a hole

Topic **3** 57

2 POEM The frog on the log 🎧

There once
Was a green
    Little frog, frog, frog –

Who played
In the wood
    On a log, log, log!

A screech owl
Sitting
    In a tree, tree, tree –

Came after
The frog
    With a scree, scree, scree!

When the frog
Heard the owl –
    In a flash, flash, flash –

He leaped
In the pond
    With a splash, splash, splash

by Ilo Orleans

▷ 👥 Partner A: learn the green verses.
Partner B: learn the brown verses.
Act out the poem for the class. Which pair is best?

3 POEM The song of a mole 🎧

All I did this afternoon was
Dig, dig, dig,
And all I'll do tomorrow will be
Dig, dig, dig,
And yesterday from dusk till dawn
I dug, dug, dug.
I sometimes think I'd rather be
A slug, slug, slug.

by Richard Edwards

▷ Think of more verbs like 'dig' – there are some ideas in the box below. Then write your own poem. You can put another animal at the end. (It doesn't have to rhyme.)

> drink/drank • fly/... • read/... • ride/... •
> sing/... • sit/... • write/...

> All I did this afternoon was
> Write, write, write.
> And all I'll do tomorrow will be
> Write, write, write
> And yesterday from dusk till dawn
> I wrote, wrote, wrote.
> I sometimes think I'd rather be
> A goat, goat, goat.

Unit 4
A weekend in Wales

1 Talking about weekend trips
Where would you like to go?
A: I'd like to go to …
B: Why would you like to go there?
A: Because it's fun / my aunt lives there / …
   What about you?
B: …

2 Town and country
a) Look at the words and phrases in the box. Can you find examples in the photos?

> beautiful • CD and DVD shop • church •
> cinema • clean • cow • dirty • factory • farm •
> field • forest • go shopping • green • hill •
> horse • house • lots of people • lots of traffic •
> noisy • quiet • ride your bike • river • sheep •
> station • train • tree • valley • village

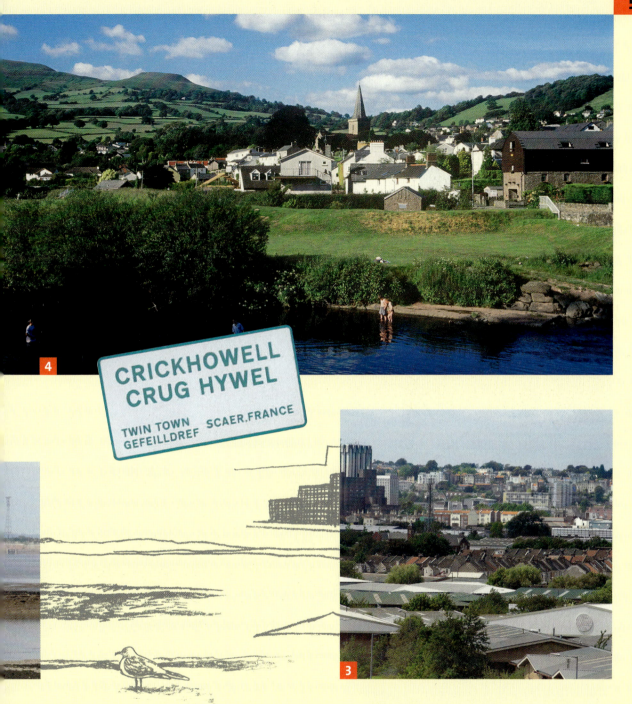

b) 👥 *What can you see or do in a town? And in the country? Which do you like better?*

A: You see lots of shops in towns. You can buy CDs and clothes there. That's fun.
B: I don't like shopping. I like animals. You see lots of farms and animals in the country.

3 👥 Dan and Jo's trip to Wales 🎧

Listen to Dan and Jo. They're going to their grandparents' new house in Wales. Choose a title for dialogues A–D.
- New country, new language
- Have you got your pyjamas?
- Welcome to Crickhowell
- Towns all look the same

Then match the photos to the dialogues.

▶ *P 1 (p. 64)* • *WB 1–2 (p. 42)*

1 Friday dinner 🎧

It was late when the twins and their grandparents got to Crickhowell. 'Grandpa will show you your room, boys,' Grandma said. 'Dinner will be on the table in a few minutes.'
'It smells great,' Jo said when they came into the kitchen. 'What are you cooking?'
'Cawl mamgu,' Grandma answered. 'That's Welsh for "Granny's soup".'

'You're very quiet, Daniel,' Grandpa Thompson said. 'Are you all right?'
'Yes, I'm fine.'
'That's good,' Grandpa Thompson said, 'because we're planning a trip to the Brecon Beacons in the morning. We want to go on the Brecon Mountain Railway. And we can have a picnic near Caerphilly Castle in the afternoon.'

> Where will Dan and Jo be when?
They'll be on ... in the morning. They'll be at ...

▶ GF 8: Word order (p. 133) • P 2–3 (p. 64) • WB 3 (p. 43)

2 Caerphilly Castle 🎧

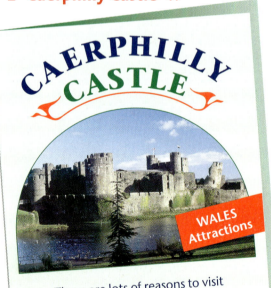

STUDY SKILLS Topic sentence

*In jedem Absatz (Englisch: paragraph) steckt ein Satz, der ins Thema einführt und die zentrale Aussage des Absatzes enthält. Meistens ist das der erste Satz. Man nennt ihn **topic sentence**. Alle anderen Sätze geben weitere Informationen oder Begründungen.*

*Schau dir den Prospekt für Caerphilly Castle an. Ist dort der erste Satz der **topic sentence**? Warum?*

3 Brecon Mountain Railway

The sentences in this paragraph are mixed up. Can you find the topic sentence?
It goes through beautiful mountains – the Brecon Beacons. From the train you have a fantastic view of the valley. Brecon Mountain Railway is one of the finest railways in Wales.

▶ SF Topic sentence (p. 121) • P 4 (p. 65) • WB 4 (p. 44)

4 'I've cooked your breakfast!' 🎧

Grandma — Daniel! Jonah! I've cooked your breakfast! And Grandpa has already packed a picnic! Hurry up!

Grandpa — Don't worry, dear. I haven't cleaned the car yet, but I can do that now. Oh, look, here comes Gwyneth.

5 GAME I've packed my bag

Play this game. Use ideas from the box.

- clean – the cage, my room, the board
- finish – my homework, my essay, my picture
- pack – my bag, the parcel, a suitcase
- wash – dad's car, my hair, the dog

A: I've packed my bag and now I can play.
B: I've packed my bag and I've finished my essay and now I can play.
C: I've packed my bag and I've finished my essay and I've …

6 A visit from the neighbours 🎧

Gwyneth — Bore da!
Grandma — Bore da, Gwyneth! Hello, Emma.
Emma — We've just made this pie for you.
Grandma — Thank you – the twins love pie!
Emma — But we haven't seen the twins yet.
Grandma — Here's one of them now. Jonah, this is Mrs Evans, our neighbour …
Jo — Hello … Sorry, Grandma, Dan hasn't come down because he doesn't feel well. Can you come upstairs please?

▶ P 5 (pp. 65)

Looking at language

Find sentences in 4 and 6 with a form of *have*. Write them down and add the infinitive.
I've cooked your breakfast. (to) cook
And Grandpa has already packed a picnic.
I haven't cleaned the car yet.

▶ GF 9, 10a–b, 11: Present perfect (pp. 134–136) •
P 6–10 (pp. 66–67) • WB 5–8 (pp. 45–47)

Extra Background File

Croeso i Gymru!
That means 'Welcome to Wales' – in Welsh. And this is the Welsh flag. About 3 million people live in Wales. The capital of Wales is Cardiff. One in five people in Wales speaks Welsh. All school children learn it as their first or second language.

7 Poor Dan 🎧

'What's the matter, dear? Are you feeling ill?' Grandma asked.
'Yes, Grandma,' Dan said.
Grandma felt Dan's face. 'Oh dear!' she said.
'I think you have a temperature. Here, put the thermometer in your mouth. Now, do you have a sore throat?'
Dan took the thermometer out. 'Yes I ...'
'No, no, dear, don't take it out. Just nod.'
Dan put the thermometer back and nodded.
'What about your arms and legs: do they hurt?'
Dan nodded.
'And do you have a headache too? Dan! Please don't take the thermometer out!'
'But Grandma, it hurts when I move my head!'
'Oh dear, why isn't Bryn at home?' Grandma said.
'Who?' Jo asked.
'Bryn Evans, our neighbour. He's a paramedic.'

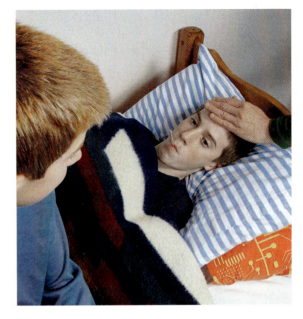

▷ What's wrong with Dan?

8 👥 What's the matter?

a) *Tell your partner what's wrong with the boy. Take turns. You can use sentences from the box.*

> He has a cold. • He has an earache •
> He has a headache. • He has a stomach ache. •
> He has a temperature. • He has a toothache.

b) Extra 👥 *One student mimes something: a headache, a sore knee ... The others guess what's wrong.*

A: Do you have a sore leg?
B: No, that's wrong.
C: Do you have a sore knee?
B: Yes, that's right. Your turn.

9 Extra Can you move your ...? 🎧

Imagine you've fallen over your neighbour's dog. Your neighbour comes to help you. Listen and act.

▶ P 11–12 (p. 68) • WB 9 (p. 47)

10 Grandma's new software 🎧

Grandma I'm so sorry about our trip, Jonah.
Jo That's OK, Grandma. I know we can't go when Dan is ill.
Grandma Jonah ... Have you ever installed software?
Jo Yes, of course I have, Grandma.
Grandma Well, I'd like to try this chat thing. Can you install it for me?
Jo Sure, Grandma. No problem.
Grandma Oh good. I've already printed out the instructions. It says here: 'Click on "Download".' Have you clicked on 'Download', dear?
Jo Yes, I have, Grandma. And –
Grandma Good. Then it says: 'The software will download.' Has it downloaded?
Jo Yes, it has, Grandma. And –

▶ Continue the dialogue. Use numbers 3–7 on the right.

Grandma Good. Then it says: 'Double-click on ... .' Have you ...?
Jo Yes, I ... . And – ...
Grandma Great, Jonah. Now we can chat!
Jo I know, Grandma. And I'm already chatting with Mum in New Zealand. She wants to talk to you!

▶ GF 10c, 11: Present perfect – questions (pp. 135–136) •
P 13–14 (p. 68) • WB 10–16 (pp. 48–51)

Quick start instructions

1 Click on 'Download'.
2 The software will download.
3 Double-click on 'setup.exe'.
4 The installation will start.
5 Click on 'Finish the installation'.
6 The software will start.
7 Enter a chat name and click 'OK'.

Now you can chat – have fun! :-))

11 Grandma's first chat

WelshGranny	Hello, Catherine!
CathNZ	hi mum. how's the weather?
WelshGranny	Cool, dear. It's winter.
CathNZ	summer here. was 27° today!
WelshGranny	Why does it say 'Welsh Granny' when I write something?
CathNZ	ask jo. lol
WelshGranny	What has Jonah done? And what does 'lol' mean?
CathNZ	lol = laughing out loud. don't worry, ur just starting. next we'll buy u a webcam :-)
WelshGranny	Please write in English, dear. I can't understand you.

▶ Write CathNZ's chat in complete sentences for Grandma Thompson.

▶ P 15–17 (p. 69) • WB 17–18 (p. 52)

4 Practice

1 WORDS Travel

a) *Read the sentences and find the travel words.*
1 Lots of kids go to school together on one. b - - *bus*
2 Cars travel on this between towns. r - - -
3 It travels from one station to another, usually from town to town. t - - - -
4 Trains stop here. s - - - - - -
5 A road goes over a river on this. b - - - - -
6 Many students ride this to school. b - - -
7 If you go to an island, you can travel on this. b - - -
8 You can fly to New York on this. p - - - -

b) *Copy and complete the networks.*

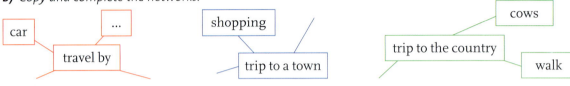

c) *Write about your last trip to a town or the country. You can use ideas from b).*
In December I went on a trip to my Grandma's. She lives in the country. I like it there. You can go riding ...

2 REVISION I can't go because ... (Word order in subordinate clauses)

Write about you, your family and friends. Remember the word order: subject – verb – object.

1 I can't go to the party this weekend	because	
2 My dad usually has a shower	before	
3 My mum sometimes gets angry with me	when	...
4 My best friend often phones me	after	
5 I never eat ...	if	
6 I sometimes watch ...		

I can't go to the party this weekend because I won't be here.

3 Where will they be tomorrow afternoon? (Word order: place before time)

a) *Say where they'll be tomorrow afternoon.*

1 Dan and Jo will be at Caerphilly Castle tomorrow afternoon.   2 Ananda ...

b) *Write five sentences about where you'll be when.*
I'll be at school on Friday morning. I'll be ...

c) **Extra** *Think of an activity. Ask five people where and when they do it. Report to the class.*
A: Where and when do you ride your bike/...?
B: I ride my bike to school every morning.

4 STUDY SKILLS Topic sentence

a) *Find the topic sentence in 1–3. Put the sentences in the right order to make a paragraph. Remember: the topic sentence usually comes first.*

1 Cardiff Castle
After your visit you can have tea in the Castle Tea Rooms.
Cardiff Castle is one of the top attractions in Wales.
Each room is different, and the gardens are beautiful too.

2 Museum of Welsh Life
It opened in 1948.
Today you can see over 30 buildings from all around Wales.
The Museum of Welsh Life shows how the people of Wales lived in the past.

3 Techniquest
There are many exciting things to see and do.
Techniquest is a science centre for young and old.
The centre usually has great projects too, for example about life on Mars.

b) *Write a short paragraph about where you live. Start with the topic sentence:*
Heidelberg is a great place. / Friedewald is a beautiful old village near …
Add two or three more sentences.
You can see and do lots of exciting things there. For example, …

c) **Extra** *Read your paragraph to the class. Then add a photo and put it in your DOSSIER.*

5 LISTENING Accents 🎧

a) *Listen to four different people. Say where they are from: London (1), Scotland (2), Wales (3) or the West Country (4).*

b) *Listen again and find the right answers.*
1 How many languages does Gwyneth speak?
2 Who are her new neighbours?
3 Does Thomas live in Exeter?
4 Thomas likes where he lives. What reasons does he give?
5 Does Angus live on a lake or an island?
6 Does he like whisky?
7 'I love London: Maybe that's because I'm a …'
8 Caroline says London has got everything. Name two things.

6 Mr Shaw has painted the kitchen door (Present perfect: regular verbs)

a) Write about the pictures.

1 Mr Shaw
paint – kitchen door

2 The twins
pack – suitcases

3 Jack
tidy – desk

4 Mr Kingsley
finish – book

5 The Kapoors
count – money

6 Ananda and Sophie
watch – DVD

7 The Thompsons
cook – lunch

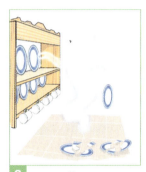
8 Prunella
drop – plates

1 *Mr Shaw has painted the kitchen door.*   2 *The twins have …*

b) Match a sentence from a) to a sentence from the box.

> Now they can go up to the flat. • He really likes the new colour. •
> They're ready to go to the station. • The Carter-Browns will need new ones. •
> Today they're having chicken and chips. • Now he can go to bed. •
> Now he can find everything again. • They liked it a lot.

1 *Mr Shaw has painted the kitchen door. He really likes the new colour.*   2 *The twins have …*

7 Grandma has made breakfast, so … (Present perfect: irregular verbs)

Put the verbs in the present perfect. You can look up the irregular forms on pp. 208–209.
1 Grandma *has made* (make) breakfast, so they can leave soon.
2 Jo … (take) lots of photos because he wants to mail them to his mum.
3 Grandpa … (go) out to the car because he wants to clean it.
4 Ananda and Jack … (be) to the cinema and now they're sitting in a café.
5 Sophie … (be) ill, so now she has to do lots of homework.
6 We … (come) to see you today because we can't come to your party tomorrow.
7 I … (do) my homework, so I can go out and play.
8 I … (see) the new sofa, but I don't like it.

Practice **4**

8 Mr and Mrs Kapoor make a list (Present perfect: negative sentences)

a) Complete the dialogue. Use **haven't** or **hasn't** and the correct form of the verbs in brackets.

Mr Kapoor   Let's go for a walk. It's a nice day.
Mrs Kapoor But I ... (make) dinner.
Mr Kapoor   Oh, Ananda can do it.
Mrs Kapoor And we ... (answer) our e-mails.
Mr Kapoor   Don't worry. We can do that later.
Mrs Kapoor And you ... (paint) the kitchen shelf.
Mr Kapoor   Don't worry. Dilip can do that.
Mrs Kapoor And what about the shop windows? I ... (clean) them.
Mr Kapoor   Dilip can do that too.
Mrs Kapoor OK. I'll make a list of jobs. Let me see – Ananda ... (tidy) her room.
Mr Kapoor   Dilip's room is a mess too.
Mrs Kapoor Look! They ... (make) their beds.
Mr Kapoor   And Dilip ... (take) out the rubbish.
Mrs Kapoor Any other jobs?

b) **Extra**   Act out the dialogue. Take turns to play the different parts.

9 They've already made their beds (Present perfect: already and not ... yet)

a) Say what Ananda and Dilip have already done.
Ananda and Dilip have already made their beds.
Ananda has already ...
Dilip ...

b) Now say what they haven't done yet.
Dilip hasn't cleaned the shop windows yet.
Ananda hasn't ... yet.
Ananda and Dilip ...

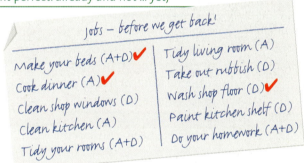

Jobs – before we get back!
Make your beds (A+D) ✔
Cook dinner (A) ✔
Clean shop windows (D)
Clean kitchen (A)
Tidy your rooms (A+D)
Tidy living room (A)
Take out rubbish (D)
Wash shop floor (D) ✔
Paint kitchen shelf (D)
Do your homework (A+D)

10 What's different? (Present perfect: just)

Partner B: Go to p. 110.
Partner A: Tell your partner about the people in the picture.
Ask about his/her picture. Take turns. Use ideas from the box.
A: In my picture Sophie has just made popcorn. What about your picture?
B: In my picture Sophie has just ...

1 Sophie – make
2 Ananda – open
3 Dan – eat
4 Jo – take
5 Jack – drop
6 Prunella – find

11 WORDS The body

Draw a 'word body': Use words from the box to draw a person.

> arm • ear • eye • finger • foot • hair •
> hand • head • knee • leg • mouth • nose •
> shoulder • stomach • toe • tooth

12 MEDIATION Phoning a doctor

Imagine you've got an English guest, Sally, in your home. When she feels ill, you phone the doctor for her.

You	Guten Morgen, Frau Doktor Becker. Wir haben eine englische Gastschülerin. Sie fühlt sich krank.	Sally	Well, my throat is sore.
		You	…
		Ärztin	Und hat sie auch Fieber?
Ärztin	Aha. Frag sie bitte, was ihr fehlt.	You	And do you have …?
You	The doctor asks: what's …?	Sally	I think maybe a bit, yes.
Sally	I have a terrible headache and my legs hurt.	You	…
		Ärztin	Sag ihr, ich komme heute Nachmittag zu euch.
You	Frau Doktor, …		
Ärztin	Und der Hals?	You	Vielen Dank, Frau Doktor. – Sally, she says she'll …
You	What about …?		

13 Have you done your homework? (Present perfect: questions)

Complete the questions with the verbs in brackets. Then complete the answers.

1. Mr Hanson: *Have you done* (you/do) your homework, Jack?
   Jack: Yes, *I have,* Dad.
2. Mr Hanson: And … (Dan and Jo/finish) their project yet?
   Jack: No, ….
3. Jack: I'm hungry. … (mum/cook) dinner?
   Mr Hanson: No, …
4. Jack: Well, … (she/buy) the food yet?
   Mr Hanson: Yes, …
5. Mr Hanson: And … (you/feed) Polly?
   Polly: No, … Hurry up! Hurry up!

14 GAME Have you …? (Present perfect: questions)

a) Four students leave the room. The others change five things (open a window, move a bag, …). Use ideas from the box.

> close • move • open •
> put • take away • write

b) The four students come back in. They ask questions to find out what has changed.
A: Have you opened the cupboard?
Class: No, we haven't.
B: Have you written on the board?
Class: Yes, we have.

15 REVISION If it's sunny ... (Conditional sentences)

Work in groups of four. Each partner starts with one of these if-clauses on a piece of paper:
Partner A: If it's sunny this afternoon, ...
Partner B: If I work hard for school every day, ...
Partner C: If I have a party, ...
Partner D: If I do sport every day, ...
Each partner finishes the sentence and passes the paper to the right:
If it's sunny this afternoon, I'll go to the pool.
The next person continues: *If I go to the pool, I'll ...* Go on.

16 PRONUNCIATION Silent letters 🎧

In some English words you don't pronounce all the letters – they are silent.

a) Read the words quietly. Then write them in your exercise book. Underline the silent letters.
two, knee, talk, know, would, climb, wrong, calm, sandwich, answer, half, who, could, walk, knock

b) Check with your partner.

c) Listen and say the words.

d) Read these sentences out loud:
1 Who is knocking on the door?
2 Do you know the answer to my question? Well, you can talk to your partner.
3 Would you like to climb the mountain with me or would you like to go for a walk?

17 GETTING BY IN ENGLISH Are you all right?

a) Can you say these things in English?
1 Ist mit dir alles OK? – Mir geht's gut. (p. 60)
2 Er fühlt sich nicht gut. (p. 61)
3 Was fehlt dir? (p. 62)
4 Es tut mir leid mit unserem Ausflug. (p. 63)
5 Hast du schon mal Software installiert? (p. 63)

b) Partner A: You're visiting Mike. Partner B: You're Mike's brother/sister. Prepare a dialogue. Act it out.

Partner A	Partner B
Grüß Partner B. Frag, ob Mike zu Hause ist.	Grüß zurück und sag, dass Mike sich nicht gut fühlt.
Du fragst, was ihm fehlt.	Mike hat Halsschmerzen.
Du fragst, ob mit B alles in Ordnung ist.	Ja, dir geht es gut.
Du fragst B, ob er/sie schon mal einen *Harry Potter*-Film gesehen hat.	Das hast du noch nicht.
Du fragst B, ob er/sie eine *Harry Potter*-DVD mit dir ansehen möchte.	Es tut dir leid mit dem *Harry Potter*-Film, aber du hast keine Zeit.

All in a day's work 🎧

> Look at the title and the pictures. What do you think the story is about?

▶ SF Understanding new words (p. 114)

Bryn hated his mobile. It always rang when he was really tired – like this morning. Before he picked it up, he looked at the clock: 6.25.

'Morning, Bryn. Elaine here. We need you on the road to Tredegar – there has been a car accident. It's quite bad.'
'Oh, Elaine,' Bryn said. 'Can't Mike and Drew go? I was on a rescue till after ten last night.'
'I know, I know. But Mike and Drew have just gone to another accident in Llanfoist. I'm afraid *you'll* have to go.'
Bryn put on his uniform and was in his car in four minutes. 'If Elaine says it's quite bad, it'll be very bad,' Bryn thought.
When Bryn got to the accident, he saw a red car on its side. Two policemen were with the driver, and Bryn could see that he wasn't hurt badly. 'They didn't call me for this,' he knew.

'Are you the paramedic?' It was one of the firemen. 'We've got a car down there.' He pointed to the side of the hill. 'We're trying to secure it, but they need you down there – fast.'
Bryn followed the fireman. He could see that the car was in some trees about ten metres down. It was another 70 or 80 metres to the valley floor.
'This is Beth. She'll go down with you,' the fireman told him.
'Hi,' said Beth. 'Are you ready?'
'I'm ready if you are,' he answered. 'Let's just hope those trees will hold till we get there.'

Bryn and Beth quickly climbed down to the car. There they found four very scared people: a man, a woman and two children. 'We're here to help you,' Beth said. 'Is everybody OK?'
The children and the woman weren't hurt badly; the man had a broken leg. But they had a much bigger problem: the trees weren't strong enough.

Five minutes later the driver was out of the car. Bryn started to climb out. He had one foot in the tree when the car fell.
'That was close,' Beth said.
'Yeah,' said Bryn. 'Too close.'

Bryn worked on the man, and Beth started with the children. She took the little boy up the hill, then the girl. Then she came back for the woman.
'Beth,' Bryn said from the other side of the car, 'take her up fast. Then come back – I need your help here.'
'OK, I'll just …'
But before Beth could finish her sentence, the car started to fall. It stopped after another three metres. When Beth and Bryn got to the car again, the man was unconscious. The woman didn't want to leave her husband, but Beth said, 'Think of the children. They need you.'

'The rescue helicopter is coming,' Beth said when she got back to Bryn and the man. 'If we can get him out, we'll have to get him to hospital fast!'
'I'll have to go inside the car, Beth,' Bryn said. 'Or I won't get him out.'
'But, Bryn, with two people in the car …' She didn't have to finish.
'I hope the trees will hold for just a few more minutes,' Bryn said.

It was 5 pm when Bryn got home – after one more car accident, a woman with a broken arm and a new baby.

His wife Gwyneth came to the door. 'How was work, dear?' she asked.
'It was all right.'
'Oh good. Can you just go over to the Thompsons' and look at their grandson? Jonah – or is it Daniel? – well, one of the twins is ill.'
'Of course,' he said, and put on his jacket again. 'All in a day's work!'

Working with the text

1 The rescue
Find seven mistakes in the picture.
The text says there is a red car on its side. In the picture it's a blue car.
In the text there are two …

2 Extra 👥 Who said what?
Partner B: Go to p. 110.
Partner A: Ask your partner who said these things and when.

1 'Morning, Bryn.' (Elaine, l. 4)
A: Who said 'Morning, Bryn' and when?
B: Elaine said that when … That's in line …

2 'They need you.' (Beth, l. 60)
3 'Yeah, too close.' (Bryn, l. 74)
4 'How was work, dear?' (Gwyneth, ll. 78–9)

Now listen to your partner's questions. Scan the text for the correct answers.
B: Who said 'Is everybody OK?'
A: Beth said that when … That's in line …

▶ *SF Scanning (p. 118)*

3 A report on the accident
a) *Imagine you are a reporter for Radio South Wales. Write your 'live' report about the rescue. The ideas below can help you.*

This is … for Radio South Wales. I'm on the road to … There's been an accident here.
One of the cars is on … A second car has gone … down.
Now a paramedic and a firewoman are climbing … Now they're talking to …
Now the firewoman is coming up the hill with …
Now her partner has gone inside …
I'll have more for you in just a few minutes.
This is Simon Bader for Radio South Wales. I'm on …

b) *Continue your report about the end of the rescue (lines 70–85).*

c) Extra *Record your report or read it to the class.*

Checkpoint 4 ▶ WB (pp. 53–55) • Activity page 2

Topic 4

Extra The red dragon and the white dragon – a Welsh legend 🎧

> Why is the red dragon the symbol of Wales? Find out here.

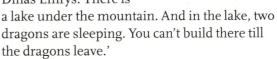

A long, long time ago, Vortigern was the king of Wales. He was a good and fair king, and his people loved him.
But there was trouble in Vortigern's country. The Saxons came, and Vortigern and his people had to hide in the mountains. The king wanted to build a very strong castle – strong enough that the Saxons could not hurt his people. So he called twelve wise men and asked, 'Where can I build this great castle?'
The wise men all agreed: 'The best place for the castle is Dinas Emrys.' The king's men started to take wood for the castle to Dinas Emrys the same day.
But the next day, the wood wasn't there! The same thing happened the next day and the next. The king called his wise men again, and the wise men all agreed: 'Before you can build in this place, you have to kill a boy there. But it must be a boy without a father.'
The king's men soon found a boy and brought him to Vortigern. The boy's name was Merlin. His mother was a woman, but his father was from the Otherworld, the world of magic. Merlin wasn't like other boys: he could do magic, and he could see the future.
Before the king's men could kill Merlin, he spoke to the king.
'But I know why the wood for your castle disappeared.'
'How do you know about the castle, boy?' the king asked.

'I know many things. And I know why you can't build a castle on Dinas Emrys. There is a lake under the mountain. And in the lake, two dragons are sleeping. You can't build there till the dragons leave.'
'Is that right?' the king asked his wise men.
'No, it isn't,' they answered. 'We must kill the boy.'
'I'm not so sure,' the king said. 'Dig in this place. Then we will know. If there is a lake, the boy may live.'
The king's men dug and dug. Then suddenly: water! There really was a lake under Dinas Emrys. But what about the dragons?
'Get all the water out!' the king shouted, and his men did what he told them. When there was no more water, a terrible noise came from the hole.
'Those are the dragons,' Merlin said. 'They are fighting.' And a moment later, a white dragon and a red dragon flew out of the hole.
'The white dragon is like the Saxons,' Merlin explained. 'It will fight for many years. But the red dragon – like the Welsh – will win.'
'You are very wise for a young boy,' Vortigern said, 'From now on, you will be my adviser.' And so Merlin became the adviser to many Welsh kings. And the red dragon became the symbol of Wales.

Unit 5

Teamwork

The Bristol Game

Play the game in groups of four. You will need a dice and four counters. Use phrases from the box.

> Can I have the dice, please?
> Whose turn is it? • It's my/your turn.
> Hey, you had a three, not a four.
> Wait, that's my counter. Yours is blue.

Bristol Tourist Information
Lots of good ideas for your time in Bristol!
Start here.

Explore-at-Bristol
You learn about science at this exciting museum.
Move on one space.

Temple Meads Station
Stop and look at the station. Britain's greatest engineer, Brunel, built it.
Move on two spaces.

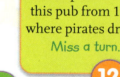

Llandoger Trow
You stop and look at this pub from 1664 where pirates drank.
Miss a turn.

Bristol Ice Rink
An hour on the ice gives you more energy.
Mime skating. Then go again.

St Nicholas Market
You get a healthy snack here.
Name four foods and two drinks.
Move on two spaces.

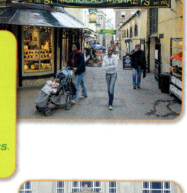

Cotham School
You want to visit the SHoCK Team, but the school is closed.
Move back two spaces.

28

Pretty Polly B & B
You go back to your room and sleep.
Miss a turn.

British Empire and Commonwealth Museum
Many rich people in Bristol had land in the Caribbean. Learn how slaves helped them to grow sugar and tobacco there.
Move on one space.

29
30
31
32
33

44 **45** **46** **47**
48
49
50

43

The Downs
You stop and sit in this beautiful park.
What do people do here? Mime two things. Can your group guess? Then move on two spaces.

Georgian House
The Pinney family lived here with their black slaves. Take the free tour.
Miss a turn.

Cabot Tower
Arrive here first, and you're the

winner!

34
35
36

42

41

40

Clifton Suspension Bridge
You walk over the River Avon on this famous bridge.
Move on three spaces.

Aardman Studios
You want to see where they make the Wallace and Gromit films, but they don't have tours.
Move back two spaces.

37 **38** **39**

River Avon
Oops! You've fallen into the water.
Sing a song in English or miss a turn.

▶ P 1–2 (p. 80) •
WB 1–2 (p. 56)

1 The Bristol Quiz 🎧

Mr Kingsley has made a quiz as part of a mini-project about Bristol. His class is working in groups.

THE BRISTOL QUIZ

Find the answers to the following questions. For each answer make one A4 page with texts and pictures. Add a title page to make a Bristol booklet.

Question 1 – a PLACE
This is one of the oldest houses in Bristol (1664). Some very bad people were here.
– Write about them. What did they do? Where did they go?

Jack	OK, let's go over the plan again. Ananda, you're going to do the computer work. Jo is going to take the photos.
Dan	Of course!
Ananda	And I'm going to find out about the Georgian House. I think it's the answer to the first question. The Pinney family lived there. They had slaves – and people with slaves were bad people!
Sophie	I'm sorry Ananda, but I think you're wrong. I think the bad men were pirates.
Jack	So what are we going to do?
Jo	Let's all go and check: first the Georgian House and then that famous pirate pub with the difficult name. Does anybody remember it?
Jack	The Llandoger Trow?
Jo	That's it!
Dan	Well, I'm not going to check anything this afternoon because I've got lots of homework.
Ananda	OK, let's go tomorrow then.

▶ P3 (p. 80)

2 👥 I'm going to play football

What are you going to do on Saturday afternoon? Find three classmates with the same plans.
A: I'm going to play football. What are you going to do?
B: I'm not going to play football. I'm going to meet friends. / I'm going to play football too.

Looking at language

Find sentences in **1** and **2** with **going to** in them.

Ananda, you're	going to	do	…
Jo is	going to	…	…
I'm	…	…	…

How do you form the **going to-future**?

▶ GF 12: going to-future (p. 137) • P 4–6 (pp. 81–82) • WB 3–6 (pp. 57–58)

3 Mini-project (1) – a place

Prepare a mini-booklet like Form 8PK's.
First find a place (building/park/museum/…).
Think: What's the most interesting place in your area? Where is it? What can you do/see there? How big/old is it?
Pair 👥: Agree on one place with your partner.
Share 👥👥: Agree on one place with your group. Write down reasons for your choice. Collect material and/or take photos of your place.

Our place: Spaßbad Elsetal
Where? Elsetalstr. 2, Giesecke
What? go swimming, four pools, outside and inside, 5-metre tower, volleyball, football pitch, table tennis, snacks
How big? very big

4 Who is he? 🎧

> **Question 2 – a PERSON**
> He did great things for Bristol, so the town gave him a statue. It's near the station.
> – Who is he? When did he live? What things did he build in Bristol? Find at least three.

'Well,' said Jack, 'we've found the answer. It's Brunel.'
'Now we have to find out when he lived,' Ananda added.
'And what he built in Bristol,' Jo said.
'That's easy,' said Dan, 'the Clifton Suspension Bridge.'
'And I've heard that he built Temple Meads Station,' Sophie said.
'But what's the third thing?' asked Ananda.
'Don't ask me,' Jo answered. 'I'm just the photographer.'
'Well, let's go to the library then,' Sophie said.

▶ P 7 (p. 82)

5 Brunel – Bristol's engineer 🎧

The SHoCK Team had to find out: When did Brunel live? What did he build in Bristol? Sophie found this text in the library.

Isambard Kingdom Brunel was born in Portsmouth in 1806. He became an engineer like his father.

Brunel was a man with a dream. He wanted to link London with New York – with bridges, tunnels, stations and of course ships. London's Paddington Station and Bristol's Temple Meads Station are results of his dream.

The most famous of Brunel's ships was the SS Great Britain. It was one of the biggest and fastest ships of its time. He built it in Bristol.

Brunel also had an idea for a bridge over the River Avon in Bristol. The people liked his idea, and work on the Clifton Suspension Bridge started in 1831. Brunel died in 1859. The bridge opened five years later.

The people of Bristol are still proud of the bridge and of 'their' engineer, Brunel.

STUDY SKILLS Marking up a text

Wenn du einen Text mit vielen Fakten liest, wird es dir helfen, nur die für dich wichtigen Informationen zu markieren.
Warum hat Sophie diese Stellen im Text über Brunel markiert?

▶ SF Marking up a text (p. 119) • P 8 (p. 83) • WB 7–8 (pp. 59–60)

6 Mini-project (2) – a person

Think: What interesting people live or have lived in your area? Why are they interesting? What have they done?
Pair 👥 : Agree on one person with your partner.
Share 👥👥 : Agree on one person with your group.
Write down reasons for your choice.
famous model, was on TV, …
Collect material about your person.

7 Healthy *and* delicious? 🎧

Mr Kingsley's last quiz question was the hardest for the team.

> **Question 3 – time for a Break**
> Find a healthy and delicious drink in St Nicholas Market.
> – What is the smallest drink? The cheapest? The most interesting?

Jo   Healthy and delicious?! That's impossible!
Sophie   You're joking, aren't you? Of course it's possible.

The team walked slowly round St Nicholas Market and looked … and looked … and looked. At last …

Extra ▶ GF 13: Question tags (p. 138) • P 9 (p. 84)

▶ P 10 (p. 84) • WB 9–11 (p. 60–61)

8 A role play – customer and waiter

a) Who says what at the juice bar?

- What flavour?
- That's £…, please.
- Can I have …, please?
- Here you are.
- Small, medium or large?
- How can I help you?
- I'd like …, please.
- Have you got …?

b) 👥 Prepare a dialogue at a juice bar/ice-cream place. Act it out for the class.

9 Mini-project (3) – time for a break

Think: Where can you go for a break in your area (a park, an ice-cream place, a juice bar, …)?
Pair 👥 : Agree on one place with your partner.
Share 👥👥 : Agree on one place with your group. Write down reasons for your choice…
lots of flavours, friendly people, cheap prices, …
Collect material and/or take photos of your place.

10 Ananda at the computer 🎧

Ananda was the last one at the computer club that evening. She now had three pages with the team's texts and Jo's photos.
'I'm afraid I have to lock up now,' somebody said. It was Mrs Pitt, the IT teacher.
'Of course, Mrs Pitt,' Ananda said. She took her things and got up to leave.
'Oh, Mrs Pitt,' she remembered, 'have you seen a black and blue mobile anywhere?'
'No, Ananda. Why?'
'David has lost his mobile. Or maybe somebody has stolen it?'

▶ What are Ananda's three pages about? (You'll find the answers on pp. 76–79.)

11 A page from the booklet 🎧

The Llandoger Trow

The Llandoger Trow is one of the oldest buildings in Bristol. It's from 1664, when Bristol still had a real harbour.
Some of the men in the Llandoger Trow were pirates. Probably the most famous of them was Blackbeard. He was born in Bristol in 1677. At 16 he sailed away to the Caribbean and became a pirate. He got his name from his black hair and from smoke: he put fireworks into his beard so that it smoked! Blackbeard never came back to Bristol. But the Llandoger Trow is still there. It's a great place in the summer. You can sit outside this beautiful old pub with a cola and a packet of crisps and chat with your friends.

STUDY SKILLS | Structuring a text

Wenn du einen Text schreibst, solltest du ihn gliedern:
Beginning *(Einleitung)*
Middle *(Mittelteil)*
End *(Schluss).*
Finde Einleitung, Mittelteil und Schluss in dem Text über Blackbeard.

▶ SF Structuring a text (p. 121) • P 11 (p. 84) • WB 13 (p. 62)

12 👥 Mini-project (4) – the booklet

– Make three pages: one about your place, one about your person and one about your place for a break.
– Write at least eight sentences.
– Use your notes, photos and other material.
– Make the pages on a computer or write out your texts and add your material.
– Make a title page. Put your booklet together.

▶ P 12–13 (p. 85) • WB 14–15 (p. 63)

5 Practice

1 WORDS A Bristol mind map

a) Make a mind map about Bristol. Use as many words and phrases as you can. Here are some ideas.

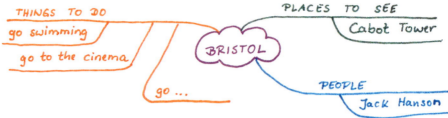

b) Would you like to visit Bristol? Why/Why not?

c) **Extra** Start a mind map like the one in a) for your area. Add more ideas as you go through the unit.

2 LISTENING The slave girl's story

a) Listen to Binta's story.
– Where did her family come from?
– Where was she before she came to Bristol?

b) Listen again. Find out:
1 How old was Binta when she left Africa?
2 How long was she on the ship?
3 What happened when the ship arrived in the Caribbean?
4 What was Binta's new name?

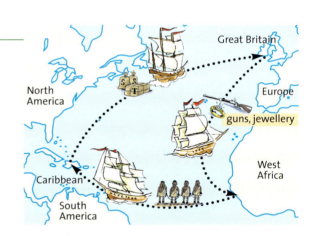

3 WORDS Discussion

a) Talk about these statements. Use the phrases in the green box. Try to give reasons.
1 English is the most interesting subject.
2 Pop songs are better in German than in English.
3 Borussia Dortmund is a great team.
4 We live in a fantastic place.

Yes	No
I agree (with you). ⟷	I don't agree (with you).
Yes, you're right. ⟷	Sorry, I think you're wrong.
That's right. ⟷	Sorry, I don't think that's right.

Partner A

I agree with number 1. I think it's interesting to hear about another country.

Hmm, maybe you're right. OK, your turn.

Partner B

Sorry, I don't agree with you. I think Art is more interesting. You can do things with your hands.

I don't agree with number 2. I think German pop songs are …

b) Tell the class about your partner and yourself.
I think English is the most interesting subject because it's interesting to hear about another country. Anna doesn't agree with me. She thinks …

Practice **5**   81

4 Dan is going to watch TV (going to-future: positive statements)

a) *Say what the people are going to do this evening.*

1 watch TV

2 play cards

3 write a letter

4 open the window

5 help Toby

6 read a book

1 *Dan is going to watch TV.*

b) *Write down what you are going to do at the time in the box.*

c) *Walk round the classroom. Try to find somebody who is going to do the same things as you.*
I'm going to play tennis this afternoon. What about you?

> this afternoon •
> tomorrow morning •
> on Saturday night •
> on Sunday afternoon

5 Next week … (going to-future: positive and negative statements)

a) *Write down your plans for next week. Here are some ideas.*

b) 👥 *Talk to your partner. Take notes.*
A: Next week I'm going to visit my aunt. What about you?
B: I'm not going to do that. Next week I'm …

c) *Make a 'window' like the one below and fill it in.*

> visit my grandma • see the
> new film at the cinema •
> play computer games •
> watch a basketball game •
> chat with my friends

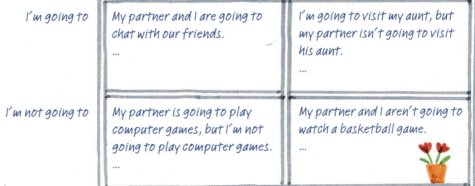

d) *Report to the class.*

6 What are you going to do? (going to-future: questions)

a) *Partner B: Look at p. 111.*
Partner A: Look at the chart. Ask your partner about Jo and Sophie and Ananda. Answer your partner's questions about Jack and Mr and Mrs Hanson.

Name	Is/Are … going to do anything nice tomorrow?	What … going to do?	Where … going to do it?	Why … going to do it?
Jo				
Jack	Yes, he is.	read	in his room	loves books
Sophie and Ananda				
Mr and Mrs Hanson	No, they aren't.	clean cupboards	in the kitchen	they're dirty
You				
Your partner				

b) *In a copy of the chart write down your plans. Ask your partner about his/her plans. Then answer his/her questions about your plans.*

c) **Extra** *Write about what two of the people plan to do.*

7 REVISION What has just happened? (present perfect)

Look at the picture. Say what has just happened. Use these verbs.

Three men from Mars have just landed and Ananda has … with her bike. Jo …

8 STUDY SKILLS Marking up a text

Use a copy of the text for these tasks.

a) Read the text. What are the 3–4 most interesting or important statements
– about Wallace
– about Gromit
– about Nick Park?
Mark them up.

b) Write down key words in your exercise book.

c) Discuss different marked texts in class.

Wallace & Gromit

Wallace and Gromit are the stars of three famous short films and one long one by Aardman Studios. But the two aren't like most stars – they're plasticine models! Everybody in the Wallace and Gromit films is a plasticine model.

Wallace lives at 62 West Wallaby Street in Wigan. He usually wears the same clothes. He loves cheese. He invents things all the time, but many of his ideas aren't very good. Wallace is a very nice man, and he thinks everything will be fine in the future.

Gromit is a dog and lives with Wallace. He has no voice, his birthday is on 12th February, and he's very clever. He even studied – at 'Dogwarts University'! (Do you know 'Hogwarts' from the Harry Potter books?) Gromit is cleverer than Wallace and often helps him with his work.

Nick Park came to Aardman Studios in 1985, and he brought Wallace and Gromit with him. As a little boy Nick liked making models with plasticine. He even used his parents' camera to make a film with his models.

When he left school, Nick went to the National Film and Television School. He started his first Wallace and Gromit film, *A Grand Day Out*[1] (1989), there. In 1993 he made *The Wrong Trousers*[2] and two years later *A Close Shave*[3]. In 2005 Wallace and Gromit came back in *The Curse of the Were-Rabbit*[4]. All three films won Oscars.

In October 2005 a fire destroyed an old warehouse, and Aardman lost lots of models from the Wallace and Gromit films. The good news is: All the Aardman films were safe in another building. So Wallace and Gromit live on!

■

Deutsche Titel: [1] Alles Käse   [2] Die Techno-Hose   [3] Unter Schafen   [4] Auf der Jagd nach dem Riesenkaninchen

9 Extra There's an ice-cream place in your town, isn't there? (Question tags)

a) Complete the sentences with question tags from the box.
1 There's an ice-cream place in your town, …
2 The flavours there are interesting, …
3 You were there last week, …
4 You were there with your friend, …
5 He/She's very nice, …
6 He/She was very happy there, …
7 There are lots of nice students at your school, …
There's an ice-cream place in your town, isn't there?

question tags
isn't he/she?
isn't there?
aren't they?
aren't there?
wasn't he/she?
weren't you?

b) Take turns and ask your partner the questions from a). Answer his/her questions. You can use answers from the box.

Yes, there is/are. • No, there isn't/aren't. • Yes, he/she is. • No, he/she isn't. • Yes, … • No, …

10 REVISION They found the answers quickly (Adverbs of manner)

a) Make adverbs from the adjectives in brackets and complete the sentences.
1 The SHoCK Team found the first two answers to Mr Kingsley's quiz … (quick).
The SHoCK Team found the first two answers to Mr Kingsley's quiz quickly.
2 The kids in 8PK thought the quiz was fun, so they did it … (happy).
3 Everybody in Bristol knows Brunel, so the SHoCK Team found his statue very … (fast).
4 They got the information on him … (easy).
5 At the juice bar, they chose their drinks … (careful).
6 They're going to work … (hard) on their booklet.
7 They want to do it … (good).

b) Use five of the adverbs from above in five new sentences.

11 STUDY SKILLS Structuring a text

a) Read the three paragraphs below. Put them in the right order: beginning, middle and end.

1 My friends and I go there quite often. I think it's the most exciting place in town.
2 My favourite place in Bristol is Explore-at-Bristol. It's a cool place, and there's always a lot to do there.
3 The building is pretty new – the museum opened in 2000. I like it because you can try out so many things. For example, you can walk through a tornado, play volleyball against a computer or become the star of your own TV show. I think the live science room is the best.

b) Look at the text in a) again. Collect useful phrases for your own text about a place.

Practice **5** 85

12 MEDIATION A tour of Bristol

The Meiers are on a tour of Bristol. But they don't
understand much English. Answer Herr and Frau Meier's
questions. Only pass on the most important parts.

Guide _____ Hi, everybody! Welcome to our Bristol Open Top
Bus tour. My name is Carol, and I'll be your guide.
I hope you'll have fun on our tour. OK then, let's go.

You _____ Sie heißt Carol und wünscht viel Spaß.

Guide _____ On the left you can see Bristol's famous harbour. The big ship over there is the SS Great
Britain. You maybe know that this ship was the work of Bristol's great engineer,
Isambard Kingdom Brunel. It's open to visitors.

Frau Meier __ Was ist mit dem Schiff?

You _____ ...

Guide _____ When we come to the top of the hill, the driver will turn left. Then, on your right, you'll
see a large green area. We call this area the Downs. As you will see, it's a popular place
on a sunny day like this. It's usually cooler than the city centre.

Herr Meier __ Wir biegen wohl ab, aber was ist dann?

You _____ ...

Guide _____ Now we're in Clifton Village. There are lots of nice little shops and cafés in the village.
We're going to stay here for thirty minutes. You can go to the shops or get something to
drink. But please don't be late – there's lots more to see.

Frau Meier __ Alle steigen aus. Ist die Fahrt schon zu Ende?

You _____ ...

13 GETTING BY IN ENGLISH At the juice bar

a) *Can you say these things in English?*

1 Es tut mir leid, aber ich glaube, du hast
Unrecht. (p. 76)
2 Frag mich nicht. (p. 77)
3 Gesund *und* lecker? (p. 78)

4 Du machst Witze, oder? (p. 78)
5 Es sieht ziemlich cool aus. (p. 78)
6 Welche Sorte hättest du gern? (p. 78)
7 Klein, mittel oder groß? (p. 78)

b) *Imagine you are walking round Bristol when you see a juice bar. Prepare the dialogue and act it out.*

Partner A

Sag B, dass die Juice Bar ganz gut aussieht.
Schlag vor, dass ihr reingeht.

Sag freundlich, dass du das anders siehst.
Saft kann sehr lecker sein.

Frag B, was er/sie gerne hätte.

Sag, dass du keine Ahnung hast.

Frag, ob klein, mittel oder groß.

Partner B

Frag A, ob er/sie Witze macht. Saft ist
gesund, aber langweilig.

Sag OK, du kannst es probieren.

Sag, dass du einen Smoothie möchtest.
Frag, welche Sorten sie haben.

Sag, dass du gerne Erdbeere hättest, wenn
sie das haben.

Du hättest gerne einen mittleren.

To catch a thief

'Well,' said Jack the next day, 'It was good teamwork on the booklet. Now we need good teamwork on our new case: Who is stealing things from Form 8PK?'
'Well, it can only be one person,' Jo said.
'Who do you mean?' Sophie asked.
'Lesley, of course!' Jo said. 'I mean, before she came, nothing disappeared in our class. Now things disappear all the time. First there was Ananda's lunch money …'
'And then Simon's pen,' Ananda added.
'And now David's mobile. I think it's Lesley.'
Jack was angry: 'That's not fair, Jo. There's no proof.'
'But Jack, you told us about Lesley and how her mum hasn't got much money,' said Ananda.
'So? We haven't got much money,' said Jack, 'but you don't think I'm a thief – or do you?'
'No, of course we don't think that,' said Dan.
'And I don't think Lesley's a thief!'
'This is the point, isn't it?' said Sophie.
'Somebody is stealing things and we don't know who.'
'No, we don't,' said Dan.
'So,' Sophie went on, 'we have to catch the thief – and we need proof.'

'Right!' said Jack.
'And how are we going to get proof?' asked Jo.
Jack smiled: 'We're going to set a trap.'
'And how are we going to do that?' asked Jo.
'Well,' said Jack, 'why don't we leave a purse in the classroom at break tomorrow?'
'But we have to go outside at break. So we can't watch it,' said Ananda.
'Hey,' said Sophie, 'I've got an idea. My mum always loses her keys. So my dad bought her a key ring – it bleeps when you whistle. So you can always find it.'
'Great idea!' said Jo. 'We put the key ring in the purse …'
'… we leave the purse in the classroom,' Dan added.
'And after break we whistle and Lesley's school bag bleeps!' finished Jo.
'Shut up, Jo!' they all said.

The next day Ananda brought an old purse to school, and Sophie brought her mum's key ring. At break, Sophie left the purse on her desk and they all went outside.
'Have you left the purse?' asked Jack.
'Yes, I have,' said Sophie.

'And is the key ring in it?' asked Jo.
'Yes, it is,' said Sophie.
'And yes, before you ask – I put some money in the purse too: five pounds,' said Ananda. 'Now all we have to do is wait.'

At the end of break, the SHoCK Team went to Sophie's desk.
'It has disappeared!' whispered Sophie.
'Right!' said Jo.
He started to whistle as he walked slowly towards Lesley's desk.

'What's wrong with you?' Lesley asked as Jo came nearer.
'Nothing. I'm just looking for Ananda's purse – somebody has stolen it,' said Jo.
'And I suppose you think that somebody is me,' said Lesley angrily. Jo just whistled again. Nothing happened. No bleep.

'I told you it wasn't Lesley,' said Jack when Jo came back. 'I'm going to try over there.'
'And I'm going to try there,' said Ananda.
Just then Mr Kingsley came into the classroom.
'We'll have to look in other places at lunch break,' whispered Ananda.
So, at lunch break:

'And?' asked Jack as they all met outside.
'Nothing,' said Jo.
'Nothing,' said Dan. He started to whistle again.
'Wait a minute,' said Sophie. 'Listen everybody.'
Jack smiled: 'A bleep! Whistle some more, Dan. Let's walk this way.'
They all walked towards the school. But the bleeps faded.
'We're walking the wrong way. Let's walk over there,' said Sophie.
They walked away from the school and …
'Bleep! Bleep!' the bleeps got louder and louder.
'Look!' said Jack. 'We're following Mr Smith.'
'It can't be Mr Smith!' said Jo. 'He's the caretaker. He doesn't steal things!'
But, as they got nearer to Mr Smith, the bleeps got louder.
'Ah, there you are, Mr Kingsley!' The SHoCK Team stopped as Mr Smith started to talk to Mr Kingsley.
'Hello, Mr Smith,' said Mr Kingsley. 'What can I do for you?'
'It's your form – 8PK. They don't look after their things very well,' answered Mr Smith. He opened his bag and took out a mobile phone.
'The cleaners found this on the floor last night. And look …' He took out a purse. Jo whistled.

'I found this purse when I went in to check the broken window at break this morning. Oh no, now it's bleeping!'

Jo stopped whistling. The rest of the SHoCK Team just stood there. Mr Kingsley turned. 'Ah, here's a group from 8PK. Do any of you know who this purse belongs to?'
'Er ... me, Mr Kingsley,' said Ananda.
'And this mobile?'
'I think it's David's, Mr Kingsley,' said Jack.
'You really have to look after your things better, you know,' said Mr Smith. 'If a thief gets into the school, it'll be very easy for him.'
'Mr Smith is right,' said Mr Kingsley.
'Remember how your lunch money disappeared, Ananda?'
'Yes, Mr Kingsley. And Simon's pen.'
'Right! So listen to Mr Smith or you'll really lose something important. See you later.'
Mr Kingsley and Mr Smith walked away together.

'Oh dear,' said Jack. 'Not one of the SHoCK Team's great cases, eh?'
'Well,' laughed Jo, 'you can't win them all!'
'No,' said Jack, 'But we have learned something.'
'Er ... have we?' asked Dan.
'Yes, we have,' said Sophie. 'There isn't a bank robber or spy behind every little mystery, right Jack?'
'Right!'
'And,' added Sophie, 'we've learned that you always need proof before you go round and say people have stolen things, right Jo?'
'Er ... right.' Jo looked at the floor. 'I suppose I have to say sorry to Lesley then?'
'Yes,' said Jack. 'She's over there.'

Working with the text

1 The story – what happened?

Put these sentences in the right order.
1. So then Jo started to whistle and walked towards Lesley. There were no bleeps.
2. The purse disappeared at break.
3. They tried again at lunch break and the bleeps started when they followed Mr Smith.
4. So the SHoCK Team set a trap to find the thief and to get proof. At break they left a purse on a desk, with Sophie's mum's key ring in it.
5. Before Lesley came to Cotham School nothing disappeared. Jo thought Lesley was the thief.
6. Mr Smith gave Mr Kingsley David's mobile and the purse.
7. At the end Jo had to say sorry to Lesley.
8. The SHoCK Team met outside to talk about their new case. They wanted to catch a thief.
9. Mr Kingsley and Mr Smith told the SHoCK Team to look after their things better.

2 The end of the story

Look at the pictures . Then write the end of the story. Here's some help:

Jo – go over to Lesley – try to explain – Lesley very angry/ not want to listen / not want friends like Jo – SHoCK Team try to help Jo – want to be friends – at the end Lesley ...

DOSSIER *Lesley's diary*

How did Lesley see the day? Write 6–10 sentences from her diary. You can put them in your dossier.

Today something mad happened after break. Jo Shaw came towards me and whistled ...

▶ WB 16 (p. 64)
Checkpoint 5 ▶ WB (p. 65)

Extra EXTENSIVE READING Robinson Crusoe

1 Imagine you're going to live alone on an island. What five things do you want to take with you?
2 Look at the pictures. What do you think the story is about?

I was born in the year 1632 in the city of York. When I was 18, I told my father that I wanted to be a sailor. He tried to stop me; my mother did too. But in 1651, when I was 19, I left home.
I travelled a lot, learned about ships and became rich. Later I bought a farm in Brazil, where I planned to live for the rest of my life. But then some friends wanted my help. They had to go to West Africa, and I knew that part of the world. So I went with them.
Our ship left on 1st September 1659. After about ten days, there was a terrible storm. We had to go with the winds for almost two weeks – we had no idea where we were.
Then one day, one of the men saw land. We tried to get there, but the water wasn't very deep and we hit a sandbank. The waves came down on our ship, and we couldn't move. At last we took the small boat from the ship. We hoped we could get to land with it!
But the wind and the waves were stronger than us. 'We'll never get to shore,' I thought. Then a wave like a mountain came down on our small boat. That was the end. The boat turned over. I couldn't find it again, and I couldn't see the other men.
I tried to ride the waves to shore. Again and again the waves took me under the water, but I was getting nearer. Suddenly I felt land under me. I ran as fast and as far as I could, but the waves pulled me out to sea again. This happened three more times before I was safe at last; the waves could not get me.
I was very afraid. I didn't know where I was, but I knew there were cannibals in that part of the world. 'How can I survive?' I thought. 'I've got nothing – only my clothes.'

I looked out to sea and saw the wreck of my ship. It was very far away. I needed food and water, and I needed a place to sleep. I was scared, but I walked round a bit. I found a little river and drank. There was a tree near the river, so I climbed it and slept there.
The next morning I saw that the storm was over. But the biggest surprise was that my ship was now only about a mile away, on some rocks. It was on its side, but it was still in one piece.
When the tide went out, I could walk most of the way to the ship. The rest of the way I swam. When I got there, I climbed up. I found food, guns, tools and clothes. I took a sail from the ship too. I wanted to make a tent with it. But how could I get everything to shore? I had to make a raft.
I used some of the tools from the ship. It wasn't a very good raft, but it helped me to take my things to shore.
I went to the ship eleven times in my first thirteen days and I brought back lots of things.

When I went the next time, I found more things, like silver from the captain's cabin. I wanted to take more, but I saw that there were clouds in the sky, and the wind was getting stronger.
I got to shore before the storm and took everything to my tent. The storm went on all night. When I looked the next morning, the ship wasn't there.

I still didn't know where I was. About a mile from my tent there were some hills. One was higher than the others, so I walked to it and climbed. It was hard work, but I got to the top. There I could see that I was on an island. There were no houses or farms, just trees and wild animals.

'I'll probably be here a long time,' I thought. So I had to build a house. And my house had to be a fort. It was difficult to find a good place: I needed water, shelter from the sun and rain, and a place where I was safe from wild animals or cannibals. And I wanted to see the sea. 'If a ship comes, I have to see it and send a signal.' It was hard work, but with the tools from the ship, I built my fort. Now I felt safe when I slept at night.

One day, as I was walking round my island, I suddenly saw it: a footprint! A man's footprint in the sand. I was very scared. I looked for more footprints, but there was only one.

I walked very quickly back to my house, my fort – I looked behind me all the time. When I got back, I thought: 'How is this possible? Where is the man's ship? Why is there only one footprint?'

After a time, I started to think that the footprint was really mine. I felt much better. But I had to go back and see. I went to the place, and the footprint was still there. I put my own foot next to it: my foot was much smaller!

Over the next months and years I learned many things. I went to different parts of my island and found the best place for fruit. I learned to kill or catch the wild goats on the island. I made clothes and candles from them. I made my own tables and chairs too. And I became a farmer. When I ate, I sat down with my pets. I had a parrot, a dog and two cats from the ship, and I had a baby goat. I wanted real friends, but my pets were better than nothing.

I even taught Poll – that was my name for the parrot – to talk. He learned to say his name. Fifteen years came and went. And then ...

In my 15 years on the island, I was the only person there. Who was this other man? What was he doing on my island? I went back to my house and started work to make my fort stronger and safer.

Then one day, as I was looking after my goats, I found something terrible: a place with bones – people's bones – around a fire. Cannibals! They weren't there now, but I thought, 'Maybe they'll come back! I don't want to be food for cannibals.'

I often went back to the place to look for the cannibals. I always had my guns with me.

Then one day, they were there. There were 20 or more, and they had two prisoners. They killed one and started to cook him. Just then the other prisoner ran. He ran, and three of the cannibals followed him.

When the prisoner got to the little river near my house, he quickly swam to the other side. Two of the cannibals followed. The prisoner was faster than the other men, and soon I was between him and the cannibals.

I had to kill one of the cannibals before he could kill me. The prisoner killed the other cannibal. Then he came towards me and spoke to me. I couldn't understand his language, but I knew he wanted to say thank you and be my servant. I gave my servant the name Friday because that was the day when I saved him. Friday became a friend. I taught him to speak our language, to use a gun and to eat meat, not people. Yes, he was a cannibal too before I saved him.
The time with Friday was my best time on the island. Then one day, he hurried into the fort. 'They have come,' he shouted. 'They have come!'
I followed Friday to a place where we could watch the shore. There was a small boat – an English boat. And out in the sea there was an English ship. But something wasn't right. The men were English, but they had three prisoners. Friday thought the men were cannibals, but I told him they weren't.
The men brought the prisoners to the island. When the prisoners sat down under some trees, not far from us, I talked to them quietly from behind the trees. They were very surprised. Then they told me their story.

One of the prisoners was the captain of the ship. But a group of bad men was now in control of it. 'I will help you,' I told the captain, 'if you promise to take me and my man Friday to England.' He quickly agreed.
I gave the captain and his men guns, and they killed one of the bad men and injured another. The others agreed to help the captain to take back his ship.
The captain went back to his ship and took control again. Then he sent a boat for me and Friday.
I took with me a few souvenirs and the silver from my ship. It was 19th December 1686 when I left my island – after 28 years, two months and 19 days.

Background File

The real Robinson Crusoe
Daniel Defoe's book Robinson Crusoe came out in 1719.
Most people agree that the 'real' Robinson Crusoe was Alexander Selkirk. Selkirk was born in Scotland in 1676. He became a sailor when he was 19.
When Selkirk argued with his captain, the captain left him on an island near Chile. He was there for four and a half years. A rich Englishman brought Selkirk back to Bristol, where he met Defoe at the Llandoger Trow Pub and told him his story. You can still visit the pub today.

1 What happened when?
Continue the sentences.
In 1632 *Robinson was born in York.*
In 1651 …
On 1st Sep 1659 …
In his first 13 days …
After 15 years …
After twelve more years …
On 19th Dec 1686 …

2 A message in a bottle
Imagine Robinson writes a message in a bottle and asks for help. Write his message.

Unit 6

A trip to Bath

1 **The Roman Baths**
Talk about the drawing of the Roman Baths in the city of Bath.
a) What can you see?
I can see a round pool/...
It's in the middle/ ...

b) What are the people doing?
The people are ...

> having a bath • having a sauna •
> jumping into ... • playing games • relaxing

2 A journey through time 🎧
a) Close your eyes, relax and listen. Take a time machine to the Roman Baths in the year 200. What can you see, hear and feel?

b) Did you enjoy the journey? What did you see, hear and feel?
I enjoyed / didn't enjoy the journey because ...
I saw ... / I heard ... / I felt ...

Extra **Background File**

Bath and the Roman Empire
Bath is about 20 km southeast of Bristol. The beautiful city is famous for its Roman Baths. The Romans found hot springs and built the Baths there. They were in the area for almost 400 years till about the year 450. The map shows the Roman Empire in the year 107.

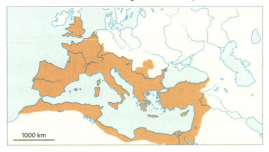

▶ WB 1 (p. 66)

statue

sandals   mosaic floor

1 8PK's school trip to Bath 🎧

It was a beautiful, sunny day. Form 8PK cycled happily along the Bristol and Bath Railway Path. They were on a school trip with Mr Kingsley and Miss White.

STUDY SKILLS | **Talking to people**

Wenn du ein Gespräch führst:
– *Fang nett an:*
  Hello! • How are you? • Can I sit with you?
– *Frag, was der/die andere denkt/fühlt:*
  What do you think/know about …? • What about you?
– *Am Ende verabschiede dich:*
  Bye then!

Finde andere nützliche Redewendungen in 1. Denk daran: Im Englischen gilt es meistens als unhöflich, nur mit einem Wort zu antworten.

▶ SF Talking to people (p. 120)

Mr Kingsley	Hi Ananda. How are you?
Ananda	I'm fine, thank you Mr Kingsley. What about you?
Mr Kingsley	I'm fine, thanks. We're lucky with the weather, aren't we?
Ananda	Yes, we are.
Mr Kingsley	Well, see you later.
Jack	It's a great day, isn't it?
Lesley	Yes. And I've never been to Bath. Have you been there before? Do you know how far it is?
Jack	Yes, about 14 miles. But we only have to cycle seven, then we're going to take the bus. Oh, here comes Jo.
Jo	Hi, Jack. Er … hello, Lesley.
Jack	Hi Jo!
Jo	Can you tell me what the time is?
Jack	It's 9.20.
Jo	Thanks. Er … can I cycle with you?
Jack	What do you think, Lesley?
Lesley	Are you going to be nice to me, Jo?
Jo	Of course, Lesley.
Lesley	Oh, all right then. Tell me what you know about Bath, Jo.
Jo	My grandma took us to the Theatre Royal when I was little.
Lesley	That sounds interesting. Tell me more.

▶ P 1–2 (p. 98) • WB 2 (p. 67)

2 👥 Now you

*Imagine you're on a school trip.
On the bus you're sitting next to your English teacher. Talk to him/her. Here are some ideas.*

Teacher	Hi, … How are you?
Student	I'm fine, thank you. What about you?
Teacher	I'm fine, thanks. Have you been to … before?
Student	Yes, I have. My dad took us to the … last year.
Teacher	That sounds interesting. Tell me more.
Student	It's … They've got … / You can … there.
Teacher	What else do you know/like about …?
Student	…
Teacher	Oh look, we're there.
Student	Great!

▶ P 3 (p. 98) • WB 3 (p. 67)

3 Which way?

When they got to Bath, they went to the Roman Baths first. After lunch Mr Kingsley said, 'Let's make two groups. Who is going to the Herschel Museum? OK, Miss White is waiting for you opposite the Abbey. The others, stay here with me.'

I think I'll go with Mr Kingsley, not with Miss White. Jo, can you tell her, please?

Sure, Dan, no problem.

Some of the students left to go with Miss White.
'Now, please look at your maps,' Mr Kingsley went on. 'The Museum of Costume is at the top. OK, you've read a map before: who can tell me the way? Lesley?'
'Well,' Lesley said, 'we're at the Abbey. So, first we turn left into Cheap Street and walk to Union Street. We turn right into Union Street, cross Upper Borough Walls and go straight on. We go past the post office and walk along Milsom Street to the end.'
'Very good, Lesley,' Mr Kingsley said. 'Sophie, do you want to go on?'
'Sure, Mr Kingsley,' said Sophie. 'From there we turn right into George Street, then left into Bartlett Street. We cross Alfred Street and the museum is on the corner.'
'Very good, Sophie. Well then, let's go!'

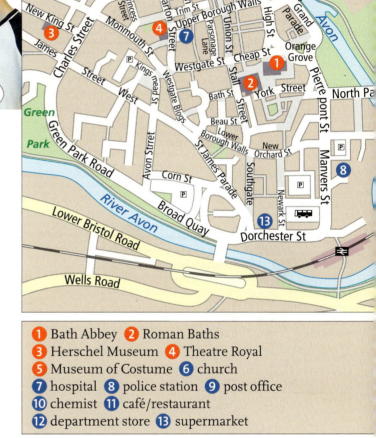

❶ Bath Abbey ❷ Roman Baths
❸ Herschel Museum ❹ Theatre Royal
❺ Museum of Costume ❻ church
❼ hospital ❽ police station ❾ post office
❿ chemist ⓫ café/restaurant
⓬ department store ⓭ supermarket

▶ Follow Mr Kingsley's group on the map.

4 Directions

a) How do Lesley and Sophie describe the route to the Museum of Costume? Collect the phrases and draw pictures to explain them.

turn left ↰   go past

b) Find a route for Miss White from the Abbey to the Herschel Museum. Write down the directions.

c) Choose a place on the map. Make notes on how you can get there from the Abbey. Give your partner directions. Can he/she find it?
A: ... and then you go straight on. The place is on the left.
B: Oh, you mean the supermarket! My turn.

▶ GF 14 Present progressive (p. 138)
▶ P 4–6 (p. 99–100) • WB 4–6 (pp. 68–69)

5 Who's missing?

At 1.30 Miss White and her group were walking through Bath. At Beauford Square Miss White stopped. 'I must check that everybody's here,' she said. 'Hmm, I only count 15. Who's missing?'
She looked at Jo. 'Where's your brother?' she asked.
'Dan?' Jo said. 'Oh, er … we were going past the theatre, and then Dan stopped to look at the posters. You needn't worry, Miss White – Dan is always slow. Oh, I can see him. He's coming.'
'All right then, but please stay together.'
A bit later, Miss White counted again: 14. She was just counting a second time when Jo came round the corner. 'Jo, I said, "Stay together."'
'Jo? I'm Dan. I'm sorry. I was looking in a shop window, and suddenly you weren't there any more.'
'You're Dan? But then where's Jo?'
'I don't know, Miss White.'
Ananda and some of the other kids were laughing quietly.
'This isn't funny!' Miss White said. She took out her mobile and made a call.

Hello, Paul? This is Isabel. I've lost Jo!

Oh dear.

We were walking along the street and then he disappeared. Dan told me …

Did you say Dan? But Dan is with me. It's a trick, Isabel. Your 'Dan' is really Jo!

A trick? Jo! You're in trouble now!

6 Now you

Talk to different partners.
A: What were you doing at …?
B: I was watching …/ talking to …/…
You can use ideas from the box.

> at 8 o'clock on Saturday night •
> at 3.30 yesterday afternoon • at …

Looking at language

a) What were Miss White and her group doing at 1.30?
They … through Bath.
What was Miss White doing when Jo came round the corner?
She … a second time.
b) How do you make this new verb form?

▶ GF 15: Past progressive (p. 139) • P 7–8 • (pp. 100–101) • WB 7–9 (pp. 70–72)

7 What planets can you name? 🎧

THE WILLIAM HERSCHEL MUSEUM

Miss White was in the museum with her group. Nicola, from the museum, was talking to the students.
'... and please don't touch anything. Right, now before we go round William Herschel's house, let's see what you know about astronomy. First, what planets can you name?'
'Mars!' called Jo. 'And Saturn, Venus ... and Jupiter.'
'Wow!' said Ananda. 'You really know about astronomy.'
'Well, astronomy is interesting!' said Jo. 'Not bad,' said Nicola to Jo. 'Now, does anybody know what planet William Herschel discovered?'

'Uranus!' said Jo.
'Very good! OK then, now we're going to look at Herschel's telescope, but please remember: you mustn't touch it. This way!'

8 William and Caroline 🎧

a) 👥 At the museum Form 8PK watched a short film about William Herschel and his sister Caroline. Look at the words in the box. Can you say what they mean? Check in the Dictionary (pp. 168–188).

> instrument • play the organ • star • comet • astronomer

b) Listen. What two things most interested William and Caroline? Where did they work together? How did they work together?

c) Look at the questions:
1 Where were the Herschels born?
2 Was Caroline older or younger than William?
3 What were William's hobbies?
4 How old was he when he went to England?
5 What did Caroline discover?
Listen again and find the answers.

d) **Extra** With the help of your answers write a short text about William and Caroline.

9 Jo's report 🎧

> We went on a trip to Bath yesterday. We cycled a bit and then we took a bus.
> When we arrived we first went to the Roman Baths. They were OK. Then we had lunch. After that we made two groups. My group went to the Herschel Museum. It was really interesting – all about stars and planets. I really enjoyed that. Before we left Bath, Miss White bought us all an ice cream. And the sun was still shining when we got home at six o'clock. It was a great day.

DOSSIER A school trip

Write about a school trip.
1 First collect ideas.
2 Then start with a sentence like this:
Last year/a few years ago ... I went on a school trip to ...
3 Write about what happened on the trip.
4 Finish with sentences like these:
It was a great/... trip. I'll remember it for a long time.

▶ P 9–12 (pp. 101–102) • WB 11–13 (pp. 73–74)

▶ SF Structuring a text (p. 121)

6 Practice

1 How to sound friendly (Indirect questions)

a) *Indirect questions often sound friendlier than direct questions. Look at the* **indirect questions** *in 1–6. What's the direct question?*

1 Please tell me **when the holidays start**.
   When do the holidays start?
2 I'd like to know **what the weather is like in New Zealand**.
   What's the weather like in New Zealand?
3 Can you remember **what the phone number is?**
4 Please tell me **why you like Robbie Williams**.
5 Do you know **where the café is?**
6 I'd like to know **why she said that.**

b) Extra *Try to make these questions sound friendlier.*

1 How far is it to Warmley?
   Do you know how far …?
2 Where does Miss White live?
3 How does she get to school?

2 WORDS Word building

a) *Which words go together?*

cycle path, family …

cycle	bag		bath	ache
family	money		dish	bin
felt	path	*bathroom, …*	dust	board
form	room		skate	chair
jumble	teacher		sweat	room
living	tip		time	shirt
pocket	tree		tooth	table
school	sale		wheel	washer

b) *Use words from a) to fill in the gaps in the story.*

Mr Kingsley jumped out of bed. Oh no! It was already 7.30. Mr Kingsley was a … at Cotham, so he had to be at school at 8.30. He went into the …, had a quick shower and put on his favourite jeans and … Then he looked in the kitchen: all his glasses and plates were in the … Ah well, no breakfast. What was his first lesson? He checked his … : Ah yes, Sport with 7IW. 8.15 already – time to go – Ouch! he fell over his old … 'That's an idea!' he thought. 'I can skate to school today. And if I skate on the …, I'll even be early!'

3 STUDY SKILLS Talking to people 🎧

a) *Listen to two more dialogues on the cycle path to Bath. Which goes well? Which doesn't?*

b) *Look at the phrases in the box. Listen again. Which phrases do you hear?*

c) *Write a dialogue between two people about their favourite hobby/… You can use phrases from the box.*

What do you think of …? • What about you? • That's nice. My … • …, right? •
That sounds interesting. • OK? • Have you got any …? • Have you … before? • Why's that?

Practice **6** 99

4 WORDS Where in Bristol?

a) Partner B: Go to p. 111.
Partner A: Look at your map. The names of these places are missing.

> tourist information • internet café • department store • church • post office

Ask your partner where the places are. Then answer your partner's questions. The phrases in the box can help.

> It's in ... Street/Road/... • near/next to/... • opposite/in front of/behind ... • between ... and ... • on the corner of ... and ...

b) Extra Label the buildings in a copy of the map. Compare your maps.

c) You're in front of the ice rink. A tourist (your partner) asks you the way to three places on the map.
B: Excuse me please, can you tell me the way to ...?
A: First go along ... Then turn left/right into ... Cross/Go straight on ... The ... is on the left/right/corner of ...

d) Now you're the tourist. Ask your partner the way to three places too.

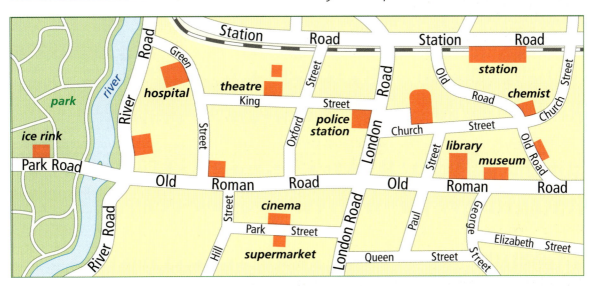

5 MEDIATION Telling the way

Your uncle wants to visit the Roman Baths. He has found a website with directions, but they're in English. Send him an e-mail with the important information in German.

By train

Take a train to BATH SPA station. There are a lot of trains from Bristol Temple Meads Station and from London Paddington (fast trains) and London Waterloo (slower but cheaper trains). When you leave the station, turn right, then left into Manvers Street. Walk along Manvers Street to York Street, where you will see a black sign to the Baths. Turn left. The Baths are on the right.

By car from Bristol

Take the A4 into Bath. For a day visit to Bath, go to Newbridge Park and Ride. It is on the A4. From there you can take a bus to the centre, where you will see signs to the Baths. To park in the city centre, drive along the A4 to Charlotte Street car park. It is easy to find – just follow the "All Attractions" signs. Go out of the car park and turn left. Walk along Charlotte Street to the end. Follow the black signs till you get to the Baths.

6 REVISION Dan is listening … *(Present progressive)*

a) Look at the pictures and say what the people are doing.

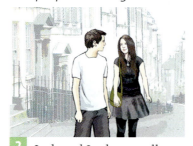

1 Dan – listen to – MP3 player
Dan is listening to his MP3 player.

2 Jack and Lesley – walk – together
Jack and Lesley …

3 Sophie – sit – next to Ananda

4 Mr Kingsley – talk to – group

5 Jo – take – photo

6 Miss White and Ananda – look at – building

b) Extra Now write down what the people are doing. Be careful with the spelling of the -ing forms.

7 Yesterday they were working *(Past progressive)*

Look at the picture. What were the people doing?

At ten o'clock yesterday Sophie was making a poster. Jo … a report. At eleven o'clock …

Practice **6** 101

8 What were they doing when …? (Past progressive)

Write down what the different people in the picture were doing when Mrs Harper came home. These verbs will help you.

build • do • feed • play • read • ride • sleep • talk • take • watch

When Mrs Harper came home, Adam was building a tower.

9 WORDS A school trip

a) Find words and phrases in the word snake.

b) **Extra** Put the words and phrases into groups:
'Getting there' • 'What we did' • 'How it was'
You can use them to write your report about a school trip for your dossier (p. 97).

10 STUDY SKILLS Correcting mistakes

a) *There are twelve spelling mistakes in the text. Write out the text and correct the mistakes.*

> **STUDY SKILLS | Correcting mistakes**
>
> Ein Text ist nicht gleich fertig, wenn du ihn zu Ende geschrieben hast. Du solltest ihn am besten noch zweimal durchsehen:
> – einmal, um zu sehen, ob dein Text Sinn ergibt
> – einmal Wort für Wort und Buchstabe für Buchstabe, um Fehler zu finden.

▸ SF Correcting mistakes (p. 122) • WB 10 (p. 73)

b) Swap texts with a partner and check.

8PK's trip to Bath

On a beautiful <u>suny</u> morning 8PK cycled <u>happyly</u> from Bristol to a village on the way to Bath. There they left <u>there</u> bikes and took the bus into Bath, where they first visited the <u>roman</u> Baths. They <u>where</u> there for about ninety minutes. <u>Than</u> they had lunch at a great café. Most of them <u>tryd</u> the 'Roman <u>santwich</u>'.
Later Miss White went with her group of <u>fivteen</u> students to the Herschel Museum. On the way <u>their</u> Jo <u>dissapeared</u>.
Miss White started to worry. She <u>stoped</u> and phoned Mr Kingsley. He told her, 'Jo is playing a trick on you.'

11 REVISION Plans (going to-future)

a) *What are your plans for the rest of the year? Write down as many things as you can.*
I'm going to finish my book before the end of the month. I'm going to save some ...

b) *For at least three of your plans find another student with the same plans.*
A: I'm going to finish my book before the end of the month. What about you?
B: Yes, I'm going to do that too. / No, that's not on my list.

12 WORDS Prepositions

a) *Choose the right preposition.*
1 Dan and Jo are students at/on/in Cotham School.
2 They're both under/on/in Form 8PK.
3 They usually go to school with/by/on their bikes.
4 They don't like waiting on/for/with the bus.
5 School starts at/on/for 8.45 and finishes at/on/for 3.30.
6 They've got PE with/under/by Mr Kingsley.
7 They live in/at/near 7 Hamilton Street.
8 Jo plays football at/on/for Mondays.
9 At/In/By the weekends he often goes to/on/after the pool with his brother Dan.
10 He listens at/on/to music too.

b) **Extra** *Draw a funny picture for one of the wrong answers in a).*

Dan and Jo aren't students <u>on</u> Cotham School ... they're students <u>at</u> Cotham School!

A trip to Bath – a play for the end of term 🎧

> Look at the pictures. How many people are there in this play? Who are they? What are they doing?

Jack	Hello, I'm Jack …
Lesley	I'm Lesley …
Jo	I'm Jo …
Ananda	I'm Ananda …
5 Dan	I'm Dan …
Sophie	And I'm Sophie. We're all students at Cotham School in Bristol.
Jack	Welcome to our little play:
10 Lesley	'A trip to Bath'.
Jo	Not 'bath' as in 'I have a bath every evening' … *(He mimes.)*
Ananda	Do you really have a bath every evening, Jo? I only have a bath every second evening. But I like a shower better anyway. I …
Jack	When you two have finished, maybe we can go on?
Ananda	Oh, sorry. Right.
20 Dan	The city of Bath is just 14 miles from Bristol, so our teacher …
Sophie	Mr Kingsley, our teacher, *(she points)* said:
'Mr Kingsley'	Let's cycle to Bath!
25	*(All grumble.)*
Sophie	Luckily our Music teacher, Miss White, *(she points)* had a good idea. *('Miss White' walks over to 'Mr Kingsley'.)*
'Miss White'	Paul, dear, let's cycle to Warmley. That's only seven miles. We can leave our bikes there and take the bus into Bath.
'Mr Kingsley'	What a good idea, Isabel.
All	Good idea!
'Mr Kingsley'	Everybody here? Then let's go! *(Each actor sits on a chair and mimes cycling.)*
Jack	We cycled … *(very fast)*
Lesley	… and cycled *(fast)*
Jo	… and cycled *(slower)*
Ananda	… and cycled *(and slower)*
Dan	… and … cycled … *(He stops and falls off.)*

Sophie	And then we arrived in Warmley … *(all get up)* … and got on the bus.

		Jack — After lunch we divided into two groups ... and we walked ... *(fast)*
		Lesley — ... and walked ... *(slower)*
		Dan — ... and walked ... *(very slowly)*
		Jack — ... and walked ... *(He falls to the floor.)*
		'Mr Kingsley' — Come on, everybody!
		Lesley — We went to the Museum of Costume ...
	(All sit the other way round on their chairs. They mime the movement of the bus and wave. The bus stops and all jump up and take their chairs to the back. They make a group round 'Mr Kingsley'.)	Sophie — And that's when things started to get interesting.
		'Mr Kingsley' — Now, let's start here with the clothes from the 18th century.
		Lesley — There was so much work in these dresses – look.
'Mr Kingsley'	Now here we are in the Roman Baths. The Romans built them almost two thousand years ago. They were a bit like our leisure centres – you know, swimming pools, saunas, cold pools ...	Dan — Hey, what are those things? Look!
		Sophie — They're corsets.
		Dan — Corsets?
		Lesley — Yes, corsets. In those days all the women wore corsets under their clothes, poor things.
Sophie	*(She shivers.)* Very healthy!	Dan — But not the men, right!
Ananda	Very nice.	Sophie — No, not the men.
Dan	Very interesting.	Dan — I wonder what they feel like ...
Jo	Very old! *(He yawns, then turns to audience.)* We were in there for two hours! And then, at last, Miss White said:	*(Dan tries to put on a corset. Jack helps him, then moves back to look at Dan. They all laugh.)*
'Miss White'	Time for lunch, Paul?	Dan — Lesley is right: the poor women. Get me out of here!
All	Yes! Hooray! Lunch!	
'Mr Kingsley'	I know a great sandwich place. Follow me!	
	(They walk, they choose, they pay, they sit down on the floor and eat.)	
Lesley	There were sandwiches with brown bread with salad ...	
Sophie	Very healthy!	
Lesley	... tomato, cheese and lettuce ...	
Ananda	Very nice!	
Lesley	... chicken tikka in a brown roll ...	
Dan	Very interesting ...	
Lesley	... tuna and mayonnaise ...	
Jo	Very old! Hey Dan, that bread really looks very old!	
Dan	It's a Roman sandwich!	
	(They all get up and make two groups, Miss White's group walks to one corner.)	

Dan — *(He tries to get out of the corset.)* Help!
(Jack tries to help.)
'Mr Kingsley' — Come on there! Hurry up!
Lesley — We're coming, Mr Kingsley!
Dan — You can't leave me here!
Lesley — *(She smiles.)* Can't we?
Dan — Please! Jack, Lesley, Sophie ...

Sophie	*(She turns to audience.)* Did we leave Dan? Well … *(She laughs.)* … No, we didn't. Here's the rest of the story – in pictures – Jo's pictures, of course.
	(Jo on stage with camera. Lesley is opening Dan's corset. They freeze.)

Jo	Click!
Sophie	'Lesley saves Dan.'
Dan	Thank you, Lesley.
Lesley	You're welcome, Dan.
Sophie	After the museum there was ice cream …
	(All come on stage and cheer.)
All	Hooray! Chocolate for me! I'd like strawberry!
Jo	OK, say ice C R E E E E A M !
	(They freeze.)
All	Ice C R E E E E E A M !
Jo	Click!
Sophie	And then we all took the bus back to Warmley. Miss White sat with Mr Kingsley.

	('Mr Kingsley' looks into 'Miss White's' eyes.)
'Mr Kingsley'	Tired, Isabel?
'Miss White'	Yes, Paul.
Sophie	Sweet.
	(They freeze.)
Jo	Click!
'Mr Kingsley'	Jo Shaw!
Sophie	And then we cycled home … Click!
Jo	End of trip!
Lesley	Click!
Jo	End of term!
Jack	Click!
Jo	Happy holidays!
All	*(They sing.)*

> We're all going on a summer holiday.
> No more working for a week or two.
> Fun and laughter on a summer holiday.
> No more worries for me and you.
> For a week or two.
> We're going where the sun shines brightly.
> We're going where the sea is blue.
> We've seen it in the movies.
> Now let's see if it's true.

by Bruce Welch, Brian Bennett

Working with the text

1 One play, seven scenes
Read the play. Divide it into seven scenes. Choose a title for each scene from the box on the right.

2 Extra **Act out the play**
Make groups of 8. Think about what you need for the play: costumes, chairs, a corset, …
Learn the words. Act out the play or your favourite scene(s).

- Welcome to 'A trip to Bath'
- Sandwiches
- On the way to Bath
- Hooray! The summer holidays
- This group for clothes and corsets!
- The end in photos
- At the Roman Baths

Checkpoint 6 ▶ *WB (pp. 75–77)* • *Activity page 3*

106 **6** Topic

Extra Dan and Jo's summer holidays in New Zealand

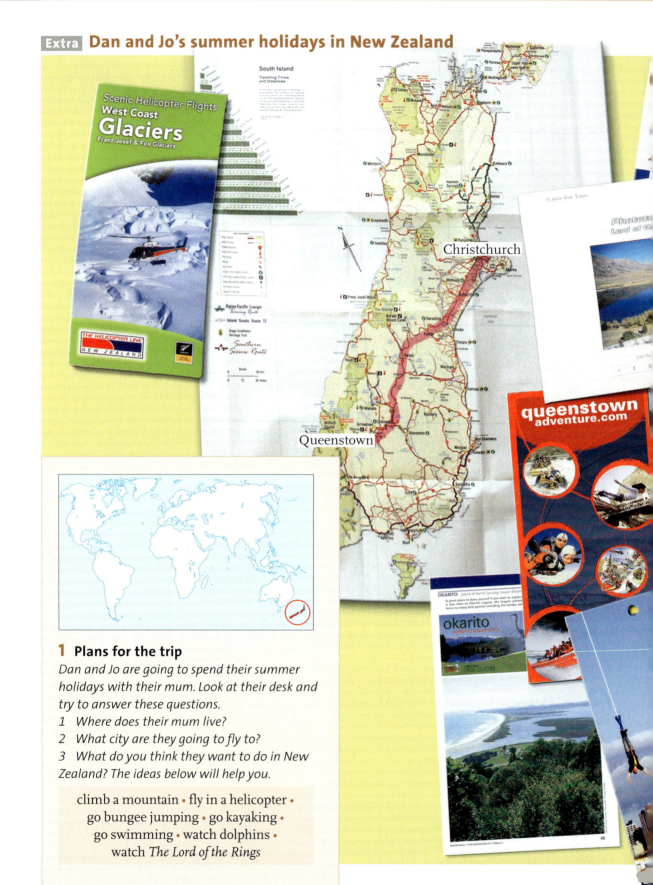

1 Plans for the trip

Dan and Jo are going to spend their summer holidays with their mum. Look at their desk and try to answer these questions.
1 Where does their mum live?
2 What city are they going to fly to?
3 What do you think they want to do in New Zealand? The ideas below will help you.

climb a mountain • fly in a helicopter • go bungee jumping • go kayaking • go swimming • watch dolphins • watch *The Lord of the Rings*

Topic **6**   107

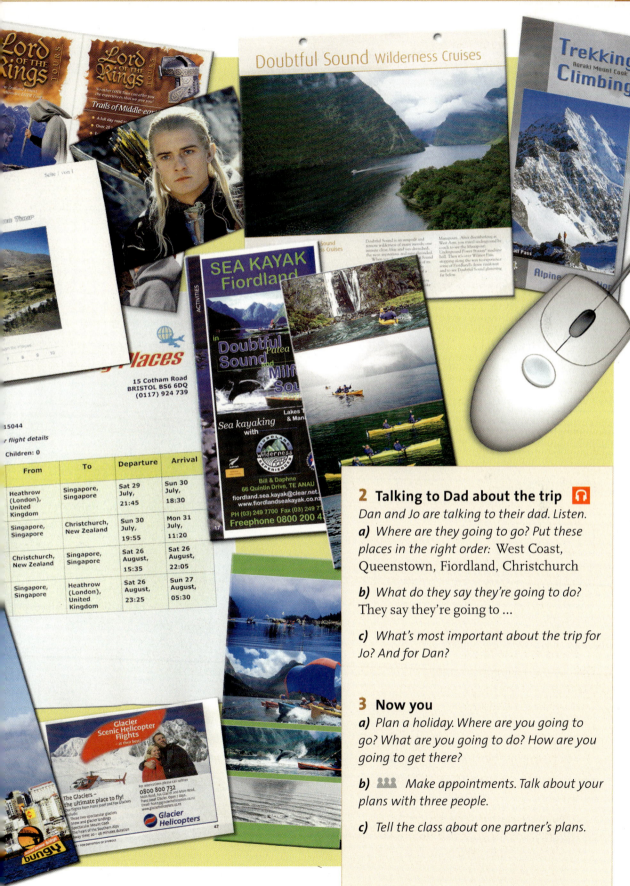

2 Talking to Dad about the trip 🎧
Dan and Jo are talking to their dad. Listen.
a) Where are they going to go? Put these places in the right order: West Coast, Queenstown, Fiordland, Christchurch

b) What do they say they're going to do? They say they're going to …

c) What's most important about the trip for Jo? And for Dan?

3 Now you
a) Plan a holiday. Where are you going to go? What are you going to do? How are you going to get there?

b) 👥 Make appointments. Talk about your plans with three people.

c) Tell the class about one partner's plans.

B Partner

Unit 1

4 SKILLS Describing pictures

a) Draw a picture with one person, a table and a chair, a cupboard and a tortoise.
(There are two examples on the rigth.)

b) First your partner describes his/her picture. You draw it. Compare your drawing with your partner's picture.

c) Now describe your picture to your partner (Do not show him/her your picture!):
There's a table in the middle of the picture. On the left, there's …
Your partner draws the picture. Then compare.

14 Yesterday afternoon (The simple past: wh-questions)

a) Answer your partner's questions. Then ask him/her about the gaps in your chart.
Fill in a copy of the chart.

	Where did … go?	How … go?	What … do?	When … go to bed?
Ananda	home			10.00
Dan and Jo			play football	
Jack	home	by bus	do his homework + write a story	
Sophie		by car		9.15
You				
Your partner				

b) Fill in the answers for 'you' in your chart. Ask your partner and add his/her answers.

c) Write about your partner or one of the Bristol kids. Then swap and check.

Partner **B** 109

Unit 2

8 How many computer games, how much time? (much/many – more – most)

a) Read the information about Christine. Answer your partner's questions about her. Then ask your partner about Lennart. Write the answers in a copy of the chart.

	Lennart	Christine	You	Your partner
computer games – know		15		
time – need for homework		90 minutes		
TV – watch every day		1 hour		
money – spend on sweets		€5 every week		
comics – buy every week		2		
books – read		one every week		

B: How many computers games does Lennart know?
A: He knows ten computers games.
B: How much time does …?

b) Fill in the answers for 'You' in your chart. Ask your partner and add his/her answers.

c) `Extra` Report to the class. Make comparisons. Use more and most.
My partner knows more computer games than Lennart. I know more computer games than my partner. But Christine knows the most.

Unit 3

6 What will they do if …? (Conditional sentences)

a) Answer your partner's questions.
Then ask him or her for the missing information.
A: What will Maike do if she finds a baby squirrel?
B: She'll take it …

	find a baby squirrel	get a 5 in English	need a new mobile
Maike	take it to an animal clinic		ask her parents
Jan		get help from his dad	
Christoph			wait till his birthday
You			
Your partner			

b) `Extra` Write three sentences: one about one of the people, one about your partner and one about you.
If Maike finds a baby squirrel, she'll take it to an animal clinic.
If my partner Nele finds a baby squirrel, she'll … If I …

Unit 4

10 What's different? (Present perfect: just)

Answer your partner's question about the people in the picture.
Then ask about his/her picture. Take turns. Use ideas from the box.
A: In my picture Sophie has just made popcorn. What about your picture?
B: In my picture Sophie has just ... And in my picture Ananda has just ...

1 Sophie – make
2 Ananda – open
3 Dan – eat
4 Jo – take
5 Jack – drop
6 Prunella – find

2 Extra Who said what?

Listen to your partner's questions. Scan the text for the correct answers.
A: Who said 'Morning, Bryn' and when?
B: Elaine said that when ... That's in line ...

Now ask your partner who said these things and when.
1 'Is everybody OK?' (Beth, l. 35)
2 'I hope the trees will hold for just a few more minutes.' (Bryn, ll. 68–69)
3 'Can you just go over to the Thompsons'?' (Gwyneth, ll. 81–82)
4 'All in a day's work!' (Bryn, l. 85)

B: Who said 'Is everybody OK?'
A: Beth said that when ... That's in line ...

Partner **B** 111

Unit 5

6 What are you going to do? (going to-future: questions)

a) Look at the chart. Answer your partner's questions about Jo and Sophie and Ananda. Then ask your partner about Jack and Mr and Mrs Hanson.

Name	Is/Are ... going to do anything nice tomorrow?	What ... going to do?	Where ... going to do it?	Why ... going to do it?
Jo	Yes, he is.	play football	on the Downs	it's his hobby
Jack				
Sophie and Ananda	Yes, they are.	watch a DVD	at Sophie's house	love the actor
Mr and Mrs Hanson				
You				
Your partner				

b) In a copy of the chart write down your plans. Answer your partner's questions about your plans. Then ask your partner about his/her plans.

c) **Extra** Write about what two of the people plan to do.

Unit 6

4 WORDS Where in Bristol?

a) Partner B: Look at your map. Answer your partner's questions. The phrases in the box can help.

> It's in ... Street/Road/... • near/next to/... •
> opposite/in front of/behind ... •
> between ... and ... • on the corner of ... and ...

The names of these places are missing in your map. Ask your partner where the places are.

> supermarket • hospital • police station •
> chemist • library

b) **Extra** Label the buildings in a copy of the map. Compare your maps.

c) Imagine you're a tourist. You're in front of the ice rink. Ask your partner the way to three places. Excuse me please, can you tell me the way to ...?

d) Now your partner is the tourist. Help him/her. First go along ... Then turn left/right into ... Cross/Go straight on ... The ... is on the left/right/corner of ...

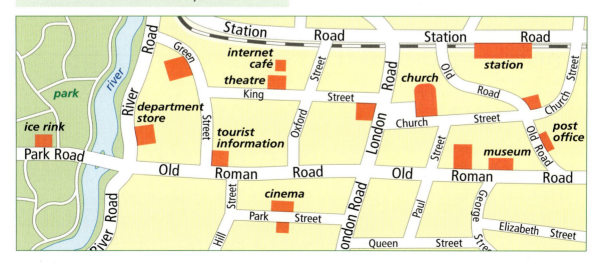

Skills File – Inhalt

Seite

STUDY AND LANGUAGE SKILLS
REVISION Stop – Check – Go	112
REVISION Learning words – Step 1	113
Learning words – Step 2	113
REVISION Mind maps	114
REVISION Understanding new words	114
REVISION Working with a dictionary	115
Describing pictures	115
Multiple-choice exercises	116
REVISION Giving a presentation	116

LISTENING AND READING SKILLS
Listening	117
Scanning	118
REVISION Taking notes	119
Marking up a text	119

SPEAKING AND WRITING SKILLS
Talking to people	120
Linking words	121
Topic sentence	121
Structuring a text	121
Correcting mistakes	122

MEDIATION SKILLS
Mediation	123

Im **Skills File** findest du Hinweise zu Arbeits- und Lerntechniken. Was du in den Skills-Kästen der Units gelernt hast, wird hier näher erläutert.

Was du bereits aus Band 1 von English G 21 kennst, ist mit **REVISION** gekennzeichnet, z.B.
– **REVISION   Stop – Check – Go**, Seite 112
– **REVISION   Learning words – Step 1**, Seite 113.

Viele neue Hinweise helfen dir bei der Arbeit mit Hör- und Lesetexten, beim Sprechen, beim Schreiben von eigenen Texten, bei der Sprachmittlung und beim Lernen von Methoden.

STUDY AND LANGUAGE SKILLS

SF REVISION   Stop – Check – Go

Fehler bei den Hausaufgaben? Falsche oder keine Antworten im Unterricht? Die nächste Englischarbeit steht bevor? – Höchste Zeit für STOP – CHECK – GO!

Stop
Mindestens einmal pro Unit, besser häufiger.

Check
Überprüfe, ob du den Stoff der Unit verstanden hast. Was zum Stoff einer Unit gehört, kannst du z.B. im Inhaltsverzeichnis sehen oder deine/n Lehrer/in fragen. Der **Checkpoint ▶** im *Workbook* hilft dir am Ende jeder Unit bei der Überprüfung. Dort findest du Testaufgaben.

Go
Überlege, was du besser machen kannst. Du könntest
– deine/n Lehrer/in um Rat fragen,
– dir das, was du nicht verstanden hast, von einem Mitschüler/einer Mitschülerin erklären lassen,
– Übungen im Buch wiederholen,
– dir einzelne Abschnitte im *Grammar File* oder *Skills File* anschauen,
– die *Listening*-CD zum Schülerbuch oder das *Workbook* benutzen.

Skills File **113**

SF REVISION Learning words – Step 1

Worauf solltest du beim Lernen und Wiederholen von Vokabeln achten?

– Führe dein Vokabelverzeichnis, dein Vokabelheft oder deinen Karteikasten aus Klasse 5 weiter.

– Lerne immer 7–10 Vokabeln auf einmal.

– Lerne neue und wiederhole alte Vokabeln regelmäßig – am besten jeden Tag 5–10 Minuten.

– Es macht mehr Spaß, wenn du die Vokabeln mit jemandem zusammen lernst. Fragt euch gegenseitig ab.

– Finde heraus, mit welchen Methoden du am besten Vokabeln lernen kannst: durch Hören, durch Bilder, am Computer (mit deinem *e-Workbook* oder dem *English Coach*) oder indem du dir eigene Geschichten um die neuen Vokabeln ausdenkst.

round the car

SF Learning words – Step 2 ▶ Unit 2 (p. 27) • P 1 (p. 32)

Wörter kannst du besser behalten, wenn du sie in Wortgruppen sammelst und ordnest. Dazu gibt es verschiedene Möglichkeiten.

Du kannst

– **Gegensatzpaare** sammeln, z.B.
sunny – **rainy**,
happy – **sad**,
top – **bottom**,
foreground – **background**;

sunny   rainy   happy   sad

– Wörter in **Wortfamilien** sammeln, z.B.
(to) sing – **song** – **singer**;

School		
subjects	sports	things
Maths	tennis	book
Art	football	pencil
Geography	...	...
...		

– Wörter in **Wortfeldern** sammeln – dabei schreibst du alle Wörter unter Oberbegriffen (**group words**) auf;

– Wörter in **Wortnetzen** (*networks*) sammeln und ordnen.

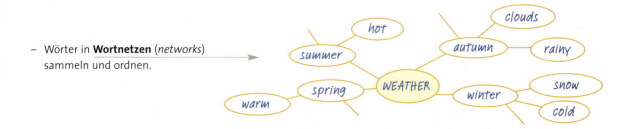

SF REVISION Mind maps

Wozu dienen Mindmaps?

Mithilfe von Mindmaps kannst du Ideen sammeln und ordnen, wenn du etwas vortragen sollst oder einen Text vorbereiten willst.

Wie mache ich eine Mindmap?

1. Schreib das Thema in die Mitte eines leeren, unlinierten Blattes Papier. Male einen Kreis oder eine Wolke drum herum.

2. Überlege dir, welche Oberbegriffe zu deiner Sammlung von Ideen passen. Verwende unterschiedliche Farben.

3. Ergänze jede Idee, die zu einem Oberbegriff passt, auf einem Nebenast. Nimm dafür nur wichtige Schlüsselwörter.
Du kannst statt Wörtern auch Symbole verwenden und Bilder ergänzen.

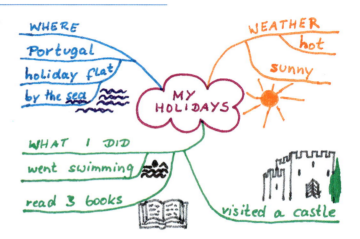

SF REVISION Understanding new words

Immer gleich im Wörterbuch nachschlagen?

Das Nachschlagen unbekannter Wörter im Wörterbuch kostet Zeit und nimmt auf Dauer den Spaß am Lesen. Oft kannst du die Bedeutung von Wörtern ohne Wörterbuch herausfinden.

Was hilft mir, unbekannte Wörter zu verstehen?

1. Bilder sind eine große Hilfe. Sie zeigen oft die Dinge, die du im Text nicht verstehst. Schau sie dir deshalb vor dem Lesen genau an.

2. Oft helfen dir die Wörter, die vor oder nach dem unbekannten Wort stehen. Erschließe die Bedeutung eines Wortes aus dem Textzusammenhang, z.B. *We must hurry. Our train* departs *in ten minutes.*

3. Viele englische Wörter werden ähnlich wie im Deutschen geschrieben oder klingen ähnlich, z.B. discussion, statue, margarine.

4. Manchmal stecken in unbekannten Wörtern bekannte Teile, z.B. sunshine, bottle opener, skater.

> • Alles klar? Dann überlege, was diese Wörter bedeuten.
> energy • discovery • builder • winner • telescope • unfair • friendly • milkshake • sprinter

Skills File **115**

SF REVISION Working with a dictionary

Du verstehst ein Wort nicht? Du brauchst ein englisches Wort, das du nicht kennst? Dann hilft Dir ein Wörterbuch weiter.
In diesem Buch findest du das **English-German dictionary** auf den Seiten 173–191 und das **German-English dictionary** auf den Seiten 191–206.

Wörter nachschlagen: Wie benutze ich ein Wörterbuch?

Denk daran:
- Stichwörter sind alphabetisch geordnet: **f** vor **g**, **fa** vor **fe** und **fle** vor **fli** usw.
- Zusammengesetzte Wörter und längere Ausdrücke findest du oft unter mehr als einem Stichwort, z.B. **ask sb. the way** unter **ask** und unter **way** und **Geh ein Feld vor** unter **gehen** und unter **Feld**.
- In eckigen Klammern steht, wie das Wort ausgesprochen und betont wird.
- Die Ziffern 1., 2. usw. zeigen, dass ein Stichwort mehrere Bedeutungen hat.

• Suche im *Dictionary* (Seiten 168–188 und 189–204) die Bedeutung der Wörter rechts heraus … • … und sprich sie deinem Partner/deiner Partnerin oder der Klasse richtig vor.	bottom • rude • service • Flug • gefährlich • Insel

Dictionary (English – German)
art [ɑːt] Kunst I
as [əz, æz]
 1. als, während II 2 (38)
 2. as old as so alt wie II 2 (30)
ask [ɑːsk] fragen I • **ask about sth.** nach etwas fragen I • **ask questions** Fragen stellen I • **ask sb. the way** jn. nach dem Weg fragen II 6 (95/170)

Dictionary (German – English)
Feld 1. field [fiːld] • **auf dem Feld** in the field
 2. *(bei Brettspielen)* **Geh ein Feld vor.** Move on one space. [speɪs] • **Geh ein Feld zurück.** Move back one space.
Fleisch meat [miːt]
fliegen fly [flaɪ]
Flug flight [flaɪt]

SF Describing pictures ▶ Unit 1 (p. 11) • P 4 (p. 17)

Wenn du ein Bild beschreibst, geht es viel besser, wenn du die folgenden Dinge beachtest.

Was hilft mir beim Bilder beschreiben?

Wo?
- Um zu sagen, wo etwas abgebildet ist, benutze:
  at the top/bottom • **in the foreground/background** • **in the middle** • **on the left/right**
- Du kannst diese *phrases* auch kombinieren:
  at the bottom on the left • **at the top on the right**
- Diese Präpositionen sind auch hilfreich:
  behind • **between** • **in front of** • **next to** • **under**

Wie?
Geh bei der Beschreibung in einer bestimmten Reihenfolge vor, z.B. von links nach rechts, von oben nach unten oder vom Vordergrund zum Hintergrund.

> **Tipp**
>
> Um zu sagen, was gerade passiert, benutze das **present progressive**.
> *Sophie **is showing** Jo a book. Ananda **is talking** to Jack.*

- Alles klar? Dann beschreib das Foto oben rechts und mach Übung 4 auf S. 17.

SF Multiple-choice exercises ▶ Unit 3 (p. 49) • P 4 (p. 49)

Was sind Multiple-Choice-Aufgaben?

Bei Multiple-Choice-Aufgaben gibt es mehrere Antworten (meist sind es drei oder vier). Meistens ist nur eine davon richtig, und die musst du auswählen.

Worauf sollte ich bei Multiple-Choice-Aufgaben achten?

– Lies die Frage sehr genau durch.
– Bevor du dir die Lösungsangebote anschaust, deck sie mit Papier ab. Überlege dir, was die richtige Antwort sein könnte. Wenn das dann auch als eine Lösungsmöglichkeit angeboten wird, ist es meistens richtig.
– Lies immer alle vorgegebenen Lösungen, bevor du dich entscheidest.
– Sprich die Sätze mit den verschiedenen Lösungsmöglichkeiten leise nach. Oft hört man heraus, was richtig ist.
– Wenn es heißt, dass nur eine Antwort richtig ist, achte darauf, dass du nur **eine** ankreuzt.
– Mach erst alle Aufgaben und geh zum Schluss zu den Fragen zurück, bei denen du unsicher bist.

• Nun probier die Aufgabe 4 auf Seite 49.

1 What did Ananda find in her yard?
 A two cats
 B a fox
 C two hedgehogs
 D three mice

2 Hedgehog babies can drink:
 A orange juice
 B water
 C milk
 D iced tea

SF REVISION Giving a presentation

Wie mache ich eine gute Präsentation?

Vorbereitung
– Schreib die wichtigsten Gedanken als Notizen auf, z.B. auf nummerierte Karteikarten oder als Mindmap (vgl. SF **Mind maps**, S. 114).
– Bereite ein Poster oder eine Folie vor. Schreib groß und für alle gut lesbar.
– Übe deine Präsentation zu Hause vor einem Spiegel. Sprich laut, deutlich und langsam.

Durchführung
– Bevor du beginnst, häng das Poster auf bzw. leg deine Folie auf den ausgeschalteten Projektor und sortiere deine Vortragskarten.
– Warte, bis es ruhig ist. Schau die Zuhörer an.
– Erkläre zu Anfang, worüber du sprechen wirst. Lies nicht von deinen Karten ab, sondern sprich frei.

My presentation is about …
First, I'd like to talk about …
Second, …

This picture/photo/… shows …

That's the end of my presentation. Have you got any questions?

Schluss
– Sag, dass du fertig bist.
– Frag die Zuhörenden, ob sie Fragen haben. Bedanke dich fürs Zuhören.

LISTENING AND READING SKILLS

SF Listening ▶ *Unit 3 (p. 43)*

Du brauchst nicht jedes Wort zu verstehen!

Bei einem Hörtext sollst du oft nur allgemein verstehen, worum es geht.

1. Bevor es losgeht, frag dich: Was weiß ich schon über das Thema? Worum wird es in dem Hörtext gehen?
2. Denk daran: *Wie* jemand etwas sagt, verrät dir viel darüber, *was* die Person sagt. Klingt er oder sie fröhlich, traurig, aufgeregt, gelangweilt …?
3. Auch Nebengeräusche sind eine Hilfe: Du hörst einen pfeifenden Teekessel? Dann weißt du, dass sich der Dialog, den du hörst, in der Küche abspielt.
4. Vor allem: Lass dich nicht verunsichern, wenn du mal einen Satz nicht verstehst. Das geht jedem so.

Was sollte ich noch beim *Listening* beachten?

Oft willst du aus einem Hörtext Einzelinformationen heraushören, z.B. auf S. 43, in welcher Reihenfolge die Fernsehsendungen ausgestrahlt werden. Das ist nicht so schwer, wenn du die folgenden Tipps beachtest.

1. **Bereite dich gut vor**
   Lies die Aufgabe zum Hörtext gut durch und bereite deine Notizen vor. Leg z.B. eine Tabelle oder Liste an.
2. **Und wenn ich eine wichtige Information nicht verstehe?**
   Auch hier gilt: keine Panik! Denk an die Aufgabe und hör weiter zu. Oft werden wichtige Informationen auch wiederholt.
3. **Stimme und Betonung helfen dir**
   Achte darauf, was der/die Sprecher/in besonders betont – das ist wichtig!
4. **Aufgepasst!**
   Die Informationen, die du suchst, kommen vielleicht in einer anderen Reihenfolge vor, als du erwartest.
5. **Notizen machen: gewusst wie**
   Mach während des Hörens nur kurze Notizen oder verwende Symbole. Du kannst sie hinterher ergänzen.
   (Vgl. SF **Taking notes**, S. 119).

SF Scanning ▸ Unit 3 (p. 47) • P 12 (p. 52)

Texte nach Informationen absuchen

Du musst einen Text manchmal gar nicht lesen, wenn du nur bestimmte Informationen brauchst. Stattdessen kannst du den Text nach Schlüsselwörtern (**key words**) absuchen und nur dort lesen, wo du sie findest.

Wie gehe ich vor?

Schritt 1: Bevor du auf den Text schaust
Denk an das Schlüsselwort, nach dem du suchst. Es hilft dir, wenn du es aufschreibst.

Schritt 2: Das Schlüsselwort finden
Geh mit deinen Augen sehr schnell durch den Text. Dabei hast du das Schriftbild oder das Bild des Wortes, nach dem du suchst, vor Augen. Das gesuchte Wort wird dir sofort „ins Auge springen".
Du kannst auch mit dem Finger in breiten Schlingen oder Bewegungen wie bei einem „S" durch die Mitte des Texts von oben bis unten gehen.
Wenn du das Schlüsselwort gefunden hast, lies nur dort weiter, um Näheres zu erfahren.

- Probier das *Scanning* am Text über Maulwürfe aus.
  Suche nach der ersten fehlenden Information (*food*) und vervollständige die Tabelle auf einem Blatt Papier.
  Suche dann nach der zweiten und nach der dritten fehlenden Information.

	moles
food	
number of babies	
enemies	

MOLES

Moles are about 17 cm long and weigh about 100 grams. They have sharp teeth, very small eyes and ears, and a hairless snout. They live underground – in tunnels in gardens, parks and woods. They don't usually come out during the day.
But at night they come out to look for food. Every day they eat 70 to 100 grams of worms and insects. They can't see colours very well, but they can see when something moves. And they can smell and hear very well. So it isn't difficult for them to find something to eat.
Female moles usually have three to five babies a year. The babies are born without any fur and are quite helpless. At first they stay underground. Then, at the age of three months, they are almost as large as their parents and are able to leave the tunnel. Moles can live up to three years. They have only a few enemies, like dogs and cats. These animals catch and kill them, but they don't eat them.

- Alles klar? Dann mach die Aufgabe 9 auf Seite 47.

Skills File **119**

SF REVISION Taking notes

Worum geht es beim Notizenmachen?

Wenn du beim Lesen oder Zuhören Notizen machst, kannst du dich später besser daran erinnern, wenn du etwas vortragen, nacherzählen oder einen Bericht schreiben sollst.

Wie mache ich Notizen?

In Texten oder Gesprächen gibt es immer wichtige und unwichtige Wörter. Die wichtigen Wörter werden Schlüsselwörter (**key words**) genannt und nur die solltest du notieren. Meist sind das Substantive und Verben, manchmal auch Adjektive oder Zahlen.

> Hmm, da hab ich wohl ein paar Symbole zu viel benutzt …

Tipp
- Verwende Ziffern (z.B. „7" statt „seven").
- Verwende Symbole und Abkürzungen, z.B. ✔ (für Ja) und + (für und) oder GB für Great Britain, A. für Ananda.
  Du kannst auch eigene Symbole erfinden.
- Verwende **not** oder ✗ statt „doesn't" oder „don't".

SF Marking up a text ▶ Unit 5 (p. 77) • P 8 (p. 83)

Wann sollte ich einen Text markieren?

Du hast einen Text mit vielen Fakten vor dir liegen und sollst später über bestimmte Dinge berichten. Dann wird es dir helfen, die für dich wichtigen Informationen im Text zu markieren.

Wie gehe ich am besten vor?

Lies den Text und markiere nur die für dein Thema wichtigen Informationen. Nicht jeder Satz enthält für deine Aufgabe wichtige Wörter, und oft reicht es aus, nur ein oder zwei Wörter in einem Satz zu markieren.

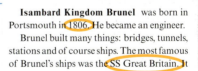

– Du kannst wichtige Wörter einkreisen.

– Du kannst sie unterstreichen.

– Du kannst sie mit einem Textmarker hervorheben.

ABER:
Markiere nur auf Fotokopien von Texten oder in deinen eigenen Büchern.

- Alles verstanden? Dann probier Aufgabe 8 auf S. 83.

120 Skills File

SPEAKING AND WRITING SKILLS

SF Talking to people ▶ Unit 6 (p. 94) • P 3 (p. 98)

Wie kann ich mich freundlich auf Englisch unterhalten?

Wenn du dich auf Englisch unterhalten willst, helfen dir ein paar einfache Redewendungen:

1. Fang nett an …	2. … und antworte nicht nur mit einem Wort.	3. Zeig, dass du wissen willst, was die anderen denken …	4. … und erzähle etwas von dir.	5. Verabschiede dich freundlich.
Hello! How are you? Can I sit with you?	Fine, thank you. Yes, of course. Yes, it is. No, I can't. Yes, thank you.	What about you? And you? What do you think? Do you like…?	I'm interested in … I often … I like … very much	Bye then. See you later. See you tomorrow. Goodbye.

Am folgenden Beispiel kannst du sehen, welchen Unterschied es macht, ob man diese Redewendungen verwendet oder nicht.

a) Jan aus Mainz ist Austauschschüler in England und spricht mit Jenny, der Tochter seiner Gasteltern.

Jenny   Hi Jan.
Jan   Hi.
Jenny   Is this your first time in England?
Jan   Yes.
Jenny   When did you arrive?
Jan   Yesterday.
Jenny   Mmm … Do you like music and dancing?
Jan   Yes.
Jenny   Well, … would you like to come to the student disco this evening?
Jan   OK.
Jenny   Well, let's meet at 7 pm then.
Jan   OK.
Jenny   Bye then, Jan.
Jan   Bye.

b) Malte ist auch zum ersten Mal in England.

Debbie   Hi Malte.
Malte   Oh, hi Debbie.
Debbie   Is this your first time in England?
Malte   Yes, it is. It's really great here.
Debbie   When did you arrive?
Malte   We arrived yesterday. So I'm a bit tired.
Debbie   Do you like music and dancing?
Malte   Oh yes, I like music a lot. What about you?
Debbie   Me too! Well, … would you like to come to the student disco this evening?
Malte   Yes, that sounds great.
Debbie   Well, let's meet at 7 pm then.
Malte   OK. Thank you.
Debbie   See you later.
Malte   Bye, Debbie. See you.

• Nun probier Nr. 2 auf S. 94 und Übung 3 auf S. 98.

Skills File **121**

SF Linking words ▶ Unit 1 (p. 18) • P 6 (p. 18)

Eine Geschichte klingt viel interessanter, wenn man die Sätze mit **linking words** miteinander verbindet. Eine Möglichkeit dazu sind **time phrases** wie **at 7 o'clock, a few minutes later, suddenly, then, next**…

At 2 o'clock in the morning David walked downstairs and opened the front door. Tim was outside. 'Follow me,' he whispered. A few minutes later the two boys were in the garden of the old house. 'We can hide behind these trees,' Tim said. They waited and watched. Suddenly somebody opened one of the windows. Then they saw a man and a woman. First the woman climbed out and jumped down. Next the man threw out a big box before he jumped down too. 'What are they doing?' David asked.

SF Topic sentence ▶ Unit 4 (p. 60) • P 4 (p. 65)

Wofür sind *topic sentences* gut?

Wenn du einen Text schreibst, sind kurze, einleitende Sätze (**topic sentences**) am Anfang jedes Absatzes gut, weil sie den Lesern sofort sagen, worum es geht. So lesen sie mit mehr Interesse weiter, wovon du berichten willst.
Folgende Wendungen können dir helfen, einen *topic sentence* zu formulieren:
1. Orte: **Bristol is famous for … / … is a great place. / There are lots of reasons to visit …**
2. Personen: **… is/was one of the greatest/most interesting …**
3. Aktivitäten: **… is great fun. / Lots of people … every day.**

• Alles verstanden? Dann probier Übung 4 auf S. 65.

SF Structuring a text ▶ Unit 5 (p. 79) • P 11 (p. 84)

Warum sollte ich meine Texte gliedern?

Ein Text ist viel besser zu verstehen, wenn er nicht einen „Textbrei", sondern mehrere Absätze enthält.

Wie sollte ich meine Texte gliedern?

Unterteile deinen Text in:
– eine Einleitung (**beginning**) – hier schreibst du, worum es in dem Text geht (vgl. SF **Topic sentence**).
– einen Mittelteil (**middle**) – hier schreibst du mehr über dein Thema.
– einen Schluss (**end**) – hier bringst du den Text zu einem interessanten Ende.

Wuppertal is famous for its overhead monorail, the 'Schwebebahn'.
 The 'Schwebebahn' is over 100 years old. It's 13.5 km long and follows the River Wupper. The people of Wuppertal built it over the river because there wasn't much room in the Wupper valley. The 'Schwebebahn' isn't very fast, but it's very safe. Lots of people use it every day.
 When you're in Wuppertal, travel by 'Schwebebahn'. It's great fun!

• Nun probier Übung 11 auf S. 84.

SF Correcting mistakes ▶ Unit 6 (p. 102) • P 10 (p. 102)

Warum sollte ich einen Text überarbeiten?

Ein Text ist noch nicht „fertig", wenn du ihn zu Ende geschrieben hast. Du solltest ihn immer mehrmals durchlesen:
Lies ihn noch einmal, um zu sehen, ob er vollständig und gut verständlich ist.

Lies ihn erneut, um ihn auf Fehler zu überprüfen. Das können unterschiedliche Fehler sein, z.B. Rechtschreibfehler (*spelling mistakes*).

Wie erkenne ich Rechtschreibfehler?

Lies deinen Text langsam, Wort für Wort, Buchstabe für Buchstabe. Wenn du unsicher bist, hilft dir ein Wörterbuch.
Einige **spelling mistakes** kannst du vermeiden, wenn du folgende Regeln beachtest.

tomato [təˈmɑːtəʊ], *pl* **tomatoes**
Tomate II 6 (104)

wife [waɪf], *pl* **wives** [waɪvz]
Ehefrau II 4 (71)

drop (-pp-) [drɒp] fallen lassen I

forget (-tt-) [fəˈget] vergessen I

> **Tipp**
>
> Einige Wörter haben Buchstaben, die geschrieben, aber nicht gesprochen werden,
>   z.B.   **walk**, **grandma**.
>
> Manchmal ändert sich die Schreibweise, wenn ein Wort eine Endung erhält,
>   z.B.   **take** —> **taking**,
>   **grumble** —> **grumbled**,
>
>   z.B.   **happy** —> **happily**,
>   **fly** —> **flies**,
>   **ABER** **stay** —> **stays**,
>
>   z.B.   **sit** —> **sitting**,
>   **plan** —> **planned**.
>
> Beim Plural reicht manchmal ein *-s* als Endung nicht aus, es muss noch ein *-e* dazu,
>   z.B.   **box** —> **boxes**,
>   **potato** —> **potatoes**.

> • Alles verstanden? Dann probier auch Aufgabe 10 auf S. 102.

Häufig sind es aber auch **Wortfehler**. – du hast vielleicht eine falsche **Präposition** benutzt.

um drei Uhr   – **at** three o'clock
im Moment   – **at** the moment
zu Hause   – **at** home

> **Tipp**
>
> • Lerne Wörter immer mit der dazugehörigen **Präposition**, z.B. nicht nur **wait**, sondern **wait for**, oder **am** Abend – **in** the evening.

> • Alles klar? Dann probier Aufgabe 12 auf S. 102.

MEDIATION SKILLS

SF Mediation ▸ Unit 2 (p. 37) • P 14 (p. 37)

Wann muss ich zwischen zwei Sprachen vermitteln?

Manchmal musst du zwischen zwei Sprachen vermitteln. Das nennt man **mediation**.

1. Du gibst englische Informationen auf Deutsch weiter: Du fährst z.B. mit deiner Familie nach Großbritannien und deine Eltern oder Geschwister wollen wissen, was jemand in einem Café gesagt hat oder was an einer Informationstafel steht.

2. Du gibst deutsche Informationen auf Englisch weiter: Vielleicht ist bei dir zu Hause eine Austauschschülerin aus England oder Dänemark zu Gast, die kein Deutsch spricht und Hilfe braucht.

3. In schriftlichen Prüfungen musst du manchmal in einem englischen Text gezielt nach Informationen suchen und diese auf Deutsch wiedergeben.

Worauf muss ich bei *mediation* achten?

Übersetze nicht alles wörtlich, gib nur das Wesentliche weiter. Du kannst Unwichtiges weglassen und Sätze anders formulieren.

> **Tipp**
> - Verwende kurze und einfache Sätze.
> - Wenn du ein Wort nicht kennst, umschreibe es oder ersetze es durch ein anderes mit ähnlicher Bedeutung.
>
> - Alles verstanden? Dann probier die Aufgabe 14 auf S. 37.

Grammar File – Inhalt

Seite

Unit 1	GF 1	**REVISION** **The simple past: positive statements** Die einfache Form der Vergangenheit: bejahte Aussagesätze		125
	GF 2	**The simple past: negative statements** Die einfache Form der Vergangenheit: verneinte Aussagesätze		126
	GF 3	**The simple past: questions and short answers** Die einfache Form der Vergangenheit: Fragen und Kurzantworten		126
Unit 2	GF 4	**The comparison of adjectives** Die Steigerung der Adjektive		127
Unit 3	GF 5	**The *will*-future** Das Futur mit *will*		129
	GF 6	**Conditional sentences (type 1)** Bedingungssätze (Typ 1)		130
	GF 7	**Adverbs of manner** Adverbien der Art und Weise		131
Unit 4	GF 8	**Word order** Wortstellung		133
	GF 9	**The present perfect: use** Das *present perfect*: Gebrauch		134
	GF 10	**The present perfect: form** Das *present perfect*: Form		134
	GF 11	**The present perfect with adverbs of indefinite time** Das *present perfect* mit Adverbien der unbestimmten Zeit		136
Unit 5	GF 12	**The *going to*-future** Das Futur mit *going to*		137
	GF 13	**Extra** **Question tags with *be*** Frageanhängsel mit *be*		138
Unit 6	GF 14	**REVISION** **The present progressive** Die Verlaufsform der Gegenwart		138
	GF 15	**The past progressive** Die Verlaufsform der Vergangenheit		139

Lösungen der Grammar-File-Aufgaben 139

Grammatical terms (Grammatische Fachbegriffe) 140

Im **Grammar File** (S. 124–140) wird zusammengefasst, was du in den sechs Units über die englische Sprache lernst.

In der **linken Spalte** findest du **Beispielsätze** und **Übersichten**, z.B.

How **did** Dan **help** her?

Fragen

Merke:
Simple present   Do you get up early?   Does Lesley get
Simple past   Did you get up earl…   Did …

In der **rechten Spalte** stehen **Erklärungen** und nützliche **Hinweise**. Das rote **Ausrufezeichen** (!) macht dich auf besondere Fehlerquellen aufmerksam.

Hinweise wie ▶ Unit 1 (p. 14) • P 11–14 (pp. 20–21) zeigen dir, zu welcher Unit und welcher Seite ein **Grammar-File**-Abschnitt gehört und welche Übungen du dazu im Practice-Teil findest.

Die **grammatischen Fachbegriffe** (*grammatical terms*) kannst du auf Seite 140 nachschlagen.

Am Ende der Abschnitte stellt dir Polly wieder kleine Aufgaben zur Selbstkontrolle. Schreib die Lösungen in dein Heft. Überprüfe sie dann auf Seite 139.

Unit 1
GF 1 REVISION The simple past: positive statements
Die einfache Form der Vergangenheit: bejahte Aussagesätze

We **were** in Spain **last summer**.
It **was** great. We **went** swimming a lot and **played** volleyball on the beach.
Wir waren letzten Sommer in Spanien / sind letzten Sommer in Spanien gewesen …

Mit dem *simple past* kannst du über Vergangenes berichten, z.B. wenn du eine Geschichte erzählst. Das *simple past* steht häufig mit Zeitangaben wie *last summer, yesterday, three weeks ago, in 2004*.

a) *(to) be* and regular verbs

Our holiday **was** fantastic.
We **were** in New York.
We **stayed** for two weeks.
And Jay **played** basketball every day!

(to) be und regelmäßige Verben

– Beim *simple past* von **be** gibt es nur zwei Formen:
  I, he/she/it   **was**
  you, we, they   **were**

– Bei **regelmäßigen Verben** bildest du das *simple past* durch Anhängen von **ed** an den Infinitiv:
  stay → stayed, play → played

  Es gibt für **alle** Personen nur eine Form.

! Merke aber:

1. It was great for Prunella without the Carter-Browns. Nobody **grumbled**.
Dan and Jo **argued** a lot.

1. Ein stummes **e** fällt weg:
grumble → grumbled, argue → argued.

2. Prunella **dropped** Emily's CDs on the floor.

2. Einige Konsonanten werden verdoppelt:
drop → dropped, plan → planned.

3. Prunella **tried** on Emily's clothes too.

3. **y** nach einem Konsonanten wird zu **ied**:
try → tried.
(Aber **y** nach einem **Vokal** bleibt: *play → played*.)

4. In August the Shaws **painted** their kitchen.
After that they **needed** a holiday.

4. Nach **t** und **d** wird die *ed*-Endung [ɪd] ausgesprochen: *painted, needed*.

b) Irregular verbs

The Carter-Browns **went** to Majorca.
    (Infinitiv: **go**)

Dan and Jo **met** a nice girl in Cornwall.
    (Infinitiv: **meet**)

The Carter-Browns **had** a very nice holiday.
    (Infinitiv: **have**)
Their hotel **had** a swimming pool.
    (Infinitiv: **have got**)

▶ Unit 1 (p. 12) • P 6 (p. 18)

Unregelmäßige Verben

Wie im Deutschen gibt es auch im Englischen eine Reihe von unregelmäßigen Verben, deren *simple past*-Formen du einzeln lernen musst.

▶ *Unregelmäßige Verben (pp. 208–209)*

! *had* ist die *simple past*-Form von *have* und von *have got*.

126 1 Grammar File

Welche dieser Formen sind simple past*-Formen?*

1 has • 2 met • 3 sit • 4 go • 5 travelled • 6 heard
7 were • 8 hear • 9 had • 10 sat • 11 went • 12 meet

GF 2 The simple past: negative statements
Die einfache Form der Vergangenheit: verneinte Aussagesätze

Sophie Lesley **didn't want** to come to Bristol.

Ananda She **didn't say** much.
         But we **didn't ask** her much.

Eine Aussage im *simple past* verneinst du immer mit **didn't** + **Infinitiv** (Langform: *did not*).

Verneinte Aussagesätze			
Merke:	**Simple present**	I **don't get up** early.	Lesley **doesn't get up** early.
	Simple past	I **didn't get up** early.	Lesley **didn't get up** early.

▶ Unit 1 (p. 13) • P 8–9 (p. 19)

Sieh dir die Bilder an und vervollständige die Sätze im simple past.

1 This morning Jo **didn't** ... his bed. (not – make)

2 Last week Dan ... ... his bike. (not – clean)

3 Yesterday Jack ... ... his homework. (not – do)

GF 3 The simple past: questions and short answers
Die einfache Form der Vergangenheit: Fragen und Kurzantworten

Did Jo **help** Jody?
– Yes, he **did**. / No, he **didn't**.

Did the girls **talk** to Lesley?
– Yes, they **did**. / No, they **didn't**.

Why **did** Jody **need** help?
How **did** Dan **help** her?

Fragen im *simple past* bildest du mit **did**:
Did Jo help?
❗ (Nicht: *Did Jo helped?*)

Das Fragewort steht wie immer am Anfang.

Fragen			
Merke:	**Simple present**	**Do** you **get up** early?	**Does** Lesley **get up** early?
	Simple past	**Did** you **get up** early?	**Did** Lesley **get up** early?

▶ Unit 1 (p. 14) • P 11–14 (pp. 20–21)

Grammar File **2**

Unit 2
GF 4 The comparison of adjectives Die Steigerung der Adjektive

a) Comparison with -er/-est

Steigerung mit *-er/-est*

Steigerungsformen verwendest du, um Personen oder Dinge miteinander zu vergleichen, z.B.:

young [jʌŋ]	jung
young**er** ['jʌŋgə]	jünger
(the) young**est** ['jʌŋgɪst]	der/die/das jüngste …; am jüngsten
old	alt
old**er**	älter
(the) old**est**	der/die/das älteste …; am ältesten

How old are the Carter-Brown children?
– Well, Sophie is young. She's twelve now.
   Toby is younger. He's nine.
   Baby Hannah is the youngest,
   and Emily is the oldest.

Prunella thinks Sophie is nicer than Emily.
Emily is bigger, but is she prettier?

▶ Unit 2 (p. 30) • P 9 (p. 35)

Die Steigerung mit *-er/-est* verwendest du für
– einsilbige Adjektive (*young, full, nice, big, …*) und
– zweisilbige Adjektive mit der Endung *-y* (*pretty, funny, easy, …*).

❗ Merke: nice – nicer – nicest
          bi**g** – bi**gg**er – bi**gg**est
          prett**y** – prett**i**er – prett**i**est

b) Comparison with *more/most*

I think tennis is **boring**.
But basketball is even **more boring**.
And mum's yoga is the **most boring** thing of all.

▶ Unit 2 (p. 31) • P 12 (p. 36)

Steigerung mit *more/most*

Andere Adjektive werden mit **more** und **most** gesteigert:

boring	langweilig
more boring	langweiliger
(the) most boring	der/die/das langweiligste …; am langweiligsten

Weitere Beispiele:
expensive – more expensive – most expensive
difficult   – more difficult   – most difficult

c) Irregular comparison

Ananda has got a good idea, but Sophie's idea is better. Lesley has got the best idea.

Jo hasn't got much money this week. Dan has got more, but Dilip has got the most.
Jo hat diese Woche nicht viel Geld. Dan hat mehr, aber Dilip hat das meiste/am meisten.

Unregelmäßige Steigerung

Einige Adjektive werden unregelmäßig gesteigert:

good	– better	– best
bad	– worse [wɜːs]	– worst [wɜːst]
much/many	– more	– most

Die Steigerung der Adjektive

Mit -er/-est:

Einsilbige Adjektive:
old – older – oldest

Adjektive auf -y:
happy – happier – happiest

Mit more/most:

Andere zwei- und mehrsilbige Adjektive:
boring – more boring – most boring
terrible – more terrible – most terrible
exciting – more exciting – most exciting

Unregelmäßig:

good – better – best

bad – worse – worst

much/many – more – most

▶ Unit 2 (pp. 30–31) • P 13 (p. 36)

d) bigger than – as big as

Sophie, Hip is so big. I think your rabbit is **bigger than** my cat.

But your cat is **faster than** Hip.

„größer als" – „so groß wie"

◀ Wenn Personen oder Dinge **unterschiedlich** groß/schnell/alt/... sind, vergleichst du sie mit der 1. Steigerungsform + **than** („als"):

Your rabbit is *bigger than* my cat.   (... größer als ...)
Your cat is *faster than* Hip.   (... schneller als ...)
                ↑
        1. Steigerungsform

❗ (Nicht: ... bigger/faster ~~as~~ ...)

Is your cat **as fast as** my rabbit?
Ist deine Katze so schnell wie mein Kaninchen?

I think she's faster. But she is**n't as big as** your rabbit.
... Aber sie ist nicht so groß wie dein Kaninchen.

◀ Wenn Personen oder Dinge **gleich** groß/schnell/alt/... sind, vergleichst du sie mit **as** big/fast/old/... **as**.
(Verneint: *not as big/fast/old/... as*)

Sophie is twelve. Emily is **older than** her.
Sophie ist zwölf. Emily ist älter als sie.

Is Sophie as old as Dan and Jo?
No, she isn't **as old as** them.
... Nein, sie ist nicht so alt wie sie.

❗ Merke:
Nach Vergleichen mit **than** und **as ... as** stehen die Personalpronomen *me/him/her* usw. (nicht: ~~I/he/she~~ usw.):
older than me/him/her/us/them
älter als **ich/er/sie/wir/sie**

▶ Unit 2 (pp. 30–31) • P 9–10, 12–13 (pp. 35–36)

 Sieh dir an, wie alt die drei Jungen in der Zeichnung sind. Schreib Vergleiche mit old *auf.*

1 Ali is ... ... Ben and Chris. He is the ...
2 Ben is ... ... Chris, but he isn't ... ... Ali.

Ali (13)   Ben (12)   Chris (12)

I'm faster than them.

Unit 3
GF 5 The *will*-future Das Futur mit *will*

The hedgehogs **will be** cold tonight. **I'll have to** take them inside.

Maybe their mother **will come**. But maybe she **won't**.

Ananda — **What will they need?** Do you know?
Will they want milk?
Sophie — **No, they won't.**

Sophie — **I think** they**'ll need** water.
Ich glaube, sie werden Wasser brauchen. /
Ich glaube, sie brauchen Wasser.
(Vermutung)

Ananda — **It will be** cold tonight.
Es wird heute Nacht kalt (werden).
(Vorhersage)

Ananda — **I don't want to** take them to the animal clinic, but **I will**.
Ich will sie nicht in die Tierklinik bringen, aber ich werde es tun.

▶ Unit 3 (p. 44) • P 2–3 (pp. 48–49)

Um auszudrücken, was in der Zukunft geschehen wird, benutzt du **will** + **Infinitiv**.
Es gibt für **alle** Personen nur eine Form.
Die Kurzform von *will* ist *'ll: I'll, you'll* usw.

Das *will-future* steht häufig mit Zeitangaben wie *tomorrow, next month, soon, in a few weeks*.

Die **verneinte Form** von *will* heißt **won't**.
(Langform: *will not*).

Fragen kannst du **mit Fragewort** (*What will they …?*) oder **ohne Fragewort** (*Will they …?*) stellen.

Die Kurzantworten lauten: *Yes, I will / No, I won't* usw.

Mit *will* kannst du eine **Vermutung** oder eine **Vorhersage** ausdrücken:

◀ Eine **Vermutung** fängt oft mit *I think, I'm sure* oder *maybe* an.

◀ Bei einer **Vorhersage** geht es oft um Dinge, die man nicht beeinflussen kann, z.B. um das Wetter.

! Im Deutschen benutzen wir oft das Präsens, wenn wir über die Zukunft sprechen:
Vielleicht kommt ihre Mutter bald.

Im Englischen steht das *will-future*:
Maybe their mother will come soon.

! Nicht verwechseln:
– *I want to* heißt „ich will".
– *I will* heißt „ich werde".

Ergänze diese Vorhersagen und Vermutungen.
Verwende **will** *oder* **'ll** *und diese Verben:*

be – like – be – survive

1 I … … 13 next month.
2 Come and visit me! I think you … … it here.
3 I'm sure the weather … … fine in August.
4 What do you think? … the baby hedgehogs …?

GF 6 Conditional sentences (type 1) Bedingungssätze (Typ 1)

If you **give** a hedgehog water, it**'ll be** happy.

Wenn du einem Igel Wasser gibst, wird er zufrieden sein.

If you **don't keep** it warm, it **won't survive**.

Wenn du ihn nicht warm hältst, wird er nicht überleben.

Bedingungssätze (Typ 1) sind „Was ist, wenn …"-Sätze: Sie beschreiben, was unter bestimmten Bedingungen geschieht oder nicht geschieht.

Die Bedingung steht im *if*-Satz, die Folge davon steht im Hauptsatz:

if-Satz (Bedingung) ↓	Hauptsatz (Folge für die Zukunft) ↓
If you **give** a hedgehog water,	it**'ll be** happy.
If you **don't keep** it warm,	it **won't survive**.
Im *if*-Satz steht das *simple present*.	Im Hauptsatz steht meist das *will-future*.

You'll find more help **if you visit our website**.
If you visit our website, you'll find more help.

◂ Wenn der Hauptsatz am Anfang steht, brauchst du kein Komma vor dem *if*-Satz.

If I **see** Jack, I'**ll show** him the babies.

Ananda:
When I see Jack, I'll tell him about the babies.
Sobald ich Jack sehe, …

If I see Jack, I'll tell him about the babies.
Falls ich Jack sehe, …

❗ Verwechsle nicht *when* und *if*:
– *when* = „sobald", „dann wenn"

– *if* = „falls", „wenn"

If you visit Ananda, you **can help** her with the hedgehogs.
If you need more information, **write** to the Animal Hotline.

◂ Im Hauptsatz können auch *can, must* oder ein Imperativ (Befehl, Aufforderung) stehen.

▸ Unit 3 (p. 45) • P 5–6 (p. 50)

Schreib die Sätze mit der richtigen Verbform in dein Heft.

1 If Jack sees the babies, he **(wants / will want)** to help them too.
2 What will happen if their mum **(won't come / doesn't come)** back?
3 If Ananda **(takes / will take)** the babies to the clinic, they **(have / will have)** a better chance of survival.

 If you add blue to yellow, you **get** green.
If the bus is late, I always **walk** home.
Immer dann, wenn …

Wenn etwas immer so ist, kann im Hauptsatz auch das *simple present* stehen.

Grammar File **3** 131

GF 7 **Adverbs of manner** Adverbien der Art und Weise

a) Use

Hedgehogs are **slow** and **quiet**.
This is Sleepy. He's a very **slow** hedgehog.
You can pick him up, but be **careful**.

Hedgehogs walk slowly and quietly.
Igel gehen langsam und leise.

You have to pick up a hedgehog very carefully.
Du musst einen Igel sehr vorsichtig hochheben.

Gebrauch

◄ Ein **Adjektiv** beschreibt ein **Nomen** näher.
Es sagt aus, wie etwas oder jemand **ist**.

◄ Ein **Adverb der Art und Weise** beschreibt ein **Verb** näher.
Es sagt aus, wie jemand etwas **tut** oder wie etwas **geschieht**.

b) Regular forms

Adjektiv				Adverb
	slow	→	slowly	
	quiet	→	quietly	
	careful	→	carefully	

Ananda was **angry** with Dilip.   (Adjektiv)
Sophie shouted at Dilip angrily. (Adverb)

▶ Unit 3 (p. 46) • P 9 (p. 51)

Regelmäßige Formen

Die meisten Adverbien der Art und Weise entstehen durch Anhängen von **-ly** an das Adjektiv.

❗ Merke aber:
1 **y** wird zu **i**:   angry → angrily
                          happy → happily
2 **le** wird zu **ly**: terrible → terribly
                          horrible → horribly
3 Nach **ic** wird **ally** angehängt:
    fantastic → fantastically

c) Irregular forms

She did a **good** job with the babies.   (Adjektiv)
She did the job well.   (Adverb)

Jo ____ The rabbits are very **fast**.   (Adjektiv)
Dan ____ Of course! All rabbits
          can run fast.   (Adverb)

Ananda _ It's **hard** work at the clinic. (Adjektiv)
Steve ___ That's right. The volunteers
          at the clinic work very hard.   (Adverb)

▶ Unit 3 (p. 47) • P 11 (p. 52)

Unregelmäßige Formen

Einige Adverbien haben eine unregelmäßige Form, die du auswendig lernen musst:

– Das Adverb zu good heißt well.

– Bei fast und hard sind Adjektiv und Adverb gleich.

d) Word order

'You killed the hedgehogs,' she shouted angrily.

Steve fed **the babies** carefully.

Steve fütterte vorsichtig die Babys.

Wortstellung

Das Adverb der Art und Weise steht direkt **nach dem Verb**.

❗ In Sätzen mit Objekt steht es **nach dem Objekt**.

Welches Wort ist richtig, Adjektiv oder Adverb?

1. When you pick up a small animal, you have to be very **careful / carefully**.
2. Squirrels and rabbits can run very **quick / quickly**.
3. Hedgehogs walk **slow / slowly** and **quiet / quietly**.
4. Ananda did a **good / well** job with the hedgehogs.
5. The woman at the animal clinic said Ananda did **good / well**.

e) Extra The comparison of adverbs of manner

Die Steigerung der Adverbien der Art und Weise

Du kannst nicht nur Adjektive, sondern auch Adverbien steigern:

◂ Adverbien, die auf **-ly** enden, steigerst du mit **more/most**:

quickly	*more* quickly	*most* quickly
schnell	schneller	am schnellsten

◂ Einsilbige Adverbien *(fast, hard)* steigerst du mit **-er/-est**:

fast	fast*er*	fast*est*
schnell	schneller	am schnellsten

◂ Die Steigerungsformen von *well* und *badly* lernst du am besten auswendig:

well	*better*	*best*
gut	besser	am besten

badly	*worse*	*worst*
schlecht, schlimm	schlechter, schlimmer	am schlechtesten, am schlimmsten

▸ Unit 3 (p. 47)

Unit 4
GF 8 Word order — Wortstellung

a) REVISION S – V – O

1 Jack **often** writes stories.
   Jack **schreibt** oft Geschichten.

2 Dilip **can play** the guitar.
   Dilip **kann** Gitarre **spielen**.

3 After school Jo **plays** football.
   Nach der Schule **spielt** Jo Fußball.

   When Jack comes home, he **feeds** Polly.
   Wenn Jack nach Hause kommt, **füttert** er Polly.

4 What do you do **when** you **come** home?
   Was machst du, **wenn du nach Hause kommst**?

▶ Unit 4 (p. 60) • P 2 (p. 64)

S – V – O

Die Wortstellung im Aussagesatz lautet
S – V – O (**S**ubjekt – **V**erb – **O**bjekt): *Jack writes stories.*

! Anders als im Deutschen …

1 … steht ein Häufigkeitsadverb *(often)* nie zwischen Verb und Objekt.

2 … dürfen Hilfsverb *(can)* und Vollverb *(play)* nicht durch ein Objekt *(the guitar)* getrennt werden.

3 … steht das Subjekt *(Jo, he)* auch dann vor dem Verb, wenn der Satz mit einer Zeitangabe *(after school)* oder einem Nebensatz *(when Jack comes home)* beginnt.

4 … ist auch im Nebensatz die Wortstellung **S – V – O**.

Denk dabei an die **Straßen-Verkehrs-Ordnung**, an die du dich immer halten musst!

---

b) Place before time

We can go **to the mountains in the morning**.
Wir können morgen Vormittag in die Berge fahren.

Great! And we can have a picnic **near the castle in the afternoon**.
… Und am Nachmittag können wir in der Nähe der Burg ein Picknick machen.

▶ Unit 4 (p. 60) • P 3 (p. 64)

Ort vor Zeit

Wenn Ortsangaben *(to the mountains)* und Zeitangaben *(in the morning)* zusammen am Satzende stehen, dann gilt: **Ort vor Zeit**.

1	2
Ort	Zeit
… to the mountains	in the morning.
… near the castle	in the afternoon.

 Welcher Satz ist richtig, 1 oder 2?

1 We have to be at six o'clock at the station.
2 We have to be at the station at six o'clock.

GF 9 The present perfect: use Das *present perfect*: Gebrauch

◀ Mit dem *present perfect* drückst du aus, dass jemand etwas getan hat oder dass etwas geschehen ist. Dabei ist **nicht wichtig, wann** es geschehen ist. Deshalb wird auch kein genauer Zeitpunkt genannt.

Wenn du aber den genauen Zeitpunkt angeben willst *(yesterday, last week, two years ago, in 2004)*, musst du das *simple past* verwenden.
(Zum *simple past* siehe GF 1–3, S. 125–126).

◀ Oft hat die Handlung Auswirkungen auf die Gegenwart oder die Zukunft:
Im Beispiel links hat Grandma das Frühstück gemacht. Ergebnis: Jetzt können alle frühstücken.

▶ Unit 4 (p. 61)

GF 10 The present perfect: form Das *present perfect*: Form

a) **The past participle**

1 Grandpa **has** packed a picnic.

They **have** planned a day in the mountains.
Dan and Jo **haven't** tidied their room.

2 The twins **haven't** seen Caerphilly Castle.
Dan doesn't feel well, so he **hasn't** eaten his breakfast.

Das Partizip Perfekt

Das *present perfect* wird mit *have/has* und der 3. Form des Verbs gebildet. Die 3. Form des Verbs heißt **Partizip Perfekt** *(past participle)*.

1 Bei regelmäßigen Verben hängst du **ed** an den Infinitiv an: pack + *ed* → pack*ed*.

◀ Beachte die Besonderheiten der Schreibung und der Aussprache (siehe GF 1, S. 125).

2 Unregelmäßige Verben haben eigene Formen, die du einzeln lernen musst.
Unregelmäßige Verben werden immer so angegeben: *(to) see, saw,* **seen**
             (to) eat, ate, **eaten**
Die 2. Form ist die *simple past*-Form *(saw, ate)*, die 3. Form ist das *past participle (seen, eaten)*.

▶ Unregelmäßige Verben (pp. 208–209)

The Thompsons **have got** very nice neighbours.
Die Thompsons **haben** sehr nette Nachbarn.

❗ Merke:
have got („haben") ist keine *present perfect*-Form.

Welche dieser Formen sind past participles?

1 eaten • 2 went • 3 gone • 4 did • 5 ate • 6 done • 7 taken • 8 took

b) Positive and negative statements

1 The neighbours have made a pie for the Thompsons.
Die Nachbarn haben einen Obstkuchen für die Thompsons gemacht.

2 Grandpa hasn't cleaned the car yet.
Opa hat das Auto noch nicht sauber gemacht.

Dan hasn't come down.
Dan ist nicht nach unten gekommen.

Bejahte und verneinte Aussagesätze

1 Bejahte Aussagesätze im *present perfect*:
have/has + Partizip Perfekt.

2 Verneinte Aussagesätze im *present perfect*:
haven't/hasn't + Partizip Perfekt.

! Beim *present perfect* musst du immer **have/has** verwenden, egal ob im Deutschen „haben" oder „sein" steht.

Present perfect

Positive statements		Negative statements		Long forms
I've packed		I haven't seen		I/You/We/They have (not) packed
You've packed		You haven't seen		He/She has (not) packed
He's packed		He hasn't seen		
She's packed	a picnic.	She hasn't seen	Dan.	I/You/We/They have (not) seen
We've packed		We haven't seen		He/She has (not) seen
You've packed		You haven't seen		
They've packed		They haven't seen		

▶ Unit 4 (p. 61) • P 6–8 (pp. 66–67)

Polly has cleaned her cage. Now she can watch TV.

c) Questions and short answers

Have the twins been to the Brecon Beacons?
– Yes, they have. / No, they haven't.

Has Jo installed the software?
– Yes, he has. / No, he hasn't.

Why has Grandma printed out the instructions?

▶ Unit 4 (p. 63) • P 13–14 (p. 68)

Fragen und Kurzantworten

Bei Fragen im *present perfect* werden Subjekt und *have/has* vertauscht.

Kurzantworten werden mit *have/has* gebildet.

Fragewörter stehen wie immer am Satzanfang.

! Merke:
Im *present perfect* gibt es **keine Fragen mit when**.
When fragt nach einem Zeitpunkt – und dafür verwendest du das *simple past*: When did …?

GF 11 The present perfect with adverbs of indefinite time
Das *present perfect* mit Adverbien der unbestimmten Zeit

I've **already** packed the car.

Ich habe schon das Auto beladen.

Oh, good. Have the twins had breakfast **yet?**

Haben ... schon gefrühstückt?

I've **just** seen Jo in the kitchen. But Dan has**n't** come down **yet.**

Ich habe gerade Jo ... gesehen. Aber Dan ist noch nicht nach unten gekommen.

I've **always** wanted to visit Caerphilly Castle. Grandma, Grandpa, have you **ever** been there?

Ich wollte schon immer ... besuchen. Oma, Opa, seid ihr jemals dort gewesen?

▶ Unit 4 (p. 61 / p. 63) • P 9–10 (p. 67) / P 13 (p. 68)

Das *present perfect* drückt aus, dass etwas **irgendwann** geschehen ist.
Daher findest du oft **Adverbien der unbestimmten Zeit** in *present perfect*-Sätzen:

already	schon, bereits
always	(schon) immer
just	gerade (eben), soeben
never	(noch) nie
not ... yet	noch nicht
often	(schon) oft
ever?	jemals? / schon mal?
yet?	schon?

Die Adverbien der unbestimmten Zeit stehen **direkt vor** dem *past participle*.

❗ Ausnahme: *yet* steht am Satzende.

 Sieh dir die Bilder an. Wie lauten die dazu passenden Sätze im *present perfect*?

1
Grandpa – just – wash – car

2
Dan – not eat – his breakfast – yet

3
The twins – already – make – their beds

Grammar File **5**   **137**

Unit 5
GF 12 The *going to*-future   Das Futur mit *going to*

I'm going to take the photos tomorrow and Ananda **is going to do** the computer work.

Ich werde morgen die Fotos machen und Ananda hat vor, die Computerarbeiten zu erledigen.

Das kennst du schon:
Du verwendest das *will-future*, wenn du Vorhersagen oder Vermutungen über die Zukunft äußern willst (siehe GF 5, S. 129).

Wenn du aber über **Absichten** und **Pläne** für die Zukunft sprechen willst, verwendest du das Futur mit **going to**. Es wird mit **am/are/is + going to + Infinitiv** gebildet. Die Kurzformen heißen *I'm/you're/he's going to* usw.

! *going to* hat hier nichts mit „gehen" zu tun. Es bedeutet „werden", „wollen", „vorhaben".

Well, **I'm not going to help** you because I've got lots of homework.

Ich werde euch nicht helfen ...

◀ Die verneinten Formen heißen *I'm not going to/ you aren't going to/he isn't going to* usw.

What are you **going to do**, Sophie? **Are** you **going to help** us?

Was hast du vor, Sophie? Wirst/Willst du uns helfen?

◀ Fragen kannst du **mit Fragewort** (*What ...?*) oder **ohne Fragewort** (*Are you ...?*) stellen.

Yes, I am. Of course!

◀ Die Kurzantworten sind *Yes, I am / No, I'm not* usw.

The *going to*-future

Positive statements		Negative statements	
I'm going to		I'm not going to	
You're going to		You aren't going to	
He's/She's going to	read.	He/She isn't going to	play.
We're going to		We aren't going to	
You're going to		You aren't going to	
They're going to		They aren't going to	

Questions and short answers

Are you going to watch TV?
– Yes, I am. / No, I'm not.

Is Jo going to watch TV?
– Yes, he is. / No, he isn't.

▶ Unit 5 (p. 76) • P 4–6 (pp. 81–82)

 Sieh dir die Bilder an. Was haben Sophie, Jo und Dan vor? Was werden sie nicht tun? Schreib zwei Sätze mit *going to* und zwei Sätze mit *not going to* in dein Heft.

1   Sophie is ...

2   She isn't ...

3   Dan and Jo ...

4   They ...

5–6 Grammar File

GF 13 Extra Question tags with *be* Frageanhängsel mit *be*

Jo **The new pizza place is** near here, **isn't it?**
Let's go there.
Die neue Pizzeria ist doch hier in der Nähe, nicht? ...

Dan Wow! **The pizzas are** really big here, **aren't they?**
Die Pizzas sind wirklich groß hier, oder?

Jo That's great, because **we're** hungry, **aren't we?** Can you see an empty table?

Wenn du von jemandem Zustimmung zu einer Aussage erwartest, benutzt du oft ein Frageanhängsel *(isn't it?, aren't they?, weren't they?)*.
Deutsche Frageanhängsel sind zum Beispiel „nicht wahr?", „oder?", „ne?", „gell?" oder „woll?".

The milkshakes were great, weren't they?

There's a table in the corner, **isn't there?**

◀ Wenn der Aussagesatz bejaht ist, ist das Frageanhängsel verneint.

verneint bejaht

It isn't too expensive here, **is it?**
Look at the prices before we sit down.

◀ Wenn der Aussagesatz verneint ist, ist das Frageanhängsel bejaht.

▶ Unit 5 (p. 78) • P 9 (p. 84)

Ordne die Frageanhängsel den Aussagen zu.

1 We're late for school, ...
2 The boys are hungry, ...
3 Jo is in the pizza place, ...
4 There was a good film on TV last night, ...
5 The pizzas were great, ...

A aren't they?
B wasn't there?
C aren't we?
D weren't they?
E isn't he?

Unit 6
GF 14 REVISION The present progressive Die Verlaufsform der Gegenwart

Du benutzt das *present progressive*, um auszudrücken, dass etwas gerade in diesem Moment geschieht.

Das *present progressive* wird mit *am/are/is* + *-ing*-Form des Verbs gebildet.
Die *-ing*-Form ist der Infinitiv + *-ing*:
do → **doing**, **wait** → **waiting**.
Beachte: **have** → **having**, **plan** → **planning**

▶ Unit 6 (p. 95) • P 6 (p. 100)

Grammar File 6

GF 15 The past progressive — Die Verlaufsform der Vergangenheit

Yesterday at one o'clock ...

Yesterday at one o'clock Form 8PK and their teachers **were having** lunch.
Gestern um ein Uhr aßen die Klasse 8PK und ihre Lehrer gerade zu Mittag.

Jack **was telling** jokes, but Jo **wasn't listening**.
Jack erzählte Witze, aber Jo hörte nicht zu.

What was Jo **doing**? **Was** he **talking** to Ananda?
Was machte Jo gerade? Redete er gerade mit Ananda?
– No, he **wasn't**. He **was planning** a trick.
– Nein. Er war gerade dabei, einen Streich zu planen.

The others **were** still **eating** and **chatting** when Jo suddenly **started** to laugh.
Die anderen waren noch dabei zu essen und sich zu unterhalten, als Jo plötzlich anfing zu lachen.

▸ Unit 6 (p. 96) • P 7–8 (pp. 100–101)

Du benutzt das *past progressive*, um auszudrücken, dass etwas zu einem bestimmten Zeitpunkt in der Vergangenheit gerade im Gange war. (Die Handlung oder der Vorgang war noch nicht abgeschlossen.)

Das *past progressive* wird mit *was/were* + *-ing*-Form gebildet.
Die verneinten Formen heißen *I wasn't listening / you weren't listening / he wasn't listening* usw.

Fragen kannst du **mit Fragewort** (*What ...?*) oder **ohne Fragewort** (*Was he ...?*) stellen.
Die Kurzantworten sind *Yes, I was / No, I wasn't* usw.

Das *past progressive* wird oft benutzt, um auszudrücken, was gerade vor sich ging (*the others were still eating ...*), als eine andere Handlung einsetzte (*Jo started to laugh*).
❗ Die zweite Handlung steht im *simple past*.

Welche Sätze drücken aus, dass jemand gerade dabei war, etwas zu tun?

1 At 6 o'clock yesterday evening Jack was reading a spy story.
2 Two days ago Sophie played tennis with Lesley.
3 At 8.30 this morning Lesley was cycling to school.
4 Last week Jo read two detective stories.
5 Emily cycled to school last Wednesday.
6 At 6.15 Jo and Dan were playing football in the park.

Lösungen der Grammar-File-Aufgaben

p.126/1 2, 5, 6, 7, 9, 10, 11
p.126/2 1 This morning Jo **didn't make** his bed.
2 Last week Dan **didn't clean** his bike.
3 Yesterday Jack **didn't do** his homework.
p.128 1 Ali is **older than** Ben and Chris. He is the **oldest**.
2 Ben is **as old as** Chris, but he isn't **as old as** Ali.
p.129 1 I'**ll be** 13 next month.
2 Come and visit me! I think you'**ll like** it here.
3 I'm sure the weather **will be** fine in August.
4 ... **Will** the baby hedgehogs **survive**?
p.130 1 If Jack sees the babies, he **will want** to help them too.
2 What will happen if their mum **doesn't come back**?
3 If Ananda **takes** the babies to the clinic, they **will have** a better chance of survival.

p.132 1 When you pick up a small animal, you have to be very **careful**.
2 Squirrels and rabbits can run very **quickly**.
3 Hedgehogs walk **slowly** and **quietly**.
4 Ananda did a **good** job with the hedgehogs.
5 The woman at the animal clinic said Ananda did **well**.
p.133 2 (We have to be at the station at six o'clock.)
p.134 1, 3, 6, 7
p.136 1 Grandpa **has** just **washed** the car.
2 Dan **hasn't eaten** his breakfast yet.
3 The twins **have already made** their beds.
p.137 1 Sophie **is going to read** a book.
2 She isn't **going to watch** TV.
3 Dan and Jo **are going to play** football.
4 They **aren't going to take** photos.
p.138 1C, 2A, 3E, 4B, 5D
p.139 1, 3, 6

140 Grammar File

Grammatical terms (Grammatische Fachbegriffe)

adjective ['ædʒɪktɪv]	Adjektiv	*good, red, new, boring, …*
adverb of frequency	Häufigkeitsadverb	*always, often, never, …*
[ˌædvɜːb_əv 'friːkwənsi]		
adverb of indefinite time [ɪnˌdefɪnət 'taɪm]	Adverb der unbestimmten Zeit	*already, ever, just, never, …*
adverb of manner ['mænə]	Adverb der Art und Weise	*badly, happily, quietly, well, …*
comparison [kəm'pærɪsn]	Steigerung	*old – older – oldest*
conditional sentence [kənˌdɪʃənl 'sentəns]	Bedingungssatz	*If I see Jack, I'll tell him.*
future ['fjuːtʃə]	Zukunft, Futur	
*going to***-future**	Futur mit *going to*	*I**'m going to watch** TV tonight.*
imperative [ɪm'perətɪv]	Imperativ (Befehlsform)	*Open your books. Don't talk.*
infinitive [ɪn'fɪnətɪv]	Infinitiv (Grundform des Verbs)	*(to) open, (to) see, (to) read, …*
irregular verb [ɪˌreɡjələ 'vɜːb]	unregelmäßiges Verb	*(to) go – went – gone*
negative statement [ˌneɡətɪv 'steɪtmənt]	verneinter Aussagesatz	*I don't like bananas.*
noun [naʊn]	Nomen, Substantiv	*Sophie, girl, brother, time, …*
object ['ɒbdʒɪkt]	Objekt	*My sister is writing **a letter**.*
object form ['ɒbdʒɪkt fɔːm]	Objektform (der Personalpronomen)	*me, you, him, her, it, us, them*
past [pɑːst]	Vergangenheit	
past participle [ˌpɑːst 'pɑːtɪsɪpl]	Partizip Perfekt	*cleaned, planned, gone, seen, …*
past progressive [ˌpɑːst prə'ɡresɪv]	Verlaufsform der Vergangenheit	*At 7.30 I **was having** dinner.*
person ['pɜːsn]	Person	
personal pronoun [ˌpɜːsənl 'prəʊnaʊn]	Personalpronomen	*I, you, he, she, it, we, they;*
	(persönliches Fürwort)	*me, you, him, her, it, us, them*
plural ['plʊərəl]	Plural, Mehrzahl	
positive statement [ˌpɒzətɪv 'steɪtmənt]	bejahter Aussagesatz	*I like oranges.*
possessive determiner	Possessivbegleiter	*my, your, his, her, its, our, their*
[pəˌzesɪv dɪ'tɜːmɪnə]	(besitzanzeigender Begleiter)	
possessive form [pəˌzesɪv fɔːm]	*s*-Genitiv	*Jo's brother; my sister's room*
possessive pronoun [pəˌzesɪv 'prəʊnaʊn]	Possessivpronomen	*mine, yours, his, hers, ours, theirs*
preposition [ˌprepə'zɪʃn]	Präposition	*after, at, in, next to, under, …*
present ['preznt]	Gegenwart	
present perfect [ˌpreznt 'pɜːfɪkt]	*present perfect*	*We**'ve made** a cake for you.*
present progressive [ˌpreznt prə'ɡresɪv]	Verlaufsform der Gegenwart	*The Hansons **are having** lunch.*
pronoun ['prəʊnaʊn]	Pronomen, Fürwort	
pronunciation [prəˌnʌnsi'eɪʃn]	Aussprache	
question ['kwestʃən]	Frage(satz)	
question tag ['kwestʃən tæɡ]	Frageanhängsel	*This place is great, **isn't it?***
question word ['kwestʃən wɜːd]	Fragewort	*what?, when?, where?, how?, …*
regular verb [ˌreɡjələ 'vɜːb]	regelmäßiges Verb	*(to) help – helped – helped*
short answer [ˌʃɔːt_'ɑːnsə]	Kurzantwort	*Yes, I am. / No, I don't. / …*
simple past [ˌsɪmpl 'pɑːst]	einfache Form der Vergangenheit	*Jo **wrote** two letters yesterday.*
simple present [ˌsɪmpl 'preznt]	einfache Form der Gegenwart	*I always **go** to school by bike.*
singular ['sɪŋɡjələ]	Singular, Einzahl	
spelling ['spelɪŋ]	Schreibweise, Rechtschreibung	
subject ['sʌbdʒɪkt]	Subjekt	***My sister** is writing a letter.*
subject form ['sʌbdʒɪkt fɔːm]	Subjektform (der Personalpronomen)	*I, you, he, she, it, we, they*
subordinate clause [səˌbɔːdɪnət 'klɔːz]	Nebensatz	*I like Scruffy **because I like dogs**.*
verb [vɜːb]	Verb	*hear, open, help, go, …*
*will***-future**	Futur mit *will*	*I think it **will be** cold tonight.*
word order ['wɜːd_ˌɔːdə]	Wortstellung	
yes/no question	Entscheidungsfrage	*Are you 13? Do you like comics?*

Vocabulary 141

Diese Wörterverzeichnisse findest du in deinem Englischbuch:

- Das **Vocabulary** (Vokabelverzeichnis – S. 141–167) enthält alle Wörter und Wendungen, die du lernen musst. Sie stehen in der Reihenfolge, in der sie in den Units vorkommen.
- Das **Dictionary** besteht aus zwei alphabetischen Wörterlisten zum Nachschlagen:
  Englisch – Deutsch: S. 168–188 / Deutsch – Englisch: S. 189–205.

So ist das Vocabulary aufgebaut:

- Hier siehst du, wo die Wörter vorkommen.
  p. 31/A 11 = Seite 31, Abschnitt 11
  p. 35/P 11 = Seite 35, Übung 11
- Die Lautschrift zeigt dir, wie ein Wort ausgesprochen und betont wird.
  (→ Englische Laute: S. 205)
- Eingerückte Wörter lernst du am besten zusammen mit dem vorausgehenden Wort, weil die beiden zusammengehören.
- Diese Kästen solltest du dir besonders gut ansehen.

Tipps zum Wörterlernen findest du im Skills File auf Seite 113.

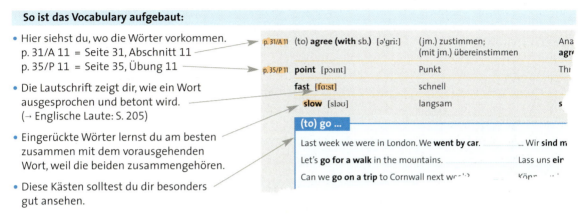

Abkürzungen:

n	= noun	v	= verb	
adj	= adjective	adv	= adverb	
prep	= preposition	conj	= conjunction	
pl	= plural	no pl	= no plural	
p.	= page	pp.	= pages	
sb.	= somebody	sth.	= something	
jn.	= jemanden	jm.	= jemandem	

Symbole:

◄► ist das „Gegenteil"-Zeichen: **slow** ◄► **fast**
(**slow** ist das Gegenteil von **fast**)

❗ Hier stehen Hinweise auf Besonderheiten, bei denen man leicht Fehler machen kann.

Welcome back – After the holidays

Remember?

p. 6

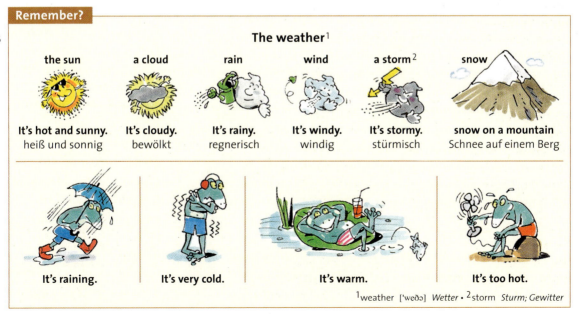

[1]weather [ˈweðə] *Wetter* • [2]storm *Sturm; Gewitter*

Personen-, Orts- und Ländernamen → S. 206–207 • Unregelmäßige Verben → S. 208–209 • Classroom English → S. 210

142 Welcome back Vocabulary

(to) **travel** ['trævl] **(-ll-)**[1]	reisen	Last year we **travelled** to Turkey in the holidays.
caravan ['kærəvæn]	Wohnwagen	*French:* la caravane
by the sea [baɪ]	am Meer	a **caravan by the sea**

Irregular simple past forms

(to) drink	**drank** [dræŋk]	trinken		(to) read [riːd]	**read** [red]	lesen
(to) eat	**ate** [et, eɪt]	essen		(to) ride	**rode** [rəʊd]	reiten; *(Rad)* fahren
(to) meet	**met** [met]	(sich) treffen		(to) swim	**swam** [swæm]	schwimmen
(to) put	**put** [pʊt]	legen, stellen, *(wohin)* tun		(to) throw	**threw** [θruː]	werfen

on the beach [biːtʃ]	am Strand	
island ['aɪlənd]	Insel	
(to) **stay** [steɪ]	bleiben; wohnen, übernachten	It rained all day so I **stayed** at home. In the holidays we **stayed** at a hotel in Cornwall.
anyway ['eniweɪ]	trotzdem	It was cold, but we went swimming **anyway**.
theatre ['θɪətə]	Theater	❗ Betonung auf der 1. Silbe: **theatre** ['θɪətə] *French:* le théâtre
cool [kuːl]	kühl	
(to) **go for a walk** [wɔːk]	spazieren gehen, einen Spaziergang machen	cold · cool · warm · hot
country ['kʌntri]	Land *(auch als Gegensatz zur Stadt)*	Germany is a big **country**. ❗ The Millers live **in the country**. (= auf dem Land)
view [vjuː]	Aussicht, Blick	This postcard shows the **view** from our hotel.
plane [pleɪn]	Flugzeug	❗ **im** Flugzeug **= on** the plane
as [əz, æz]	als, während	I ate my sandwiches **as** I waited for the bus.
(to) **fly** [flaɪ], *simple past:* **flew** [fluː]	fliegen	
round [raʊnd]	um ... (herum); in ... umher	**round** the car Walk **round** the classroom and talk to different partners.
(to) **shine** [ʃaɪn], *simple past:* **shone** [ʃɒn]	scheinen *(Sonne)*	Most people are happy when the sun **shines**.
p. 7 **sky** [skaɪ]	Himmel	❗ It was a sunny day. There wasn't a cloud **in the sky**. (= am Himmel)
our **own** pool [əʊn]	unser eigenes Schwimmbad	❗ I've got **my own** room. (*Never:* an own room)
(to) **go by car/bike/...**	mit dem Auto/Rad/... fahren	

(to) go ... (*simple past:* went)

Last week we were in London. We **went by car**.	... Wir **sind mit dem Auto gefahren**.
Let's **go for a walk** in the mountains.	Lass uns **einen Spaziergang** in den Bergen **machen**.
Can we **go on a trip** to Cornwall next week?	Können wir ... **einen Ausflug** nach Cornwall **machen**?
We **went on holiday** to Italy this summer.	Wir sind diesen Sommer nach Italien **in Urlaub gefahren**.

What was the weather like?   Wie war das Wetter?

[1] Die Angabe **(-ll-)** zeigt, dass der Endkonsonant bei der Bildung von *-ing*-Form und *-ed*-Form verdoppelt wird: **travel – travelling / travelled**.

Tipps zum Wörterlernen → S. 113 · Englische Laute → S. 205 · Alphabetische Wörterverzeichnisse → S. 168–188 / S. 189–205

Vocabulary 1

p.8	**degree** [dɪˈgriː]	Grad	It's 14 **degrees** (14°) and very cloudy in England. *French:* le degré
	foggy [ˈfɒgi]	neblig	
	fog [fɒg]	Nebel	noun: **fog** – adjective: **foggy**
	start [stɑːt]	Start, Anfang, Beginn	verb: (to) **start** – noun: **start**
p.9	(to) **go abroad** [əˈbrɔːd]	ins Ausland gehen/fahren	
	nobody [ˈnəʊbədi]	niemand	
	(to) **speak (to)** [spiːk], *simple past:* **spoke** [spəʊk]	sprechen (mit), reden (mit)	
	clothes *(pl)* [kləʊðz, kləʊz]	Kleider, Kleidung(sstücke)	! **clothes** ist ein Pluralwort: **Kleidung ist** teuer. = **Clothes are** expensive.
	lake [leɪk]	(Binnen-)See	(picture: mountains, the sea, an island, a lake) ! the **lake** = der See • the **sea** = die See, das Meer

Unit 1: Back to school

p.11	(to) **describe** sth. **(to** sb.**)** [dɪˈskraɪb]	(jm.) etwas beschreiben	! **Describe** the picture **to your partner**. = **Beschreibe** das Bild **deinem Partner**. *French:* décrire
	description [dɪˈskrɪpʃn]	Beschreibung	*French:* la description
	background [ˈbækgraʊnd]	Hintergrund	In this picture, Dan and Jo are in the **foreground**. In the **background** you can see a lake.
	foreground [ˈfɔːgraʊnd]	Vordergrund	
	at the bottom (of) [ˈbɒtəm]	unten, am unteren Ende (von)	Now do the exercise **at the bottom of** the page. ↓ **at the bottom (of)** ◄► **at the top (of)** ↑

left – right

Do you write with your **left** or your **right** hand?	Schreibst du mit der **linken** oder mit der **rechten** Hand?
Jack looks **left** and **right**, but he can't see the man.	Jack schaut **nach links** und **nach rechts**, aber …
On the left, you can see Morris, my cat.	**Links/Auf der linken Seite** …
My dog Alice is **on the right**.	… **rechts/auf der rechten Seite**.

Where's the rabbit? (Prepositions)

| **behind**[1]
the cage | **in front of**
the cage | **in**
the cage | **between**[2]
the girls | **near**
the cat | **next to**
the cat | [1] **behind** [bɪˈhaɪnd]
hinter
[2] **between** [bɪˈtwiːn]
zwischen |

Personen-, Orts- und Ländernamen → S. 206–207 • Unregelmäßige Verben → S. 208–209 • Classroom English → S. 210

144 1 Vocabulary

p. 12/A 1	**flight** [flaɪt]	Flug	verb: (to) **fly** – noun: **flight**
	time(s) [taɪm(z)]	Mal(e); -mal	We went surfing four **times** last week.
	a bit [ə ˈbɪt]	ein bisschen, etwas	The tea was **a bit** hot, so I added some milk.
	the underground [ˈʌndəgraʊnd]	die U-Bahn	*American English:* **the subway** [ˈsʌbweɪ]

Irregular simple past forms

(to) get	**got** [gɒt]	gelangen, (hin)kommen	(to) hear	**heard** [hɜːd]	hören
(to) get on/off	**got on/off**	ein-, aussteigen	(to) know	**knew** [njuː]	wissen; kennen
(to) give	**gave** [geɪv]	geben	(to) teach	**taught** [tɔːt]	unterrichten, lehren

	dangerous [ˈdeɪndʒərəs]	gefährlich	*French:* dangereux, dangereuse
	fast [fɑːst]	schnell	
	slow [sləʊ]	langsam	**fast** ◄► **slow**
	What was **the best thing about ...?**	Was war das Beste an ...?	**The best thing about** the film was the music.
	building [ˈbɪldɪŋ]	Gebäude	**buildings**
	lift [lɪft]	Fahrstuhl, Aufzug	*American English:* **elevator** [ˈelɪveɪtə]
	amazing [əˈmeɪzɪŋ]	erstaunlich, unglaublich	
	for miles [maɪlz]	meilenweit	You can see **for miles** from this tower.
	mile [maɪl]	Meile *(= ca. 1,6 km)*	
p. 13/A 2	**at the back (of** the room**)** [bæk]	hinten, im hinteren Teil (des Zimmers)	
	Mind your own business. [ˌmaɪnd jər ˌəʊn ˈbɪznəs]	Das geht dich nichts an! / Kümmere dich um deine eigenen Angelegenheiten!	How much was that mobile phone? – **Mind your own business.**
	after [ˈɑːftə]	nachdem	**!** **after** = 1. *(prep)* nach – **after** school 2. *(conj)* nachdem – **after** I came home
	before [bɪˈfɔː]	bevor	**!** **before** = 1. *(prep)* vor – **before** lunch 2. *(conj)* bevor – **before** we eat
	rude [ruːd]	unhöflich, unverschämt	It's **rude** to speak with your mouth full.
p. 14/A 4	**Do you really think so?**	Meinst du wirklich? / Glaubst du das wirklich?	Shopping is great fun. – **Do you really think so?** I think it's boring.
	No way! [ˌnəʊ ˈweɪ]	Auf keinen Fall! / Kommt nicht in Frage!	Mum, can you give me £80 for a new sweatshirt? – £80? **No way!** You can have £30.
	Come on. [ˌkʌm ˈɒn]	Ach komm! / Na hör mal!	Oh **come on** – you know that's wrong!

Tipps zum Wörterlernen → S. 113 · Englische Laute → S. 205 · Alphabetische Wörterverzeichnisse → S. 168–188 / S. 189–205

Vocabulary **1**   145

(to) **be in trouble** [ˈtrʌbl]	in Schwierigkeiten sein; Ärger kriegen	My friends helped me when I **was in trouble**. Jo **is in trouble**. He hasn't got his homework.
hero [ˈhɪərəʊ], *pl* **heroes** [ˈhɪərəʊz]	Held, Heldin	
(to) **calm down** [ˌkɑːm ˈdaʊn]	sich beruhigen	Help! There's a mouse in the kitchen. – **Calm down.** It can't hurt you.
(to) **get angry/hot/...** (-tt-), *simple past:* **got**	wütend/heiß/... werden	It**'s getting hot** in here. Can you open the window, please?
angry (about sth./**with** sb.) [ˈæŋgri]	wütend, böse (über etwas/auf jn.)	Let's be friends again. Or are you still **angry with** me?

nothing (nichts)	**something** (etwas)	**everything** (alles)

p. 15/A 6	**role play** [ˈrəʊl pleɪ]	Rollenspiel
p. 18/P 5	**vowel sound** [ˈvaʊəl saʊnd]	Vokallaut
p. 18/P 6	**linking word** [ˈlɪŋkɪŋ wɜːd]	Bindewort

Ms Travelot [mɪz, məz]	Frau Travelot	❗ Manche Frauen möchten lieber mit **Ms ...** angesprochen werden, weil am Wort **Ms** nicht zu erkennen ist, ob sie verheiratet sind oder nicht. (**Mrs ...** = verheiratet; **Miss ...** = unverheiratet)
hour [ˈaʊə]	Stunde	*French:* l'heure *(f)*

p. 20/P 10	**person** [ˈpɜːsn]	Person	❗ Betonung auf der 1. Silbe: **person** [ˈpɜːsn]
	(to) **be on**	eingeschaltet sein, an sein *(Radio, Licht usw.)*	I can't do my homework when the radio **is on**.
p. 20/P 12	**Find/Ask somebody who ...**	Finde/Frage jemanden, der ...	I've got no idea. **Ask somebody who** knows more about Bristol.

Saved!

p. 22	(to) **save** [seɪv]	retten	*French:* sauver
	through [θruː]	durch	He's climbing **through** the window.

the top **bunk**

bunk (bed) [bʌŋk]	Etagenbett, Koje	**bunk beds**
he **could ...** [kəd, kʊd]	er konnte ...	My brother **could** ride a bike when he was four.
(to) **get** (-tt-), *simple past:* **got**	holen, besorgen	

(to) get (*simple past:* got)

1. gelangen, (hin)kommen	How can I **get** to the station, please?	**Remember:**	
2. werden	My mother **got** very angry last night.	(to) **get dressed**	sich anziehen
3. holen, besorgen	Can you **get** the tickets for the theatre?	(to) **get on/off**	ein-/aussteigen
4. bekommen, kriegen	Did you **get** nice birthday presents?	(to) **get up**	aufstehen

Personen-, Orts- und Ländernamen → S. 206–207 · Unregelmäßige Verben → S. 208–209 · Classroom English → S. 210

1–2 Vocabulary

out ("hinaus, heraus", "draußen")

There's a little cat in the water. We have to pull her **out**.	... Wir müssen sie **heraus**ziehen.
Dan saw a girl swim **out**.	Dan sah ein Mädchen **hinaus**schwimmen.
Where's Sheeba? – She's **out** there in the garden.	... Sie ist da **draußen** im Garten.

Come on. [ˌkʌm_ˈɒn]	Na los, komm.	
tide [taɪd]	Gezeiten, Ebbe und Flut	**!** The **tide** is **out**. (Es ist **Ebbe**.) The **tide** is **in**. (Es ist **Flut**.)
past [pɑːst]	vorbei (an), vorüber (an)	We walked **past** theatres, cafés and shops.
(to) **wave** [weɪv]	winken	She's **waving**.
a few [fjuː]	ein paar, einige	We didn't have much money, just **a few** pounds.
all right [ɔːl ˈraɪt]	gut, in Ordnung	Let's meet tomorrow. – **All right**. Is 8.30 OK?
almost [ˈɔːlməʊst]	fast, beinahe	It's **almost** six.
(to) **drive** [draɪv], *simple past:* **drove** [drəʊv]	*(ein Auto/mit dem Auto)* fahren	Does your mother **drive** to work? – No, she usually goes by bike.
(to) **see** sb. [siː], *simple past:* **saw** [sɔː]	jn. besuchen, jn. aufsuchen	Why don't you come and **see** us next Sunday?
(to) **know about** sth., *simple past:* **knew** [njuː]	von etwas wissen; über etwas Bescheid wissen	I didn't **know about** the party, so I couldn't go.
happy ending [ˌhæpi_ˈendɪŋ]	Happyend	**!** In English you say **happy ending**. (*Not:* ~~happy end~~)
in time [ɪn ˈtaɪm]	rechtzeitig	We didn't get home **in time**, so we couldn't watch the film.
(to) **go surfing** [ˈsɜːfɪŋ]	wellenreiten gehen, surfen gehen	(to) **go surfing**
surfboard [ˈsɜːfbɔːd]	Surfbrett	surfboard
exciting [ɪkˈsaɪtɪŋ]	aufregend, spannend	**exciting** ◄► **boring**

p. 23

Unit 2: What money can buy

pocket money [ˈpɒkɪt mʌni]	Taschengeld	bags
pocket [ˈpɒkɪt]	Tasche *(an einem Kleidungsstück)*	pockets
(to) **spend money/time (on)** [spend], *simple past:* **spent** [spent]	Geld ausgeben (für) / Zeit verbringen (mit)	My brother **spends** a lot of money **on** clothes. We **spent** the weekend at my grandmother's in Rostock.
(to) **save** [seɪv]	sparen	
survey (on) [ˈsɜːveɪ]	Umfrage, Untersuchung (über)	We're doing a **survey on** free-time activities.

p. 26

Tipps zum Wörterlernen → S. 113 · Englische Laute → S. 205 · Alphabetische Wörterverzeichnisse → S. 168–188 / S. 189–205

Vocabulary 2

Irregular simple past forms

p. 27

(to) buy	**bought** [bɔːt]	kaufen
(to) find	**found** [faʊnd]	finden
(to) sell	**sold** [səʊld]	verkaufen
(to) think	**thought** [θɔːt]	glauben, meinen, denken

(to) understand	**understood** [ˌʌndəˈstʊd]	verstehen
(to) wear	**wore** [wɔː]	tragen (Kleidung)
(to) win	**won** [wʌn]	gewinnen

---

blouse [blaʊz]	Bluse		a pretty **blouse**
(baseball) cap [kæp]	(Baseball-)Mütze		a **(baseball) cap**
cinema [ˈsɪnəmə]	Kino	❗	**ins** Kino gehen = (to) go **to the** cinema *French:* le cinéma
jacket [ˈdʒækɪt]	Jacke, Jackett	❗	Betonung auf der 1. Silbe: **jacket** [ˈdʒækɪt]
make-up [ˈmeɪkʌp]	Make-up		**make-up** [ˈmeɪkʌp]
pullover [ˈpʊləʊvə]	Pullover		**pullover** [ˈpʊləʊvə]
skirt [skɜːt]	Rock		
sports gear *(no pl)* [ˈspɔːts ɡɪə]	Sportausrüstung, Sportsachen	❗	Where **is** my **sports gear**? *(singular)* = Wo **sind** meine **Sportsachen**?
a pair (of) [peə]	ein Paar		a pair of trainers
trainers *(pl)* [ˈtreɪnəz]	Turnschuhe		*French:* la paire
trousers *(pl)* [ˈtraʊzəz]	Hose	❗	**Are** your **trousers** new? – Yes, **they are**. (= **Ist** deine **Hose** neu?)

Plural words: *glasses, jeans, shorts, trousers*

She wears **glasses**.	Sie trägt **eine Brille**.	❗ Wörter wie **glasses, jeans, shorts,**
Why does he need **two pairs of glasses**?	... **zwei Brillen**?	**trousers** sind Pluralwörter – also nie
Those trousers are great. Can I have **them**?	**Die Hose da ist** toll. Kann ich **sie** haben?	~~a glasses~~, ~~two jeans~~, ~~this trousers~~!
I need **a new pair of trousers/some new trousers**.	... **eine neue Hose**.	

---

p. 28/A 1

| **What's the matter?** [ˈmætə] | Was ist los? / Was ist denn? | |
| **awful** [ˈɔːfl] | furchtbar, schrecklich | very bad, terrible |

It's mine.

| **mine** [maɪn] | meiner, meine, meins | |

Possessive pronouns (Possessivpronomen)

mine	This isn't my pencil. **Mine** is green.	meiner, meine, meins
yours	My pen doesn't write. Can I use **yours**?	deiner, deine, deins
his	Where are Mike's shoes? Those aren't **his**.	seiner, seine, seins
hers	That isn't Kate's book. **Hers** is on her desk.	ihrer, ihre, ihrs
ours	Your dog is black, **ours** is brown.	unserer, unsere, unseres
yours	Dan, Jo, what about these CDs? Are they **yours**?	eurer, eure, eures
theirs	That wasn't the Millers' car. **Theirs** is red.	ihrer, ihre, ihrs

---

Personen-, Orts- und Ländernamen → S. 206–207 • Unregelmäßige Verben → S. 208–209 • Classroom English → S. 210

148 2 Vocabulary

everybody ['evribɒdi]	jeder, alle	**nobody** (niemand) **somebody** (jemand) **everybody** (jeder, alle)
(to) **be fed up (with** sth.**)** [ˌfed_'ʌp]	die Nase voll haben (von etwas)	I**'m fed up with** comics. I think they're boring.
(to) **lose** [luːz], *simple past:* **lost** [lɒst]	verlieren	(to) **lose money** ◄► (to) **find money** (to) **lose a match** ◄► (to) **win a match**
whose? [huːz]	wessen?	**Whose** CDs are these? Are they yours, Sophie? And **whose** are these? (= Wem gehören diese?)
(to) **disappear** [ˌdɪsə'pɪə]	verschwinden	*French:* disparaître
just like you	genau wie du	You look **just like** your father.
(to) **have** [həv, hæv], *simple past:* **had** [həd, hæd]	haben, besitzen	**!** haben, besitzen = **1.** have got; **2.** (to) have (Im *simple present* wird *have got* häufiger verwendet. Das *simple past* von beiden ist *had*.)
p. 28/A 2 **fine** [faɪn]	gut, schön; in Ordnung	It was a very **fine** day, so we went swimming. Is my essay OK? – Yes, it's **fine**.
p. 28/A 3 **test** [test]	Klassenarbeit, Test, Prüfung	*French:* le test
p. 29/A 4 **problem** ['prɒbləm]	Problem	**!** Betonung auf der 1. Silbe: **problem** ['prɒbləm] *French:* le problème
(to) **look up (from)**	hochsehen, aufschauen (von)	She heard a noise and **looked up from** her book.
What for? [ˌwɒt 'fɔː]	Wofür?	I need £20. – **What for?**
moment ['məʊmənt]	Moment, Augenblick	Please call again later, Jo's out **at the moment**. **!** Betonung auf der 1. Silbe: **moment** ['məʊmənt] *French:* le moment
cheap [tʃiːp]	billig, preiswert	**cheap** ◄► expensive
my old **ones** [wʌnz]	meine alten	There are three CDs on the table: a new **one** (= a new CD) and two old **ones** (= two old CDs).
small [smɔːl]	klein	What a nice little house! But isn't it too **small** for your family?
(to) **grow** [grəʊ], *simple past:* **grew** [gruː]	wachsen	Orange trees **grow** only in hot countries.
more than ['mɔː ðən]	mehr als	**!** **more than** <u>me</u> = mehr als <u>ich</u>: My sister has got **more** CDs **than** <u>me</u>.
(to) **point (at/to** sth.**)** [pɔɪnt]	zeigen, deuten (auf etwas)	He **pointed at/to** the clock. 'We're late,' he said.
p. 30/A 8 **letter (to)** ['letə]	Brief (an)	lots of **letters** a letter *French:* la lettre
even ['iːvn]	sogar	Everybody tried to help, **even** the children.
fuller (than) ['fʊlə]	voller (als)	In the evenings the shop is **fuller than** in the afternoons.

Tipps zum Wörterlernen → S. 113 · Englische Laute → S. 205 · Alphabetische Wörterverzeichnisse → S. 168–188 / S. 189–205

Vocabulary 2

(the) fullest ['fʊlɪst]	der/die/das vollste ...; am vollsten	On Sunday mornings the shop is **fullest**. **full – fuller – (the) fullest**	
stuff [stʌf]	Zeug, Kram	What's that red **stuff** on your T-shirt? Ketchup?	
surprise [sə'praɪz]	Überraschung	*French:* la surprise	
as big/exciting **as**	so groß/aufregend wie	Bristol is not **as big as** New York.	

good – better – best • bad – worse – worst

good	gut	**bad**	schlecht, schlimm
better	besser	**worse** [wɜːs]	schlechter, schlimmer
(the) best	am besten; der/die/das beste ...	**(the) worst** [wɜːst]	am schlechtesten, schlimmsten; der/die/das schlechteste, schlimmste ...

My computer is **better** than yours, but Mr Scott's computer is **the best**.
Our school uniform is **bad**, but theirs is **worse**.
What do you think: What's **the best** pop group at the moment? What's **the worst**?

p. 31/A 10	(to) **put** sth. **on** [ˌpʊt_'ɒn] (-tt-), *simple past:* **put on**	etwas anziehen *(Kleidung)*	**Put on** a pullover. It's cold outside.

	(to) **take** sth. **off** [ˌteɪk_'ɒf], *simple past:* **took off**	etwas ausziehen *(Kleidung)*	(to) **take off** a pullover ◂▸ (to) **put on** a pullover
	more boring **(than)**	langweiliger (als)	My home town is smaller and **more boring than** New York.
	(the) most boring [məʊst]	der/die/das langweiligste ...; am langweiligsten	This village must be **the most boring** place in Britain.
	charity ['tʃærəti]	Wohlfahrtsorganisation	
	recycling [ˌriː'saɪklɪŋ]	Wiederverwertung, Recycling	
	recycled [ˌriː'saɪkld]	wiederverwertet, wiederverwendet, recycelt	
p. 31/A 11	(to) **agree (with** sb.**)** [ə'griː]	(jm.) zustimmen; (mit jm.) übereinstimmen	Ananda thinks sport is fun but Jack doesn't **agree with** her.
p. 35/P 10	**about** [ə'baʊt]	ungefähr	There were **about** 300 people in the park. **!** about = 1. über – a book **about** pets 2. ungefähr – **about** 300 people
p. 35/P 11	**point** [pɔɪnt]	Punkt	Three **points** for the right answer! *French:* le point

The Clothes Project

p. 38	**fashion** ['fæʃn]	Mode	
	(to) **join** sb. [dʒɔɪn]	sich jm. anschließen; bei jm. mitmachen	We're going shopping. Do you want to **join** us? I like computers, so I **joined** the computer club.
	presenter [prɪ'zentə]	Moderator/in	
	over to ...	hinüber zu/nach ...	Dan saw Jo in the park and walked **over to** him.
	(to) **love** [lʌv]	lieben, sehr mögen	(to) **love** ◂▸ (to) **hate**
	love	Liebe	noun: **love** – verb: (to) **love**

Personen-, Orts- und Ländernamen → S. 206–207 • Unregelmäßige Verben → S. 208–209 • Classroom English → S. 210

2–3 Vocabulary

careful [ˈkeəfl]	vorsichtig; sorgfältig	Please be **careful** – this road is very dangerous. The poster looks great, Ananda. Thank you for your **careful** work.
(to) **design** [dɪˈzaɪn]	entwerfen, gestalten	
hat [hæt]	Hut	a **hat**
mirror [ˈmɪrə]	Spiegel	a **mirror** *French:* le miroir
(to) **stand** [stænd], *simple past:* **stood** [stʊd]	stehen; sich (hin)stellen	**Stand** on the chair, Tom. Tom **is standing** on the chair now.
(to) **hurry** [ˈhʌri]	eilen; sich beeilen	It was cold and windy so we **hurried** to the car. **Hurry (up)**, we haven't got much time.
(to) **land** [lænd]	landen	
p. 39 (to) **prepare** [prɪˈpeə]	vorbereiten; sich vorbereiten	(to) **prepare** a presentation / a show / a report ❗ **sich vorbereiten auf** = (to) **prepare for**: I can't help you. I have to **prepare for** a test. *French:* préparer
puzzled [ˈpʌzld]	verwirrt	
bin [bɪn], **dustbin** [ˈdʌstbɪn]	Mülltonne	a **dustbin**
point of view [ˌpɔɪnt_əv ˈvjuː]	Standpunkt	❗ from my **point of view** = von meinem **Standpunkt** aus gesehen; aus meiner **Sicht**

Unit 3:   Animals in the city

p. 42 **animal** [ˈænɪml]	Tier	*French:* l'animal *(m)*
fox [fɒks]	Fuchs	a **fox**
series, *pl* **series** [ˈsɪəriːz]	(Sende-)Reihe, Serie	It's my favourite **series**. I watch it every week.
wild [waɪld]	wild	❗ Pronunciation: **wild** [waɪld]

tonight's programme – Zeitangaben mit *s*-Genitiv

tonight's programme	das Programm von heute Abend; das heutige Abendprogramm
yesterday's homework	die Hausaufgaben von gestern
tomorrow's weather	das Wetter von morgen

(to) **survive** [səˈvaɪv]	überleben	*French:* survivre
survival [səˈvaɪvl]	Überleben	verb: (to) **survive** – noun: **survival**
channel [ˈtʃænl]	Kanal, Sender	

Tipps zum Wörterlernen → S. 113 · Englische Laute → S. 205 · Alphabetische Wörterverzeichnisse → S. 168–188 / S. 189–205

Vocabulary **3**   151

p. 43	**deer**, *pl* **deer** [dɪə]	Reh, Hirsch
	woodpecker ['wʊdpekə]	Specht
	grey [greɪ]	grau
	squirrel ['skwɪrəl]	Eichhörnchen
	mole [məʊl]	Maulwurf
	hedgehog ['hedʒhɒg]	Igel
	frog [frɒg]	Frosch

woodpecker · *deer* · *squirrels* · *hedgehog* · *mole* · *frog*

	interview ['ɪntəvjuː]	Interview	*French:* l'interview *(f)*
p. 44/A 1	**rubbish** ['rʌbɪʃ]	(Haus-)Müll, Abfall	Where's my old cap? – Dad put it in the **rubbish**.
	you'll be cold (= you **will be cold**) [wɪl]	du wirst frieren; ihr werdet frieren	**❗** I'**ll** (= I **will**) help Dan. = Ich **werde** Dan helfen. I **want to** help Dan. = Ich **will** Dan helfen.
	you won't be cold [wəʊnt] (= you **will not be cold**)	du wirst nicht frieren; ihr werdet nicht frieren	
	yard [jɑːd]	Hof	**❗** After school we always play **in the yard**. (= auf dem Hof)
	probably ['prɒbəbli]	wahrscheinlich	*French:* probablement
	(to) **mail** sb. [meɪl]	jn. anmailen	
	(to) **sit down** (-tt-), *simple past:* **sat down**	sich hinsetzen	(to) **sit down** ◄► (to) **stand up**

Irregular simple past forms

(to) bring	**brought** [brɔːt]	(mit-, her)bringen	(to) lay the table	**laid** [leɪd]	den Tisch decken
(to) choose	**chose** [tʃəʊz]	(aus)wählen, (sich) aussuchen	(to) let	**let** [let]	lassen
			(to) sing	**sang** [sæŋ]	singen
(to) feed	**fed** [fed]	füttern	(to) sleep	**slept** [slept]	schlafen
(to) hide	**hid** [hɪd]	(sich) verstecken	(to) write	**wrote** [rəʊt]	schreiben

p. 44/A 2	**moon** [muːn]	Mond
p. 45/A 4	**Thanks very much!**	Danke sehr! / Vielen Dank!	(to) like/love sth. **very much** = etwas **sehr** mögen/**sehr** lieben
	if [ɪf]	falls, wenn	**❗** **If** I see him, I'll ask him. (**Falls** ich ihn sehe …) **When** I see him, … (**Dann wenn** … / **Sobald** …)
	ill [ɪl]	krank	Susan is **ill**.
	(to) **pick** sth. **up** [ˌpɪk_'ʌp]	etwas hochheben, aufheben	Who dropped this paper on the floor? Come and **pick it up**, please.
	important [ɪm'pɔːtnt]	wichtig	*French:* important, e
	(to) **keep** sth. warm/cool/ open/… [kiːp], *simple past:* **kept** [kept]	etwas warm/kühl/offen/… halten	It's important to **keep** hedgehog babies **warm**. **Keep** your eyes **open** when you're on the road.
	hot-water bottle	Wärmflasche	
	fine [faɪn]	*(gesundheitlich)* gut	**❗** I'm/He's **fine**. = Es geht mir/ihm gut.

Personen-, Orts- und Ländernamen → S. 206–207 · Unregelmäßige Verben → S. 208–209 · Classroom English → S. 210

	(to) **visit** [ˈvɪzɪt]	besuchen, aufsuchen	
	chance [tʃɑːns]	Chance, Möglichkeit, Aussicht	
	clinic [ˈklɪnɪk]	Klinik	❗ Pronunciation: **clinic** [ˈklɪnɪk] *(kurzes „i")* *French:* la clinique
	as soon as [əz ˈsuːn_əz]	sobald, sowie	I'll call you **as soon as** I'm home.
p. 46/A 6	(to) **explain** sth. **to** sb. [ɪkˈspleɪn]	jm. etwas erklären, erläutern	If you don't understand, I'll **explain it to you**. ❗ Kannst du **mir** das **erklären**? = Can you **explain** that **to me**? (*Not:* Can you ~~explain me~~ ...)
	explanation [ˌekspləˈneɪʃn]	Erklärung	*French:* expliquer; l'explication *(f)*
	Guess what! [ˌges ˈwɒt]	Stell dir vor! / Stellt euch vor!	
	(to) **guess** [ges]	raten, erraten, schätzen	**Guess** how old I am. – 13? – No, I'm 14.
	at break	in der Pause *(zwischen Schulstunden)*	
	just then	genau in dem Moment; gerade dann	At three o'clock we wanted to go swimming, and **just then** it started to rain.
	(to) **jump** [dʒʌmp]	springen	Can you **jump** over your desk?
	horrible [ˈhɒrəbl]	scheußlich, grauenhaft	a **horrible** day; **horrible** weather *French:* horrible
	garage [ˈgærɑːʒ]	Garage	❗ Betonung auf der 1. Silbe: **garage** [ˈgærɑːʒ] *French:* le garage
	safe (from) [seɪf]	sicher, in Sicherheit (vor)	❗ Will the hedgehogs be **safe**? (= **in Sicherheit**) – **I'm sure** they'll be fine. (= **sicherlich**)
p. 47/A 8	(to) **do a good job**	gute Arbeit leisten	I like your essay. You **did a** really **good job**.
	You did **well**. *(adv)* [wel]	Das hast du gut gemacht.	adjective: **good** – adverb: **well**
	broken *(adj)* [ˈbrəʊkən]	gebrochen; zerbrochen, kaputt	a **broken** arm a **broken** plate
	woods *(pl)* [wʊdz]	Wald, Wälder	Let's go for a walk in the **woods**.
	wood [wʊd]	Holz	a piece of **wood**
	hard [hɑːd]	hart; schwer, schwierig	**hard** work; a **hard** piece of bread This exercise isn't **hard**. You can do it.
	(to) **work hard**	hart arbeiten	
	I'm afraid [əˈfreɪd]	leider	❗ • I have to go now, **I'm afraid**. = **Leider** muss ich jetzt gehen. • My sister **is afraid of** dogs. = Meine Schwester **hat Angst** vor Hunden.
	quite quickly/well/... [kwaɪt]	ziemlich schnell/gut/...	I play hockey **quite well**, but I'm not good enough for the school team.
p. 47/A 9	(to) **scan** a text [skæn] (-nn-)	einen Text schnell nach bestimmten Wörtern/ Informationen absuchen	
	enemy [ˈenəmi]	Feind/in	**enemy** ◂▸ **friend** *French:* l'ennemi *(m)*
	(to) **have a baby**	ein Baby/Kind bekommen	❗ ein Kind **bekommen** = (to) **have** a baby

Tipps zum Wörterlernen → S. 113 · Englische Laute → S. 205 · Alphabetische Wörterverzeichnisse → S. 168–188 / S. 189–205

Vocabulary 3 153

p. 49/P 4	**fire** [ˈfaɪə]	Feuer, Brand	
p. 50/P 6	**(to) ask** sb. **for** sth.	jn. um etwas bitten	She **asked** her mother **for** help / **for** some money.
p. 52/P 12	**(to) cook** [kʊk]	kochen, zubereiten	
	news *(no pl)* [njuːz]	Nachrichten	❗ Das **sind** gute **Nachrichten**! = That**'s** good **news**! *(singular)* *Never:* The news ~~are~~ ... *or* ~~a news~~

Remember?

p. 52/P 13

1 **crocodile** [ˈkrɒkədaɪl]
2 **monkey** [ˈmʌŋki]
3 **camel** [ˈkæml]
4 **zebra** [ˈzebrə]
5 one **wolf** [wʊlf], two **wolves** [wʊlvz]
6 **tiger** [ˈtaɪgə]
7 **giraffe** [dʒəˈrɑːf]
8 **lion** [ˈlaɪən]
9 **rhino** [ˈraɪnəʊ]
10 **hippo** [ˈhɪpəʊ]
11 **bear** [beə]
12 **elephant** [ˈelɪfənt]
13 **kangaroo** [ˌkæŋgəˈruː]

| p. 53/P 14 | **word building** [ˈwɜːd ˌbɪldɪŋ] | Wortbildung | |

El's best friend

p. 54	**angel** [ˈeɪndʒl]	Engel	*French:* l'ange *(m)*
	(to) bully [ˈbʊli]	einschüchtern, tyrannisieren	
	suitcase [ˈsuːtkeɪs]	Koffer	a **suitcase**
	(to) pack [pæk]	packen, einpacken	
	(to) leave [liːv], *simple past:* **left** [left]	gehen, weggehen; abfahren	I said 'Goodbye' and **left**.

(to) leave (*simple past:* left)

1. **(weg)gehen; abfahren**	Get your suitcase. We**'re leaving**. Hurry up, the train **leaves** in an hour.
2. **verlassen**	El's mum wanted to **leave** her dad. I took my bags and **left** the room.
3. **zurücklassen**	He **left** his dog in the car when he went into the shop.

| | **sad** [sæd] | traurig | **sad** 🙁 🙂 **happy** |

Personen-, Orts- und Ländernamen → S. 206–207 · Unregelmäßige Verben → S. 208–209 · Classroom English → S. 210

3–4 Vocabulary

(to) **miss** [mɪs]	vermissen	It was great in England, but I **missed** my friends.
(to) **promise** ['prɒmɪs]	versprechen	I'll come and visit you. I **promise**. ❗ Ich **verspreche es**! = I **promise**! (*not:* I promise ~~it~~) *French:* promettre
neat and tidy [niːt], ['taɪdi]	schön ordentlich	My room is always **neat and tidy**.
neat	gepflegt	Your hair looks very **neat**, but isn't it a bit short?
tidy	ordentlich, aufgeräumt	verb: (to) **tidy** (aufräumen) – adjective: **tidy**
sweetheart ['swiːthɑːt]	Liebling, Schatz	
heart [hɑːt]	Herz	a **heart**
(to) **move out** [ˌmuːv_'aʊt]	ausziehen	(to) **move out** ◄► (to) **move in** We had to **move out** of our house, so we **moved to** London, **to** a small flat in Camden.
(to) **move (to)**	umziehen (nach, in)	
p. 55 (to) **count** [kaʊnt]	zählen	Jack **counted** his money. He had £6.50. *French:* compter
return ticket [rɪ'tɜːn ˌtɪkɪt]	Rückfahrkarte	
Oh dear!	Oje!	
(to) **search (for)** [sɜːtʃ]	suchen (nach)	When we got to London, we **searched for** a cheap hotel.
good	brav	If you're a **good** boy, you can have an ice cream. ❗ **good** = **1.** gut – a **good** film/story **2.** brav – a **good** boy/dog
(to) **turn** [tɜːn]	sich umdrehen	
towards sb./sth. [tə'wɔːdz]	auf jn./etwas zu	Jo turned and walked slowly **towards** the door. 'Bye,' he said.
shy [ʃaɪ]	schüchtern, scheu	Come on, ask that man over there. Don't be **shy**.
line [laɪn]	Zeile	I don't know the second word in **line** 12. Abkürzung: **l.** 5 = **line** 5 · **ll.** 5–9 = **lines** 5–9 *French:* la ligne
(to) **feel** [fiːl], *simple past:* **felt** [felt]	sich fühlen; fühlen	I always **feel** good when I hear that song. Take my hand. Can you **feel** how cold it is?

Unit 4: A weekend in Wales

p. 58 **clean** [kliːn]	sauber	verb: (to) **clean** – adjective: **clean**
cow [kaʊ]	Kuh	
dirty ['dɜːti]	schmutzig	**dirty** ◄► **clean**
factory ['fæktri]	Fabrik	My parents work in a **factory**. They make cars.
farm [fɑːm]	Bauernhof, Farm	*French:* la ferme
field [fiːld]	Feld, Acker, Weide	❗ **auf** dem Feld = **in the field**
forest ['fɒrɪst]	Wald	*French:* la forêt
hill [hɪl]	Hügel	
traffic ['træfɪk]	Verkehr	Look at all those cars. The **traffic** here is terrible.
noisy ['nɔɪzi]	laut, lärmend	noun: **noise** – adjective: **noisy**

Tipps zum Wörterlernen → S. 113 · Englische Laute → S. 205 · Alphabetische Wörterverzeichnisse → S. 168–188 / S. 189–205

Vocabulary 4

river	['rɪvə]	Fluss	
sheep, *pl* sheep	[ʃiːp]	Schaf	
valley	['væli]	Tal	

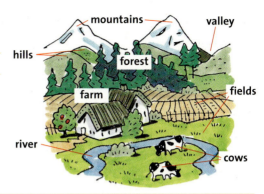

p. 59	pyjamas *(pl)* [pə'dʒɑːməz]	Schlafanzug	!	Where **are** my **pyjamas**? (= Wo **ist** mein **Schlafanzug**?) *French:* le pyjama
p. 60/A 1	(to) smell [smel]	riechen		I could **smell** Mum's cake in the kitchen. 'Mmmm, that **smells** great,' I said.

Verbs and nouns with the same form

(to) glue	(auf-, ein)kleben	(to) name	nennen; benennen	(to) ride a bike	Rad fahren
glue	Klebstoff	name	Name	(bike) ride	(Rad-)Fahrt
(to) interview	interviewen, befragen	(to) phone	anrufen	(to) smell	riechen
interview	Interview	phone	Telefon	smell	Geruch
(to) joke	scherzen, Witze machen	(to) plan (-nn-)	planen	(to) smile	lächeln
joke	Witz	plan	Plan	smile	Lächeln
(to) list	auflisten, aufzählen	(to) report (to)	berichten	(to) visit	besuchen
list	Liste	report	Bericht, Reportage	visit	Besuch

Welsh	[welʃ]	walisisch; Walisisch	Some people in Wales speak English and **Welsh**.
soup	[suːp]	Suppe	*French:* la soupe
railway	['reɪlweɪ]	Eisenbahn	
picnic	['pɪknɪk]	Picknick	*French:* le pique-nique
castle	['kɑːsl]	Burg, Schloss	a **castle**

p. 60/A 2	attraction [ə'trækʃn]	Attraktion, Anziehungspunkt	Disney World is a big **attraction** for kids. *French:* l'attraction *(f)*
	football/hockey pitch [pɪtʃ]	Fußball-/Hockeyplatz, -feld	
	all around the castle ['ɔːl_ə,raʊnd]	ganz um die Burg herum	It was a nice day, so we walked **all around** the lake.
	(to) miss [mɪs]	verpassen	She got up late, so she **missed** the bus. ! (to) **miss** = 1. vermissen – I **miss** my friends. 2. verpassen – I **missed** the bus.
	topic sentence [,tɒpɪk 'sentəns]	Satz, der in das Thema eines Absatzes einführt	
	paragraph ['pærəgrɑːf]	Absatz *(in einem Text)*	! Betonung auf der 1. Silbe: **paragraph** ['pærəgrɑːf]
p. 61/A 4	already [ɔːl'redi]	schon, bereits	Jo was still on the beach, but Dan was **already** in the water.
	not (...) yet [jet]	noch nicht	Are you ready? – **Not yet**. I'll be ready in ten minutes.

Personen-, Orts- und Ländernamen → S. 206–207 • Unregelmäßige Verben → S. 208–209 • Classroom English → S. 210

p. 61/A 6	**just** [dʒʌst]	gerade (eben), soeben	❗ **just** = **1.** nur, bloß – Don't worry if you don't win. It's **just** a game. **2.** gerade (eben) – I'm new in Berlin. I've **just** moved here.

The present perfect: statements

In Aussagesätzen im *present perfect* findet man oft diese unbestimmten Zeitangaben:

already	Please tidy your room. – But I've **already** tidied it.	**schon**
not ... yet	I've tidied my room, but I have**n't** finished my homework **yet**.	**noch nicht**
never	I often play football but I've **never** played basketball.	**(noch) nie**
just	Your room looks great. – Yes, I've **just** tidied it.	**gerade (eben), soeben**

made [meɪd]	*3. Form von „make"*	(to) make – made – **made**
pie [paɪ]	Obstkuchen; Pastete	
seen [siːn]	*3. Form von „see"*	(to) see – saw – **seen**
come [kʌm]	*3. Form von „come"*	(to) come – came – **come**

Irregular past participles[1]

(to) be	was/were	**been** [biːn]	sein		(to) have (have got)	had	**had** [hæd]	haben, besitzen
(to) do	did	**done** [dʌn]	tun, machen					
(to) eat	ate	**eaten** [ˈiːtn]	essen		(to) take	took	**taken** [ˈteɪkən]	nehmen, (weg-, hin)bringen
(to) find	found	**found** [faʊnd]	finden					
(to) go	went	**gone** [gɒn]	gehen, fahren		[1] Die dritte Form des Verbs nennt man *past participle* (Partizip Perfekt).			

well *(adj)*	*(gesundheitlich)* gut; gesund, wohlauf	❗ **well** = **1.** *(adv)* gut – She sang **well**. *(Adverb zu „good")* **2.** *(adj)* gesund – He doesn't feel **well**. I'm **well** again.
p. 62/A 7	(to) **have a temperature** [ˈtemprətʃə]	Fieber haben	I feel very hot. I think I **have a temperature**. ❗ Betonung auf der 1. Silbe: **temperature** [ˈtemprətʃə]
	temperature	Temperatur	*French:* la température
	thermometer [θəˈmɒmɪtə]	Thermometer	❗ Betonung auf der 2. Silbe: **thermometer** [θəˈmɒmɪtə]	*French:* le thermomètre

(to) **have a sore throat** [sɔːˈθrəʊt]	Halsschmerzen haben	She **has a sore throat**.
(to) **be sore**	wund sein, wehtun	Your eyes are very red. **Are** they **sore**?
throat	Hals, Kehle	
(to) **nod** [nɒd] **(-dd-)**	nicken (mit)	❗ Er **nickte mit dem Kopf**. = He **nodded his head**.
headache [ˈhedeɪk]	Kopfschmerzen	I have a **headache**. I often get **headaches**.
(to) **move** [muːv]	bewegen; sich bewegen	Don't **move**.

Tipps zum Wörterlernen → S. 113 · Englische Laute → S. 205 · Alphabetische Wörterverzeichnisse → S. 168–188 / S. 189–205

Vocabulary **4**   **157**

paramedic [ˌpærə'medɪk]   Sanitäter/in

❗ Englische Berufsangaben mit unbestimmtem Artikel: My dad is **a** paramedic / **a** teacher.
(Mein Vater ist Sanitäter / Lehrer.)

What's wrong with you? („Was fehlt dir?")

(to) have **a headache / a toothache / an earache / a stomach[1] ache**	Kopfschmerzen / Zahnschmerzen / Ohrenschmerzen / Magenschmerzen haben
(to) have **a cold**	eine Erkältung haben, erkältet sein

I don't feel well. / I feel ill.   Ich fühle mich nicht gut. / Ich fühle mich krank.
– What's wrong with you?   – Was fehlt dir?
I have a terrible headache and my throat is sore.   Ich habe schreckliche Kopfschmerzen und mein Hals tut weh.
– Maybe you have a cold.   – Vielleicht hast du eine Erkältung / bist du erkältet.
  Do you have a temperature too?   Hast du auch Fieber?

Statt I **have** a cold / a headache / a temperature usw. kannst du auch I**'ve got** a cold / a headache / a temperature usw. sagen.

[1]stomach ['stʌmək] *Magen*

p. 63/A 10 **ever** ['evə]   je, jemals, schon mal   Have you **ever** visited England?

The present perfect: questions

In Fragen im *present perfect* findet man oft diese unbestimmten Zeitangaben:

ever?	Have you **ever** played tennis? – No, never.	**schon mal? / jemals?**
yet?	Have you done your homework **yet**? – Yes, I have.	**schon?**

(to) **install** [ɪn'stɔːl]	installieren, einrichten	verb: (to) **install** –	*French:* installer
installation [ˌɪnstə'leɪʃn]	Installation, Einrichtung	noun: **installation**	*French:* l'installation (f)
(to) **chat** [tʃæt] **(-tt-)**	chatten, plaudern	We sat in the park and **chatted** for a few hours.	
chat [tʃæt]	Chat, Unterhaltung		
(to) **print** sth. **out** [ˌprɪnt_'aʊt]	etwas ausdrucken	If you've finished the letter, you can **print** it **out** now.	
instructions (pl) [ɪn'strʌkʃnz]	(Gebrauchs-)Anweisung(en), Anleitung(en)	Read the **instructions** before you use the new dishwasher.	
It says here: ...	Hier steht: ... / Es heißt hier: ...		

The text says ...

The text says (that) the castle is 700 years old.	Im Text steht, dass ...
It says here / in line 4 / on page 3 that London is older than Berlin.	Hier / In Zeile 4 / Auf Seite 3 steht, dass ...
The poster says (that) it's only £1 for children.	Auf dem Poster steht, dass ...

(to) **click on** sth. [klɪk]	etwas anklicken	What do I do next? – Just **click on** 'OK'.
(to) **enter** sth. ['entə]	etwas eingeben, eintragen	Please **enter** your name on this list.

Computer words and phrases

You can ...

– **surf** the internet and **download** music or pictures.   – **print out** pictures or texts.

– **install** software on your computer.   – **copy** texts and pictures.

– **chat** with friends in a chat room.   – **send**[1] e-mails to your friends.

[1](to) send [send], sent, sent [sent] *senden, schicken*

Personen-, Orts- und Ländernamen → S. 206–207 · Unregelmäßige Verben → S. 208–209 · Classroom English → S. 210

4 Vocabulary

Irregular past participles

(to) buy	bought	**bought** [bɔːt]	kaufen		(to) put	put	**put** [pʊt]	legen, stellen
(to) feed	fed	**fed** [fed]	füttern		(to) say	said	**said** [sed]	sagen
(to) give	gave	**given** ['gɪvn]	geben		(to) think	thought	**thought** [θɔːt]	denken, glauben
(to) know	knew	**known** [nəʊn]	wissen; kennen		(to) write	wrote	**written** ['rɪtn]	schreiben

p. 63/A 11	(to) **mean** [miːn], **meant, meant** [ment]	bedeuten	What does 'forest' **mean**? – It **means** 'Wald'. ❗ *Never:* ~~What means~~ ...?
p. 65/P 4	**from all around Wales**	aus ganz Wales	
p. 65/P 5	**accent** ['æksənt]	Akzent	❗ Betonung auf der 1. Silbe: <u>ac</u>cent ['æksənt]
p. 69/P 16	**silent letter** [ˌsaɪlənt 'letə]	„stummer" Buchstabe *(nicht gesprochener Buchstabe)*	You can't hear the 'w' in 'answer' – it's a **silent letter**.

All in a day's work

p. 70	(to) **ring** [rɪŋ], **rang** [ræŋ], **rung** [rʌŋ]	klingeln, läuten	Listen – I think the phone **is ringing**.
	accident ['æksɪdənt]	Unfall	Drive carefully or you'll have an **accident**. *French:* l'accident *(m)*
	side [saɪd]	Seite	How can we get to the other **side** of the river? ❗ Seite (im Buch) = **page**
	policeman [pə'liːsmən] / **policewoman** [pə'liːswʊmən]	Polizist/Polizistin	
	hurt [hɜːt]	verletzt	❗ **hurt** = 1. *(v)* verletzen; wehtun; 2. *(adj)* verletzt
	fireman ['faɪəmən] / **firewoman** ['faɪəˌwʊmən]	Feuerwehrmann/-frau	
	metre ['miːtə]	Meter	*French:* le mètre
	(to) **hope** [həʊp]	hoffen	John is late. I **hope** he hasn't had an accident.
	(to) **hold** [həʊld], **held, held** [held]	halten	Can you **hold** the baby for a moment, please?

strong [strɒŋ]	stark
weak [wiːk]	schwach

He's very **strong**. ◄► He's **weak**.

p. 71	(to) **fall** [fɔːl], **fell** [fel], **fallen** ['fɔːlən]	fallen, stürzen; hinfallen	Oh no! Toby **has fallen** into the pool. I **fell** and hurt my leg yesterday.
	unconscious [ʌn'kɒnʃəs]	bewusstlos	He isn't dead. He's just **unconscious**.
	husband ['hʌzbənd]	Ehemann	❗ mein **Mann** = my **husband** (*not:* ~~my man~~)
	wife [waɪf], *pl* **wives** [waɪvz]	Ehefrau	❗ meine **Frau** = my **wife** (*not:* ~~my woman~~)

Tipps zum Wörterlernen → S. 113 · Englische Laute → S. 205 · Alphabetische Wörterverzeichnisse → S. 168–188 / S. 189–205

Vocabulary **4–5**

(to) think

think	I **think** you're right.	denken, glauben, meinen
think about	**Think about** these questions: ...	nachdenken über
think of	**Think of** the children. They need you. **Think of** a word with five letters.	denken an sich ausdenken
think about/of	What do you **think about / think of** the story?	denken über, halten von

hospital ['hɒspɪtl]	Krankenhaus	*French:* l'hôpital *(m)*
That was close. [kləʊs]	Das war knapp.	❗ Pronunciation: (to) **close** („schließen") [kləʊz] **close** („knapp") [kləʊs]
grandson ['grænsʌn] / **granddaughter** ['grændɔːtə]	Enkel/Enkelin	a son of your child / a daughter of your child

Unit 5: Teamwork

p. 74 **dice**, *pl* **dice** [daɪs]	Würfel	
counter ['kaʊntə]	Spielstein	
Move on one space.	Geh ein Feld vor.	
Move back one space.	Geh ein Feld zurück.	
engineer [ˌendʒɪ'nɪə]	Ingenieur/in	
(to) **build** [bɪld], **built**, **built** [bɪlt]	bauen	
pub [pʌb]	Kneipe, Lokal	where people go to drink and talk
Miss a turn.	Einmal aussetzen.	
ice rink ['aɪs rɪŋk]	Schlittschuhbahn	
energy ['enədʒi]	Energie; Kraft	❗ Betonung auf der 1. Silbe: **energy** ['enədʒi] *French:* l'énergie *(f)*
(to) **mime** [maɪm]	pantomimisch darstellen, vorspielen	Can you say a poem or **mime** something for me?
(to) **skate** [skeɪt]	Schlittschuh laufen, eislaufen	❗ (to) **skate** = **1.** Schlittschuh laufen; **2.** Inliner fahren; **3.** Skateboard fahren
closed [kləʊzd]	geschlossen	**closed** ◄► **open**
market ['mɑːkɪt]	Markt	*French:* le marché
healthy ['helθi]	gesund	It's very **healthy** to do sports.
snack [snæk]	Snack, Imbiss	
p. 75 **famous (for)** ['feɪməs]	berühmt (für, wegen)	Bristol is **famous for** the Clifton Suspension Bridge.
slave [sleɪv]	Sklave, Sklavin	*French:* l'esclave *(m, f)*
British ['brɪtɪʃ]	britisch; Brite, Britin	There's a lot of **British** music on German radio. I'm German, but my mother is **British**.
rich [rɪtʃ]	reich	a **rich** person = a person with lots of money **rich** ◄► **poor** *French:* riche
land [lænd]	Land, Grund und Boden	❗ Land/Staat = **country**

Personen-, Orts- und Ländernamen → S. 206–207 · Unregelmäßige Verben → S. 208–209 · Classroom English → S. 210

5 Vocabulary

(to) **grow** [grəʊ], **grew** [gruː], **grown** [grəʊn]	*(Getreide usw.)* anbauen, anpflanzen	We have a garden and **grow** our own potatoes. **!** (to) **grow** = 1. wachsen; 2. anbauen, anpflanzen
sugar [ˈʃʊgə]	Zucker	Tea with milk and **sugar**? *French:* le sucre
tobacco [təˈbækəʊ]	Tabak	**!** Schreibung: **tobacco** *French:* le tabac
(to) **arrive** [əˈraɪv]	ankommen, eintreffen	(to) **arrive** ◄► (to) **leave**

as

p. 76/A 1

„als"
- Last week we did a quiz **as** part of a project.
  As a child, my father didn't have a computer.
- 'Hi,' Jo said **as** (= when) Jack opened the door.

„wie"
- I go to the same school **as** my brother.
- **As** you can see, the plate is broken.

booklet [ˈbʊklət]	Broschüre	
(to) **be wrong**	sich irren, Unrecht haben	Cotham School is in Bath. – You're **wrong**. It's in Bristol. (to) **be wrong** ◄► (to) **be right**
Does **anybody** remember the name? [ˈenɪbɒdi]	Erinnert sich (irgend)jemand an den Namen?	

somebody – anybody / something – anything / somewhere – anywhere

Für die Zusammensetzungen mit **some-** und **any-** gelten dieselben Regeln wie für *some* und *any*:

somebody, something, somewhere stehen vor allem in bejahten Aussagesätzen,
anybody, anything, anywhere stehen vor allem in verneinten Aussagesätzen und in Fragen.

+	Listen. There's **somebody** at the door.	... Da ist **jemand** an der Tür.
–	I heard a noise in the garden, but I can't see **anybody**.	... aber ich kann **niemanden** sehen.
?	Can you see **anybody** in the garden?	Kannst du **(irgend)jemanden** im Garten sehen?
+	Let's go to the shops and get **something** to eat.	... **etwas** zu essen
–	I'm too nervous – I can't eat **anything** at the moment.	... ich kann im Moment **nichts** essen.
?	Do you need **anything** from the shops?	Brauchst du **(irgend)etwas** ...?
+	This summer I'd like to go **somewhere** where it's hot.	... **irgendwohin**, wo es warm ist.
–	I don't want to go **anywhere**, I want to stay at home.	Ich möchte **nirgendwohin** fahren ...
?	Are you going to go **anywhere** this summer?	Fährst du diesen Sommer **irgendwohin**?

p. 77/A 4 **statue** [ˈstætʃuː] Statue *French:* la statue

Irregular past participles

(to) drive	drove	**driven** [ˈdrɪvn]	*(ein Auto)* fahren	(to) meet	met	**met** [met]	(sich) treffen
(to) hear	heard	**heard** [hɜːd]	hören	(to) run	ran	**run** [rʌn]	rennen, laufen
(to) leave	left	**left** [left]	(weg)gehen, abfahren; verlassen; zurücklassen	(to) sell	sold	**sold** [səʊld]	verkaufen
				(to) sit	sat	**sat** [sæt]	sitzen; sich setzen
				(to) sleep	slept	**slept** [slept]	schlafen

photographer [fəˈtɒgrəfə]	Fotograf/in	**!** Betonung auf der 2. Silbe: **photographer** [fəˈtɒgrəfə]
p. 77/A 5 (to) **be born** [bɪ ˈbɔːn]	geboren sein/werden	**!** I **was born** in 1997. = Ich **bin** 1997 geboren. Never: I ~~am born~~ in 1997.
(to) **become** [bɪˈkʌm], **became** [bɪˈkeɪm], **become**	werden	Kate Walker **became** a singer five years ago. **!** Nicht verwechseln: (to) **become** = werden (to) **get** = bekommen

Tipps zum Wörterlernen → S. 113 • Englische Laute → S. 205 • Alphabetische Wörterverzeichnisse → S. 168–188 / S. 189–205

Vocabulary 5   161

tunnel [ˈtʌnl]	Tunnel	**!** Pronunciation: **tunnel** [ˈt‿ʌnl] *French:* le tunnel
also [ˈɔːlsəʊ]	auch	Jack had an idea and Ananda had an idea too. = Ananda **also** had an idea.
(to) **die (of)** [daɪ]	sterben (an)	**!** -ing form: **dying** – This tree is **dying**.
proud (of sb./sth.**)** [praʊd]	stolz (auf jn./etwas)	Our daughter is the best student in her class. We're very **proud of** her.
(to) **mark** sth. **up** [ˌmɑːk‿ˈʌp]	etwas markieren, kennzeichnen	

p. 78/A 7

delicious [dɪˈlɪʃəs]	köstlich, lecker	What's the pizza like? – Mmmm. It's **delicious**. *French:* délicieux,se
impossible [ɪmˈpɒsəbl]	unmöglich	It's **impossible** to run a mile in two minutes. *French:* impossible
possible [ˈpɒsəbl]	möglich	**possible** ◄► **impossible** *French:* possible
You're joking, aren't you?	Du machst Witze, nicht wahr? / Das ist nicht dein Ernst, oder?	I don't want to go on holiday. – **You're joking, aren't you?**
pretty cool/good/... [ˈprɪti]	ziemlich cool/gut/...	**!** **pretty** = 1. *(adj)* hübsch – Polly is a **pretty** parrot. 2. *(adv)* ziemlich – This place looks **pretty** cool.
flavour [ˈfleɪvə]	Geschmack, Geschmacks- richtung	Two ice creams, please. – What **flavour**? – Chocolate, please.
strawberry [ˈstrɔːbəri]	Erdbeere	

waiter **customers** **shop assistant**

p. 78/A 8

customer [ˈkʌstəmə]	Kunde, Kundin
waiter [ˈweɪtə]	Kellner
waitress [ˈweɪtrəs]	Kellnerin

medium [ˈmiːdiəm]	mittel(groß)	We sell this T-shirt in three sizes: small, **medium** and **large**.
large [lɑːdʒ]	groß	

---

big – large – great

big / large	**big** und **large** sind oft austauschbar.	▶ a **big/large** family, a **big/large** house
	big ist umgangssprachlicher als **large**. In eher förmlichen Texten solltest du daher **large** schreiben.	
	large wird in der Regel <u>nicht</u> verwendet, um Menschen zu beschreiben.	▶ a very **big** man
great	**great** drückt aus, dass jemand oder etwas **wichtig, bedeutend, großartig** ist.	▶ a **great** actor/singer/engineer a **great** new CD We were in **great** danger.

---

p. 78/A 9 **friendly** [ˈfrendli]	freundlich	noun: **friend** – adjective: **friendly**
p. 79/A 10 (to) **lock up** [ˌlɒk‿ˈʌp]	abschließen	Please **lock up** before you leave the building.

Personen-, Orts- und Ländernamen → S. 206–207 · Unregelmäßige Verben → S. 208–209 · Classroom English → S. 210

IT [ˌaɪ 'tiː] **(information technology)** [tek'nɒlədʒi] — IT (Informationstechnologie)

Irregular past participles

(to) bring	brought	**brought** [brɔːt]	(mit-, her)bringen
(to) choose	chose	**chosen** ['tʃəʊzn]	(aus)wählen, (sich) aussuchen
(to) drink	drank	**drunk** [drʌŋk]	trinken
(to) lose	lost	**lost** [lɒst]	verlieren

(to) speak	spoke	**spoken** ['spəʊkən]	sprechen
(to) swim	swam	**swum** [swʌm]	schwimmen
(to) teach	taught	**taught** [tɔːt]	unterrichten, lehren
(to) tell	told	**told** [təʊld]	erzählen

(to) steal [stiːl], **stole** [stəʊl], **stolen** ['stəʊlən] — stehlen
Where's your new bike?
– Somebody **has stolen** it.

p. 79/A 11 **harbour** ['hɑːbə] — Hafen

at 16 — mit 16, im Alter von 16 Jahren
You have to go to school till you're 16, but **at 16** you can leave and get a job.

(to) sail [seɪl] — segeln

smoke [sməʊk] — Rauch

smoke

(to) smoke [sməʊk] — rauchen
No **smoking**!

fireworks *(pl)* ['faɪəwɜːks] — Feuerwerk(skörper)

beard [bɪəd] — Bart
a man with a **beard**

(to) structure ['strʌktʃə] — strukturieren, aufbauen
French: structurer

beginning [bɪ'gɪnɪŋ] — Beginn, Anfang; Einleitung
beginning ◄► end

p. 80/P 2 **gun** [gʌn] — (Schuss-)Waffe

jewellery ['dʒuːəlri] — Schmuck
I've got some earrings, but no other **jewellery**.

p. 80/P 3 **discussion** [dɪ'skʌʃn] — Diskussion
! Betonung auf der 2. Silbe: **discussion** [dɪ'skʌʃn]
French: la discussion

p. 84/P 11 **tornado** [tɔː'neɪdəʊ] — Tornado, Wirbelsturm

To catch a thief

p. 86 **(to) catch** [kætʃ], **caught, caught** [kɔːt] — fangen; erwischen
You throw the ball and I'll **catch** it.
The police are trying to **catch** a bank robber.

thief [θiːf], *pl* **thieves** [θiːvz] — Dieb/in

case [keɪs] — Fall
'This will be a difficult **case**,' the detective said.
French: le cas

who? — wen? / wem?

who? = „wer?" / „wen?" / „wem?"

„wer?"

„Wer?"-Fragen werden ohne do/does/did gebildet:

Who loves Polly? – Jack.
Wer liebt Polly? – Jack.

Who helped Toby? – Emily.
Wer half Toby? – Emily.

◄ Jack loves Polly. ►

◄ Emily helped Toby. ►

„wen?" / „wem?"

„Wen?"-Fragen und „Wem?"-Fragen werden im *simple present* mit *do/does* und im *simple past* mit *did* gebildet:

Who does Jack love? – Polly.
Wen liebt Jack? – Polly.

Who did Emily help? – Toby.
Wem half Emily? – Toby.

Tipps zum Wörterlernen → S. 113 · Englische Laute → S. 205 · Alphabetische Wörterverzeichnisse → S. 168–188 / S. 189–205

Vocabulary 5

(to) **mean** [miːn], **meant, meant** [ment]	meinen	I hate that man. – Who do you **mean**? I said Tuesday, but I **meant** Thursday. ❗ (to) **mean** = **1.** bedeuten; **2.** meinen
proof *(no pl)* [pruːf]	Beweis(e)	Is she really a thief? We need **proof**. ❗ *Never:* ~~a proof~~
So?	Und? / Na und?	It's very cold today. – **So?** You can wear a pullover when you go out.
(to) **set a trap (for** sb.**), set, set** [ˌset_ə ˈtræp] **(-tt-)**	(jm.) eine Falle stellen	
purse [pɜːs]	Geldbörse	a **purse**
ring [rɪŋ]	Ring	
(to) **bleep** [bliːp]	piepsen	
bleep [bliːp]	Piepton	
(to) **whistle** [ˈwɪsl]	pfeifen	
Shut up. [ˌʃʌt_ˈʌp]	Halt den Mund!	**Shut up**, Toby. I want to watch this film. ❗ (to) **shut – shut – shut**
p. 87 **all we have to do now …**	alles, was wir jetzt (noch) tun müssen, …	
(to) **look for** [ˈlʊk fɔː]	suchen	I'm **looking for** my purse. Do you know where it is?
(to) **suppose** [səˈpəʊz]	annehmen, vermuten	Anne wasn't at school today. I **suppose** she's ill. *French:* supposer
Wait a minute.	Warte mal! / Moment mal!	
this way [ˈðɪs weɪ]	hier entlang, in diese Richtung	Excuse me. Where's 8PK's classroom? – **This way**, please. It's on the right.
the wrong way	in die falsche Richtung	Stop! You're going **the wrong way**. We have to go this way.
caretaker [ˈkeəteɪkə]	Hausmeister/in	
(to) **look after** sth./sb. [ˌlʊk_ˈɑːftə]	auf etwas/jn. aufpassen; sich um etwas/jn. kümmern	Emily often **looks after** Baby Hannah.
cleaner [ˈkliːnə]	Putzfrau, -mann	
p. 88 **rest** [rest]	Rest	*French:* le reste
(to) **belong (to)** [bɪˈlɒŋ]	gehören (zu)	Who does this book **belong to**? (= Whose book is this?) – I think it's Jo's.
mystery [ˈmɪstri]	Rätsel, Geheimnis	My grandfather doesn't understand computers. They're a **mystery** to him. *French:* le mystère
(to) **tell** sb. **to do** sth.	jn. auffordern, etwas zu tun; jm. sagen, dass er/sie etwas tun soll	Mr Kingsley **told** Jack **to close** the window.

Personen-, Orts- und Ländernamen → S. 206–207 · Unregelmäßige Verben → S. 208–209 · Classroom English → S. 210

6 Vocabulary

Unit 6: A trip to Bath

p. 92	**Roman** ['rəʊmən]	römisch; Römer, Römerin	*French:* romain,e
	bath [bɑːθ]	Bad, Badewanne	**!** (to) **have a bath** = baden, ein Bad nehmen
	round [raʊnd]	rund	r**o**und
	(to) **have a sauna** ['sɔːnə]	in die Sauna gehen	
	(to) **relax** [rɪ'læks]	(sich) entspannen, sich ausruhen	rela**x**
	journey ['dʒɜːni]	Reise, Fahrt	Is it a long **journey** from your home to your school?
	(to) **enjoy** [ɪn'dʒɔɪ]	genießen	Lunch was very good. I really **enjoyed** it.
	sandal ['sændl]	Sandale	**sandals** **!** Betonung auf der 1. Silbe: **sandal** ['sændl]
p. 93	**wall** [wɔːl]	Wand; Mauer	A room has got four **walls**.
	stone [stəʊn]	Stein	Can you climb that **stone** wall?
p. 94/A 1	(to) **cycle** ['saɪkl]	(mit dem) Rad fahren	(to) ride a bike
	along the road [ə'lɒŋ]	entlang der Straße / die Straße entlang	
	path [pɑːθ]	Pfad, Weg	a **cycle path along** the river
	How are you? [ˌhaʊ_'ɑː jʊ]	Wie geht es dir/Ihnen/euch?	**How are you**, Mr Kingsley**?** – I'm fine, thank you.
	(to) **be lucky (with)** ['lʌki]	Glück haben (mit)	**!** • We **were lucky** with the weather. (Wir **hatten Glück** mit dem Wetter.) • We**'re happy** when the sun shines. (Wir **sind glücklich**, wenn die Sonne scheint.)
	luckily ['lʌkɪli]	zum Glück, glücklicherweise	I dropped a plate yesterday. **Luckily**, it wasn't very expensive.
	I've never been **to** Bath.	Ich bin noch nie in Bath gewesen.	
	before [bɪ'fɔː]	(vorher) schon mal	Have you been to Bath **before** or is it your first visit?

Höflich um Auskunft bitten

Direkte Fragen können unhöflich wirken. Höflicher ist es, wenn du deine Bitten um Auskunft mit *Can you tell me ...?, I'd like to know ..., Do you know ...?* einleitest:

Direkte Fragen	Höflicher: indirekte Fragen	
Where**'s** Dan?	Can you tell me **where Dan is**?	..., wo Dan ist?
When **does** the museum open?	I'd like to know **when the museum opens**.	..., wann das Museum öffnet.
Why **did** he call you?	Do you know **why he called** you?	..., warum er dich angerufen hat?

! Kein *do/does/did* nach dem Fragewort!
Wortstellung in indirekten Fragen: Fragewort + Subjekt + Verb.

Tipps zum Wörterlernen → S. 113 · Englische Laute → S. 205 · Alphabetische Wörterverzeichnisse → S. 168–188 / S. 189–205

Vocabulary 6

p. 94/A 2	**What else** do you know …?	Was weißt du sonst noch …?	
p. 95/A 3	**opposite** [ˈɒpəzɪt]	gegenüber (von)	The bathroom is **opposite** the bedroom.
	map [mæp]	Landkarte, Stadtplan	

Irregular past participles

(to) feel	felt	**felt** [felt]	(sich) fühlen	(to) read [riːd]	read [red]	**read** [red]	lesen
(to) fly	flew	**flown** [fləʊn]	fliegen	(to) ride	rode	**ridden** [ˈrɪdn]	reiten; (Rad) fahren
(to) get	got	**got** [gɒt]	bekommen; holen; werden; (hin)kommen	(to) sing	sang	**sung** [sʌŋ]	singen
(to) hide	hid	**hidden** [ˈhɪdn]	(sich) verstecken	(to) throw	threw	**thrown** [θrəʊn]	werfen
(to) hit	hit	**hit** [hɪt]	schlagen	(to) win	won	**won** [wʌn]	gewinnen

(to) **tell** sb. **the way**	jm. den Weg beschreiben
(to) **ask** sb. **the way**	jn. nach dem Weg fragen

way („Richtung", „Weg")

Stop. You're going **the wrong way**.	Halt! Du gehst **in die falsche Richtung**.
We have to go **this way**.	Wir müssen **hier entlang / in diese Richtung**.
Which way is the station, please?	**In welcher Richtung liegt** der Bahnhof, bitte? / **Wo geht's** zum Bahnhof, bitte?
I don't know where we are. Let's **ask** somebody **the way**.	… Lass uns jemanden **nach dem Weg fragen**.
'Excuse me. Can you **tell** us **the way** to Bath?'	„… Können Sie uns **den Weg** nach Bath **beschreiben**?"
The group had a lot of fun **on their way** to Bath.	… **auf ihrem Weg** nach Bath.

(to) **turn left/right**	(nach) links/rechts abbiegen	Turn left. Turn right.

French: tourner à gauche/à droite

(to) turn

The way to the station? No problem – **turn left** at the church, then **turn right** into Elm Street.	abbiegen
Suddenly the woman **turned** and looked at me.	sich umdrehen
Mrs Hanson **turned to** Jack and asked, 'Why?'	sich jm. zuwenden; sich an jn. wenden
Jo **turned off** the radio and **turned on** the TV.	aus-, einschalten

(to) **cross** [krɒs]	überqueren; (sich) kreuzen	Don't **cross** the road here. It's too dangerous. The two roads **cross** in the city centre.
straight on [streɪt ˈɒn]	geradeaus weiter	The hospital? Turn left here, and then go **straight on**.
post office [ˈpəʊst ˌɒfɪs]	Postamt	
corner [ˈkɔːnə]	Ecke	**!** **on the corner of** Sand Street and London Road (= Sand Street, Ecke London Road)
police station [pəˈliːs ˌsteɪʃn]	Polizeiwache, Polizeirevier	
restaurant [ˈrestrɒnt]	Restaurant	**!** Betonung auf der 1. Silbe: **restaurant** [ˈrestrɒnt] *French:* le restaurant
chemist [ˈkemɪst]	Drogerie, Apotheke	

Personen-, Orts- und Ländernamen → S. 206–207 • Unregelmäßige Verben → S. 208–209 • Classroom English → S. 210

	department store [dɪˈpɑːtmənt stɔː]	Kaufhaus	
p. 95/A 4	**directions** *(pl)* [dəˈrekʃnz]	Wegbeschreibung(en)	I couldn't find the station, but then a policeman gave me **directions**.
p. 96/A 5	(to) **be missing** [ˈmɪsɪŋ]	fehlen	Almost all my friends were at the party. Only Robbie **was missing**.
	square [skweə]	Platz *(in der Stadt)*	
	needn't do [ˈniːdnt]	nicht tun müssen, nicht zu tun brauchen	I can do the exercise. You **needn't** help me. **needn't** ◄► **must**
	not (…) any more	nicht mehr	The Greens do**n't** live here **any more**. They've moved to London.
	This is Isabel**.**	Hier spricht Isabel. / Hier ist Isabel. *(am Telefon)*	*(on the phone)* Am I speaking to Laura? – No, **this is** Emma.
	(to) **play a trick on** sb.	jm. einen Streich spielen	
p. 97/A 7	**planet** [ˈplænɪt]	Planet	❗ Betonung auf der 1. Silbe: **planet** [ˈplænɪt] *French:* la planète
	(to) **touch** [tʌtʃ]	berühren, anfassen	Don't **touch** the plates! They're hot.
	(to) **discover** [dɪˈskʌvə]	entdecken; herausfinden	*French:* découvrir
	mustn't do [ˈmʌsnt]	nicht tun dürfen	You **mustn't** touch the plates. They're hot.

must – needn't – mustn't

must (müssen)	**needn't** (nicht müssen)	**mustn't** (nicht dürfen)
Mit **must** drückt man aus, dass jemand etwas tun muss:	Mit **needn't** drückt man aus, dass jemand etwas nicht zu tun braucht:	Mit **mustn't** drückt man aus, dass jemand etwas nicht tun darf:
I **must** clean the hamster's cage today. It's very dirty.	I **needn't** clean the rabbits' cage. It isn't dirty.	You **mustn't** give hedgehogs milk. It's bad for them.
(Ich muss … sauber machen.)	(Ich muss … nicht sauber machen / brauche … nicht sauber zu machen.)	(Du darfst Igeln keine Milch geben.)

p. 97/A 8	**instrument** [ˈɪnstrəmənt]	Instrument	❗ Betonung auf der 1. Silbe: **instrument** [ˈɪnstrəmənt] *French:* l'instrument *(m)*
	organ [ˈɔːgən]	Orgel	❗ (to) **play the organ** (Orgel spielen)
	star [stɑː]	Stern	a **star**
p. 102/P 10	(to) **correct** [kəˈrekt]	berichtigen, korrigieren	

A trip to Bath – a play for the end of term

p. 103	**term** [tɜːm]	Trimester	The school year has three **terms** in Britain.
	(to) **like** sth. **better**	etwas lieber mögen	Tim's favourite sport is tennis, but I **like** football **better**.
	(to) **fall off** [ˌfɔːl ˈɒf]	herunterfallen (von)	Liz **fell off** her horse, but luckily she wasn't hurt.
p. 104	**the other way round**	anders herum	So your name is John James. – No, **the other way round**: James John.
	movement [ˈmuːvmənt]	Bewegung	*French:* le mouvement
	leisure centre [ˈleʒə sentə]	Freizeitzentrum, -park	
	(to) **shiver** [ˈʃɪvə]	zittern	

Tipps zum Wörterlernen → S. 113 · Englische Laute → S. 205 · Alphabetische Wörterverzeichnisse → S. 168–188 / S. 189–205

(to) **yawn** [jɔːn]	gähnen		She**'s yawning**.
audience [ˈɔːdɪəns]	Publikum; Zuschauer/innen, Zuhörer/innen		
Hooray! [huˈreɪ]	Hurra!		
(to) **pay (for)** [peɪ], **paid, paid** [peɪd]	bezahlen	❗ (to) **pay for a sandwich** (ein Sandwich bezahlen)	
tomato [təˈmɑːtəʊ], *pl* **tomatoes**	Tomate		*French:* la tomate
lettuce [ˈletɪs]	(Kopf-)Salat	lettuce tomatoes	
century [ˈsentʃəri]	Jahrhundert	Martin Luther was born in the 15th **century**.	
(to) **wonder** [ˈwʌndə]	sich fragen, gern wissen wollen	Do you know that boy over there? I **wonder** who he is.	
(to) **cheer** [tʃɪə]	jubeln, Beifall klatschen	At the end of the play, the audience **cheered** loudly.	
laughter [ˈlɑːftə]	Gelächter	verb: (to) **laugh** – noun: **laughter**	
worry [ˈwʌri]	Sorge, Kummer	verb: (to) **worry** – noun: **worry**	
bright [braɪt]	hell, leuchtend	It's a very **bright** room. It gets the sun all day.	
if	ob	❗ **if** = **1**. ob – I don't know **if** I can come to your party. **2**. falls, wenn – But I'll come **if** I can.	
true [truː]	wahr	The twins' mother lives in Australia. – That's not **true**. She lives in New Zealand.	

p. 105 (to) **cheer**

Irregular past participles

(to) hurt	hurt	**hurt** [hɜːt]	wehtun; verletzen	(to) spend	spent	**spent** [spent]	*(Geld)* ausgeben; *(Zeit)* verbringen
(to) keep	kept	**kept** [kept]	*(warm/offen/...)* halten	(to) stand	stood	**stood** [stʊd]	stehen; sich (hin)stellen
(to) lay the table	laid	**laid** [leɪd]	den Tisch decken	(to) under-stand	under-stood	**under-stood** [ˌ-ˈstʊd]	verstehen
(to) let	let	**let** [let]	lassen	(to) wear	wore	**worn** [wɔːn]	tragen *(Kleidung)*
(to) shine	shone	**shone** [ʃɒn]	scheinen *(Sonne)*				
(to) show	showed	**shown** [ʃəʊn]	zeigen				

Personen-, Orts- und Ländernamen → S. 206–207 · Unregelmäßige Verben → S. 208–209 · Classroom English → S. 210

168 Dictionary (English – German)

Das Dictionary besteht aus zwei alphabetischen Wörterlisten:

Englisch – Deutsch (S. 168–188)
Deutsch – Englisch (S. 189–205).

Das **English – German Dictionary** enthält den Wortschatz der Bände 1 und 2 von *English G 21*.
Wenn du wissen möchtest, was ein Wort bedeutet, wie man es ausspricht oder wie es genau geschrieben wird, kannst du hier nachschlagen.

Im **English – German Dictionary** werden folgende **Abkürzungen** und **Symbole** verwendet:

jm. = jemandem	sb. = somebody	*pl* = *plural* (Mehrzahl)	*AE = American English*
jn. = jemanden	sth. = something	*no pl = no plural*	

° Mit diesem Kringel sind Wörter markiert, die nicht zum Lernwortschatz gehören.
▶ Der Pfeil verweist auf Kästchen im Vocabulary (S. 141–167), in denen du weitere Informationen zu diesem Wort findest.

Die **Fundstellenangaben** zeigen, wo ein Wort zum ersten Mal vorkommt.
Die Ziffern in Klammern bezeichnen Seitenzahlen:

I	= Band 1
II Welc (6)	= Band 2, Welcome back, Seite 6
II Welc (6/141)	= Band 2, Welcome back, Seite 141 (im Vocabulary, zu Seite 6)
II 1 (22)	= Band 2, Unit 1, Seite 22
II 1 (22/145)	= Band 2, Unit 1, Seite 145 (im Vocabulary, zu Seite 22)

Tipps zur Arbeit mit dem Dictionary findest du im Skills File auf Seite 115.

A

a [ə] ein, eine I • **a bit** ein bisschen, etwas II 1 (12) • **a few** ein paar, einige II 1 (23) • **a lot (of)** eine Menge, viel, viele II 2 (30) • **He likes her a lot.** Er mag sie sehr. I
°**abbey** ['æbi] Abtei
about [ə'baʊt]
1. über I
2. ungefähr II 2 (35)
ask about sth. nach etwas fragen I • **This is about Mr Green.** Es geht um Mr Green. I • **What about …? 1.** Was ist mit …? / Und …? I; **2.** Wie wär's mit …? I • **What are you talking about?** Wovon redest du? I • °**What are the pages about?** Wovon handeln die Seiten? • **What was the best thing about …?** Was war das Beste an …? II 1 (12) • °**Say what you like about …** Sag, was du an … magst
°**above** [ə'bʌv]: **from above** von oben
abroad [ə'brɔːd] im Ausland II Welc (9) • **go abroad** ins Ausland gehen/fahren II Welc (9)
°**absurd** [əb'sɜːd] absurd, lächerlich
accent ['æksənt] Akzent II 4 (65)
accident ['æksɪdənt] Unfall II 4 (70)
act [ækt] aufführen, spielen I
°**Act out …** Spiele/Spielt … vor.

activity [æk'tɪvəti] Aktivität, Tätigkeit I
actor ['æktə] Schauspieler/in II 3 (53)
add (to) [æd] hinzufügen, ergänzen, addieren (zu) I
adjective ['ædʒɪktɪv] Adjektiv I
adverb ['ædvɜːb] Adverb I
°**adviser** [əd'vaɪzə] Berater/in
afraid [ə'freɪd]
1. be afraid (of) Angst haben (vor) I
2. I'm afraid leider II 3 (47)
°**Afro-Caribbean** [ˌæfrəʊˌkærə'biːən] afro-karibisch
after ['ɑːftə] nach *(zeitlich)* I
after that danach I • °**come after sb.** hinter jm. herkommen
after ['ɑːftə] nachdem II 1 (13)
afternoon [ˌɑːftə'nuːn] Nachmittag I • **in the afternoon** nachmittags, am Nachmittag I • **on Friday afternoon** freitagnachmittags, am Freitagnachmittag I
again [ə'gen] wieder; noch einmal I
against [ə'genst] gegen I
ago [ə'gəʊ]: **a minute ago** vor einer Minute I
agree (on) [ə'griː] sich einigen (auf) I • **agree with sb./sth.** jm./etwas zustimmen; mit jm./etwas übereinstimmen II 2 (31)
°**alien** ['eɪliən] Außerirdische(r)

all [ɔːl] alle; alles I • **all around the castle** ganz um die Burg herum II 4 (60) • **all day** den ganzen Tag (lang) I • °**all I did** alles, was ich tat • °**All in a day's work.** *etwa:* Mach ich doch gern.
all right [ɔːl 'raɪt] gut, in Ordnung II 1 (23) • **all the time** die ganze Zeit I • **all we have to do now …** alles, was wir jetzt (noch) tun müssen, … II 5 (87) • **from all around Wales** aus ganz Wales II 4 (65) • **This is all wrong.** Das ist ganz falsch. I
almost ['ɔːlməʊst] fast, beinahe II 1 (23)
alone [ə'ləʊn] allein I
along the road [ə'lɒŋ] entlang der Straße / die Straße entlang II 6 (94)
alphabet ['ælfəbet] Alphabet I
°**alphabetical** [ˌælfə'betɪkl] alphabetisch
already [ɔːl'redi] schon, bereits II 4 (61)
▶ S.156 The present perfect: statements
also ['ɔːlsəʊ] auch II 5 (77)
always ['ɔːlweɪz] immer I
am [ˌeɪ'em]: **7 am** 7 Uhr morgens/ vormittags I
amazing [ə'meɪzɪŋ] erstaunlich, unglaublich II 1 (12)
American football [əˌmerɪkən 'fʊtbɔːl] Football I

Dictionary (English – German) 169

an [ən] ein, eine I

and [ənd, ænd] und I

angel ['eɪndʒl] Engel II 3 (54)

angry (about sth./with sb.) ['æŋgri] wütend, böse (über etwas/auf jn.) II 1 (14)

animal ['ænɪml] Tier II 3 (42)

another [ə'nʌðə] ein(e) andere(r, s); noch ein(e) I • **another 45p** weitere 45 Pence, noch 45 Pence II 3 (55)

answer ['ɑːnsə] antworten; beantworten I

answer (to) ['ɑːnsə] Antwort (auf) I

any [eni]: **any ...?** (irgend)welche ...? I • **not (...) any** kein, keine I • **not (...) any more** nicht mehr II 6 (96)

anybody ['enibɒdi] (irgend)jemand II 5 (76) • **not (...) anybody** niemand II 5 (76/160)
▶ S.160 somebody – anybody

anything ['eniθɪŋ] (irgend)etwas II 5 (76/160) • **not (...) anything** nichts II 5 (76/160)
▶ S.160 something – anything

anyway ['eniweɪ]
1. sowieso I
2. trotzdem II Welc (6)

anywhere ['eniweə] irgendwo(hin) II 5 (76/160) • **not (...) anywhere** nirgendwo(hin) II 5 (76/160)
▶ S.160 somewhere – anywhere

apple ['æpl] Apfel I

appointment [ə'pɔɪntmənt] Termin, Verabredung I

April ['eɪprəl] April I

are [ɑː] bist; sind; seid I • **How are you?** [ˌhaʊ_'ɑː jʊ] Wie geht es dir/Ihnen/euch? II 6 (94) • **The pencils are 35p.** Die Bleistifte kosten 35 Pence. I • **You're joking, aren't you?** Du machst Witze, nicht wahr? / Das ist nicht dein Ernst, oder? II 5 (78)

°**area** ['eəriə] Gegend, Gebiet

argue ['ɑːgjuː] sich streiten, sich zanken I

arm [ɑːm] Arm I

armchair ['ɑːmtʃeə] Sessel I

around [ə'raʊnd]: **all around the castle** ganz um die Burg herum II 4 (60) • °**around the world** in/auf der ganzen Welt • **from all around Wales** aus ganz Wales II 4 (65)

arrive [ə'raɪv] ankommen, eintreffen II 5 (75)

art [ɑːt] Kunst I

article ['ɑːtɪkl] (Zeitungs-)Artikel I

as [əz, æz]
1. als, während II Welc (6)
2. as a child als Kind II 5 (76/160)
3. as you can see wie du sehen kannst II 5 (76/160)
4. as big/exciting as so groß/aufregend wie II 2 (30) • **as soon as** sobald, sowie II 3 (45)
▶ S.160 so

ask [ɑːsk] fragen I • **ask about sth.** nach etwas fragen I • **ask questions** Fragen stellen I • **ask sb. for sth.** jn. um etwas bitten II 3 (50) • **ask sb. the way** jn. nach dem Weg fragen II 6 (95/165)

asleep [ə'sliːp]: **be asleep** schlafen I

°**astronomer** [ə'strɒnəmə] Astronom/in

°**astronomy** [ə'strɒnəmi] Astronomie

at [ət, æt]: **at 7 Hamilton Street** in der Hamiltonstraße 7 I • **at 8.45** um 8.45 I • **at 16** mit 16, im Alter von 16 Jahren II 5 (79) • **at break** in der Pause (zwischen Schulstunden) II 3 (46) • **at home** daheim, zu Hause I • **at last** endlich, schließlich I • **at least** zumindest, wenigstens I • **at night** nachts, in der Nacht I • **at school** in der Schule I • **at that table** an dem Tisch (dort) / an den Tisch (dort) I • **at the back (of the room)** hinten, im hinteren Teil (des Zimmers) II 1 (13) • **at the bottom (of)** unten, am unteren Ende (von) II 1 (11) • **at the end (of)** am Ende (von) I • **at the moment** im Moment, gerade II 2 (29/148) • **at the Shaws' house** im Haus der Shaws / bei den Shaws zu Hause I • **at the station** am Bahnhof I • **at the top (of)** oben, am oberen Ende, an der Spitze (von) I • **at the weekend** am Wochenende I • **at work** bei der Arbeit / am Arbeitsplatz I

ate [et, eɪt] siehe eat

°**attic** ['ætɪk] Dachboden

attraction [ə'trækʃn] Attraktion, Anziehungspunkt II 4 (60)

audience ['ɔːdiəns] Publikum; Zuschauer/innen, Zuhörer/innen II 6 (104)

August ['ɔːgəst] August I

aunt [ɑːnt] Tante I • **auntie** ['ɑːnti] Tante II 2 (30)

autumn ['ɔːtəm] Herbst I

away [ə'weɪ] weg, fort I

awful ['ɔːfl] furchtbar, schrecklich II 2 (28)

B

baby ['beɪbi] Baby I • **have a baby** ein Baby/Kind bekommen II 3 (47)

back [bæk]: **at the back (of the room)** hinten, im hinteren Teil (des Zimmers) II 1 (13)

back (to) [bæk] zurück (nach) I °**Jo went back to the game.** Jo wandte sich wieder dem Spiel zu.

back door [ˌbæk 'dɔː] Hintertür II 3 (44)

background ['bækgraʊnd] Hintergrund II 1 (11) • **background file** etwa: Hintergrundinformation II (3)

bad [bæd] schlecht, schlimm I

badminton ['bædmɪntən] Badminton, Federball I

bag [bæg] Tasche, Beutel, Tüte I

ball [bɔːl] Ball I

°**ball dress** ['bɔːl dres] Ballkleid I

banana [bə'nɑːnə] Banane I

band [bænd] Band, (Musik-)Gruppe I

°**Bang!** [bæŋ] Peng!

bank [bæŋk] Bank, Sparkasse I **bank robber** ['bæŋk ˌrɒbə] Bankräuber/in I

bar [bɑː] Bar II 5 (78)

°**barbecue** ['bɑːbɪkjuː] Grillparty

°**barn** [bɑːn] Scheune

°**barrel** ['bærəl] Fass, Tonne

baseball ['beɪsbɔːl] Baseball I **baseball cap** Baseballmütze II 2 (27)

basket ['bɑːskɪt] Korb I • **a basket of apples** ein Korb Äpfel I

basketball ['bɑːskɪtbɔːl] Basketball I

bath [bɑːθ] Bad, Badewanne II 6 (92) • **have a bath** baden, ein Bad nehmen II 6 (92)

bathroom ['bɑːθruːm] Badezimmer I

be [biː], **was/were, been** sein I

beach [biːtʃ] Strand II Welc (6) **on the beach** [biːtʃ] am Strand II Welc (6)

bear [beə] Bär II 3 (52/153)

beard [bɪəd] Bart II 5 (79)

beautiful ['bjuːtɪfl] schön I

became [bɪ'keɪm] siehe become

because [bɪ'kɒz] weil I

become [bɪ'kʌm], **became, become** werden II 5 (77)

bed [bed] Bett I • **Bed and Breakfast (B&B)** [ˌbed_ən 'brekfəst] Frühstückspension (wörtlich: Bett und Frühstück) I • **go to bed** ins Bett gehen I

bedroom ['bedruːm] Schlafzimmer I

170 Dictionary (English – German)

been [biːn] *siehe* **be**
before [bɪˈfɔː] vor *(zeitlich)* I
before [bɪˈfɔː] bevor II 1 (13/144)
before [bɪˈfɔː] (vorher) schon mal II 6 (94)
beginning [bɪˈgɪnɪŋ] Beginn, Anfang; Einleitung II 5 (79)
behind [bɪˈhaɪnd] hinter II 1 (11/143)
bell [bel] Klingel, Glocke I
belong (to) [bɪˈlɒŋ] gehören (zu) II 5 (88)
°**below** [bɪˈləʊ] unten
°**bend over** [ˌbendˈˈəʊvə] sich bücken
best [best] am besten II 2 (30)
  the best ... der/die/das beste ...; die besten I • °**like sth. best** etwas am liebsten mögen • **What was the best thing about ...?** Was war das Beste an ...? II 1 (12)
better [ˈbetə] besser I • **like sth. better** etwas lieber mögen II 6 (103)
between [bɪˈtwiːn] zwischen II 1 (11/143)
big [bɪg] groß I
  ▶ S.161 big – large – great
bike [baɪk] Fahrrad I • **ride a bike** Rad fahren I
bin [bɪn] Mülltonne II 2 (39)
°**binoculars** *(pl)* [bɪˈnɒkjələz] Fernglas
biology [baɪˈɒlədʒi] Biologie I
bird [bɜːd] Vogel I
birthday [ˈbɜːθdeɪ] Geburtstag I
  Happy birthday. Herzlichen Glückwunsch zum Geburtstag. I • **My birthday is in May.** Ich habe im Mai Geburtstag. I • **My birthday is on 13th June.** Ich habe am 13. Juni Geburtstag. I • **When's your birthday?** Wann hast du Geburtstag? I
biscuit [ˈbɪskɪt] Keks, Plätzchen I
bit: a bit [əˈbɪt] ein bisschen, etwas II 1 (12)
black [blæk] schwarz I
bleep [bliːp] piepsen II 5 (86)
bleep [bliːp] Piepton II 5 (87)
blouse [blaʊz] Bluse II 2 (27)
blue [bluː] blau I
board [bɔːd] (Wand-)Tafel I • **on the board** an der/die Tafel I
boat [bəʊt] Boot, Schiff I
body [ˈbɒdi] Körper I
°**bone** [bəʊn] Knochen
°**bonfire** [ˈbɒnfaɪə] (Freuden-)Feuer
book [bʊk] Buch I
booklet [ˈbʊklət] Broschüre II 5 (76)
boot [buːt] Stiefel I
boring [ˈbɔːrɪŋ] langweilig I
born [bɔːn] **be born** geboren sein/ werden II 5 (77)

both [bəʊθ] beide I
bottle [ˈbɒtl] Flasche I • **a bottle of milk** eine Flasche Milch I
bottom [ˈbɒtəm] unteres Ende II 1 (11) • **at the bottom (of)** unten, am unteren Ende (von) II 1 (11)
bought [bɔːt] *siehe* **buy**
bowl [bəʊl] Schüssel I • **a bowl of cornflakes** eine Schale Cornflakes I
box [bɒks] Kasten, Kästchen, Kiste I
boy [bɔɪ] Junge I
°**bracket** [ˈbrækɪt] Klammer *(in Texten)*
bread *(no pl)* [bred] Brot I
break [breɪk] Pause I • **at break** in der Pause *(zwischen Schulstunden)* II 3 (46)
breakfast [ˈbrekfəst] Frühstück I
  have breakfast frühstücken I
bridge [brɪdʒ] Brücke I
bright [braɪt] hell, leuchtend II 6 (105)
bring [brɪŋ]**, brought, brought** (mit-, her)bringen I
British [ˈbrɪtɪʃ] britisch; Brite, Britin II 5 (75)
broken [ˈbrəʊkən] gebrochen; zerbrochen, kaputt II 3 (47)
brother [ˈbrʌðə] Bruder I
brought [brɔːt] *siehe* **bring**
brown [braʊn] braun I
budgie [ˈbʌdʒi] Wellensittich I
build [bɪld]**, built, built** bauen II 5 (74)
building [ˈbɪldɪŋ] Gebäude II 1 (12)
built [bɪlt] *siehe* **build**
bully [ˈbʊli] einschüchtern, tyrannisieren II 3 (54)
°**bungee jumping** [ˈbʌndʒiˈdʒʌmpɪŋ] Bungeejumping
bunk (bed) [bʌŋk] Etagenbett, Koje II 1 (22)
°**burn** [bɜːn] verbrennen; brennen
bus [bʌs] Bus I
business: Mind your own business. [ˌmaɪndjɔːˈˈəʊnˈbɪznəs] Das geht dich nichts an! / Kümmere dich um deine eigenen Angelegenheiten! II 1 (13)
but [bət, bʌt] aber I
buy [baɪ]**, bought, bought** kaufen I
°**buzz** [bʌz] *hier:* den Summer/die Glocke betätigen
by [baɪ]
  1. von I
  2. an; (nahe) bei II Welc (6)
  3. by car/bike/... mit dem Auto/ Rad/... II Welc (7)
Bye. [baɪ] Tschüs! I

C

°**cabin** [ˈkæbɪn] Kajüte
café [ˈkæfeɪ] *(kleines)* Restaurant, Imbissstube, Café I
cage [keɪdʒ] Käfig I
cake [keɪk] Kuchen, Torte I
°**calabash** [ˈkæləbæʃ] Kalebasse *(aus einem Kürbis hergestelltes Gefäß)*
calendar [ˈkælɪndə] Kalender I
call [kɔːl] rufen; anrufen; nennen I
call [kɔːl] Anruf, Telefongespräch I
  make a call ein Telefongespräch führen II 6 (96)
calm down [ˌkɑːmˈdaʊn] sich beruhigen II 1 (14)
came [keɪm] *siehe* **come**
camel [ˈkæml] Kamel II 3 (52/153)
camera [ˈkæmərə] Kamera, Fotoapparat I
can [kən, kæn]
  1. können I
  2. dürfen I
  Can I help you? Kann ich Ihnen helfen? / Was kann ich für Sie tun? *(im Geschäft)* I
°**candle** [ˈkændl] Kerze
°**cannibal** [ˈkænɪbl] Kannibale, Kannibalin
cap [kæp] Mütze, Kappe II 2 (27)
°**capital** [ˈkæpɪtl] Hauptstadt
°**captain** [ˈkæptɪn] Kapitän/in
°**caption** [ˈkæpʃn] Bildunterschrift
car [kɑː] Auto I
caravan [ˈkærəvæn] Wohnwagen II Welc (6)
card [kɑːd] (Spiel-, Post-)Karte I
careful [ˈkeəfl]
  1. vorsichtig II 2 (38)
  2. sorgfältig II 2 (38)
caretaker [ˈkeəteɪkə] Hausmeister/in II 5 (87)
carrot [ˈkærət] Möhre, Karotte I
cartoon [kɑːˈtuːn] Cartoon (Zeichentrickfilm; Bilderwitz) II 3 (42)
case [keɪs] Fall II 5 (86)
castle [ˈkɑːsl] Burg, Schloss II 4 (60)
cat [kæt] Katze I
catch [kætʃ]**, caught, caught** fangen; erwischen II 5 (86)
°**Catholic** [ˈkæθlɪk] katholisch; Katholik/in
caught [kɔːt] *siehe* **catch**
CD [ˌsiːˈdiː] CD I • **CD player** CD-Spieler I
°**celebrate** [ˈselɪbreɪt] feiern
cent (c) [sent] Cent I
centre [ˈsentə] Zentrum, Mitte I
century [ˈsentʃəri] Jahrhundert II 6 (104)
°**chain** [tʃeɪn] Kette
chair [tʃeə] Stuhl I

Dictionary (English – German)   171

champion ['tʃæmpiən] Meister/in, Champion I

chance [tʃɑːns] Chance, Möglichkeit, Aussicht II 3 (45)

change [tʃeɪndʒ] Wechselgeld I

°**change** [tʃeɪndʒ] (ver)ändern

channel ['tʃænl] Kanal, Sender II 3 (42)

charity ['tʃærəti] Wohlfahrtsorganisation II 2 (31) • °**charity shop** *Geschäft, in dem Sachen für eine Wohlfahrtsorganisation verkauft werden*

°**chart** [tʃɑːt] Schaubild, Diagramm, Tabelle

chat (-tt-) [tʃæt] chatten, plaudern II 4 (63)
► S.157 Computer words and phrases

chat [tʃæt] Chat, Unterhaltung II 4 (63)

cheap [tʃiːp] billig, preiswert II 2 (29)

check [tʃek] (über)prüfen, kontrollieren I

checkpoint ['tʃekpɔɪnt] Kontrollpunkt *(hier: zur Selbstüberprüfung)* I

cheer [tʃɪə] jubeln, Beifall klatschen II 6 (105)

cheese [tʃiːz] Käse I

chemist ['kemɪst] Drogerie, Apotheke II 6 (95)

chicken ['tʃɪkɪn] Huhn; (Brat-)Hähnchen I • °**chicken tikka** [ˌtʃɪkɪn 'tɪkə] *indisches Gericht (mariniertes gegrilltes Hühnerfleisch)*

child [tʃaɪld], *pl* **children** ['tʃɪldrən] Kind I

chips *(pl)* [tʃɪps] Pommes frites I

chocolate ['tʃɒklət] Schokolade I

°**choice** [tʃɔɪs] (Aus-)Wahl

choir ['kwaɪə] Chor I

choose [tʃuːz], **chose, chosen** (sich) aussuchen, (aus)wählen I

°**chorus** ['kɔːrəs] Refrain

chose [tʃəʊz] *siehe* **choose**

chosen ['tʃəʊzn] *siehe* **choose**

°**Christmas** ['krɪsməs] Weihnachten °**Father Christmas** der Weihnachtsmann • °**Merry Christmas.** Frohe Weihnachten.

church [tʃɜːtʃ] Kirche I

cinema ['sɪnəmə] Kino II 2 (27) **go to the cinema** ins Kino gehen II 2 (27/147)

city ['sɪti] Stadt, Großstadt I **city centre** [ˌsɪti 'sentə] Stadtzentrum, Innenstadt I

class [klɑːs] (Schul-)Klasse I **class teacher** Klassenlehrer/in I

classmate ['klɑːsmeɪt] Klassenkamerad/in, Mitschüler/in I

classroom ['klɑːsruːm] Klassenzimmer I

clean [kliːn] sauber II 4 (58)

clean [kliːn] sauber machen, putzen • **I clean my teeth.** Ich putze mir die Zähne.

cleaner ['kliːnə] Putzfrau, -mann II 5 (87)

clear [klɪə] klar, deutlich I

clever ['klevə] klug, schlau I

click on sth. [klɪk] etwas anklicken II 4 (63)

climb [klaɪm] klettern; hinaufklettern (auf) I • **Climb a tree.** Klettere auf einen Baum. I

clinic ['klɪnɪk] Klinik II 3 (45)

clock [klɒk] (Wand-, Stand-, Turm-)Uhr I

close [kləʊs]: **That was close.** Das war knapp. II 4 (71) • °**a close shave** [ˌkləʊs 'ʃeɪv] *etwa:* Das ging beinahe ins Auge. *(wörtlich:* eine glatte Rasur)

close [kləʊz] schließen, zumachen I

closed [kləʊzd] geschlossen II 5 (74)

clothes *(pl)* [kləʊðz, kləʊz] Kleider, Kleidung(sstücke) II Welc (9)

cloud [klaʊd] Wolke II Welc (6/141)

cloudy ['klaʊdi] bewölkt II Welc (6/141)

club [klʌb] Klub; Verein I

°**coast** [kəʊst] Küste

cola ['kəʊlə] Cola I

cold [kəʊld] kalt I • **be cold** frieren I

cold [kəʊld] Erkältung II 4 (62/157) **have a cold** erkältet sein, eine Erkältung haben II 4 (62/157)
► S.157 What's wrong with you?

°**collage** ['kɒlɑːʒ] Collage

collect [kə'lekt] sammeln I

collector [kə'lektə] Sammler/in II 3 (53)

colour ['kʌlə] Farbe I • **What colour is ...?** Welche Farbe hat ...? I

°**coloured** ['kʌləd] farbig, bunt

°**combine** [kəm'baɪn] kombinieren, verbinden

come [kʌm], **came, come** kommen I °**come after sb.** hinter jm. herkommen • **come home** nach Hause kommen I • **come in** hereinkommen I • **Come on. 1.** Na los, komm. II 1 (22); **2.** Ach komm! / Na hör mal! II 1 (14)

°**comet** ['kɒmɪt] Komet

comic ['kɒmɪk] Comic-Heft I

°**Commonwealth** ['kɒmənwelθ]: **the Commonwealth** *Gemeinschaft der Länder des ehemaligen britischen Weltreichs*

°**compare** [kəm'peə] vergleichen

comparison [kəm'pærɪsn] Steigerung; Vergleich II 2 (30) / II 2 (127) °**make comparisons** Vergleiche anstellen, vergleichen

°**complete** [kəm'pliːt] vollständig, komplett

°**complete** [kəm'pliːt] vervollständigen, ergänzen

computer [kəm'pjuːtə] Computer I

°**continue** [kən'tɪnjuː] fortsetzen; weitermachen (mit)

°**control** [kən'trəʊl]: **be in control of sth.** etwas unter Kontrolle haben; die Gewalt über etwas haben **take control** die Kontrolle/Gewalt übernehmen

cook [kʊk] kochen, zubereiten II 3 (52)

cooker ['kʊkə] Herd I

cool [kuːl]
1. kühl II Welc (6)
2. cool I

copy ['kɒpi] kopieren II 4 (63/157)
► S.157 Computer words and phrases

°**copy** ['kɒpi] Kopie

corner ['kɔːnə] Ecke I • **on the corner of Sand Street and London Road** Sand Street, Ecke London Road II 6 (95/165)

°**corner shop** ['kɔːnə ʃɒp] Tante-Emma-Laden *(wörtlich:* Eck-Geschäft)

cornflakes ['kɔːnfleɪks] Cornflakes I

correct [kə'rekt] berichtigen, korrigieren II 6 (102)

°**correct** [kə'rekt] richtig, korrekt

°**corset** ['kɔːsɪt] Korsett

°**cost** [kɒst], **cost, cost** kosten

°**costume** ['kɒstjuːm] Kostüm

could [kəd, kʊd]: **he could ...** er konnte ... II 1 (22)

count [kaʊnt] zählen II 3 (55)

counter ['kaʊntə] Spielstein II 5 (74)

country ['kʌntri] Land *(auch als Gegensatz zur Stadt)* II Welc (6) **in the country** auf dem Land II Welc (6/142)

course: of course [əv 'kɔːs] natürlich, selbstverständlich I

cousin ['kʌzn] Cousin, Cousine I

cover ['kʌvə] (CD-)Hülle I

cow [kaʊ] Kuh II 4 (58)

°**Crash!** [kræʃ] Krach!

crisps *(pl)* [krɪsps] Kartoffelchips I

Dictionary (English – German)

crocodile ['krɒkədaɪl] Krokodil II 3 (52/153)

cross [krɒs] überqueren; (sich) kreuzen II 6 (95)

°**cruel** ['kruːəl]: **be cruel to animals** Tiere quälen

°**cruelty to animals** ['kruːəlti] Tierquälerei

cupboard ['kʌbəd] (Küchen-)Schrank I

°**curse** [kɜːs] Fluch

customer ['kʌstəmə] Kunde, Kundin II 5 (78)

cycle ['saɪkl] (mit dem) Rad fahren II 6 (94) • **cycle path** Radweg II 6 (94/164)

D

dad [dæd] Papa, Vati; Vater I

dance [dɑːns] tanzen I

dance [dɑːns] Tanz I

dancer ['dɑːnsə] Tänzer/in II 3 (53)

dancing ['dɑːsɪŋ] Tanzen I **dancing lessons** Tanzstunden, Tanzunterricht I

danger ['deɪndʒə] Gefahr I

dangerous ['deɪndʒərəs] gefährlich II 1 (12)

dark [dɑːk] dunkel I

date [deɪt] Datum I

daughter ['dɔːtə] Tochter I

°**dawn** [dɔːn] (Morgen-)Dämmerung

day [deɪ] Tag I • **one day** eines Tages I • **days of the week** Wochentage I

dead [ded] tot I

dear [dɪə] Schatz, Liebling I **Oh dear!** Oje! II 3 (55)

dear [dɪə]: **Dear Jay …** Lieber Jay, … I

December [dɪ'sembə] Dezember I

°**decide (on)** [dɪ'saɪd] sich entscheiden (für), beschließen

°**deep** [diːp] tief

deer, *pl* **deer** [dɪə] Reh, Hirsch II 3 (53)

degree [dɪ'griː] Grad II Welc (8)

delicious [dɪ'lɪʃəs] köstlich, lecker II 5 (78)

department store [dɪ'pɑːtmənt stɔː] Kaufhaus II 6 (95)

describe sth. (to sb.) [dɪ'skraɪb] (jm.) etwas beschreiben II 1 (11)

description [dɪ'skrɪpʃn] Beschreibung II 1 (11/143)

design [dɪ'zaɪn] entwerfen, gestalten II 2 (38)

desk [desk] Schreibtisch I

°**destroy** [dɪ'strɔɪ] zerstören

detective [dɪ'tektɪv] Detektiv/in I

°**dialogue** ['daɪəlɒg] Dialog

diary ['daɪəri] Tagebuch; Terminkalender I • °**keep a diary** ein Tagebuch führen

dice, *pl* **dice** [daɪs] Würfel II 5 (74)

dictionary ['dɪkʃənri] Wörterbuch, *(alphabetisches)* Wörterverzeichnis I

did [dɪd] *siehe* **do** • **Did you know …?** Wusstest du …? I • **we didn't go** ['dɪdnt] wir gingen nicht / wir sind nicht gegangen I

°**difference** ['dɪfrəns] Unterschied

different (from) ['dɪfrənt] verschieden, unterschiedlich; anders (als) I

difficult ['dɪfɪkəlt] schwierig, schwer I

°**dig (-gg-)** [dɪg], **dug, dug** graben

dining room ['daɪnɪŋ ruːm] Esszimmer I

dinner ['dɪnə] Abendessen, Abendbrot I • **have dinner** Abendbrot essen I

direct question [dəˌrekt 'kwestʃən] direkte Frage II 6 (98)

▶ S.164 Höflich um Auskunft bitten

directions *(pl)* [də'rekʃnz] Wegbeschreibung(en) II 6 (95)

dirty ['dɜːti] schmutzig II 4 (58)

disappear [ˌdɪsə'pɪə] verschwinden II 2 (28)

disco ['dɪskəʊ] Disko I

discover [dɪ'skʌvə] entdecken; herausfinden II 6 (97)

°**discuss** [dɪ'skʌs] diskutieren

discussion [dɪ'skʌʃn] Diskussion II 5 (80)

dishwasher ['dɪʃwɒʃə] Geschirrspülmaschine I

°**divide (into)** [dɪ'vaɪd] auf-, einteilen (in)

divorced [dɪ'vɔːst] geschieden I

do [duː], **did, done** tun, machen I **Do you like …?** Magst du …? I **do a good job** gute Arbeit leisten II 3 (47) • **do a project** ein Projekt machen, durchführen II 2 (33) • **do an exercise** eine Übung machen II 2 (33) • °**do magic** zaubern • **do sport** Sport treiben I

doctor ['dɒktə] Doktor; Arzt/Ärztin II 3 (49)

dog [dɒg] Hund I

°**dolphin** ['dɒlfɪn] Delfin

done [dʌn] *siehe* **do**

don't [dəʊnt]: **Don't listen to Dan.** Hör/Hört nicht auf Dan. I • **I don't like …** Ich mag … nicht. / Ich mag kein(e) … I

door [dɔː] Tür I

doorbell ['dɔːbel] Türklingel I

dossier ['dɒsieɪ] Mappe, Dossier *(des Sprachenportfolios)* I

double ['dʌbl] zweimal, doppelt, Doppel- I

double-click ['dʌblklɪk] doppelklicken II 4 (63)

down [daʊn] hinunter, herunter, nach unten I • **down there** dort unten II 4 (70) • **fall down** hinfallen II 5 (82)

download [ˌdaʊn'ləʊd] runterladen, downloaden II 4 (63)

▶ S.157 Computer words and phrases

downstairs [ˌdaʊn'steəz] unten; nach unten I

°**Down Under** [ˌdaʊn_'ʌndə] *umgangssprachliche Bezeichnung für Australien und Neuseeland*

°**dragon** ['drægən] Drache

drama ['drɑːmə] Schauspiel, darstellende Kunst I

drank [dræŋk] *siehe* **drink**

°**draw** [drɔː] zeichnen

°**drawing** ['drɔːɪŋ] Zeichnung

dream [driːm] Traum I • **dream house** Traumhaus I

dress [dres] Kleid I

dressed [drest]: **get dressed** sich anziehen I

drink [drɪŋk] Getränk I

drink [drɪŋk], **drank, drunk** trinken I

drive [draɪv], **drove, driven** *(ein Auto/mit dem Auto)* fahren II 1 (23)

driven ['drɪvn] *siehe* **drive**

driver ['draɪvə] Fahrer/in II 4 (70)

drop (-pp-) [drɒp] **1.** fallen lassen I **2.** fallen I

drove [drəʊv] *siehe* **drive**

drunk [drʌŋk] *siehe* **drink**

°**duck** [dʌk] Ente

°**dug** [dʌg] *siehe* **dig**

°**dusk** [dʌsk] (Abend-)Dämmerung

dustbin ['dʌstbɪn] Mülltonne II 2 (39)

DVD [ˌdiː viː' diː] DVD I

E

each [iːtʃ] jeder, jede, jedes (einzelne) I • °**Ask each other questions.** Stellt euch gegenseitig Fragen.

ear [ɪə] Ohr I

earache ['ɪəreɪk] Ohrenschmerzen II 4 (62/157)

▶ S.157 What's wrong with you?

early ['ɜːli] früh I

Dictionary (English – German) 173

earring ['ɪərɪŋ] Ohrring I
easy ['iːzi] leicht, einfach I
eat [iːt], **ate, eaten** essen I
eaten ['iːtn] *siehe* eat
e-friend ['iːfrend] Brieffreund/in *(im Internet)* I
°**either ... or ...** ['aɪðə ɔː, 'iːðə ɔː] entweder ... oder
elephant ['elɪfənt] Elefant I
elevator ['elɪveɪtə] *(AE)* Fahrstuhl, Aufzug II 1 (12)
else [els]: **What else do you know ...?** Was weißt du sonst noch ...? II 6 (94)
e-mail ['iːmeɪl] E-Mail I
°**empire** ['empaɪə] (Welt-)Reich
empty ['empti] leer I
end [end] Ende, Schluss I • **at the end (of)** am Ende (von) I
enemy ['enəmi] Feind/in II 3 (47)
energy ['enədʒi] Energie; Kraft II 5 (74)
engineer [,endʒɪ'nɪə] Ingenieur/in II 5 (74)
English ['ɪŋglɪʃ] Englisch; englisch I
enjoy [ɪn'dʒɔɪ] genießen II 6 (92)
enough [ɪ'nʌf] genug I
enter sth. ['entə] etwas eingeben, eintragen II 4 (63)
°**entry** ['entri] Eintrag *(im Tagebuch)*
essay (about, on) ['eseɪ] Aufsatz (über) I
°**etc.** [et'setərə] usw.
euro (€) ['jʊərəʊ] Euro I
even ['iːvn] sogar II 2 (30)
evening ['iːvnɪŋ] Abend I • **in the evening** abends, am Abend I
on Friday evening freitagabends, am Freitagabend I
ever? ['evə] je? / jemals? / schon mal? II 4 (63)
▶ S.157 The present perfect: questions
every ['evri] jeder, jede, jedes I
everybody ['evribɒdi] jeder, alle II 2 (28)
everything ['evriθɪŋ] alles I
everywhere ['evriweə] überall I
example [ɪg'zɑːmpl] Beispiel I
for example zum Beispiel I
°**excited** [ɪk'saɪtɪd] aufgeregt
exciting [ɪk'saɪtɪŋ] aufregend, spannend II 1 (23)
Excuse me, ... [ɪk'skjuːz miː] Entschuldigung, ... / Entschuldigen Sie, ... I
exercise ['eksəsaɪz] Übung, Aufgabe I • **exercise book** ['eksəsaɪz bʊk] Schulheft, Übungsheft I
expensive [ɪk'spensɪv] teuer I
explain sth. to sb. [ɪk'spleɪn] jm. etwas erklären, erläutern II 3 (46)

explanation [,eksplə'neɪʃn] Erklärung II 3 (46)
explore [ɪk'splɔː] erkunden, erforschen I
explorer [ɪk'splɔːrə] Entdecker/in, Forscher/in II 3 (53)
°**extensive reading** [ɪk'stensɪv] extensives Lesen *(das Lesen längerer Texte mit dem Ziel des allgemeinen Verständnisses, nicht des Detailverständnisses)*
extra ['ekstrə] zusätzlich I
eye [aɪ] Auge I

F

face [feɪs] Gesicht I
factory ['fæktri] Fabrik II 4 (58)
°**fade** [feɪd] schwächer werden
fair [feə] fair, gerecht II 1 (18)
fall [fɔːl], **fell, fallen** fallen, stürzen; hinfallen II 4 (71) • **fall down** hinfallen II 5 (82) • **fall off** [,fɔːl 'ɒf] herunterfallen (von) II 6 (103)
fallen ['fɔːlən] *siehe* fall
family ['fæməli] Familie I
family tree (Familien-)Stammbaum I
famous (for) ['feɪməs] berühmt (für, wegen) II 5 (75)
fan [fæn] Fan I
fantastic [fæn'tæstɪk] fantastisch, toll I
far [fɑː] weit (entfernt) I • **so far** bis jetzt, bis hierher I
farm [fɑːm] Bauernhof, Farm II 4 (58)
°**farmer** ['fɑːmə] Bauer, Bäuerin
fashion ['fæʃn] Mode II 2 (38)
fast [fɑːst] schnell II 1 (12) / II 3 (47)
father ['fɑːðə] Vater I • °**Father Christmas** der Weihnachtsmann
favourite ['feɪvərɪt] Lieblings- I
my favourite colour meine Lieblingsfarbe I
February ['februəri] Februar I
fed [fed] *siehe* feed • **be fed up (with sth.)** [,fed 'ʌp] die Nase voll haben (von etwas) II 2 (28)
feed [fiːd], **fed, fed** füttern I
feel [fiːl], **felt, felt** sich fühlen; fühlen II 3 (55); sich anfühlen II 6 (104)
▶ S.157 What's wrong with you?
feet [fiːt] *Plural von „foot"* I
fell [fel] *siehe* fall
felt [felt] *siehe* feel
felt tip ['felt tɪp] Filzstift I
°**festival** ['festɪvl] Fest, Festival
few: a few [ə 'fjuː] ein paar, einige II 1 (23)

field [fiːld] Feld, Acker, Weide II 4 (58) • **in the field** auf dem Feld II 4 (58/154)
°**fight** [faɪt], **fought, fought** kämpfen
file [faɪl]: **background file** *etwa:* Hintergrundinformation II (3)
grammar file *Grammatikanhang* I
skills file *Anhang mit Lern- und Arbeitstechniken* I
°**fill in** [,fɪl 'ɪn]
1. einsetzen
2. ausfüllen
film [fɪlm] Film I • **film star** Filmstar I
find [faɪnd], **found, found** finden I
find out (about) herausfinden (über) I
finder ['faɪndə] Finder I
fine [faɪn]
1. gut, schön; in Ordnung II 2 (28)
2. *(gesundheitlich)* gut II 3 (45)
I'm/He's fine. Es geht mir/ihm gut. II 3 (45/151)
finger ['fɪŋgə] Finger I
finish ['fɪnɪʃ] beenden, zu Ende machen; enden I
fire ['faɪə] Feuer, Brand II 3 (49)
fireman ['faɪəmən] Feuerwehrmann II 4 (70)
firewoman ['faɪə,wʊmən] Feuerwehrfrau II 4 (70)
fireworks *(pl)* ['faɪəwɜːks] Feuerwerk(skörper) II 5 (79)
first [fɜːst]
1. erste(r, s) I
2. zuerst, als Erstes I
be first der/die Erste sein I
fish, *pl* **fish** [fɪʃ] Fisch I
fit (-tt-) [fɪt] passen I
°**flag** [flæg] Flagge, Fahne I
°**flash** [flæʃ]: **in a flash** blitzartig, wie der Blitz I
flat [flæt] Wohnung I
flavour ['fleɪvə] Geschmack, Geschmacksrichtung II 5 (78)
flew [fluː] *siehe* fly
flight [flaɪt] Flug II 1 (12)
°**float** [fləʊt] schweben
°**floor** [flɔː]
1. Fußboden I
°2. Stockwerk
flow chart ['fləʊ tʃɑːt] Flussdiagramm I
°**flower** ['flaʊə] Blüte; Blume
flown [fləʊn] *siehe* fly
fly [flaɪ], **flew, flown** fliegen II Welc (6)
°**fly** [flaɪ] Fliege
fog [fɒg] Nebel II Welc (8/143)
foggy ['fɒgi] neblig II Welc (8)

follow ['fɒləʊ] folgen; verfolgen I
the following ... die folgenden ... II 5 (76)
food [fuːd]
1. Essen; Lebensmittel I
2. Futter I
foot [fʊt], pl **feet** [fiːt] Fuß I
football ['fʊtbɔːl] Fußball I
football boots ['fʊtbɔːl buːts] Fußballschuhe, -stiefel I
football pitch ['fʊtbɔːl pɪtʃ] Fußballplatz, -feld II 4 (60)
°**footprint** ['fʊtprɪnt] Fußabdruck
for [fə, fɔː] für I • **for breakfast/lunch/dinner** zum Frühstück/Mittagessen/Abendbrot I • **for example** zum Beispiel I • **for lots of reasons** aus vielen Gründen I • **for miles** meilenweit II 1 (12) **for three days** drei Tage (lang) I **just for fun** nur zum Spaß I **What for?** Wofür? II 2 (29) **What's for homework?** Was haben wir als Hausaufgabe auf? I
foreground ['fɔːɡraʊnd] Vordergrund II 1 (11)
forest ['fɒrɪst] Wald II 4 (58)
form [fɔːm]
1. (Schul-)Klasse I • **form teacher** Klassenlehrer/in I
°**2.** Form
°**form** [fɔːm] bilden
°**fort** [fɔːt] Fort
°**fortune-teller** ['fɔːtʃuːn telə] Wahrsager/in
°**fought** [fɔːt] siehe **fight**
found [faʊnd] siehe **find**
fox [fɒks] Fuchs II 3 (42)
free [friː]
1. frei I • **free time** Freizeit, freie Zeit I
2. kostenlos I
°**freeze** [friːz], **froze, frozen** einfrieren, gefrieren; hier: stillstehen, erstarren
French [frentʃ] Französisch I
Friday ['fraɪdeɪ, 'fraɪdi] Freitag I
fridge [frɪdʒ] Kühlschrank I
friend [frend] Freund/in I
friendly ['frendli] freundlich II 5 (78)
frog [frɒɡ] Frosch II 3 (43)
from [frəm, frɒm]
1. aus I
2. von I
°**from above** von oben • **from all around Wales** aus ganz Wales II 4 (65) • °**from ... to ...** von ... bis ... **from my point of view** aus meiner Sicht; von meinem Standpunkt aus gesehen II 2 (39/150) • **I'm from ...** Ich komme aus ... / Ich bin aus ... I

Where are you from? Wo kommst du her? I
°**front** [frʌnt] Vorderseite
front [frʌnt]: **in front of** vor (räumlich) I • **to the front** nach vorn I
front door [,frʌnt 'dɔː] Wohnungstür, Haustür I
°**froze** [frəʊz] siehe **freeze**
°**frozen** ['frəʊzn] siehe **freeze**
fruit [fruːt] Obst, Früchte; Frucht I
fruit salad ['fruːt ,sæləd] Obstsalat I
full [fʊl] voll I
fun [fʌn] Spaß I • **have fun** Spaß haben, sich amüsieren I • **Have fun!** Viel Spaß! I • **just for fun** nur zum Spaß I • **Riding is fun.** Reiten macht Spaß. I
funny ['fʌni] witzig, komisch I
future ['fjuːtʃə] Zukunft I

G

game [ɡeɪm] Spiel I • **a game of football** ein Fußballspiel II 1 (22)
°**gap** [ɡæp] Lücke
garage ['ɡærɑːʒ] Garage II 3 (46)
garden ['ɡɑːdn] Garten I
gave [ɡeɪv] siehe **give**
gear: sports gear (no pl) ['spɔːts ɡɪə] Sportausrüstung, Sportsachen II 2 (27)
geography [dʒi'ɒɡrəfi] Geografie, Erdkunde I
°**Georgian** ['dʒɔːdʒən] georgianisch (aus der Zeit der britischen Könige Georg I–IV)
German ['dʒɜːmən] Deutsch; deutsch; Deutsche(r) I
Germany ['dʒɜːməni] Deutschland I
get (-tt-) [ɡet], **got, got**
1. bekommen, kriegen II 1 (22/145)
2. holen, besorgen II 1 (22)
3. gelangen, (hin)kommen I
4. get angry/hot/... wütend/heiß/... werden II 1 (14)
5. get off (the train/bus) (aus dem Zug/Bus) aussteigen I • **get on (the train/bus)** (in den Zug/Bus) einsteigen I
6. get up aufstehen I
get dressed sich anziehen I
get ready (for) sich fertig machen (für), sich vorbereiten (auf) I • **get things ready** Dinge fertig machen, vorbereiten I
▶ S.145 (to) get
getting by in English [,ɡetɪŋ 'baɪ] etwa: auf Englisch zurechtkommen I

°**giant** ['dʒaɪənt] riesig
giraffe [dʒə'rɑːf] Giraffe II 3 (52/153)
girl [ɡɜːl] Mädchen I
give [ɡɪv], **gave, given** geben I
given ['ɡɪvn] siehe **give**
glass [ɡlɑːs] Glas I • **a glass of water** ein Glas Wasser I
glasses (pl) ['ɡlɑːsɪz] (eine) Brille I
▶ S.147 Plural words
glue [ɡluː] (auf-, ein)kleben II 4 (60/155)
glue [ɡluː] Klebstoff I • **glue stick** ['ɡluː stɪk] Klebestift I
go [ɡəʊ], **went, gone** gehen I; fahren II Welc (7) • **go abroad** ins Ausland gehen/fahren II Welc (9) **go by car/train/bike/...** mit dem Auto/Zug/Rad/... fahren II Welc (7) **go for a walk** spazieren gehen, einen Spaziergang machen II Welc (6) **go home** nach Hause gehen I **go on** weitermachen I • **Go on.** Mach weiter. / Erzähl weiter. I **go on a trip** einen Ausflug machen II Welc (7/142) • **go on holiday** in Urlaub fahren II Welc (7/142) • **go out** weg-, raus-, ausgehen I • **go riding** reiten gehen I • **go shopping** einkaufen gehen I • **go surfing** wellenreiten gehen, surfen gehen II 1 (23) • **go swimming** schwimmen gehen I • **go to bed** ins Bett gehen I • **go to the cinema** ins Kino gehen II 2 (27/147) **Let's go.** Auf geht's! I • °**go well** gut (ver)laufen • °**go with** passen zu
▶ S.142 (to) go
°**goat** [ɡəʊt] Ziege
gone [ɡɒn] siehe **go**
good [ɡʊd]
1. gut I • **Good afternoon.** Guten Tag. (nachmittags) I • **Good luck (with ...)!** Viel Glück (bei/mit ...)! I **Good morning.** Guten Morgen. I
2. brav II 3 (55)
Goodbye. [,ɡʊd'baɪ] Auf Wiedersehen I • **say goodbye** sich verabschieden I
got [ɡɒt] siehe **get**
got [ɡɒt]: **I've got ...** Ich habe ... I **I haven't got a chair.** Ich habe keinen Stuhl. I
grammar ['ɡræmə] Grammatik I **grammar file** Grammatikanhang I
°**grand** [ɡrænd] prachtvoll, großartig
grandchild ['ɡræntʃaɪld], pl **grandchildren** ['-tʃɪldrən] Enkel/in I
granddaughter ['ɡrændɔːtə] Enkelin II 4 (71)

Dictionary (English – German) 175

grandfather ['grænfɑːðə] Großvater I

grandma ['grænmɑː] Oma I

grandmother ['grænmʌðə] Großmutter I

grandpa ['grænpɑː] Opa I

grandparents ['grænpeərənts] Großeltern I

grandson ['grænsʌn] Enkel II 4 (71)

granny ['græni] Oma II 2 (30)

great [greɪt] großartig, toll I
▸ S.161 big – large – great

green [griːn] grün I

grew [gruː] siehe **grow**

grey [greɪ] grau II 3 (43)

group [gruːp] Gruppe I • **group word** Oberbegriff II 2 (27)

grow [grəʊ], **grew, grown**
1. wachsen II 2 (29)
2. (Getreide usw.) anbauen, anpflanzen II 5 (75)

grown [grəʊn] siehe **grow**

grumble ['grʌmbl] murren, nörgeln I

guess [ges] raten, erraten, schätzen II 3 (46) • **Guess what!** Stell dir vor! / Stellt euch vor! II 3 (46)

guest [gest] Gast I

°**guide** [gaɪd] Fremdenführer/in, Reiseleiter/in

guinea pig ['gɪni pɪg] Meerschweinchen I

guitar [gɪ'tɑː] Gitarre I • **play the guitar** Gitarre spielen I

gun [gʌn] (Schuss-)Waffe II 5 (80)

°**gunpowder** ['gʌnpaʊdə] Schießpulver

H

had [hæd] siehe **have**

hair (no pl) [heə] Haar, Haare I

half [hɑːf]: **half past 11** halb zwölf (11.30 / 23.30) I

hall [hɔːl] Flur, Diele I

hamburger ['hæmbɜːgə] Hamburger I

hamster ['hæmstə] Hamster I

hand [hænd] Hand I

happen (to) ['hæpən] geschehen, passieren (mit) I

happy ['hæpi] glücklich, froh I
Happy birthday. Herzlichen Glückwunsch zum Geburtstag. I
happy ending Happyend II 1 (23)

harbour ['hɑːbə] Hafen II 5 (79)

hard [hɑːd] hart; schwer, schwierig II 3 (47) • **work hard** hart arbeiten II 3 (47)

hat [hæt] Hut II 2 (38)

hate [heɪt] hassen, gar nicht mögen I

have [həv, hæv], **had, had** haben, besitzen II 2 (28) • **have a baby** ein Baby/Kind bekommen II 3 (47) **have a bath** baden, ein Bad nehmen II 6 (92) • **have a cold** erkältet sein, eine Erkältung haben II 4 (62/157) • **have a party** eine Party feiern/veranstalten II 1 (14) **have a sauna** in die Sauna gehen II 6 (92) • **have a shower** (sich) duschen I • **have a sore throat** Halsschmerzen haben II 4 (62) **have a temperature** Fieber haben II 4 (62) • **have breakfast** frühstücken I • **have dinner** Abendbrot essen I • **have ... for breakfast** ... zum Frühstück essen/trinken I • **have fun** Spaß haben, sich amüsieren I • **Have fun!** Viel Spaß! I • **have to do** tun müssen I

have got: I've got ... [aɪv 'gɒt] Ich habe ... I • **I haven't got a chair.** ['hævnt gɒt] Ich habe keinen Stuhl. I

he [hiː] er I

head [hed] Kopf I • °**heads and tails** wörtlich: Köpfe und Schwänze; hier: (Satz-)Anfänge und Enden

headache ['hedeɪk] Kopfschmerzen II 4 (62)
▸ S.157 What's wrong with you?

°**heading** ['hedɪŋ] Überschrift

°**heads and tails** [ˌhedz_ən 'teɪlz] wörtlich: Köpfe und Schwänze; hier: (Satz-)Anfänge und Enden

healthy ['helθi] gesund II 5 (74)

hear [hɪə], **heard, heard** hören I

heard [hɜːd] siehe **hear**

heart [hɑːt] Herz II 3 (54/154)

hedgehog ['hedʒhɒg] Igel II 3 (43)

held [held] siehe **hold**

helicopter ['helɪkɒptə] Hubschrauber, Helikopter II 4 (71)

Hello. [hə'ləʊ] Hallo. / Guten Tag. I

help [help] helfen I • **Can I help you?** Kann ich Ihnen helfen? / Was kann ich für Sie tun? (im Geschäft) I

help [help] Hilfe I

her [hə, hɜː]
1. ihr, ihre I
2. sie; ihr I

here [hɪə]
1. hier I
2. hierher I

Here you are. Bitte sehr. / Hier bitte. I

hero ['hɪərəʊ], pl **heroes** ['hɪərəʊz] Held, Heldin II 1 (14)

hers [hɜːz] ihrer, ihre, ihrs II 2 (28/147)
▸ S.147 Possessive pronouns

Hi! [haɪ] Hallo! I • **Say hi to Dilip for me.** Grüß Dilip von mir. I

hid [hɪd] siehe **hide**

hidden ['hɪdn] siehe **hide**

hide [haɪd], **hid, hidden** sich verstecken; (etwas) verstecken I

°**high** [haɪ] hoch

°**high school** ['haɪ skuːl] Gesamtschule in den USA mit den Klassen 7–12 für 13- bis 18-Jährige

hill [hɪl] Hügel II 4 (58)

him [hɪm] ihn; ihm I

hippo ['hɪpəʊ] Flusspferd II 3 (52/153)

his [hɪz]
1. sein, seine I
2. seiner, seine, seins II 2 (28/147)
▸ S.147 Possessive pronouns

history ['hɪstri] Geschichte I

hit (-tt-) [hɪt], **hit, hit** schlagen I
°**hit a sandbank** auf eine Sandbank laufen (Schiff)

hobby ['hɒbi] Hobby I

hockey ['hɒki] Hockey I

hockey pitch ['hɒki pɪtʃ] Hockeyplatz, -feld II 4 (60)

hockey shoes ['hɒki ʃuːz] Hockeyschuhe I

°**hog** [hɒg] Schwein

hold [həʊld], **held, held** halten II 4 (70) • °**hold up** hochhalten

hole [həʊl] Loch I

holiday(s) ['hɒlədeɪ(z)] Ferien I
be on holiday in Urlaub sein; Ferien haben/machen II 1 (14)
go on holiday in Urlaub fahren II Welc (7/142)

home [həʊm] Heim, Zuhause I
at home daheim, zu Hause I
come home nach Hause kommen I • **get home** nach Hause kommen I • **go home** nach Hause gehen I

homework (no pl) ['həʊmwɜːk] Hausaufgabe(n) I • **do homework** die Hausaufgabe(n) machen I • **What's for homework?** Was haben wir als Hausaufgabe auf? I

Hooray! [hu'reɪ] Hurra! II 6 (104)

°**hop (-pp-)** [hɒp] hüpfen

hope [həʊp] hoffen II 4 (70)

horrible ['hɒrəbl] scheußlich, grauenhaft II 3 (46)

horse [hɔːs] Pferd I

hospital ['hɒspɪtl] Krankenhaus II 4 (71)

hot [hɒt] heiß I • **hot chocolate** heiße Schokolade I • **hot-water bottle** Wärmflasche II 3 (45)

176 Dictionary (English – German)

hotel [həʊˈtel] Hotel II Welc (7)
hotline [ˈhɒtlaɪn] Hotline II 3 (44)
hour [ˈaʊə] Stunde II 1 (18)
house [haʊs] Haus I • **at the Shaws' house** im Haus der Shaws / bei den Shaws zu Hause I
how [haʊ] wie I • **How are you?** Wie geht es dir/Ihnen/euch? II 6 (94) • **How do you know ...?** Woher weißt/kennst du ...? I **how many?** wie viele? I • **how much?** wie viel? I • **How much is/are ...?** Was kostet/kosten ...? / Wie viel kostet/kosten ...? I **How old are you?** Wie alt bist du? I • **How was ...?** Wie war ...? I
hundred [ˈhʌndrəd] hundert I
hungry [ˈhʌŋgri] hungrig I • **be hungry** Hunger haben, hungrig sein I
hurry [ˈhʌri] eilen; sich beeilen II 2 (38) • **hurry up** sich beeilen I
hurry [ˈhʌri]: **be in a hurry** in Eile sein, es eilig haben I
hurt [hɜːt], **hurt, hurt** wehtun; verletzen I
hurt [hɜːt] verletzt II 4 (70)
husband [ˈhʌzbənd] Ehemann II 4 (71)
hutch [hʌtʃ] (Kaninchen-)Stall I

I

I [aɪ] ich I • **I'm** [aɪm] ich bin I **I'm from ...** Ich komme aus ... / Ich bin aus ... I • **I'm ... years old.** Ich bin ... Jahre alt. I • **I'm sorry.** Entschuldigung. / Tut mir leid. I
ice [aɪs] Eis II 5 (74) • **ice cream** [ˌaɪs ˈkriːm] (Speise-)Eis I • **ice rink** [ˈaɪs rɪŋk] Schlittschuhbahn II 5 (74)
idea [aɪˈdɪə] Idee, Einfall I
if [ɪf]
  1. falls, wenn II 3 (45)
  2. ob II 6 (105)
ill [ɪl] krank II 3 (45)
  ▶ S.157 What's wrong with you?
°**imagine sth.** [ɪˈmædʒɪn] sich etwas vorstellen I
important [ɪmˈpɔːtnt] wichtig II 3 (45)
impossible [ɪmˈpɒsəbl] unmöglich II 5 (78)
in [ɪn] in I • **in 1948** im Jahr 1948 II 4 (65) • **in ... Street** in der ...straße I • **in English** auf Englisch I • **in front of** vor (räumlich) I • **in here** hier drinnen I • °**in one piece** heil, ganz • **in the afternoon** nachmittags, am

Nachmittag I • **in the country** auf dem Land II Welc (6/142) • **in the evening** abends, am Abend I **in the field** auf dem Feld II 4 (58/154) • **in the morning** am Morgen, morgens I • **in the photo** auf dem Foto I • **in the picture** auf dem Bild I • **in the sky** am Himmel II Welc (7/142) • **in there** dort drinnen I • **in the yard** auf dem Hof II 3 (44/151) • **in time** rechtzeitig II 1 (23) • °**one in five people** jede(r) Fünfte, eine(r) von fünf(en) I
°**including** [ɪnˈkluːdɪŋ] einschließlich I
°**independence** [ˌɪndɪˈpendəns] Unabhängigkeit I
indirect question [ˌɪndərekt ˈkwestʃən] indirekte Frage II 6 (98)
  ▶ S.164 Höflich um Auskunft bitten
infinitive [ɪnˈfɪnətɪv] Infinitiv (Grundform des Verbs) I
information (about/on) (no pl) [ˌɪnfəˈmeɪʃn] Information(en) (über) I
°**injure** [ˈɪndʒə] (sich) verletzen I
inside [ˌɪnˈsaɪd]
  1. innen (drin), drinnen I
  2. nach drinnen II 3 (44)
  3. inside the car ins Auto (hinein), ins Innere des Autos II 4 (71)
°**inside cover** [ˌɪnsaɪd ˈkʌvə] Umschlaginnenseite I
install [ɪnˈstɔːl] installieren, einrichten II 4 (63)
  ▶ S.157 Computer words and phrases
installation [ˌɪnstəˈleɪʃn] Installation, Einrichtung II 4 (63)
instructions (pl) [ɪnˈstrʌkʃnz] (Gebrauchs-)Anweisung(en), Anleitung(en) II 4 (63)
instrument [ˈɪnstrəmənt] Instrument II 6 (97)
°**interest sb.** [ˈɪntrəst] jn. interessieren
interesting [ˈɪntrəstɪŋ] interessant I
internet [ˈɪntənet] Internet I
interview [ˈɪntəvjuː] interviewen, befragen II 4 (60/155)
interview [ˈɪntəvjuː] Interview II 3 (43)
into [ˈɪntə, ˈɪntʊ] in ... (hinein) I
°**invent** [ɪnˈvent] erfinden I
invitation (to) [ˌɪnvɪˈteɪʃn] Einladung (zu) I
invite (to) [ɪnˈvaɪt] einladen (zu) I
irregular [ɪˈregjələ] unregelmäßig I
is [ɪz] ist I
island [ˈaɪlənd] Insel II Welc (6)

it [ɪt] er/sie/es I • **It's £1.** Er/Sie/Es kostet 1 Pfund. I • **It says here: ...** Hier steht: ... / Es heißt hier: ... II 4 (63)
IT [ˌaɪ ˈtiː], **information technology** [tekˈnɒlədʒi] IT, Informationstechnologie II 5 (79)
its [ɪts] sein/seine; ihr/ihre I

J

jacket [ˈdʒækɪt] Jacke, Jackett II 2 (27)
January [ˈdʒænjuəri] Januar I
jazz [dʒæz] Jazz I
jeans (pl) [dʒiːnz] Jeans I
  ▶ S.147 Plural words
jewellery [ˈdʒuːəlri] Schmuck II 5 (80)
°**jiggle** [ˈdʒɪgl] herumhampeln I
job [dʒɒb] Aufgabe, Job I
join sb. [dʒɔɪn] sich jm. anschließen; bei jm. mitmachen II 2 (38)
joke [dʒəʊk] Witz I
joke [dʒəʊk] scherzen, Witze machen II 4 (60/155)
journey [ˈdʒɜːni] Reise, Fahrt II 6 (92)
judo [ˈdʒuːdəʊ] Judo I • **do judo** Judo machen I
jug [dʒʌg] Krug I • **a jug of milk** ein Krug Milch I
juice [dʒuːs] Saft I
July [dʒuˈlaɪ] Juli I
°**jumble** [ˈdʒʌmbl] gebrauchte Sachen, Trödel I
jumble sale [ˈdʒʌmbl seɪl] Wohltätigkeitsbasar I
jump [dʒʌmp] springen II 3 (46)
June [dʒuːn] Juni I
junior [ˈdʒuːniə] Junioren-, Jugend- I
just [dʒʌst]
  1. (einfach) nur, bloß I • °**they just don't fit** sie passen einfach nicht I
  2. gerade (eben), soeben II 4 (61) **just then** genau in dem Moment; gerade dann II 3 (46)
  3. just like you genau wie du II 2 (28)
  ▶ S.156 The present perfect: statements

K

kangaroo [ˌkæŋgəˈruː] Känguru II 3 (52/153)
°**kayaking** [ˈkaɪækɪŋ] Kajak fahren I
keep [kiːp], **kept, kept: keep sth. warm/cool/open/...** etwas warm/kühl/offen/... halten

Dictionary (English – German) 177

II 3 (45) • °**keep a diary** ein Tagebuch führen

kept [kept] *siehe* **keep**

key [kiː] Schlüssel I • **key word** Stichwort, Schlüsselwort I

kid [kɪd] Kind, Jugendliche(r) I

kill [kɪl] töten I

°**kilometre (km)** [ˈkɪləmiːtə, kɪˈlɒmɪtə] Kilometer (km)

king [kɪŋ] König I

kitchen [ˈkɪtʃɪn] Küche I

kite [kaɪt] Drachen I

knee [niː] Knie I

knew [njuː] *siehe* **know**

knock (on) [nɒk] (an)klopfen (an) I

know [nəʊ], **knew, known**
1. wissen I
2. kennen I
know about sth. von etwas wissen; über etwas Bescheid wissen II 1 (23) • **How do you know ...?** Woher weißt du ...? / Woher kennst du ...? I • **I don't know.** Ich weiß es nicht. I • **..., you know.** ..., wissen Sie. / ..., weißt du. I • **You know what, Sophie?** Weißt du was, Sophie? I

known [nəʊn] *siehe* **know**

L

°**label** [ˈleɪbl] beschriften, etikettieren

°**ladder** [ˈlædə] *(die)* Leiter

°**lady** [ˈleɪdi] Dame

laid [leɪd] *siehe* **lay**

lake [leɪk] (Binnen-)See II Welc (9)

lamp [læmp] Lampe I

land [lænd] Land, Grund und Boden II 5 (75)

land [lænd] landen II 2 (38)

language [ˈlæŋgwɪdʒ] Sprache I

large [lɑːdʒ] groß II 5 (78)
▶ S.161 big – large – great

lasagne [ləˈzænjə] Lasagne I

last [lɑːst] letzte(r, s) I • **the last day** der letzte Tag I • **at last** endlich, schließlich I

late [leɪt] spät; zu spät I • **be late** zu spät sein/kommen I • **Sorry, I'm late.** Entschuldigung, dass ich zu spät bin/komme. I

later [ˈleɪtə] später I

laugh [lɑːf] lachen I • **laugh out loud** laut lachen II 4 (63)

laughter [ˈlɑːftə] Gelächter II 6 (105)

lay the table [leɪ], **laid, laid** den Tisch decken I

°**lean** [liːn] sich neigen

°**leaning tower** [ˌliːnɪŋ ˈtaʊə] schiefer Turm

°**leap** [liːp] springen

learn [lɜːn] lernen I • **learn sth. about sth.** etwas über etwas erfahren, etwas über etwas herausfinden II 5 (74)

least: at least [ət ˈliːst] zumindest, wenigstens I

leave [liːv], **left, left**
1. (weg)gehen; abfahren II 3 (54)
2. verlassen II 3 (54/153)
3. zurücklassen II 3 (54/153)
▶ S.153 (to) leave

left [left] *siehe* **leave**

left [left] linke(r, s) II 1 (11/143)
look left nach links schauen II 1 (11/143) • **on the left** links, auf der linken Seite I • **turn left** (nach) links abbiegen II 6 (95)
▶ S.143 left – right

leg [leg] Bein I

°**legend** [ˈledʒənd] Legende, Sage

leisure centre [ˈleʒə sentə] Freizeitzentrum, -park II 6 (104)

lemonade [ˌleməˈneɪd] Limonade I

lesson [ˈlesn] (Unterrichts-)Stunde I • **lessons** *(pl)* [ˈlesnz] Unterricht I

let [let], **let, let** lassen II 3 (44/151)
Let's ... Lass uns ... / Lasst uns ... I
Let's go. Auf geht's! (*wörtlich:* Lass uns gehen.) I • **Let's look at the list.** Sehen wir uns die Liste an. / Lasst uns die Liste ansehen. I

letter [ˈletə]
1. Buchstabe I
2. **letter (to)** Brief (an) II 2 (30)

lettuce [ˈletɪs] (Kopf-)Salat II 6 (104)

library [ˈlaɪbrəri] Bibliothek, Bücherei I

life [laɪf], *pl* **lives** [laɪvz] Leben I

°**lifeboat** [ˈlaɪfbəʊt] Rettungsboot, -schiff

°**lifeboatmen** *(pl)* [ˈlaɪfbəʊtmən] *die Besatzung eines Rettungsbootes*

lift [lɪft] Fahrstuhl, Aufzug II 1 (12)

like [laɪk] wie I • **just like you** genau wie du II 2 (28) • **What was the weather like?** Wie war das Wetter? II Welc (7) • °**like that / like this** so

like [laɪk] mögen, gernhaben I
like sth. better etwas lieber mögen II 6 (103) • **I like swimming/ dancing/...** Ich schwimme/tanze/ ... gern. I • **I'd like ... (= I would like ...)** Ich hätte gern ... / Ich möchte gern ... I • **I'd like to go (= I would like to go)** Ich würde gern gehen / Ich möchte gehen I • **I wouldn't like to go** Ich würde nicht gern gehen / Ich möchte nicht gehen I
Would you like ...? Möchtest du

...? / Möchten Sie ...? I • °**Say what you like about ...** Sag, was du an ... magst

line [laɪn]
1. Zeile II 3 (55)
°2. Linie

link [lɪŋk] verbinden, verknüpfen I

linking word [ˈlɪŋkɪŋ wɜːd] Bindewort II 1 (20)

lion [ˈlaɪən] Löwe II 3 (52/153)

list [lɪst] Liste I

list [lɪst] auflisten, aufzählen II 4 (60/155)

listen (to) [ˈlɪsn] zuhören; sich *etwas* anhören I

listener [ˈlɪsnə] Zuhörer/in II 3 (53)

little [ˈlɪtl] klein I

live [lɪv] leben, wohnen I • °**live on** weiterleben

live music [laɪv] Livemusik II 1 (20)

lives [laɪvz] *Plural von „life"* I

living room [ˈlɪvɪŋ ruːm] Wohnzimmer I

°**local** [ˈləʊkl] lokal, örtlich, Lokal-

lock up [ˌlɒk ˈʌp] abschließen II 5 (79)

°**log** [lɒg] Holzscheit, Baumstamm

long [lɒŋ] lang I

look [lʊk]
1. schauen, gucken I
2. **look different/great/old** anders/ toll/alt aussehen I
look after sth./sb. auf etwas/jn. aufpassen; sich um etwas/jn. kümmern II 5 (87) • **look at** ansehen, anschauen I • **look for** suchen II 5 (87) • **look left/right** nach links/rechts schauen II 1 (11/143)
look round sich umsehen I
look up (from) hochsehen, aufschauen (von) II 2 (29) • °**look up words** Wörter nachschlagen

lose [luːz], **lost, lost** verlieren II 2 (28)

lost [lɒst] *siehe* **lose**

lot [lɒt]: **a lot (of)** eine Menge, viel, viele II 2 (30) • **Thanks a lot!** Vielen Dank! I • **He likes her a lot.** Er mag sie sehr. I • **lots more** viel mehr I • **lots of ...** eine Menge ..., viele ..., viel ... I

loud [laʊd] laut I

love [lʌv] lieben, sehr mögen II 2 (38)

love [lʌv] Liebe II 2 (38/149)
Love ... Liebe Grüße, ... (*Briefschluss*) I

luck [lʌk]: **Good luck (with ...)!** Viel Glück (bei/mit ...)! I

luckily [ˈlʌkɪli] zum Glück, glücklicherweise II 6 (94/164)

lucky ['lʌki]: **be lucky (with)** Glück haben (mit) II 6 (94)
lunch [lʌntʃ] Mittagessen I
lunch break Mittagspause I

M

°**machine** [mə'ʃiːn] Maschine
mad [mæd] verrückt I
made [meɪd] siehe **make**
magazine [ˌmægə'ziːn] Zeitschrift, Magazin I
°**magic** ['mædʒɪk] Magie, Zauberkunst • °**do magic** zaubern
mail [meɪl] schicken, senden (per Post oder E-Mail) I • **mail sb.** jn. anmailen II 3 (44)
make [meɪk], **made, made** machen; bauen I • **make a call** ein Telefongespräch führen II 6 (96) **make a mess** alles durcheinanderbringen, alles in Unordnung bringen I • °**make comparisons** Vergleiche anstellen, vergleichen °**make notes** (sich) Notizen machen
make-up ['meɪkʌp] Make-up II 2 (27)
man [mæn], pl **men** [men] Mann I
many ['meni] viele I • **how many?** wie viele? I
map [mæp] Landkarte, Stadtplan II 6 (95)
March [mɑːtʃ] März I
mark sth. up [ˌmɑːk_'ʌp] etwas markieren, kennzeichnen II 5 (77)
°**marked** [mɑːkt] markiert
market ['mɑːkɪt] Markt II 5 (74)
marmalade ['mɑːməleɪd] (Orangen-)Marmelade I
married (to) ['mærɪd] verheiratet (mit) I
match [mætʃ] Spiel, Wettkampf I
°**match** [mætʃ]
  1. passen zu
  2. zuordnen
  °**Match the letters and numbers.** Ordne die Buchstaben den Zahlen zu.
°**mate** [meɪt] Kumpel
°**material** [mə'tɪəriəl] Material
maths [mæθs] Mathematik I
matter ['mætə]: **What's the matter?** Was ist los? / Was ist denn? II 2 (28)
may [meɪ] dürfen I
May [meɪ] Mai I
maybe ['meɪbi] vielleicht I
°**mayonnaise** [ˌmeɪə'neɪz] Majonäse
me [miː] mir; mich I • **Me too.** Ich auch. I • **more than me** mehr als ich II 2 (29/148) • **That's me.**

Das bin ich. I • **Why me?** Warum ich? I
mean [miːn], **meant, meant**
  1. bedeuten II 4 (63)
  2. meinen (sagen wollen) II 5 (86)
meant [ment] siehe **mean**
meat [miːt] Fleisch I
mediation [ˌmiːdi'eɪʃn] Vermittlung, Sprachmittlung, Mediation II (3)
medium ['miːdiəm] mittel(groß) II 5 (78)
meet [miːt], **met, met**
  1. treffen; kennenlernen I
  2. sich treffen I
men [men] Plural von „man" I
°**Merry Christmas.** [ˌmeri 'krɪsməs] Frohe Weihnachten.
mess [mes]: **be a mess** sehr unordentlich sein; fürchterlich aussehen II 4 (67) • **make a mess** alles durcheinanderbringen, alles in Unordnung bringen I
°**message** ['mesɪdʒ] Nachricht, Botschaft • °**message in a bottle** Flaschenpost
met [met] siehe **meet**
metre ['miːtə] Meter II 4 (70)
mice [maɪs] Plural von „mouse" I
middle (of) ['mɪdl] Mitte I; Mittelteil II 5 (79)
mile [maɪl] Meile (= ca. 1,6 km) II 1 (12) • **for miles** meilenweit II 1 (12)
milk [mɪlk] Milch I
°**million** ['mɪljən] Million
mime [maɪm] pantomimisch darstellen, vorspielen II 5 (74)
°**mime** [maɪm] Pantomime
mind map ['maɪnd mæp] Mindmap („Gedankenkarte", „Wissensnetz") I
Mind your own business. [ˌmaɪnd jər_ˌəʊn 'bɪznəs] Das geht dich nichts an! / Kümmere dich um deine eigenen Angelegenheiten! II 1 (13)
mine [maɪn] meiner, meine, meins II 2 (28)
  ▶ S.147 Possessive pronouns
mini- ['mɪni] Mini- II 5 (76)
°**minister** ['mɪnɪstə] Minister/in
mints (pl) [mɪnts] Pfefferminzbonbons I
minute ['mɪnɪt] Minute I • **Wait a minute.** Warte mal! / Moment mal! II 5 (87)
mirror ['mɪrə] Spiegel II 2 (38)
miss [mɪs]
  1. vermissen II 3 (54)
  2. verpassen II 4 (60)
  3. Miss a turn. Einmal aussetzen. II 5 (74)

Miss White [mɪs] Frau White (unverheiratet) I
°**missing** ['mɪsɪŋ]: **be missing** fehlen II 6 (96) • °**the missing information/words** die fehlenden Informationen/Wörter
mistake [mɪ'steɪk] Fehler I
°**mix up** [ˌmɪks_'ʌp] durcheinanderbringen • °**be mixed up** durcheinander/in der falschen Reihenfolge sein
°**mobile** ['məʊbaɪl] Mobile
mobile (phone) ['məʊbaɪl] Mobiltelefon, Handy I
model ['mɒdl] Modell(-flugzeug, -schiff usw.) I; (Foto-)Modell II 2 (39)
mole [məʊl] Maulwurf II 3 (43)
moment ['məʊmənt] Moment, Augenblick II 2 (29) • **at the moment** im Moment, gerade II 2 (29/148)
Monday ['mʌndeɪ, 'mʌndi] Montag I • **Monday morning** Montagmorgen I
money ['mʌni] Geld I
monkey ['mʌŋki] Affe II 3 (52/153)
month [mʌnθ] Monat I
moon [muːn] Mond II 3 (44)
more [mɔː] mehr I • **lots more** viel mehr I • **more boring (than)** langweiliger (als) II 2 (31) • **more quickly (than)** schneller (als) II 3 (47) • **more than** mehr als II 2 (29) • **more than me** mehr als ich II 2 (29/148) • **no more music** keine Musik mehr I • **not (...) any more** nicht mehr II 6 (96) • **one more** noch ein(e), ein(e) weitere(r, s) I
morning ['mɔːnɪŋ] Morgen, Vormittag I • **in the morning** morgens, am Morgen I • **Monday morning** Montagmorgen I • **on Friday morning** freitagmorgens, am Freitagmorgen I
°**mosaic** [məʊ'zeɪɪk] Mosaik
most [məʊst] (der/die/das) meiste ...; am meisten II 2 (127) • **most people** die meisten Leute I **(the) most boring** der/die/das langweiligste ...; am langweiligsten II 2 (31)
mother ['mʌðə] Mutter I
mountain ['maʊntən] Berg II Welc (6/141)
mouse [maʊs], pl **mice** [maɪs] Maus I
mouth [maʊθ] Mund I
move [muːv]
  1. bewegen; sich bewegen II 4 (62)
  Move back one space. Geh ein Feld zurück. II 5 (74) • **Move on one**

Dictionary (English – German)

space. Geh ein Feld vor. II 5 (74)
2. move (to) umziehen (nach, in) II 3 (54/154) • **move in** einziehen II 3 (54/154) • **move out** ausziehen II 3 (54)
movement ['muːvmənt] Bewegung II 6 (104)
°**movies** *(pl)* ['muːviz] Kino
MP3 player [ˌempiːˈθriː ˌpleɪə] MP3-Spieler I
Mr ... ['mɪstə] Herr ... I
Mrs ... ['mɪsɪz] Frau ... I
Ms ... [mɪz, məz] Frau ... II 1 (18)
much [mʌtʃ] viel I • **how much?** wie viel? I • **How much is/are ...?** Was kostet/kosten ...? / Wie viel kostet/kosten ...? I • **like/love sth. very much** etwas sehr mögen/sehr lieben II 3 (45/151)
multiple choice [ˌmʌltɪpl 'tʃɔɪs] Multiple-Choice II 3 (49)
mum [mʌm] Mama, Mutti; Mutter I
museum [mjuˈziːəm] Museum I
music ['mjuːzɪk] Musik I
musical ['mjuːzɪkl] Musical I
must [mʌst] müssen I
▶ S.166 must – needn't – mustn't
mustn't do ['mʌsnt] nicht tun dürfen II 6 (97)
▶ S.166 must – needn't – mustn't
my [maɪ] mein/e I • **My name is ...** Ich heiße ... / Mein Name ist ... I **It's my turn.** Ich bin dran / an der Reihe. I
mystery ['mɪstri] Rätsel, Geheimnis II 5 (88)

N

name [neɪm] Name I • **My name is ...** Ich heiße ... / Mein Name ist ... I • **What's your name?** Wie heißt du? I
name [neɪm] nennen; benennen II 4 (60/155)
°**national** ['næʃnəl] national
°**Natural History Unit** [ˌnætʃrəl 'hɪstri juːnɪt] Naturkundeabteilung
near [nɪə] in der Nähe von, nahe (bei) I
neat [niːt] gepflegt II 3 (54) • **neat and tidy** schön ordentlich II 3 (54)
need [niːd] brauchen, benötigen I
needn't do ['niːdnt] nicht tun müssen, nicht zu tun brauchen II 6 (96)
▶ S.166 must – needn't – mustn't
neighbour ['neɪbə] Nachbar/in I
nervous ['nɜːvəs] nervös, aufgeregt I
°**network** ['netwɜːk] (Wörter-)Netz

never ['nevə] nie, niemals I
▶ S.156 The present perfect: statements
new [njuː] neu I
news *(no pl)* [njuːz] Nachrichten II 3 (52)
newspaper ['njuːspeɪpə] Zeitung I
next [nekst]: **be next** der/die Nächste sein I • **the next morning/day** am nächsten Morgen/Tag I • **the next photo** das nächste Foto I • **What have we got next?** Was haben wir als Nächstes? I
next to [nekst] neben I
nice [naɪs] schön, nett I
night [naɪt] Nacht, später Abend I **at night** nachts, in der Nacht I **on Friday night** freitagnachts, Freitagnacht I
no [nəʊ] nein I
no [nəʊ] kein, keine I • **no more music** keine Musik mehr I • **No way!** Auf keinen Fall! / Kommt nicht in Frage! II 1 (14)
nobody ['nəʊbədi] niemand II Welc (9)
nod (-dd-) [nɒd] nicken (mit) II 4 (62)
noise [nɔɪz] Geräusch; Lärm I
noisy ['nɔɪzi] laut, lärmend II 4 (58)
nose [nəʊz] Nase I
not [nɒt] nicht I • **not (...) any** kein, keine I • **not (...) any more** nicht mehr II 6 (96) • **not (...) anybody** niemand II 5 (76/160) • **not (...) anything** nichts II 5 (76/160) **not (...) anywhere** nirgendwo(hin) II 5 (76/160) • **not (...) yet** noch nicht II 4 (61)
note [nəʊt] Mitteilung, Notiz I °**make notes** sich Notizen machen **take notes** sich Notizen machen I
nothing ['nʌθɪŋ] nichts II 1 (14) °**There's nothing like a mate.** *etwa:* Nichts geht über einen guten Kumpel.
°**notice** ['nəʊtɪs] Notiz, Mitteilung
November [nəʊ'vembə] November I
now [naʊ] nun, jetzt I
number ['nʌmbə] Zahl, Ziffer, Nummer I

O

o [əʊ] null I
°**observatory** [əb'zɜːvətri] Observatorium; Aussichtsplattform
o'clock [ə'klɒk]: **eleven o'clock** elf Uhr I
October [ɒk'təʊbə] Oktober I

°**odd** [ɒd]: **What word is the odd one out?** Welches Wort passt nicht dazu? / Welches Wort gehört nicht dazu?
of [əv, ɒv] von I • **of the summer holidays** der Sommerferien I
of course [əv 'kɔːs] natürlich, selbstverständlich I
off [ɒf]: **take 10c off** 10 Cent abziehen I
often ['ɒfn] oft, häufig I
Oh dear! [əʊ 'dɪə] Oje! II 3 (55)
Oh well ... [əʊ 'wel] Na ja ... / Na gut ... I
OK [əʊ'keɪ] okay, gut, in Ordnung I
old [əʊld] alt I • **How old are you?** Wie alt bist du? I • **I'm ... years old.** Ich bin ... Jahre alt. I
on [ɒn]
1. auf I
2. be on eingeschaltet sein, an sein *(Radio, Licht usw.)* II 1 (20) **on 13th June** am 13. Juni I • **on Friday** am Freitag I • **on Friday afternoon** freitagnachmittags, am Freitagnachmittag I • **on Friday evening** freitagabends, am Freitagabend I • **on Friday morning** freitagmorgens, am Freitagmorgen I • **on Friday night** freitagnachts, Freitagnacht I • **on the beach** am Strand II Welc (6) • **on the board** an die Tafel I • **on the corner of Sand Street and London Road** Sand Street, Ecke London Road II 6 (95/165) • **on the left** links, auf der linken Seite I • **on the phone** am Telefon I • **on the plane** im Flugzeug II Welc (6/142) **on the radio** im Radio I • **on the right** rechts, auf der rechten Seite I • **on the train** im Zug I • **on TV** im Fernsehen I • **What page are we on?** Auf welcher Seite sind wir? I • **be on holiday** in Urlaub sein; Ferien haben/machen II 1 (14) **go on holiday** in Urlaub fahren II Welc (7/142) • **straight on** geradeaus weiter II 6 (95)
°**once** [wʌns] einst; (früher) einmal
one [wʌn] eins, ein, eine I • **one day** eines Tages I • °**one in five people** jede(r) Fünfte, eine(r) von fünf(en) • **one more** noch ein/e, ein/e weitere(r, s) I • **a new one** ein neuer / eine neue / ein neues II 2 (29/148) • **my old ones** meine alten II 2 (29)
only ['əʊnli]
1. nur, bloß I
2. the only guest der einzige Gast I

180 Dictionary (English – German)

open ['əʊpən]
1. öffnen, aufmachen I
2. sich öffnen I
open ['əʊpən] offen, geöffnet II 2 (38)
°**opening hours** ['əʊpnɪŋ‿ˌaʊəz] Öffnungszeiten
opposite ['ɒpəzɪt] gegenüber (von) II 6 (95)
opposite ['ɒpəzɪt] Gegenteil I
or [ɔː] oder I • °**either … or …** ['aɪðə ɔː, 'iːðə ɔː] entweder … oder
orange ['ɒrɪndʒ] orange(farben) I
orange ['ɒrɪndʒ] Orange, Apfelsine I • **orange juice** ['ɒrɪndʒ dʒuːs] Orangensaft I
°**order** ['ɔːdə] Reihenfolge • °**in the right order** in der richtigen Reihenfolge • °**word order** Wortstellung
organ ['ɔːgən] Orgel II 6 (97)
°**organization** [ˌɔːgənaɪ'zeɪʃn] Organisation
other ['ʌðə] andere(r, s) I • **the others** die anderen I • **the other way round** anders herum II 6 (104)
°**Otherworld** ['ʌðəwɜːld]: **the Otherworld** etwa: das Reich der Elfen und Feen
Ouch! [aʊtʃ] Autsch! I
our ['aʊə] unser, unsere I
ours ['aʊəz] unserer, unsere, unseres II 2 (28/147)
▶ S.147 Possessive pronouns
out [aʊt] heraus, hinaus; draußen II 1 (22/146) • **be out** weg sein, nicht da sein I • **out of …** aus … (heraus/hinaus) I
▶ S.146 out
outfit ['aʊtfɪt] Outfit (Kleidung; Ausrüstung) II 2 (38)
outside [ˌaʊt'saɪd]
1. draußen I
2. nach draußen II 1 (14)
3. **outside his room** vor seinem Zimmer; außerhalb seines Zimmers I
over ['əʊvə]
1. über, oberhalb von I • **over there** da drüben, dort drüben I **over to …** hinüber zu/nach … II 2 (38)
2. über, mehr als II 4 (65)
3. **be over** vorbei sein, zu Ende sein I
°**owl** [aʊl] Eule
own [əʊn]: **our own pool** unser eigenes Schwimmbad II Welc (7)
°**owner** ['əʊnə] Besitzer/in

P

pack [pæk] packen, einpacken II 3 (54)
packet ['pækɪt] Päckchen, Packung, Schachtel I • **a packet of mints** ein Päckchen/eine Packung Pfefferminzbonbons I
page [peɪdʒ] (Buch-, Heft-)Seite I **What page are we on?** Auf welcher Seite sind wir? I
paid [peɪd] siehe **pay**
paint [peɪnt] malen, anmalen I
painter ['peɪntə] Maler/in II 3 (53)
pair [peə]: **a pair (of)** ein Paar II 2 (27)
°**pants** (pl) [pænts] (AE) Hose
paper ['peɪpə]
1. Papier I
2. Zeitung II 2 (29)
°**parade** [pə'reɪd] Parade, Umzug
paragraph ['pærəgrɑːf] Absatz (in einem Text) II 4 (60)
paramedic [ˌpærə'medɪk] Sanitäter/in II 4 (62)
parcel ['pɑːsl] Paket I
parents ['peərənts] Eltern I
park [pɑːk] Park I
°**parliament** ['pɑːləmənt] Parlament
parrot ['pærət] Papagei I
part [pɑːt] Teil I
partner ['pɑːtnə] Partner/in I
party ['pɑːti] Party I • **have a party** eine Party feiern/veranstalten II 1 (14)
pass [pɑːs] (herüber)reichen, weitergeben I • **pass round** herumgeben I • °**pass sth. on** etwas weitergeben
past [pɑːst] Vergangenheit II 4 (65)
past [pɑːst] vorbei (an), vorüber (an) II 1 (22) • **half past 11** halb zwölf (11.30 / 23.30) I • **quarter past 11** Viertel nach 11 (11.15 / 23.15) I
path [pɑːθ] Pfad, Weg II 6 (94)
pay (for sth.) [peɪ], **paid, paid** etwas bezahlen II 6 (104)
PE [ˌpiː‿'iː], **Physical Education** [ˌfɪzɪkəl‿edʒu'keɪʃn] Sportunterricht, Turnen I
pen [pen] Kugelschreiber, Füller I
pence (p) (pl) [pens] Pence (Plural von „penny") I
pencil ['pensl] Bleistift I • **pencil case** ['pensl keɪs] Federmäppchen I • **pencil sharpener** ['pensl ʃɑːpnə] Bleistiftanspitzer I
penny ['peni] kleinste britische Münze I
people ['piːpl] Menschen, Leute I
°**perfect** ['pɜːfɪkt] perfekt
°**perhaps** [pə'hæps] vielleicht
person ['pɜːsn] Person II 1 (20)

pet [pet] Haustier I • **pet shop** Tierhandlung I
phone [fəʊn] Telefon I • **on the phone** am Telefon I • **phone call** Anruf, Telefongespräch I • **phone number** Telefonnummer I
phone [fəʊn] anrufen II 4 (60/155)
photo ['fəʊtəʊ] Foto I • **in the photo** auf dem Foto I • **take photos** Fotos machen, fotografieren I
photographer [fə'tɒgrəfə] Fotograf/in II 5 (77)
phrase [freɪz] Ausdruck, (Rede-)Wendung I
piano [pi'ænəʊ] Klavier, Piano I **play the piano** Klavier spielen I
pick sth. up [ˌpɪk‿'ʌp] etwas hochheben, aufheben II 3 (45)
picnic ['pɪknɪk] Picknick II 4 (60)
picture ['pɪktʃə] Bild I • **in the picture** auf dem Bild I
pie [paɪ] Obstkuchen; Pastete II 4 (61)
piece [piːs]: **a piece of** ein Stück I • **a piece of paper** ein Stück Papier I • °**in one piece** heil, ganz
pink [pɪŋk] pink(farben), rosa I
°**piranha** [pɪ'rɑːnə] Piranha
pirate ['paɪrət] Pirat, Piratin I
pitch [pɪtʃ]: **football/hockey pitch** Fußball-/Hockeyplatz, -feld II 4 (60)
pizza ['piːtsə] Pizza I
place [pleɪs] Ort, Platz I • °**take place** stattfinden
°**placemat** ['pleɪsmæt] Set, Platzdeckchen
plan [plæn] Plan I
plan (-nn-) [plæn] planen II 4 (60/155)
plane [pleɪn] Flugzeug II Welc (6) **on the plane** im Flugzeug Welc (6/142)
planet ['plænɪt] Planet II 6 (97)
°**plasticine** ['plæstəsiːn] Knetmasse
plate [pleɪt] Teller I • **a plate of chips** ein Teller Pommes frites I
play [pleɪ] spielen I • **play a trick on sb.** jm. einen Streich spielen II 6 (96) • **play football** Fußball spielen I • **play the guitar** Gitarre spielen I • **play the piano** Klavier spielen I
play [pleɪ] Theaterstück I
player ['pleɪə] Spieler/in I
please [pliːz] bitte (in Fragen und Aufforderungen) I
pm [ˌpiː‿'em]: **7 pm** 7 Uhr abends/ 19 Uhr I
pocket ['pɒkɪt] Tasche (an Kleidungsstück) II 2 (26/146) • **pocket money** Taschengeld II 2 (26)

Dictionary (English – German) 181

poem [ˈpəʊɪm] Gedicht I
°**pohutukawa tree** [pəˌhuːtəˈkaːwə] Eisenholzbaum
point [pɔɪnt] Punkt II 2 (35) • **point of view** [ˌpɔɪnt_əv ˈvjuː] Standpunkt II 2 (39) • **from my point of view** aus meiner Sicht; von meinem Standpunkt aus gesehen II 2 (39/150)
point (at/to sth.) [pɔɪnt] zeigen, deuten (auf etwas) II 2 (29)
police *(pl)* [pəˈliːs] Polizei I
police station [pəˈliːs steɪʃn] Polizeiwache, Polizeirevier II 6 (95)
policeman [pəˈliːsmən] Polizist II 4 (70)
policewoman [pəˈliːswʊmən] Polizistin II 4 (70)
poltergeist [ˈpəʊltəɡaɪst] Poltergeist I
°**pond** [pɒnd] Teich I
poor [pɔː, pʊə] arm I • **poor Sophie** (die) arme Sophie I
popcorn [ˈpɒpkɔːn] Popcorn II 4 (67)
°**popular** [ˈpɒpjələ] beliebt, populär
possible [ˈpɒsəbl] möglich II 5 (78)
post office [ˈpəʊst_ɒfɪs] Postamt II 6 (95)
postcard [ˈpəʊstkɑːd] Postkarte II Welc (6)
poster [ˈpəʊstə] Poster I
potato [pəˈteɪtəʊ], *pl* **potatoes** Kartoffel I
pound (£) [paʊnd] Pfund *(britische Währung)* I
°**powder** [ˈpaʊdə] Pulver I
practice [ˈpræktɪs] *hier:* Übungsteil I
practise [ˈpræktɪs] üben; trainieren I
prepare [prɪˈpeə] vorbereiten; sich vorbereiten II 2 (39) • **prepare for** sich vorbereiten auf II 2 (39/150)
present [ˈpreznt]
1. Gegenwart I
2. Geschenk I
present sth. (to sb.) [prɪˈzent] (jm.) etwas präsentieren, vorstellen I
presentation [ˌprezn̩ˈteɪʃn] Präsentation, Vorstellung I
presenter [prɪˈzentə] Moderator/in II 2 (38)
pretty [ˈprɪti] hübsch I
pretty cool/good/... [ˈprɪti] ziemlich cool/gut/... II 5 (78)
price [praɪs] (Kauf-)Preis I
print sth. out [ˌprɪnt_ˈaʊt] etwas ausdrucken II 4 (63)
▶ S.157 Computer words and phrases
°**prisoner** [ˈprɪznə] Gefangene(r) I
prize [praɪz] Preis, Gewinn I

probably [ˈprɒbəbli] wahrscheinlich II 3 (44)
problem [ˈprɒbləm] Problem II 2 (29)
programme [ˈprəʊɡræm] Programm I
project (about, on) [ˈprɒdʒekt] Projekt (über, zu) I
promise [ˈprɒmɪs] versprechen II 3 (54)
°**pronounce** [prəˈnaʊns] aussprechen
pronunciation [prəˌnʌnsiˈeɪʃn] Aussprache I
proof *(no pl)* [pruːf] Beweis(e) II 5 (86)
°**Protestant** [ˈprɒtɪstənt] protestantisch; Protestant/in
proud (of sb./sth.) [praʊd] stolz (auf jn./etwas) II 5 (77)
pub [pʌb] Kneipe, Lokal II 5 (74)
pull [pʊl] ziehen I
pullover [ˈpʊləʊvə] Pullover II 2 (27)
purple [ˈpɜːpl] violett; lila I
purse [pɜːs] Geldbörse II 5 (86)
push [pʊʃ] drücken, schieben, stoßen I
put (-tt-) [pʊt], **put, put** legen, stellen, *(etwas wohin)* tun I • **put sth. on** etwas anziehen *(Kleidung)* II 2 (31) • °**put on a show** eine Show aufführen, zeigen • °**Put up your hand.** Heb deine Hand. / Hebt eure Hand.
puzzled [ˈpʌzld] verwirrt II 2 (39)
pyjamas *(pl)* [pəˈdʒɑːməz] Schlafanzug II 4 (59)

Q

quarter [ˈkwɔːtə]: **quarter past 11** Viertel nach 11 (11.15 / 23.15) I **quarter to 12** Viertel vor 12 (11.45 / 23.45) I
question [ˈkwestʃn] Frage I • **ask questions** Fragen stellen
°**question word** [ˈkwestʃn wɜːd] Fragewort
quick [kwɪk] schnell I
quiet [ˈkwaɪət] leise, still, ruhig I
quite quickly/well/... [kwaɪt] ziemlich schnell/gut/... II 3 (47)
quiz [kwɪz], *pl* **quizzes** [ˈkwɪzɪz] Quiz, Ratespiel I

R

rabbit [ˈræbɪt] Kaninchen I
radio [ˈreɪdiəʊ] Radio I • **on the radio** im Radio I

°**raft** [rɑːft] Floß
railway [ˈreɪlweɪ] Eisenbahn II 4 (60)
rain [reɪn] Regen II Welc (6/141)
rain [reɪn] regnen II Welc (6/141)
rainy [ˈreɪni] regnerisch II Welc (6/141)
ran [ræn] *siehe* **run**
rang [ræŋ] *siehe* **ring**
rap [ræp] Rap *(rhythmischer Sprechgesang)* I
°**rather** [ˈrɑːðə]: **I'd rather be ...** Ich wäre lieber ...
RE [ˌɑːr_ˈiː], **Religious Education** [rɪˌlɪdʒəs_edʒʊˈkeɪʃn] Religion, Religionsunterricht I
read [riːd], **read, read** lesen I °**read on** weiterlesen • °**read out** vorlesen • °**Read out loud.** Lies laut vor. • °**Read the poem to a partner.** Lies das Gedicht einem Partner/einer Partnerin vor.
read [red] *siehe* **read**
reader [ˈriːdə] Leser/in II 2 (26)
ready [ˈredi] bereit, fertig I • **get ready (for)** sich fertig machen (für), sich vorbereiten (auf) I • **get things ready** Dinge fertig machen, vorbereiten I
real [rɪəl] echt, wirklich I
really [ˈrɪəli] wirklich I
reason [ˈriːzn] Grund, Begründung I • **for lots of reasons** aus vielen Gründen I
°**record** [rɪˈkɔːd] aufzeichnen, aufnehmen *(auf Band)*
recycled [ˌriːˈsaɪkld] wiederverwertet, wiederverwendet, recycelt II 2 (31)
recycling [ˌriːˈsaɪklɪŋ] Wiederverwertung, Recycling II 2 (31)
red [red] rot I
rehearsal [rɪˈhɜːsl] Probe *(am Theater)* I
rehearse [rɪˈhɜːs] proben *(am Theater)* I
relax [rɪˈlæks] (sich) entspannen, sich ausruhen II 6 (92)
remember sth. [rɪˈmembə]
1. sich an etwas erinnern I
2. sich etwas merken I
°**Remember ...** Denk dran, ...
°**remind** [rɪˈmaɪnd]: **That reminds me ...** Dabei fällt mir ein ...
°**rent** [rent] leihen, mieten
report (on) [rɪˈpɔːt] Bericht, Reportage (über) I
report (to sb.) [rɪˈpɔːt] (jm.) berichten II 4 (60/155)
°**rescue** [ˈreskjuː] Rettung(saktion)
rest [rest] Rest II 5 (88)
restaurant [ˈrestrɒnt] Restaurant II 6 (95)

result [rɪ'zʌlt] Ergebnis, Resultat I
°**retell** [ˌriː'tel]**, retold, retold** nacherzählen
°**retold** [ˌriː'təʊld] *siehe* **retell**
return ticket [rɪ'tɜːn ˌtɪkɪt] Rückfahrkarte II 3 (55)
revision [rɪ'vɪʒn] Wiederholung *(des Lernstoffs)* I
rhino ['raɪnəʊ] Nashorn II 3 (52/153)
°**rhyme** [raɪm] (sich) reimen
rich [rɪtʃ] reich II 5 (75)
ridden ['rɪdn] *siehe* **ride**
ride [raɪd]**, rode, ridden** reiten I
go riding ['raɪdɪŋ] reiten gehen I
ride a bike Rad fahren I
ride [raɪd]**: (bike) ride** (Rad-)Fahrt, (Rad-)Tour II 4 (60/155)
right [raɪt] richtig I • **all right** [ɔːl 'raɪt] gut, in Ordnung II 1 (23)
be right Recht haben I • **That's right.** Das ist richtig. / Das stimmt. I • **You need a school bag, right?** Du brauchst eine Schultasche, stimmt's? / nicht wahr? I
right [raɪt] rechte(r, s) II 1 (11/143)
look right nach rechts schauen II 1 (11/143) • **on the right** rechts, auf der rechten Seite I • **turn right** (nach) rechts abbiegen II 6 (95)
▶ S.143 left – right
right [raɪt]**: right after lunch** direkt/ gleich nach dem Mittagessen I
right now jetzt sofort; jetzt gerade I • **right behind you** direkt/genau hinter dir II 1 (14)
ring [rɪŋ] Ring II 5 (86)
ring [rɪŋ]**, rang, rung** klingeln, läuten II 4 (70)
river ['rɪvə] Fluss II 4 (58)
road [rəʊd] Straße I • **Park Road** [ˌpɑːk 'rəʊd] Parkstraße I
°**rock** [rɒk] Fels, Felsen
rode [rəʊd] *siehe* **ride**
role play ['rəʊl pleɪ] Rollenspiel II 1 (15)
roll [rəʊl] Brötchen I
Roman ['rəʊmən] römisch; Römer, Römerin II 6 (92)
room [ruːm, rʊm] Raum, Zimmer I
round [raʊnd] rund II 6 (92)
round [raʊnd] um ... (herum); in ... umher II Welc (6) • **the other way round** anders herum II 6 (104)
°**route** [ruːt] Route, Weg
°**RSPCA (Royal Society for the Prevention of Cruelty to Animals)** [ˌrɔɪəl sə'saɪəti fə ðə prɪ'venʃn əv 'kruːəlti tuˈ_ˈænɪmlz] *britischer Tierschutzverein*
rubber ['rʌbə] Radiergummi I

rubbish ['rʌbɪʃ] (Haus-)Müll, Abfall II 3 (44) • °**rubbish collection** ['rʌbɪʃ kəˌlekʃn] Müllabfuhr
rude [ruːd] unhöflich, unverschämt II 1 (13)
ruler ['ruːlə] Lineal I
run [rʌn] (Wett-)Lauf II 3 (47)
run (-nn-) [rʌn]**, ran, run** laufen, rennen I
rung [rʌŋ] *siehe* **ring**
runner ['rʌnə] Läufer/in II 3 (53)

S

sad [sæd] traurig II 3 (54)
safe (from) [seɪf] sicher, in Sicherheit (vor) II 3 (46)
said [sed] *siehe* **say**
sail [seɪl] segeln II 5 (79)
°**sail** [seɪl] Segel
°**sailor** ['seɪlə] Seemann, Matrose
salad ['sæləd] Salat *(als Gericht oder Beilage)* I
same [seɪm]**: the same ...** der-/die-/ dasselbe ...; dieselben ... I • **be/ look the same** gleich sein/aussehen I
sandal ['sændl] Sandale II 6 (92)
°**sandbank** ['sændbæŋk] Sandbank
sandwich ['sænwɪtʃ, 'sænwɪdʒ] Sandwich, *(zusammengeklapptes)* belegtes Brot I • °**sandwich box** Brotdose
sang [sæŋ] *siehe* **sing**
sat [sæt] *siehe* **sit**
Saturday ['sætədeɪ, 'sætədi] Samstag, Sonnabend I
sauna ['sɔːnə] Sauna II 6 (92)
have a sauna in die Sauna gehen II 6 (92)
sausage ['sɒsɪdʒ] (Brat-, Bock-) Würstchen, Wurst I
save [seɪv]
1. retten II 1 (22)
2. sparen II 2 (26)
°**saved** [seɪvd] gerettet
saw [sɔː] *siehe* **see**
°**Saxon** ['sæksn]**: the Saxons** die Sachsen
say [seɪ]**, said, said** sagen I • **It says here: ...** Hier steht: ... / Es heißt hier: ... II 4 (63) • **say goodbye** sich verabschieden I • **Say hi to Dilip for me.** Grüß Dilip von mir. I
say sorry sich entschuldigen II 5 (88)
▶ S.157 The text says ...
scan a text (-nn-) [skæn] einen Text schnell nach bestimmten Wörtern/ Informationen absuchen II 3 (47)

scared [skeəd] verängstigt II 4 (70)
be scared (of) Angst haben (vor) I
scary ['skeəri] unheimlich; gruselig I
scene [siːn] Szene I
school [skuːl] Schule I • **at school** in der Schule I • **school bag** Schultasche I • **school subject** Schulfach I
science ['saɪəns] Naturwissenschaft I
°**screech owl** ['skriːtʃˌaʊl] Kreischeule
sea [siː] Meer, *(die)* See I
search (for) [sɜːtʃ] suchen (nach) II 3 (55)
second ['sekənd] zweite(r, s) I
°**second-hand** gebraucht; aus zweiter Hand
°**second** ['sekənd] Sekunde
°**section** ['sekʃn] Abschnitt
°**secure** [sɪ'kjʊə] sichern, absichern
see [siː]**, saw, seen**
1. sehen I
2. see sb. jn. besuchen, jn. aufsuchen II 1 (23)
See? Siehst du? I • **See you.** Tschüs. / Bis bald. I
°**seem (to be/do)** [siːm] (zu sein/ tun) scheinen
seen [siːn] *siehe* **see**
sell [sel]**, sold, sold** verkaufen I
send [send]**, sent, sent** senden, schicken II 4 (63/157)
▶ S.157 Computer words and phrases
sent [sent] *siehe* **send**
sentence ['sentəns] Satz I
September [sep'tembə] September I
series, *pl* **series** ['sɪəriːz] (Sende-) Reihe, Serie II 3 (42)
°**servant** ['sɜːvənt] Diener/in
°**service** ['sɜːvɪs] Dienst, Service
set a trap (for sb.) (-tt-) [set]**, set, set** (jm.) eine Falle stellen II 5 (86)
share (with) [ʃeə] sich *etwas* teilen (mit) I
°**shave: a close shave** [ˌkləʊs 'ʃeɪv] *etwa:* Das ging beinahe ins Auge. *(wörtlich:* eine glatte Rasur)
she [ʃiː] sie I
sheep, *pl* **sheep** [ʃiːp] Schaf II 4 (58)
shelf [ʃelf]**,** *pl* **shelves** [ʃelvz] Regal(brett) I
°**shelter (from)** ['ʃeltə] Schutz (vor)
shine [ʃaɪn]**, shone, shone** scheinen *(Sonne)* II Welc (6)
ship [ʃɪp] Schiff I
shirt [ʃɜːt] Hemd I
shiver ['ʃɪvə] zittern II 6 (104)
shoe [ʃuː] Schuh I
shone [ʃɒn] *siehe* **shine**

Dictionary (English – German)   **183**

shop [ʃɒp] Laden, Geschäft I
shop assistant [ˈʃɒp_ə‚sɪstənt] Verkäufer/in I • **shop window** Schaufenster II 4 (67)
shop (-pp-) [ʃɒp] einkaufen (gehen) I
shopping [ˈʃɒpɪŋ] (das) Einkaufen I • **go shopping** einkaufen gehen I • **shopping list** Einkaufsliste I
°**shore** [ʃɔː] Ufer, Strand
short [ʃɔːt] kurz I
shorts *(pl)* [ʃɔːts] Shorts, kurze Hose I
▶ S.147 Plural words
shoulder [ˈʃəʊldə] Schulter I
shout [ʃaʊt] schreien, rufen I • **shout at sb.** jn. anschreien I
show [ʃəʊ] Show, Vorstellung I • °**put on a show** eine Show aufführen, zeigen
show [ʃəʊ], **showed, shown** zeigen I
shower [ˈʃaʊə] Dusche I • **have a shower** (sich) duschen I
shown [ʃəʊn] *siehe* **show**
shut up [ˌʃʌt_ˈʌp], **shut, shut** den Mund halten II 5 (86)
shy [ʃaɪ] schüchtern, scheu II 3 (55)
side [saɪd] Seite II 4 (70)
°**signal** [ˈsɪgnəl] Signal, Zeichen
silent letter [ˌsaɪlənt ˈletə] „stummer" Buchstabe *(nicht gesprochener Buchstabe)* II 4 (69)
°**silver** [ˈsɪlvə] Silber
sing [sɪŋ], **sang, sung** singen I
singer [ˈsɪŋə] Sänger/in II 3 (53)
single [ˈsɪŋgl] ledig, alleinstehend I
sink [sɪŋk] Spüle, Spülbecken I
sister [ˈsɪstə] Schwester I
sit (-tt-) [sɪt], **sat, sat** sitzen; sich setzen I • **sit down** sich hinsetzen II 3 (44) • **Sit with me.** Setz dich zu mir. / Setzt euch zu mir. I
size [saɪz] Größe I
skate [skeɪt] Inliner/Skateboard fahren I; Schlittschuh laufen, eislaufen II 5 (74)
skateboard [ˈskeɪtbɔːd] Skateboard I
skates *(pl)* [skeɪts] Inliner I
sketch [sketʃ] Sketch I
skills file [ˈskɪlz faɪl] *Anhang mit Lern- und Arbeitstechniken* I
skirt [skɜːt] Rock II 2 (27)
sky [skaɪ] Himmel II Welc (7) • **in the sky** am Himmel II Welc (7/142)
slave [sleɪv] Sklave, Sklavin II 5 (75)
sleep [sliːp], **slept, slept** schlafen I
°**sleep** [sliːp] Schlaf
°**sleeve** [sliːv] Ärmel
slept [slept] *siehe* **sleep**

slow [sləʊ] langsam II 1 (12/144)
°**slug** [slʌg] Nacktschnecke
small [smɔːl] klein II 2 (29)
smell [smel] riechen II 4 (60)
smell [smel] Geruch II 4 (60/155)
smile [smaɪl] lächeln I • **smile at sb.** jn. anlächeln II 3 (55)
smile [smaɪl] Lächeln II 4 (60/155)
smoke [sməʊk] rauchen II 5 (79)
smoke [sməʊk] Rauch II 5 (79)
°**smoothie** [ˈsmuːði] *dickflüssiger Fruchtshake mit Milch, Joghurt oder Eiscreme*
snack [snæk] Snack, Imbiss II 5 (74)
snake [sneɪk] Schlange I
snow [snəʊ] Schnee II Welc (6/141)
so [səʊ]
1. also; deshalb, daher I • **So?** Und? / Na und? II 5 (86)
2. **so sweet** so süß I • **so far** bis jetzt, bis hierher I
3. **I think so.** Ich glaube (ja). I • **I don't think so.** Das finde/glaube ich nicht. I • **Do you really think so?** Meinst du wirklich? / Glaubst du das wirklich? II 1 (14)
soap [səʊp] Seife I
sock [sɒk] Socke, Strumpf I
sofa [ˈsəʊfə] Sofa I
software [ˈsɒftweə] Software II 4 (63)
sold [səʊld] *siehe* **sell**
some [səm, sʌm] einige, ein paar I • **some cheese/juice/money** etwas Käse/Saft/Geld I
somebody [ˈsʌmbədi] jemand I **Find/Ask somebody who ...** Finde/Frage jemanden, der ... II 1 (20)
▶ S.160 somebody – anybody
something [ˈsʌmθɪŋ] etwas I **something to eat** etwas zu essen I
▶ S.160 something – anything
sometimes [ˈsʌmtaɪmz] manchmal I
somewhere [ˈsʌmweə] irgendwo(hin) II 5 (76/160)
▶ S.160 somewhere – anywhere
son [sʌn] Sohn I
song [sɒŋ] Lied, Song I
soon [suːn] bald I • **as soon as** sobald, sowie II 3 (45)
sore [sɔː]: **be sore** wund sein, wehtun II 4 (62) • **have a sore throat** Halsschmerzen haben II 4 (62)
▶ S.157 What's wrong with you?
sorry [ˈsɒri]: **(I'm) sorry.** Entschuldigung. / Tut mir leid. I • **Sorry, I'm late.** Entschuldigung, dass ich zu spät bin/komme. I • **Sorry?** Wie bitte? I • **say sorry** sich entschuldigen II 5 (88)

°**sort (of)** [sɔːt] Art, Sorte
sound [saʊnd] klingen, sich *(gut usw.)* anhören I
sound [saʊnd] Laut; Klang I
soup [suːp] Suppe II 4 (60)
°**southeast (of)** [ˌsaʊθˈiːst] südöstlich (von)
°**souvenir** [ˌsuːvəˈnɪə] Andenken, Souvenir
space [speɪs]: **Move back one space.** Geh ein Feld zurück. II 5 (74) **Move on one space.** Geh ein Feld vor. II 5 (74)
spaghetti [spəˈgeti] Spaghetti II Welc (9)
speak (to) [spiːk], **spoke, spoken** sprechen (mit), reden (mit) II Welc (9)
°**special** [ˈspeʃl] besondere(r, s)
°**speech bubble** [ˈspiːtʃ bʌbl] Sprechblase
spell [spel] buchstabieren I
°**spelling** [ˈspelɪŋ] (Recht-) Schreibung, Schreibweise I
spend [spend], **spent, spent**: **spend money (on)** Geld ausgeben (für) II 2 (26) • **spend time (on)** Zeit verbringen (mit) II 2 (26)
spent [spent] *siehe* **spend**
°**spider** [ˈspaɪdə] Spinne
°**splash** [splæʃ] Klatschen, Platschen
spoke [spəʊk] *siehe* **speak**
spoken [ˈspəʊkən] *siehe* **speak**
sport [spɔːt] Sport; Sportart I **do sport** Sport treiben I
sports gear *(no pl)* [ˈspɔːts gɪə] Sportausrüstung, Sportsachen II 2 (27)
°**Spot the mistakes. (-tt-)** [spɒt] Entdecke/Finde die Fehler.
spring [sprɪŋ]
1. Frühling I
°2. Quelle
spy [spaɪ] Spion/in I
square [skweə] Platz *(in der Stadt)* II 6 (96)
squirrel [ˈskwɪrəl] Eichhörnchen II 3 (43)
stage [steɪdʒ] Bühne I
stairs *(pl)* [steəz] Treppe; Treppenstufen I
stamp [stæmp] Briefmarke I
stand [stænd], **stood, stood** stehen; sich (hin)stellen II 2 (38) • **stand up** aufstehen II 3 (44/151)
star [stɑː]
1. Stern II 6 (97)
2. (Film-, Pop-)Star I
start [stɑːt] starten, anfangen, beginnen (mit) I
start [stɑːt] Start, Anfang, Beginn II Welc (8)

184 Dictionary (English – German)

°**statement** ['steɪtmənt] Aussage

station ['steɪʃn] Bahnhof Ⅰ • **at the station** am Bahnhof Ⅰ

statue ['stætʃuː] Statue Ⅱ5 (77)
°**Statue of Liberty** [ˌstætʃuː_əv 'lɪbəti] Freiheitsstatue

stay [steɪ] bleiben; wohnen, übernachten Ⅱ Welc (6)

steal [stiːl], **stole, stolen** stehlen Ⅱ5 (79)

step [step]
1. Schritt Ⅰ
°**2.** Stufe

still [stɪl] (immer) noch Ⅰ

stole [stəʊl] *siehe* **steal**

stolen ['stəʊlən] *siehe* **steal**

stomach ['stʌmək] Magen Ⅱ4 (62/157) • **stomach ache** Magenschmerzen, Bauchweh Ⅱ4 (62/157)
▶ S.157 What's wrong with you?

stone [stəʊn] Stein Ⅱ6 (93)

stood [stʊd] *siehe* **stand**

stop (-pp-) [stɒp]
1. aufhören Ⅰ
2. anhalten Ⅰ
Stop that! Hör auf damit! / Lass das! Ⅰ

storm [stɔːm] Sturm; Gewitter Ⅱ Welc (6/141)

stormy ['stɔːmi] stürmisch Ⅱ Welc (6/141)

story ['stɔːri] Geschichte, Erzählung Ⅰ

straight on [streɪt_'ɒn] geradeaus weiter Ⅱ6 (95)

strawberry ['strɔːbəri] Erdbeere Ⅱ5 (78)

street [striːt] Straße Ⅰ • **at 7 Hamilton Street** in der Hamiltonstraße 7 Ⅰ

strong [strɒŋ] stark Ⅱ4 (70)

structure ['strʌktʃə] strukturieren, aufbauen Ⅱ5 (79)

student ['stjuːdənt] Schüler/in; Student/in Ⅰ

studio ['stjuːdiəʊ] Studio Ⅰ

°**study** ['stʌdi] studieren

study skills *(pl)* ['stʌdi skɪlz] Lern- und Arbeitstechniken Ⅰ

stuff [stʌf] Zeug, Kram Ⅱ2 (30)

subject ['sʌbdʒɪkt] Schulfach Ⅰ

subway ['sʌbweɪ]: **the subway** *(AE)* die U-Bahn Ⅱ1 (12)

suddenly ['sʌdnli] plötzlich, auf einmal Ⅰ

sugar ['ʃʊgə] Zucker Ⅱ5 (75)

suitcase ['suːtkeɪs] Koffer Ⅱ3 (54)

°**summarize** ['sʌməraɪz] zusammenfassen

summer ['sʌmə] Sommer Ⅰ

°**summertime** ['sʌmətaɪm] Sommer Ⅰ

sun [sʌn] Sonne Ⅱ Welc (6/141)

Sunday ['sʌndeɪ, 'sʌndi] Sonntag Ⅰ

sung [sʌŋ] *siehe* **sing**

sunglasses *(pl)* ['sʌnglɑːsɪz] (eine) Sonnenbrille Ⅰ
▶ S.147 Plural words

sunny ['sʌni] sonnig Ⅱ Welc (6/141)

supermarket ['suːpəmɑːkɪt] Supermarkt Ⅱ6 (95)

suppose [sə'pəʊz] annehmen, vermuten Ⅱ5 (87)

sure [ʃʊə, ʃɔː] sicher Ⅰ

surf the internet [sɜːf] im Internet surfen Ⅱ4 (63/157)
▶ S.157 Computer words and phrases

surfboard ['sɜːfbɔːd] Surfbrett Ⅱ1 (23)

surfing ['sɜːfɪŋ]: **go surfing** wellenreiten gehen, surfen gehen Ⅱ1 (23)

surprise [sə'praɪz] Überraschung Ⅱ2 (30)

°**surprised** [sə'praɪzd] überrascht

survey (on) ['sɜːveɪ] Umfrage, Untersuchung (über) Ⅱ2 (26)

survival [sə'vaɪvl] Überleben Ⅱ3 (42/150)

survive [sə'vaɪv] überleben Ⅱ3 (42)

°**swallow** ['swɒləʊ] verschlucken, hinunterschlucken

swam [swæm] *siehe* **swim**

°**swap (-pp-)** [swɒp] tauschen

sweatshirt ['swetʃɜːt] Sweatshirt Ⅰ

sweet [swiːt] süß Ⅰ

sweetheart ['swiːthɑːt] Liebling, Schatz Ⅱ3 (54)

sweets *(pl)* [swiːts] Süßigkeiten Ⅰ

swim (-mm-) [swɪm], **swam, swum** schwimmen Ⅰ • **go swimming** schwimmen gehen Ⅰ

swimmer ['swɪmə] Schwimmer/in Ⅱ1 (22) / Ⅱ3 (53)

swimming pool ['swɪmɪŋ puːl] Schwimmbad, Schwimmbecken Ⅰ

swum [swʌm] *siehe* **swim**

syllable ['sɪləbl] Silbe Ⅰ

°**symbol** ['sɪmbl] Symbol

T

table ['teɪbl] Tisch Ⅰ • **table tennis** ['teɪbl tenɪs] Tischtennis Ⅰ

take [teɪk], **took, taken**
1. nehmen Ⅰ
2. (weg-, hin)bringen Ⅰ
°**take control** die Kontrolle/Gewalt übernehmen • **take notes** sich Notizen machen Ⅰ • **take photos** Fotos machen, fotografieren Ⅰ • °**take place** stattfinden Ⅰ • **take sth. off** etwas ausziehen (Kleidung) Ⅱ2 (31) • **take 10c off** 10 Cent abziehen Ⅰ • °**Take turns.** Wechselt euch ab. • **I'll take it.** *(beim Einkaufen)* Ich nehme es (ihn, sie). / Ich werde es (ihn, sie) nehmen. Ⅰ

taken ['teɪkən] *siehe* **take**

talk [tɔːk]: **talk (about)** reden (über), sich unterhalten (über) Ⅰ • **talk (to)** reden (mit), sich unterhalten (mit) Ⅰ

°**talk** [tɔːk] Vortrag, Referat, Rede

°**tall** [tɔːl] groß (gewachsen)

°**task** [tɑːsk] Aufgabe

taught [tɔːt] *siehe* **teach**

tea [tiː] Tee; *(auch:)* leichte Nachmittags- oder Abendmahlzeit Ⅰ

teach [tiːtʃ], **taught, taught** unterrichten, lehren Ⅰ

teacher ['tiːtʃə] Lehrer/in Ⅰ

team [tiːm] Team, Mannschaft Ⅰ

teenager ['tiːneɪdʒə] Teenager, Jugendliche(r) Ⅱ1 (23)

teeth [tiːθ] *Plural von „tooth"* Ⅰ

telephone ['telɪfəʊn] Telefon Ⅰ
telephone number Telefonnummer Ⅰ

°**telescope** ['telɪskəʊp] Teleskop

television (TV) ['telɪvɪʒn] Fernsehen Ⅰ

tell (about) [tel], **told, told** erzählen (von), berichten (über) Ⅰ • **Tell me your names.** Sagt mir eure Namen. Ⅰ • **tell sb. the way** jm. den Weg beschreiben Ⅱ6 (95) **tell sb. to do sth.** jn. auffordern, etwas zu tun; jm. sagen, dass er/sie etwas tun soll Ⅱ5 (88)

temperature ['temprətʃə] Temperatur Ⅱ4 (62) • **have a temperature** Fieber haben Ⅱ4 (62)
▶ S.157 What's wrong with you?

tennis ['tenɪs] Tennis Ⅰ

°**tent** [tent] Zelt

term [tɜːm] Trimester Ⅱ6 (103)

terrible ['terəbl] schrecklich, furchtbar Ⅰ

°**territory** ['terətriː] Revier, Gebiet, Territorium

test [test] Klassenarbeit, Test, Prüfung Ⅱ2 (28)

°**test** [test] prüfen, testen

text [tekst] Text Ⅰ

than [ðæn, ðən] als Ⅱ2 (29/148)
more than ['mɔː ðən] mehr als Ⅱ2 (29) • **more than me** mehr als ich Ⅱ2 (29/148)

Thank you. ['θæŋk juː] Danke (schön). Ⅰ • **Thanks.** [θæŋks] Danke. Ⅰ • **Thanks a lot!** Vielen Dank! Ⅰ • **Thanks very much!** Danke sehr! / Vielen Dank! Ⅱ3 (45)

Dictionary (English – German) 185

that [ðət, ðæt]
1. das (dort) I
2. jene(r, s) I
°**like that** so • **That's me.** Das bin ich. I • **That's right.** Das ist richtig. / Das stimmt. I • **that's why** deshalb, darum I

that [ðət, ðæt] dass I

°**that** [ðət, ðæt]: **a spider that wriggled inside her** eine Spinne, die in ihr herumzappelte

the [ðə, ði] der, die, das; die I

theatre ['θɪətə] Theater II Welc (6)

their [ðeə] ihr, ihre (Plural) I

theirs [ðeəz] ihrer, ihre, ihrs II 2 (28/147)
▶ S.147 Possessive pronouns

them [ðəm, ðem] sie; ihnen I

then [ðen] dann, danach I

there [ðeə]
1. da, dort I
2. dahin, dorthin I
down there dort unten II 4 (70)
in there dort drinnen I • **over there** da drüben, dort drüben I • **there are** es sind (vorhanden); es gibt I • **there's** es ist (vorhanden); es gibt I • **there isn't a ...** es ist kein/e ...; es gibt kein/e ... I

thermometer [θə'mɒmɪtə] Thermometer II 4 (62)

these [ði:z] diese, die (hier) I

they [ðeɪ] sie (Plural) I

thief [θi:f], pl **thieves** [θi:vz] Dieb/in II 5 (86)

thing [θɪŋ] Ding, Sache I • **What was the best thing about ...?** Was war das Beste an ...? II 1 (12)

think [θɪŋk], **thought, thought** glauben, meinen, denken I • **I think so.** Ich glaube (ja). I • **I don't think so.** Das finde/glaube ich nicht. I • **think about 1.** nachdenken über II 4 (71/159); **2.** denken über, halten von II 4 (71/159) • **think of 1.** denken über, halten von II 4 (71/159); **2.** denken an; sich ausdenken II 4 (71/159)
▶ S.159 (to) think

third [θɜːd] dritte(r, s) I

thirsty ['θɜːsti] durstig I • **be thirsty** Durst haben, durstig sein I

this [ðɪs]
1. dies (hier) I
2. diese(r, s) I
This is Isabel. Hier spricht Isabel. / Hier ist Isabel. (am Telefon) II 6 (96)
this morning/afternoon/evening heute Morgen/Nachmittag/Abend I • **this way** hier entlang, in diese Richtung II 5 (87)

those [ðəʊz] die (da), jene (dort) I

thought [θɔːt] siehe **think**

thousand ['θaʊznd] tausend I

threw [θruː] siehe **throw**

throat [θrəʊt] Hals, Kehle II 4 (62)
have a sore throat Halsschmerzen haben II 4 (62)
▶ S.157 What's wrong with you?

through [θruː] durch II 1 (22)

throw [θrəʊ], **threw, thrown** werfen I

thrown [θrəʊn] siehe **throw**

Thursday ['θɜːzdeɪ, 'θɜːzdi] Donnerstag I

°**tick** [tɪk] Häkchen

ticket ['tɪkɪt]
1. Eintrittskarte I
2. Fahrkarte II 3 (55) • **return ticket** Rückfahrkarte II 3 (55)

°**tickle** ['tɪkl] kitzeln

tide [taɪd] Gezeiten, Ebbe und Flut II 1 (22) • **the tide is in/out** es ist Flut/Ebbe II 1 (22/146)

tidy ['taɪdi] aufräumen I

tidy ['taɪdi] ordentlich, aufgeräumt II 3 (54)

tiger ['taɪɡə] Tiger II 3 (52/153)

°**tight** [taɪt] eng

till [tɪl] bis (zeitlich) I

time [taɪm]
1. Zeit; Uhrzeit I • **What's the time?** Wie spät ist es? I • **in time** rechtzeitig II 1 (23)
2. **time(s)** Mal(e); -mal II 1 (12)

timetable ['taɪmteɪbl] Stundenplan I

tired ['taɪəd] müde I

title ['taɪtl] Titel, Überschrift I

to [tə, tu]
1. zu, nach I • **an e-mail to** eine E-Mail an I • °**from ... to ...** von ... bis ... • **to Jenny's** zu Jenny I • **to the front** nach vorn I • **I've never been to Bath.** Ich bin noch nie in Bath gewesen. II 6 (94) **write to** schreiben an I
2. **quarter to 12** Viertel vor 12 (11.45 / 23.45) I
3. **something to eat** etwas zu essen I • **try to do** versuchen, zu tun I
4. um zu I

toast [təʊst] Toast(brot) I

tobacco [tə'bækəʊ] Tabak II 5 (75)

today [tə'deɪ] heute I

toe [təʊ] Zeh I

together [tə'ɡeðə] zusammen I

toilet ['tɔɪlət] Toilette I

told [təʊld] siehe **tell**

tomato [tə'mɑːtəʊ], pl **tomatoes** Tomate II 6 (104)

tomorrow [tə'mɒrəʊ] morgen I
tomorrow's weather das Wetter von morgen II 3 (42/150)

°**tongue-twister** ['tʌŋtwɪstə] Zungenbrecher

tonight [tə'naɪt] heute Nacht, heute Abend I • **tonight's programme** das Programm von heute Abend; das heutige Abendprogramm II 3 (42/150)

too [tuː]: **from Bristol too** auch aus Bristol I • **Me too.** Ich auch. I

too much/big/... [tuː] zu viel/groß/ ... I

took [tʊk] siehe **take**

°**tool** [tuːl] Werkzeug

tooth [tuːθ], pl **teeth** [tiːθ] Zahn I

toothache ['tuːθeɪk] Zahnschmerzen II 4 (62/157)
▶ S.157 What's wrong with you?

top [tɒp]
1. Spitze, oberes Ende I • **at the top (of)** oben, am oberen Ende, an der Spitze (von) I
2. Top, Oberteil I

topic ['tɒpɪk] Thema, Themenbereich I • **topic sentence** Satz, der in das Thema eines Absatzes einführt II 4 (60)

tornado [tɔː'neɪdəʊ] Tornado, Wirbelsturm II 5 (84)

tortoise ['tɔːtəs] Schildkröte I

touch [tʌtʃ] berühren, anfassen II 6 (97)

tour (of the house) [tʊə] Rundgang, Tour (durch das Haus) I

tourist ['tʊərɪst] Tourist/in II 5 (74)
tourist information Fremdenverkehrsamt II 5 (74)

towards sb./sth. [tə'wɔːdz] auf jn./etwas zu II 3 (55)

tower ['taʊə] Turm I

town [taʊn] Stadt I

°**tradition** [trə'dɪʃn] Tradition

°**traditional** [trə'dɪʃənl] traditionell

traffic ['træfɪk] Verkehr II 4 (58)

train [treɪn] Zug I • **on the train** im Zug I

trainers (pl) ['treɪnəz] Turnschuhe II 2 (27)

°**translate (into)** [træns'leɪt] übersetzen (in)

trap [træp] Falle II 5 (86)

travel (-ll-) ['trævl] reisen II Welc (6)

tree [triː] Baum I

trick [trɪk]
1. (Zauber-)Kunststück, Trick I • **do tricks** (Zauber-)Kunststücke machen I
2. Streich II 6 (96) • **play a trick on sb.** jm. einen Streich spielen II 6 (96)

186 Dictionary (English – German)

trip [trɪp] Reise; Ausflug I • **go on a trip** einen Ausflug machen II Welc (7/142)

trouble ['trʌbl] Schwierigkeiten, Ärger II 1 (14) • **be in trouble** in Schwierigkeiten sein; Ärger kriegen II 1 (14)

trousers (pl) ['traʊzəz] Hose II 2 (27)
▶ S.147 Plural words

°**truck** [trʌk] Lastwagen, LKW

true [truː] wahr II 6 (105)

try [traɪ]
1. versuchen I
2. probieren, kosten I
try and do sth. / try to do sth. versuchen, etwas zu tun I • **try on** anprobieren (Kleidung) I

T-shirt ['tiːʃɜːt] T-Shirt I

Tuesday ['tjuːzdeɪ, 'tjuːzdi] Dienstag I

°**tuna (fish)** ['tjuːnə] Thunfisch

tunnel ['tʌnl] Tunnel II 5 (77)

turn [tɜːn]
1. sich umdrehen II 3 (55) • **turn left/right** (nach) links/rechts abbiegen II 6 (95) • °**turn over** umkippen (Boot) • **turn to sb.** sich jm. zuwenden; sich an jn. wenden II 6 (95/165)
2. **turn sth. on** etwas einschalten I **turn sth. off** etwas ausschalten II 6 (95/165)
▶ S.165 (to) turn

turn [tɜːn]: **(It's) my turn.** Ich bin dran / an der Reihe. I • **Miss a turn.** Einmal aussetzen. II 5 (74) °**Take turns.** Wechselt euch ab. **Whose turn is it?** Wer ist dran / an der Reihe? II 5 (74)

TV [tiː'viː] Fernsehen I • **on TV** im Fernsehen I • **watch TV** fernsehen I

twin [twɪn]: **twin brother** Zwillingsbruder I • **twins** (pl) Zwillinge I • **twin town** Partnerstadt I

U

uncle ['ʌŋkl] Onkel I

unconscious [ʌn'kɒnʃəs] bewusstlos II 4 (71)

under ['ʌndə] unter I

underground ['ʌndəgraʊnd]: **the underground** die U-Bahn II 1 (12)

°**underline** [ˌʌndə'laɪn] unterstreichen

understand [ˌʌndə'stænd], **understood, understood** verstehen, begreifen I

understood [ˌʌndə'stʊd] siehe **understand**

uniform ['juːnɪfɔːm] Uniform I

unit ['juːnɪt] Kapitel, Lektion I

°**university** [ˌjuːnɪ'vɜːsəti] Universität, Hochschule

up [ʌp] hinauf, herauf, nach oben I **up (the hill)** (den Hügel) hinauf II 4 (71)

°**update** [ˌʌp'deɪt] aktualisieren, auf den neuesten Stand bringen

upstairs [ˌʌp'steəz] oben; nach oben I

us [əs, ʌs] uns I

use [juːz] benutzen, verwenden I °**used** [juːzd] gebraucht

°**useful** ['juːsfəl] nützlich

usually ['juːʒuəli] meistens, gewöhnlich, normalerweise I

V

valley ['væli] Tal II 4 (58) • **valley floor** Talboden II 4 (70)

°**veggie burger** ['vedʒi ˌbɜːgə] Gemüseburger

°**verse** [vɜːs] Strophe, Vers

very ['veri] sehr I • **like/love sth. very much** etwas sehr mögen/ sehr lieben II 3 (45/151) • **Thanks very much!** Danke sehr! / Vielen Dank! II 3 (45)

view [vjuː] Aussicht, Blick II Welc (6) **point of view** Standpunkt II 2 (39) **from my point of view** aus meiner Sicht; von meinem Standpunkt aus gesehen II 2 (39/150)

village ['vɪlɪdʒ] Dorf I

virus ['vaɪrəs] Virus I

visit ['vɪzɪt] besuchen, aufsuchen II 3 (45)

visit ['vɪzɪt] Besuch II 4 (60/155)

visitor ['vɪzɪtə] Besucher/in, Gast I

vocabulary [və'kæbjələri] Vokabelverzeichnis, Wörterverzeichnis I

voice [vɔɪs] Stimme I

volleyball ['vɒlibɔːl] Volleyball I

°**volunteer** [ˌvɒlən'tɪə] Freiwillige(r)

vowel sound ['vaʊəl saʊnd] Vokallaut II 1 (18)

W

wait (for) ['weɪt fɔː] warten (auf) I **I can't wait to see …** ich kann es kaum erwarten, … zu sehen I **Wait a minute.** Warte mal! / Moment mal! II 5 (87)

waiter ['weɪtə] Kellner II 5 (78)

waitress ['weɪtrəs] Kellnerin II 5 (78/161)

walk [wɔːk] (zu Fuß) gehen I

walk [wɔːk] Spaziergang II Welc (6) **go for a walk** spazieren gehen, einen Spaziergang machen II Welc (6)

wall [wɔːl] Wand; Mauer II 6 (93)

°**Wallop!** ['wɒləp] Schepper!

want [wɒnt] (haben) wollen I **want to do** tun wollen I

wardrobe ['wɔːdrəʊb] Kleiderschrank I

°**warehouse** ['weəhaʊs] Lagerhaus, -halle

warm [wɔːm] warm II Welc (6/141)

was [wəz, wɒz]: **(I/he/she/it) was** siehe **be**

wash [wɒʃ] waschen I; (auf)wischen (Fußboden) II 4 (67) • **I wash my face.** Ich wasche mir das Gesicht. I

watch [wɒtʃ] beobachten, sich etwas ansehen; zusehen I **watch TV** fernsehen I

watch [wɒtʃ] Armbanduhr I

water ['wɔːtə] Wasser I

wave [weɪv] winken II 1 (22)

°**wave** [weɪv] Welle

way [weɪ]
1. Weg II 6 (95/165) • **ask sb. the way** jn. nach dem Weg fragen II 6 (95/165) **on the way (to)** auf dem Weg (zu/ nach) II 6 (95/165) • **tell sb. the way** jm. den Weg beschreiben II 6 (95)
2. Richtung II 5 (87) • **the other way round** anders herum II 6 (104) **the wrong way** in die falsche Richtung II 5 (87) • **this way** hier entlang, in diese Richtung II 5 (87) **which way?** in welche Richtung? / wohin? II 6 (95/165)
3. **No way!** Auf keinen Fall! / Kommt nicht in Frage! II 1 (14)
▶ S.165 way

we [wiː] wir I

weak [wiːk] schwach II 4 (70/158)

wear [weə], **wore, worn** tragen, anhaben (Kleidung) I

weather ['weðə] Wetter II Welc (6/141)

webcam ['webkæm] Webcam, Internetkamera II 4 (63)

website ['websaɪt] Website II 3 (45)

Wednesday ['wenzdeɪ, 'wenzdi] Mittwoch I

week [wiːk] Woche I • **days of the week** Wochentage I

weekend [ˌwiːk'end] Wochenende I • **at the weekend** am Wochenende I

Dictionary (English – German) 187

welcome ['welkəm]
1. Welcome (to Bristol). Willkommen (in Bristol). I
2. You're welcome. Gern geschehen. / Nichts zu danken. I
welcome sb. (to) ['welkəm] jn. begrüßen, willkommen heißen (in) I
They welcome you to ... Sie heißen dich in ... willkommen I
well [wel]
1. gut II 3 (47) • °**go well** gut (ver)laufen • **You did well.** Das hast du gut gemacht. II 3 (47)
Oh well ... Na ja ... / Na gut ... I
Well, ... Nun, ... / Also, ... I
2. (gesundheitlich) gut; gesund, wohlauf II 4 (61)
▶ S.157 What's wrong with you?
Welsh [welʃ] walisisch; Walisisch II 4 (60)
went [went] siehe go
were [wə, wɜː]: **(we/you/they) were** siehe be
°**were-rabbit** ['weə ˌræbɪt] Werwolf-Kaninchen
°**west** [west]: **the West Country** umgangssprachliche Bezeichnung für den Südwesten Englands
what [wɒt]
1. was I
2. welche(r, s) I
What about ...? 1. Was ist mit ...? / Und ...? I; **2.** Wie wär's mit ...? I
°**What are the pages about?** Wovon handeln die Seiten? • **What are you talking about?** Wovon redest du? I • **What colour is ...?** Welche Farbe hat ...? I • **What else do you know ...?** Was weißt du sonst noch ...? II 6 (94) • **What for?** Wofür? II 2 (29) • **What have we got next?** Was haben wir als Nächstes? I • **What page are we on?** Auf welcher Seite sind wir? I **What's for homework?** Was haben wir als Hausaufgabe auf? I
What's the matter? Was ist los? / Was ist denn? II 2 (28) • **What's the time?** Wie spät ist es? I • **What's wrong with you?** Was fehlt dir? II 4 (62/157) • **What's your name?** Wie heißt du? I • **What was the weather like?** Wie war das Wetter? II Welc (7)
°**wheatgrass** ['wiːtɡrɑːs] Weizengras
wheelchair ['wiːltʃeə] Rollstuhl I
when [wen] wann I • **When's your birthday?** Wann hast du Geburtstag? I
when [wen]
1. wenn I
2. als I

where [weə]
1. wo I
2. wohin I
Where are you from? Wo kommst du her? I
which [wɪtʃ]: **Which picture ...?** Welches Bild ...? I • **which way?** in welche Richtung? / wohin? II 6 (95/165)
whisky ['wɪski] Whisky II 4 (65)
whisper ['wɪspə] flüstern I
whistle ['wɪsl] pfeifen II 5 (86)
white [waɪt] weiß I
who [huː]
1. wer I
2. wen / wem II 5 (86)
▶ S.162 who?
who [huː]: **Find/Ask somebody who ...** Finde/Frage jemanden, der ... II 1 (20) • °**a lady who swallowed a fly** eine Dame, die eine Fliege verschluckte
whose? [huːz] wessen? II 2 (28)
Whose are these? Wem gehören diese? II 2 (28/148) • **Whose turn is it?** Wer ist dran? / Wer ist an der Reihe? II 5 (74)
why [waɪ] warum I • **Why me?** Warum ich? I • **that's why** deshalb, darum I
wife [waɪf], pl **wives** [waɪvz] Ehefrau II 4 (71)
wild [waɪld] wild II 3 (42)
will [wɪl]: **you'll be cold (= you will be cold)** du wirst frieren; ihr werdet frieren II 3 (44)
win (-nn-) [wɪn], **won, won** gewinnen I
wind [wɪnd] Wind I
window ['wɪndəʊ] Fenster I
windy ['wɪndi] windig I
winner ['wɪnə] Gewinner/in, Sieger/in II 3 (53)
winter ['wɪntə] Winter I
°**wisdom** ['wɪzdəm] Weisheit I
°**wise** [waɪz] weise I
with [wɪð]
1. mit I
2. bei I
Sit with me. Setz dich zu mir. / Setzt euch zu mir. I
without [wɪˈðaʊt] ohne I
wives [waɪvz] pl von „wife" II 4 (71)
wolf [wʊlf], pl **wolves** [wʊlvz] Wolf II 3 (52/153)
woman ['wʊmən], pl **women** ['wɪmɪn] Frau I
won [wʌn] siehe win
won't [wəʊnt]: **you won't be cold (= you will not be cold)** du wirst nicht frieren; ihr werdet nicht frieren II 3 (44)

wonder ['wʌndə] sich fragen, gern wissen wollen II 6 (104)
wood [wʊd] Holz II 3 (47/152)
woodpecker ['wʊdpekə] Specht II 3 (43)
woods (pl) [wʊdz] Wald, Wälder II 3 (47)
word [wɜːd] Wort I • **word building** Wortbildung II 3 (53) °**word order** Wortstellung I
wore [wɔː] siehe wear
work [wɜːk] arbeiten I • **work hard** hart arbeiten II 3 (47) • **work on sth.** an etwas arbeiten I
work [wɜːk] Arbeit I • **at work** bei der Arbeit / am Arbeitsplatz I
worker ['wɜːkə] Arbeiter/in II 3 (53)
worksheet ['wɜːkʃiːt] Arbeitsblatt I
world [wɜːld] Welt I
worn [wɔːn] siehe wear
worry ['wʌri] Sorge, Kummer II 6 (105)
worry (about) ['wʌri] sich Sorgen machen (wegen, um) I • **Don't worry.** Mach dir keine Sorgen. I
worse [wɜːs] schlechter, schlimmer II 2 (30/149)
worst [wɜːst]: **(the) worst** am schlechtesten, schlimmsten; der/die/das schlechteste, schlimmste II 2 (30/149)
would [wəd, wʊd]: **I'd like ... (= I would like ...)** Ich hätte gern ... / Ich möchte gern ... I • **Would you like ...?** Möchtest du ...? / Möchten Sie ...? I • **I'd like to go (= I would like to go)** ich würde gern gehen / ich möchte gehen I • **I wouldn't like to go** ich würde nicht gern gehen / ich möchte nicht gehen I
°**wreck** [rek] Wrack
°**wriggle** ['rɪɡl] (herum)zappeln
write [raɪt], **wrote, written** schreiben I • **write down** aufschreiben I • **write to** schreiben an I
writer ['raɪtə] Schreiber/in; Schriftsteller/in II 3 (53)
written ['rɪtn] siehe write
wrong [rɒŋ] falsch, verkehrt I **be wrong 1.** falsch sein I; **2.** sich irren, Unrecht haben II 5 (76) **the wrong way** in die falsche Richtung II 5 (87) • **What's wrong with you?** Was fehlt dir? II 4 (62/157)
wrote [rəʊt] siehe write

Dictionary (English – German)

Y

yard [jɑːd] Hof II 3 (44) • **in the yard** auf dem Hof II 3 (44/151)
yawn [jɔːn] gähnen II 6 (104)
year [jɪə]
 1. Jahr I
 2. Jahrgangsstufe I
yellow ['jeləʊ] gelb I
yes [jes] ja I
yesterday ['jestədeɪ, 'jestədi] gestern I • **yesterday morning/afternoon/evening** gestern Morgen/Nachmittag/Abend I **yesterday's homework** die Hausaufgaben von gestern II 3 (42/150)

yet [jet]: **not (...) yet** noch nicht II 4 (61) • **yet?** schon? II 4 (63/157)
 ▶ S.156 The present perfect: statements
 ▶ S.157 The present perfect: questions
yoga ['jəʊgə] Yoga I
you [juː]
 1. du; Sie I
 2. ihr I • **you two** ihr zwei I
 3. dir; dich; euch I
young [jʌŋ] jung I
your [jɔː]
 1. dein/e I
 2. Ihr I
 3. euer/eure I
yours [jɔːz]
 1. deiner, deine, deins II 2 (28/147)

 2. Ihrer, Ihre, Ihrs II 2 (28/147)
 3. eurer, eure, eures II 2 (28/147)
 ▶ S.147 Possessive pronouns
°**yourself** [jə'self, jɔː'self]: **about yourself** über dich selbst
°**youth** [juːθ] Jugend, Jugend-
°**yuck** [jʌk] igitt

Z

zebra ['zebrə] Zebra II 3 (52/153)
zero ['zɪərəʊ] null I

Dictionary (German – English) | 189

Das **German – English Dictionary** enthält den **Lernwortschatz** der Bände 1 und 2 von *English G 21*.
Es kann dir eine erste Hilfe sein, wenn du vergessen hast, wie etwas auf Englisch heißt.

Wenn du wissen möchtest, wo das englische Wort zum ersten Mal in *English G 21* vorkommt,
dann kannst du im **English – German Dictionary** (S. 168–188) nachschlagen.

Im **German – English Dictionary** werden folgende **Abkürzungen** und **Symbole** verwendet:

jm. = jemandem	sb. = somebody	*pl* = *plural* (Mehrzahl)	BE = *British English*
jn. = jemanden	sth. = something	*no pl* = *no plural*	AE = *American English*

▸ Der Pfeil verweist auf Kästchen im Vocabulary (S. 141–167), in denen du weitere Informationen findest.

A

**abbiegen: (nach) links/rechts ab-
biegen** turn left/right [tɜːn]
  ▸ S.165 (to) turn
Abend evening ['iːvnɪŋ]; *(später
Abend)* night [naɪt] • **am Abend,
abends** in the evening
Abendbrot, -essen dinner ['dɪnə]
  Abendbrot essen have dinner
  zum Abendbrot for dinner
aber but [bət, bʌt]
abfahren *(wegfahren)* leave [liːv]
Abfall rubbish ['rʌbɪʃ]
Absatz *(in einem Text)* paragraph
  ['pærəgrɑːf]
abschließen *(Zimmer)* lock up
  [,lɒk_'ʌp]
abschreiben *(kopieren)* copy ['kɒpi]
abziehen: 10 Cent abziehen take 10c
  off [,teɪk_'ɒf]
Acker field [fiːld]
addieren (zu) add (to) [æd]
Adjektiv adjective ['ædʒɪktɪv]
Adverb adverb ['ædvɜːb]
Affe monkey ['mʌŋki]
Aktivität activity [æk'tɪvəti]
Akzent accent ['æksənt]
alle *(die ganze Gruppe)* all [ɔːl]
allein alone [ə'ləʊn]
alleinstehend single ['sɪŋgl]
alles everything ['evriθɪŋ]; all [ɔːl]
  **alles, was wir jetzt (noch) tun
  müssen, ...** all we have to do now ...
Alphabet alphabet ['ælfəbet]
als 1. *(zeitlich)* when [wen]; *(während)*
  as [əz, æz]
  2. als Kind as a child
  3. größer/teurer als bigger/more
  expensive than [ðæn, ðən] • **mehr
  als** more than • **mehr als ich**
  more than me
also *(daher, deshalb)* so [səʊ]
  Also, ... Well, ... [wel]
alt old [əʊld]
am 1. am Bahnhof at the station
  am Himmel in the sky • **am
  oberen Ende (von)** at the top (of)

am Strand on the beach • **am
Telefon** on the phone • **am
unteren Ende (von)** at the bottom
(of) ['bɒtəm]
2. *(nahe bei)* **am Meer** by the sea
3. *(zeitlich)* **am 13. Juni** on 13th June
am Morgen/Nachmittag/Abend
in the morning/afternoon/evening
am Ende (von) at the end (of)
am Freitag on Friday • **am Freitagmorgen** on Friday morning
am nächsten Morgen/Tag the
next morning/day • **am Wochenende** at the weekend
amüsieren: sich amüsieren have fun
  [hæv 'fʌn]
an 1. an dem/den Tisch (dort) at
that table • **an der Spitze** at the
top (of) • **an der/die Tafel** on the
board • **schreiben an** write to
2. *(nahe bei)* **an der See** by the sea
3. Was war das Beste an ...? What
was the best thing about ...?
4. an sein *(Radio, Licht usw.)* be on
anbauen *(Getreide usw.)* grow [grəʊ]
andere(r, s) other ['ʌðə] • **die
anderen** the others • **ein(e)
andere(r, s) ...** another ... [ə'nʌðə]
anders (als) different (from) ['dɪfrənt]
  anders herum the other way
  round
Anfang beginning [bɪ'gɪnɪŋ]; start
  [stɑːt]
anfangen (mit) start [stɑːt]
anfassen touch [tʌtʃ]
anfühlen: sich gut anfühlen feel
good [fiːl]
Angst haben (vor) be afraid (of)
  [ə'freɪd]; be scared (of) [skeəd]
anhaben *(Kleidung)* wear [weə]
anhalten stop [stɒp]
anhören 1. sich etwas anhören
  listen to sth. ['lɪsn]
  2. sich gut anhören sound good
  [saʊnd]
anklicken: etwas anklicken click on
  sth. [klɪk]
anklopfen (an) knock (on) [nɒk]

ankommen arrive [ə'raɪv]
anlächeln: jn. anlächeln smile at sb.
  [smaɪl]
Anleitung(en) *(Gebrauchsanweisun-
gen)* instructions *(pl)* [ɪn'strʌkʃnz]
anmailen: jn. anmailen mail sb.
  [meɪl]
anmalen paint [peɪnt]
annehmen *(vermuten)* suppose
  [sə'pəʊz]
anpflanzen *(Getreide usw.)* grow
  [grəʊ]
anprobieren *(Kleidung)* try on
  [,traɪ_'ɒn]
Anruf call [kɔːl]; phone call ['fəʊn kɔːl]
anrufen call [kɔːl]; phone [fəʊn]
anschauen look at [lʊk]
anschließen: sich jm. anschließen
  join sb. [dʒɔɪn]
anschreien shout at [ʃaʊt]
ansehen: sich etwas ansehen look
  at sth. [lʊk]; watch sth. [wɒtʃ]
Antwort (auf) answer (to) ['ɑːnsə]
antworten answer ['ɑːnsə]
Anweisung(en) *(Gebrauchsanwei-
sungen)* instructions *(pl)*
  [ɪn'strʌkʃnz]
anziehen: etwas anziehen *(Kleidung)*
  put sth. on [,pʊt_'ɒn] • **sich anziehen** get dressed [get 'drest]
Apfel apple ['æpl]
Apfelsine orange ['ɒrɪndʒ]
Apotheke chemist ['kemɪst]
April April ['eɪprəl]
Arbeit work [wɜːk] • **bei der Arbeit/
am Arbeitsplatz** at work
arbeiten (an) work (on) [wɜːk]
Arbeiter/in worker ['wɜːkə]
Arbeitsblatt worksheet ['wɜːkʃiːt]
Arbeits- und Lerntechniken study
  skills ['stʌdi skɪlz]
Ärger *(Schwierigkeiten)* trouble
  ['trʌbl] • **Ärger kriegen** be in
  trouble
arm poor [pɔː, pʊə]
Arm arm [ɑːm]
Armbanduhr watch [wɒtʃ]
Artikel article ['ɑːtɪkl]

190 Dictionary (German – English)

Arzt/Ärztin doctor ['dɒktə]
Attraktion attraction [ə'trækʃn]
auch: auch aus Bristol from Bristol too [tuː]; also from Bristol ['ɔːlsəʊ]
Ich auch. Me too.
auf on [ɒn] • **auf dem Bild/Foto** in the picture/photo • **auf dem Feld** in the field • **auf dem Hof** in the yard • **auf dem Land** in the country • **auf dem Weg (zu/nach)** on the way (to) • **auf einmal** suddenly ['sʌdnli] • **auf Englisch** in English • **Auf geht's!** Let's go. **auf jn./etwas zu** towards sb./sth. [tə'wɔːdz] • **Auf keinen Fall!** No way! • **Auf welcher Seite sind wir?** What page are we on? • **Auf Wiedersehen.** Goodbye. [ˌɡʊd'baɪ]
auffordern: jn. auffordern, etwas zu tun tell sb. to do sth.
aufführen (Szene, Dialog) act [ækt]
Aufgabe (im Schulbuch) exercise ['eksəsaɪz]; (Job) job [dʒɒb]
aufgeräumt (ordentlich) tidy ['taɪdi]
aufgeregt (nervös) nervous ['nɜːvəs]
aufheben: etwas aufheben (hochheben) pick sth. up [ˌpɪk_'ʌp]
aufhören stop [stɒp]
auflisten list [lɪst]
aufmachen open ['əʊpən]
aufpassen: auf etwas/jn. aufpassen look after sth./sb. [ˌlʊk_'ɑːftə]
aufräumen tidy ['taɪdi]
aufregend exciting [ɪk'saɪtɪŋ]
Aufsatz essay ['eseɪ]
aufschauen (von) look up (from) [ˌlʊk_'ʌp]
aufschreiben write down [ˌraɪt 'daʊn]
aufstehen (sich erheben) stand up [ˌstænd_'ʌp]; get up [ˌɡet_'ʌp]; (aus dem Bett) get up
aufsuchen: jn. aufsuchen see sb. [siː]
aufwischen (Fußboden) wash [wɒʃ]
aufzählen (auflisten) list [lɪst]
Aufzug lift [lɪft] (BE); elevator ['elɪveɪtə] (AE)
Auge eye [aɪ]
Augenblick moment ['məʊmənt]
August August ['ɔːɡəst]
aus: Ich komme/bin aus … I'm from … [frəm, frɒm] • **aus … (heraus/hinaus)** out of … ['aʊt_əv] • **aus dem Zug/Bus aussteigen** get off the train/bus • **aus ganz Wales** from all around Wales • **aus meiner Sicht** from my point of view • **aus vielen Gründen** for lots of reasons
ausdenken: sich etwas ausdenken think of sth. [θɪŋk]
▶ S.159 (to) think
Ausdruck ((Rede-)Wendung) phrase [freɪz]

ausdrucken: etwas ausdrucken print sth. out [ˌprɪnt_'aʊt]
Ausflug trip [trɪp] • **einen Ausflug machen** go on a trip
ausgeben: Geld ausgeben (für) spend money (on) [spend]
ausgehen (weg-, rausgehen) go out
Ausland: im Ausland abroad [ə'brɔːd] **ins Ausland gehen/fahren** go abroad
ausruhen: sich ausruhen relax [rɪ'læks]
ausschalten: etwas ausschalten turn sth. off
▶ S.165 (to) turn
aussehen: anders/toll/alt aussehen look different/great/old [lʊk] **fürchterlich aussehen** be a mess [mes] • **gleich aussehen** look the same
außerhalb seines Zimmers outside his room [ˌaʊt'saɪd]
aussetzen: Einmal aussetzen. Miss a turn. [tɜːn]
Aussicht (Blick) view [vjuː]
Aussprache pronunciation [prə,nʌnsi'eɪʃn]
aussteigen (aus dem Zug/Bus) get off (the train/bus) [ˌɡet_'ɒf]
aussuchen: (sich) etwas aussuchen choose sth. [tʃuːz]
auswählen choose [tʃuːz]
ausziehen 1. (aus Wohnung) move out [ˌmuːv_'aʊt] **2. etwas ausziehen** (Kleidung) take sth. off [ˌteɪk_'ɒf]
Auto car [kɑː]
Autsch! Ouch! [aʊtʃ]

B

Baby baby ['beɪbi] • **ein Baby bekommen** have a baby
baden (ein Bad nehmen) have a bath [bɑːθ]
Badewanne bath [bɑːθ]
Badezimmer bathroom ['bɑːθruːm]
Badminton badminton ['bædmɪntən]
Bahnhof station ['steɪʃn] • **am Bahnhof** at the station
bald soon [suːn]
Ball ball [bɔːl]
Banane banana [bə'nɑːnə]
Band (Musikgruppe) band [bænd]
Bank (Sparkasse) bank [bæŋk]
Bankräuber/in bank robber ['rɒbə]
Bar bar [bɑː]
Bär bear [beə]
Bart beard [bɪəd]
Baseball baseball ['beɪsbɔːl]
Baseballmütze baseball cap [kæp]

Basketball basketball ['bɑːskɪtbɔːl]
Bauchweh stomach ache ['stʌmək_eɪk]
▶ S.157 What's wrong with you?
bauen build [bɪld]
Bauernhof farm [fɑːm]
Baum tree [triː]
beantworten answer ['ɑːnsə]
bedeuten mean [miːn]
beeilen: sich beeilen hurry ['hʌri]; hurry up [ˌhʌri_'ʌp]
beenden finish ['fɪnɪʃ]
Beginn beginning [bɪ'ɡɪnɪŋ]; start [stɑːt]
beginnen (mit) start [stɑːt]
begreifen understand [ˌʌndə'stænd]
Begründung reason ['riːzn]
bei: bei den Shaws zu Hause at the Shaws' house • **bei der Arbeit** at work • **Englisch bei Mr Kingsley** English with Mr Kingsley
beide both [bəʊθ]
Beifall klatschen cheer [tʃɪə]
Bein leg [leɡ]
beinahe almost ['ɔːlməʊst]
Beispiel example [ɪɡ'zɑːmpl] • **zum Beispiel** for example
bekommen get [ɡet] • **ein Baby bekommen** have a baby
benennen name [kɔːl]
benötigen need [niːd]
benutzen use [juːz]
beobachten watch [wɒtʃ]
bereit ready ['redi]
bereits already [ɔːl'redi]
Berg mountain ['maʊntən]
Bericht (über) report (on) [rɪ'pɔːt]
berichten (über) tell (about) [tel] **(jm.) etwas berichten** report sth. (to sb.) [rɪ'pɔːt]
berichtigen correct [kə'rekt]
beruhigen: sich beruhigen calm down [ˌkɑːm 'daʊn]
berühmt (für, wegen) famous (for) ['feɪməs]
berühren touch [tʌtʃ]
Bescheid: über etwas Bescheid wissen know about sth. [nəʊ]
beschreiben: (jm.) etwas beschreiben describe sth. (to sb.) [dɪ'skraɪb] **jm. den Weg beschreiben** tell sb. the way
Beschreibung description [dɪ'skrɪpʃn]
besorgen (holen) get [ɡet]
besser better ['betə]
▶ S.149 good – better – best
beste: am besten (the) best [best] **der/die/das beste …; die besten …** the best … • **Was war das Beste an …?** What was the best thing about …?
▶ S.149 good – better – best

Dictionary (German – English) 191

Besuch visit ['vɪzɪt]
besuchen: jn. besuchen visit sb. ['vɪzɪt]; see sb. [si:]
Besucher/in visitor ['vɪzɪtə]
Bett bed [bed]
Beutel bag [bæg]
bevor before [bɪ'fɔ:]
bewegen: sich bewegen move [mu:v]
Bewegung movement ['mu:vmənt]
Beweis(e) proof *(no pl)* [pru:f]
bewölkt cloudy ['klaʊdi]
bewusstlos unconscious [ʌn'kɒnʃəs]
bezahlen: etwas bezahlen pay for sth. [peɪ]
Bibliothek library ['laɪbrəri]
Bild picture ['pɪktʃə] • **auf dem Bild** in the picture
billig cheap [tʃi:p]
Bindewort linking word ['lɪŋkɪŋ wɜ:d]
Biologie biology [baɪ'ɒlədʒi]
bis *(zeitlich)* till [tɪl] • **Bis bald.** See you. ['si: ju:] • **bis jetzt / bis hierher** so far
bisschen: ein bisschen a bit [bɪt]
bitte 1. *(in Fragen und Aufforderungen)* please [pli:z]
2. Bitte sehr. / Hier bitte. Here you are.
3. Bitte, gern geschehen. You're welcome. ['welkəm]
4. Wie bitte? Sorry? ['sɒri]
bitten: jn. um etwas bitten ask sb. for sth. [ɑ:sk]
blau blue [blu:]
bleiben stay [steɪ]
Bleistift pencil ['pensl]
Bleistiftanspitzer pencil sharpener ['pensl ʃɑ:pnə]
Blick *(Aussicht)* view [vju:]
bloß just [dʒʌst]; only ['əʊnli]
Bluse blouse [blaʊz]
Boot boat [bəʊt]
böse sein (über etwas/auf jn.) be angry (about sth./with sb.) ['æŋgri]
Brand fire ['faɪə]
brauchen need [ni:d] • **nicht zu tun brauchen** needn't do ['ni:dnt]
▶ S.166 must – needn't – mustn't
braun brown [braʊn]
brav good [gʊd]
Brief (an) letter (to) ['letə]
Brieffreund/in *(im Internet)* e-friend ['i:frend]
Briefmarke stamp [stæmp]
Brille: (eine) Brille glasses *(pl)* ['glɑ:sɪz]
▶ S.147 Plural words
bringen: (mit-, her)bringen bring [brɪŋ] • **(weg-, hin)bringen** take [teɪk]
britisch; Brite, Britin British ['brɪtɪʃ]

Broschüre booklet ['bʊklət]
Brot bread *(no pl)* [bred]
Brötchen roll [rəʊl]
Brücke bridge [brɪdʒ]
Bruder brother ['brʌðə]
Buch book [bʊk]
Bücherei library ['laɪbrəri]
Buchstabe letter ['letə]
buchstabieren spell [spel]
Bühne stage [steɪdʒ]
Burg castle ['kɑ:sl]
Bus bus [bʌs]

C

Café café ['kæfeɪ]
Cartoon cartoon [kɑ:'tu:n]
CD CD [,si:'di:] • **CD-Spieler** CD player [,si:'di: ,pleɪə]
Cent cent (c) [sent]
Champion champion ['tʃæmpiən]
Chance *(Gelegenheit; Aussicht)* chance [tʃɑ:ns]
Chat *(Unterhaltung)* chat [tʃæt]
chatten chat [tʃæt]
Chor choir ['kwaɪə]
Cola cola ['kəʊlə]
Comic-Heft comic ['kɒmɪk]
Computer computer [kəm'pju:tə]
cool cool [ku:l]
Cornflakes cornflakes ['kɔ:nfleɪks]
Cousin, Cousine cousin ['kʌzn]

D

da, dahin *(dort, dorthin)* there [ðeə]
  da drüben over there [,əʊvə 'ðeə]
daheim at home [ət 'həʊm]
daher so [səʊ]
danach *(zeitlich)* after that [,ɑ:ftə 'ðæt]
Danke. Thank you. ['θæŋk ju:]; Thanks.
  Danke sehr! Thanks very much!
  Vielen Dank! Thanks a lot!
dann then [ðen]
darstellende Kunst drama ['drɑ:mə]
darum that's why ['ðæts ,waɪ]
das *(Artikel)* the [ðə, ði]
das *(dort)* *(Singular)* that [ðət, ðæt]; *(Plural)* those [ðəʊz] • **Das bin ich.** That's me.
dass that [ðət, ðæt]
dasselbe the same [seɪm]
Datum date [deɪt]
decken: den Tisch decken lay the table [,leɪ ðə 'teɪbl]
dein(e) ... your ... [jɔ:]
deiner, deine, deins yours [jɔ:z]
▶ S.147 Possessive pronouns
denken think [θɪŋk] • **denken an** think of • **Was denkst du über ...?**

What do you think about/of ...?
▶ S.159 (to) think
der 1. *(Artikel)* the [ðə, ði]
  2. Finde/Frage jemanden, der ... Find/Ask somebody who ...
derselbe the same [seɪm]
deshalb so [səʊ]; that's why ['ðæts ,waɪ]
Detektiv/in detective [dɪ'tektɪv]
deuten (auf etwas) *(zeigen)* point (at/to sth.) [pɔɪnt]
deutlich clear [klɪə]
Deutsch; deutsch; Deutsche(r) German ['dʒɜ:mən]
Deutschland Germany ['dʒɜ:məni]
Dezember December [dɪ'sembə]
dich you [ju:]
die *(Artikel)* the [ðə, ði]
die (dort) *(Singular)* that [ðət, ðæt]; *(Plural)* those [ðəʊz] • **die (hier)** *(Singular)* this [ðɪs]; *(Plural)* these [ði:z]
Dieb/in thief [θi:f], *pl* thieves [θi:vz]
Diele hall [hɔ:l]
Dienstag Tuesday ['tju:zdeɪ, 'tju:zdi] *(siehe auch unter „Freitag")*
dies (hier); diese(r, s) *(Singular)* this [ðɪs]; *(Plural)* these [ði:z]
dieselbe(n) the same [seɪm]
Ding thing [θɪŋ]
dir you [ju:]
direkt hinter dir right behind you
direkte Frage direct question [də,rekt 'kwestʃən]
▶ S.164 Höflich um Auskunft bitten
Disko disco ['dɪskəʊ]
Diskussion discussion [dɪ'skʌʃn]
Doktor doctor ['dɒktə]
Donnerstag Thursday ['θɜ:zdeɪ, 'θɜ:zdi] *(siehe auch unter „Freitag")*
doppelt, Doppel- double ['dʌbl]
doppelklicken double-click ['dʌblklɪk]
Dorf village ['vɪlɪdʒ]
dort, dorthin there [ðeə] • **dort drinnen** in there • **dort drüben** over there • **dort unten** down there
Dossier dossier ['dɒsieɪ]
downloaden download [,daʊn'ləʊd]
Drachen kite [kaɪt]
dran: Ich bin dran. It's my turn. [tɜ:n] **Wer ist dran** Whose turn is it? [hu:z]
draußen outside [,aʊt'saɪd]; out [aʊt] **nach draußen** outside
▶ S.146 out
drinnen inside [,ɪn'saɪd] • **dort drinnen** in there [,ɪn 'ðeə] • **hier drinnen** in here [,ɪn 'hɪə] • **nach drinnen** inside
dritte(r, s) third [θɜ:d]
Drogerie chemist ['kemɪst]

192 Dictionary (German – English)

drüben: da/dort drüben over there [ˌəʊvə 'ðeə]

drücken push [pʊʃ]

du you [juː]

dunkel dark [dɑːk]

durch through [θruː]

durcheinander: alles durcheinander-bringen make a mess [ˌmeɪk_ə 'mes]

durchführen: ein Projekt durch-führen do a project

dürfen can [kən, kæn]; may [meɪ]
nicht dürfen mustn't ['mʌsnt]
▶ S.166 must – needn't – mustn't

Durst haben, durstig sein be thirsty [ˈθɜːsti]

Dusche shower [ˈʃaʊə]

duschen; sich duschen have a shower [ˈʃaʊə]

DVD DVD [ˌdiː viːˈ diː]

E

Ebbe und Flut *(Gezeiten)* tide [taɪd]
es ist Ebbe the tide is out

echt real [rɪəl]

Ecke corner [ˈkɔːnə] • **Sand Street, Ecke London Road** on the corner of Sand Street and London Road

Ehefrau wife [waɪf], *pl* wives [waɪvz]

Ehemann husband [ˈhʌzbənd]

Eichhörnchen squirrel [ˈskwɪrəl]

eigene(r, s): unser eigenes Schwimmbad our own pool [əʊn]

Eile: in Eile sein be in a hurry [ˈhʌri]

eilen *(sich beeilen)* hurry [ˈhʌri]

eilig: es eilig haben be in a hurry [ˈhʌri]

ein(e) a, an [ə, ən]; one [ˈwʌn]
ein(e) andere(r, s) ... another ... [əˈnʌðə] • **eine Menge** a lot (of) [lɒt]; lots (of) [lɒts] • **ein neuer / eine neue / ein neues** a new one [wʌn] • **ein paar** some [səm, sʌm]
eines Tages one day

einfach *(nicht schwierig)* easy [ˈiːzi]
einfach nur just [dʒʌst]

Einfall *(Idee)* idea [aɪˈdɪə]

eingeben: etwas eingeben *(in den Computer)* enter sth. [ˈentə]

eingeschaltet sein *(Radio, Licht usw.)* be on

einige some [səm, sʌm]; *(einige wenige)* a few [fjuː]

einigen: sich einigen (auf) agree (on) [əˈgriː]

einkaufen: einkaufen gehen go shopping [ˌgəʊ ˈʃɒpɪŋ]

Einkaufen shopping [ˈʃɒpɪŋ]

einladen (zu) invite (to) [ɪnˈvaɪt]

Einladung (zu) invitation (to) [ˌɪnvɪˈteɪʃn]

einmal: Einmal aussetzen. Miss a turn. [tɜːn] • **auf einmal** suddenly [ˈsʌdnli]

einpacken pack [pæk]

eins, ein, eine one [ˈwʌn]

einschalten *(Computer usw.)* turn on [ˌtɜːn_ˈɒn]
▶ S.165 (to) turn

einschüchtern bully [ˈbʊli]

einsteigen (in den Zug/Bus) get on (the train/bus) [ˌget_ˈɒn]

eintragen: etwas eintragen *(in Formular)* enter sth. [ˈentə]

eintreffen *(ankommen)* arrive [əˈraɪv]

Eintrittskarte ticket [ˈtɪkɪt]

einziehen *(in Wohnung)* move in [ˌmuːv_ˈɪn]

einzig: der einzige Gast the only guest [ˈəʊnli]

Eis ice [aɪs]; *(Speiseeis)* ice cream [ˌaɪs ˈkriːm]

Eisenbahn railway [ˈreɪlweɪ]

eislaufen skate [skeɪt]

Elefant elephant [ˈelɪfənt]

Eltern parents [ˈpeərənts]

E-Mail (an) e-mail (to) [ˈiːmeɪl]

Ende **1.** end [end] • **am Ende (von)** at the end (of) • **zu Ende machen** finish [ˈfɪnɪʃ] • **zu Ende sein** be over [ˈəʊvə]
2. oberes Ende *(Spitze)* top [tɒp]
am oberen Ende at the top
3. unteres Ende bottom [ˈbɒtəm]
am unteren Ende (von) at the bottom (of) [ˈbɒtəm]

enden finish [ˈfɪnɪʃ]

endlich at last [ət ˈlɑːst]

Energie energy [ˈenədʒi]

Engel angel [ˈeɪndʒl]

Englisch; englisch English [ˈɪŋglɪʃ]

Enkel grandson [ˈgrænsʌn]; grandchild [ˈgræntʃaɪld], *pl* grandchildren [ˈgræntʃɪldrən]

Enkelin granddaughter [ˈgrændɔːtə]; grandchild [ˈgræntʃaɪld], *pl* grandchildren [ˈgræntʃɪldrən]

entdecken discover [dɪˈskʌvə]

Entdecker/in *(Forscher/in)* explorer [ɪkˈsplɔːrə]

entlang der Straße / die Straße entlang along the street [əˈlɒŋ]

entschuldigen: sich entschuldigen say sorry [ˈsɒri]

Entschuldigung **1.** *(Tut mir leid)* I'm sorry. [ˈsɒri] • **Entschuldigung, dass ich zu spät komme.** Sorry, I'm late.
2. Entschuldigung, ... *(Darf ich mal stören?)* Excuse me, ... [ɪkˈskjuːz miː]

entspannen; sich entspannen relax [rɪˈlæks]

entwerfen design [dɪˈzaɪn]

er **1.** *(männliche Person)* he [hiː]; **2.** *(Ding, Tier)* it [ɪt]

Erdbeere strawberry [ˈstrɔːbəri]

Erdkunde geography [dʒiˈɒgrəfi]

erfahren: etwas über etwas erfahren learn sth. about sth. [lɜːn]

erforschen explore [ɪkˈsplɔː]

ergänzen add (to) [æd]

Ergebnis result [rɪˈzʌlt]

erinnern: sich erinnern (an) remember [rɪˈmembə]

erkältet sein have a cold [kəʊld]
▶ S.157 What's wrong with you?

Erkältung cold [kəʊld] • **eine Erkältung haben** have a cold
▶ S.157 What's wrong with you?

erklären: jm. etwas erklären explain sth. to sb. [ɪkˈspleɪn]

Erklärung explanation [ˌekspləˈneɪʃn]

erkunden explore [ɪkˈsplɔː]

erläutern: jm. etwas erläutern explain sth. to sb. [ɪkˈspleɪn]

erraten guess [ges]

erstaunlich amazing [əˈmeɪzɪŋ]

erste(r, s) first [fɜːst] • **als Erstes** first • **der erste Tag** the first day
der/die Erste sein be first

erwarten: ich kann es kaum erwarten, ... zu sehen I can't wait to see ... [weɪt]

erwischen *(fangen)* catch [kætʃ]

erzählen (von) tell (about) [tel]

Erzählung story [ˈstɔːri]

es it [ɪt] • **es gibt** *(es ist vorhanden)* there's; *(es sind vorhanden)* there are

Essen food [fuːd]

essen eat [iːt] • **Abendbrot essen** have dinner • **Toast zum Frühstück essen** have toast for breakfast

Esszimmer dining room [ˈdaɪnɪŋ ruːm]

Etagenbett bunk (bed) [bʌŋk]

etwas something [ˈsʌmθɪŋ]; *(irgendetwas)* anything [ˈeniθɪŋ]; *(ein bisschen)* a bit [bɪt] • **etwas Käse/Saft** some cheese/juice [səm, sʌm]
▶ S.160 something – anything

euch you [juː]

euer, eure ... your ... [jɔː]

eurer, eure, eures yours [jɔːz]
▶ S.147 Possessive pronouns

Euro euro [ˈjʊərəʊ]

F

Fabrik factory [ˈfæktri]

fahren go [gəʊ]; *(ein Auto/mit dem Auto)* drive [draɪv] • **in Urlaub fahren** go on holiday • **mit dem Auto/Zug/Rad/... fahren** go by car/train/bike/... • **Inliner/Skate-**

Dictionary (German – English) 193

board fahren skate [skeɪt] • **Rad fahren** cycle ['saɪkl]; ride a bike [,raɪd ə 'baɪk]

Fahrer/in driver ['draɪvə]

Fahrkarte ticket ['tɪkɪt]

Fahrrad bike [baɪk]

Fahrstuhl lift [lɪft] *(BE)*; elevator ['elɪveɪtə] *(AE)*

Fahrt: (Rad-)Fahrt (bike) ride [raɪd]

fair fair [feə]

Fall *(Kriminalfall)* case [keɪs] • **Auf keinen Fall!** No way! [,nəʊ 'weɪ]

Falle trap [træp] • **(jm.) eine Falle stellen** set a trap (for sb.) [set]

fallen fall [fɔːl]; drop [drɒp]

fallen lassen drop [drɒp]

falls if [ɪf]

falsch wrong [rɒŋ] • **in die falsche Richtung** the wrong way

Familie family ['fæməli]

Fan fan [fæn]

fangen catch [kætʃ]

fantastisch fantastic [fæn'tæstɪk]

Farbe colour ['kʌlə] • **Welche Farbe hat ...?** What colour is ...?

Farm farm [fɑːm]

fast almost ['ɔːlməʊst]

Februar February ['februəri]

Federball badminton ['bædmɪntən]

Federmäppchen pencil case ['pensl keɪs]

fehlen *(nicht da sein)* be missing ['mɪsɪŋ] • **Was fehlt dir?** *(bei Krankheit)* What's wrong with you?
▶ S.157 What's wrong with you?

Fehler mistake [mɪ'steɪk]

feiern: eine Party feiern have a party

Feind/in enemy ['enəmi]

Feld 1. field [fiːld] • **auf dem Feld** in the field
2. *(bei Brettspielen)* **Geh ein Feld vor.** Move on one space. [speɪs] • **Geh ein Feld zurück.** Move back one space.

Fenster window ['wɪndəʊ]

Ferien holidays ['hɒlədeɪz] • **Ferien haben/machen** be on holiday

Fernsehen television ['telɪvɪʒn]; TV [tiːˈviː] • **im Fernsehen** on TV

fernsehen watch TV [,wɒtʃ tiːˈviː]

fertig *(bereit)* ready ['redi] • **sich fertig machen (für)** *(sich vorbereiten)* get ready (for) • **Dinge fertig machen (für)** get things ready (for)

Feuer fire ['faɪə]

Feuerwehrfrau firewoman ['faɪə,wʊmən]

Feuerwehrmann fireman ['faɪəmən]

Feuerwerk(skörper) fireworks *(pl)* ['faɪəwɜːks]

Fieber haben have a temperature ['temprətʃə]
▶ S.157 What's wrong with you?

Film film [fɪlm]

Filmstar film star ['fɪlm stɑː]

Filzstift felt tip ['felt tɪp]

finden *(entdecken)* find [faɪnd]

Finger finger ['fɪŋgə]

Fisch fish, *pl* fish [fɪʃ]

Flasche bottle ['bɒtl] • **eine Flasche Milch** a bottle of milk

Fleisch meat [miːt]

fliegen fly [flaɪ]

Flug flight [flaɪt]

Flugzeug plane [pleɪn] • **im Flugzeug** on the plane

Flur hall [hɔːl]

Fluss river ['rɪvə]

Flussdiagramm flow chart ['fləʊ tʃɑːt]

Flusspferd hippo ['hɪpəʊ]

flüstern whisper ['wɪspə]

Flut: Ebbe und Flut *(Gezeiten)* tide [taɪd] • **es ist Flut** the tide is in

folgen follow ['fɒləʊ] • **die folgenden ...** the following ...

Football American football [ə,merɪkən 'fʊtbɔːl]

Forscher/in *(Entdecker/in)* explorer [ɪk'splɔːrə]

fort away [ə'weɪ]

Foto photo ['fəʊtəʊ] • **auf dem Foto** in the photo • **Fotos machen** take photos

Fotoapparat camera ['kæmərə]

Fotograf/in photographer [fə'tɒgrəfə]

fotografieren take photos [teɪk 'fəʊtəʊz]

Frage question ['kwestʃn] • **Fragen stellen** ask questions • **Kommt nicht in Frage!** No way!

fragen ask [ɑːsk] • **nach etwas fragen** ask about sth. • **jn. nach dem Weg fragen** ask sb. the way • **sich fragen** wonder ['wʌndə]

Französisch French [frentʃ]

Frau woman ['wʊmən], *pl* women ['wɪmɪn] • **Frau Brown** Mrs Brown ['mɪsɪz]; Ms Brown [mɪz, məz] • **Frau White** *(unverheiratet)* Miss White [mɪs]

frei free [friː] • **freie Zeit** free time

Freitag Friday ['fraɪdeɪ, 'fraɪdi] **freitagabends, am Freitagabend** on Friday evening • **freitagnachts, Freitagnacht** on Friday night

Freizeit free time [,friː 'taɪm]

Freizeitzentrum, -park leisure centre ['leʒə sentə]

Fremdenverkehrsamt tourist information ['tʊərɪst ,ɪnfə,meɪʃn]

Freund/in friend [frend]

freundlich friendly ['frendli]

frieren be cold [kəʊld]

froh happy ['hæpi]

Frosch frog [frɒg]

Frucht, Früchte fruit [fruːt]

früh early ['ɜːli]

Frühling spring [sprɪŋ]

Frühstück breakfast ['brekfəst] **zum Frühstück** for breakfast

frühstücken have breakfast

Frühstückspension Bed and Breakfast (B&B) [,bed ən 'brekfəst]

Fuchs fox [fɒks]

fühlen; sich fühlen feel [fiːl]
▶ S.157 What's wrong with you?

führen: ein Telefongespräch führen make a call ['kɔːl]

Füller pen [pen]

für for [fə, fɔː]

furchtbar terrible ['terəbl]; awful ['ɔːfl]

fürchterlich aussehen be a mess [mes]

Fuß foot [fʊt], *pl* feet [fiːt]

Fußball football ['fʊtbɔːl]

Fußballplatz, -feld football pitch [pɪtʃ]

Fußballspiel: ein Fußballspiel a game of football [geɪm]

Fußballschuhe, -stiefel football boots ['fʊtbɔːl buːts]

Fußboden floor [flɔː]

Futter food [fuːd]

füttern feed [fiːd]

G

gähnen yawn [jɔːn]

ganz: aus ganz Wales from all around Wales • **Das ist ganz falsch.** This is all wrong. • **den ganzen Tag (lang)** all day • **die ganze Zeit** all the time • **ganz um die Burg herum** all around the castle ['ɔːl ,ə,raʊnd]

Garage garage ['gærɑːʒ]

Garten garden ['gɑːdn]

Gast guest [gest]; *(Besucher/in)* visitor ['vɪzɪtə]

Gebäude building ['bɪldɪŋ]

geben give [gɪv] • **es gibt** *(es ist vorhanden)* there's; *(es sind vorhanden)* there are

geboren sein/werden be born [bɔːn]

gebrochen *(Arm, Bein)* broken ['brəʊkən]

Geburtstag birthday ['bɜːθdeɪ] **Ich habe im Mai / am 13. Juni Geburtstag.** My birthday is in May / on 13th June. • **Wann hast du Geburtstag?** When's your birthday?

Gedicht poem ['pəʊɪm]

Gefahr danger ['deɪndʒə]

gefährlich dangerous ['deɪndʒərəs]
gegen against [ə'genst]
Gegenteil opposite ['ɒpəzɪt]
gegenüber (von) opposite ['ɒpəzɪt]
Gegenwart present ['preznt]
Geheimnis *(Rätsel)* mystery ['mɪstri]
gehen 1. go [gəʊ]; *(zu Fuß gehen)* walk [wɔːk]; *(weggehen)* leave [liːv] **Auf geht's!** Let's go. • **einkaufen gehen** go shopping; shop [ʃɒp] **Geh ein Feld vor.** Move on one space. [speɪs] • **Geh ein Feld zurück.** Move back one space. **in die Sauna gehen** have a sauna **ins Ausland gehen** go abroad **ins Bett gehen** go to bed • **ins Kino gehen** go to the cinema **nach Hause gehen** go home **reiten/schwimmen gehen** go riding/swimming • **spazieren gehen** go for a walk [wɔːk]
2. Es geht mir/ihm gut. I'm/He's fine. [faɪn] • **Wie geht es dir/Ihnen/euch?** How are you?
3. Es geht um Mr Green. This is about Mr Green.
4. Das geht dich nichts an! Mind your own business. [ˌmaɪnd jər_ˌəʊn 'bɪznəs]
gehören (zu) belong (to) [bɪ'lɒŋ] **Wem gehören diese?** Whose are these? [huːz]
Gelächter laughter ['lɑːftə]
gelangen *(hinkommen)* get [get]
gelb yellow ['jeləʊ]
Geld money ['mʌni] • **Geld ausgeben (für)** spend money (on) [spend]
Geldbörse purse [pɜːs]
Gelegenheit *(Chance, Möglichkeit)* chance [tʃɑːns]
genau: genau hinter dir right behind you • **genau in dem Moment** just then • **genau wie du** just like you
genießen enjoy [ɪn'dʒɔɪ]
genug enough [ɪ'nʌf]
geöffnet open ['əʊpən]
Geografie geography [dʒi'ɒgrəfi]
gepflegt neat [niːt]
gerade at the moment; *(soeben)* just [dʒʌst] • **gerade dann** *(genau in dem Moment)* just then • **jetzt gerade** *(in diesem Moment)* right now [raɪt 'naʊ]
▶ S.156 The present perfect: statements
geradeaus weiter straight on [streɪt_'ɒn]
Geräusch noise [nɔɪz]
gerecht fair [feə]
gern: Ich hätte gern … / Ich möchte gern … I'd like … (= I would like …) **Ich schwimme/tanze/… gern.** I like

swimming/dancing/… • **Ich würde gern gehen** I'd like to go **Ich würde nicht gern gehen** I wouldn't like to go • **Gern geschehen.** You're welcome. ['welkəm]
gernhaben like [laɪk]
Geruch smell
Geschäft shop [ʃɒp]
geschehen (mit) happen (to) ['hæpən]
Geschenk present ['preznt]
Geschichte 1. story ['stɔːri] **2.** *(vergangene Zeiten)* history ['hɪstri]
geschieden divorced [dɪ'vɔːst]
Geschirrspülmaschine dishwasher ['dɪʃwɒʃə]
geschlossen closed [kləʊzd]
Geschmack(srichtung) flavour ['fleɪvə]
Gesicht face [feɪs]
gestalten design [dɪ'zaɪn]
gestern yesterday ['jestədeɪ, 'jestədi] **gestern Morgen/Nachmittag/Abend** yesterday morning/afternoon/evening • **die Hausaufgaben von gestern** yesterday's homework
▶ S.150 tonight's programme – Zeitangaben mit s-Genitiv
gesund healthy ['helθi]
▶ S.157 What's wrong with you?
Getränk drink [drɪŋk]
Gewinn prize [praɪz]
gewinnen win [wɪn]
Gewinner/in winner ['wɪnə]
Gewitter storm [stɔːm]
gewöhnlich usually ['juːʒuəli]
Gezeiten *(Ebbe und Flut)* tide [taɪd]
Giraffe giraffe [dʒə'rɑːf]
Gitarre guitar [gɪ'tɑː] • **Gitarre spielen** play the guitar
Glas glass [glɑːs] • **ein Glas Wasser** a glass of water
glauben think [θɪŋk] • **Das glaube ich nicht. / Ich glaube nicht.** I don't think so. • **Ich glaube (ja).** I think so. • **Glaubst du das wirklich?** Do you really think so?
gleich 1. gleich sein/aussehen be/look the same [seɪm] **2. gleich nach dem Mittagessen** right after lunch [raɪt]
Glocke bell [bel]
Glück: Glück haben (mit) be lucky (with) ['lʌki] • **Viel Glück (bei/mit …)!** Good luck (with …)! [gʊd 'lʌk] **zum Glück** *(glücklicherweise)* luckily ['lʌkɪli]
glücklich happy ['hæpi]
glücklicherweise luckily ['lʌkɪli]
Grad degree [dɪ'griː]
Grammatik grammar ['græmə]

grau grey [greɪ]
grauenhaft horrible ['hɒrəbl]
groß big [bɪg]; large [lɑːdʒ]
▶ S.161 big – large – great
großartig great [greɪt]
▶ S.161 big – large – great
Größe *(Schuhgröße usw.)* size [saɪz]
Großeltern grandparents ['grænpeərənts]
Großmutter grandmother ['grænmʌðə]
Großstadt city ['sɪti]
Großvater grandfather ['grænfɑːðə]
grün green [griːn]
Grund reason ['riːzn] • **aus vielen Gründen** for lots of reasons
Gruppe group [gruːp]; *(Musikgruppe)* band [bænd]
gruselig scary ['skeəri]
Gruß: Liebe Grüße, … *(Briefschluss)* Love … [lʌv]
Grüß Dilip von mir. Say hi to Dilip for me.
gucken look [lʊk]
gut good [gʊd]; *(okay)* OK [əʊ'keɪ]; *(in Ordnung)* all right [ɔːl 'raɪt]; *(gesundheitlich gut, wohlauf)* well [wel]; fine [faɪn] • **Es geht mir/ihm gut.** I'm/He's fine. • **gute Arbeit leisten** do a good job • **Guten Morgen.** Good morning. • **Guten Tag.** Hello.; *(nachmittags)* Good afternoon. • **Das hast du gut gemacht.** You did well.
▶ S.149 good – better – best
▶ S.157 What's wrong with you?

H

Haar, Haare hair *(no pl)* [heə]
haben have got ['hæv gɒt]; have [həv, hæv] • **Ich habe keinen Stuhl.** I haven't got a chair. • **Ich habe am 13. Juni/im Mai Geburtstag.** My birthday is on 13th June/in May. **Wann hast du Geburtstag?** When's your birthday? • **haben wollen** want [wɒnt] • **Was haben wir als Hausaufgabe auf?** What's for homework?
Hafen harbour ['hɑːbə]
Hähnchen chicken ['tʃɪkɪn]
halb zwölf half past 11 [hɑːf]
Hallo! Hi! [haɪ]; Hello. [hə'ləʊ]
Hals throat [θrəʊt]
Halsschmerzen haben have a sore throat [sɔː 'θrəʊt]
▶ S.157 What's wrong with you?
halten 1. hold [həʊld] **2. etwas warm/kühl/offen/…** **halten** keep sth. warm/cool/

Dictionary (German – English)   195

open/... [kiːp]
3. Halt den Mund! Shut up. [ˌʃʌt ˈʌp]
4. Was hältst du von ...? What do you think about/of ...?
▶ S.159 (to) think
Hamburger hamburger [ˈhæmbɜːgə]
Hamster hamster [ˈhæmstə]
Hand hand [hænd]
Handy mobile (phone) [ˈməʊbaɪl]
Happyend happy ending [ˌhæpiˈendɪŋ]
hart hard [hɑːd] • **hart arbeiten** work hard
hassen hate [heɪt]
häufig often [ˈɒfn]
Haus house [haʊs] • **im Haus der Shaws / bei den Shaws zu Hause** at the Shaws' house • **nach Hause gehen** go home [həʊm] • **nach Hause kommen** come home; get home • **zu Hause** at home
Hausaufgabe(n) homework (no pl) [ˈhəʊmwɜːk] • **die Hausaufgabe(n) machen** do homework • **Was haben wir als Hausaufgabe auf?** What's for homework?
Hausmeister/in caretaker [ˈkeəteɪkə]
Haustier pet [pet]
Haustür front door [ˌfrʌnt ˈdɔː]
Heim home [həʊm]
heiß hot [hɒt]
heißen 1. Ich heiße ... My name is ... **Wie heißt du?** What's your name? **2. Sie heißen dich in ... willkommen** They welcome you to ... [ˈwelkəm]
Held/in hero [ˈhɪərəʊ], pl heroes [ˈhɪərəʊz]
helfen help [help]
Helikopter helicopter [ˈhelɪkɒptə]
hell (leuchtend) bright [braɪt]
Hemd shirt [ʃɜːt]
herauf up [ʌp]
heraus out [aʊt] • **aus ... heraus** out of ... [ˈaʊt_əv]
▶ S.146 out
herausfinden find out [ˌfaɪnd_ˈaut]; (entdecken) discover [dɪˈskʌvə] • **etwas über etwas herausfinden** learn sth. about sth. [lɜːn]
herausnehmen take out [ˌteɪk_ˈaut]
herbringen bring [brɪŋ]
Herbst autumn [ˈɔːtəm]
Herd cooker [ˈkʊkə]
hereinkommen come in [ˌkʌm_ˈɪn]
Herr Brown Mr Brown [ˈmɪstə]
herum: anders herum the other way round [raʊnd] • **um ... herum** round • **ganz um die Burg herum** all around the castle [ˈɔːl_ə͵raʊnd]
herumgeben pass round [ˌpɑːs ˈraʊnd]
herunter down [daʊn]

herunterfallen (von) fall off [ˌfɔːl_ˈɒf]
Herz heart [hɑːt]
Herzlichen Glückwunsch zum Geburtstag. Happy birthday. [ˌhæpi ˈbɜːθdeɪ]
heute today [təˈdeɪ] • **heute Morgen/Nachmittag/Abend** this morning/afternoon/evening **heute Nacht** tonight [təˈnaɪt] **das Programm von heute** today's programme
▶ S.150 tonight's programme – Zeitangaben mit s-Genitiv
heutig: das heutige Programm today's programme
▶ S.150 tonight's programme – Zeitangaben mit s-Genitiv
hier here [hɪə] • **Hier bitte.** (Bitte sehr.) Here you are. • **hier drinnen** in here [ˌɪn ˈhɪə] • **hier entlang** this way [ˈðɪs weɪ] • **Hier spricht Isabel. / Hier ist Isabel.** (am Telefon) This is Isabel. • **Hier steht: ... / Es heißt hier: ...** (im Text) It says here: ...
▶ S.157 The text says ...
hierher here [hɪə]
Hilfe help [help]
Himmel sky [skaɪ] • **am Himmel** in the sky
hinauf up [ʌp] • **den Hügel hinauf** up the hill
hinaufklettern (auf) climb [klaɪm] **Klettere auf einen Baum.** Climb a tree.
hinaus out [aʊt] • **aus ... hinaus** out of ... [ˈaʊt_əv]
▶ S.146 out
hinein: in ... hinein into ... [ˈɪntə, ˈɪntʊ]
hinfallen fall [fɔːl]; fall down
hinkommen (gelangen) get [get]
hinsetzen: sich hinsetzen sit down [ˌsɪt ˈdaʊn]
hinstellen: sich hinstellen stand [stænd]
hinten (im Zimmer) at the back (of the room) [bæk]
hinter behind [bɪˈhaɪnd] • **im hinteren Teil (des Zimmers)** at the back (of the room) [bæk]
Hintergrund background [ˈbækgraʊnd]
Hintertür back door
hinüber zu/nach ... over to ... [ˈəʊvə]
hinunter down [daʊn]
hinzufügen (zu) add (to) [æd]
Hirsch deer, pl deer [dɪə]
Hobby hobby [ˈhɒbi], pl hobbies
hochheben: etwas hochheben pick sth. up [ˌpɪk_ˈʌp]
hochsehen (von) look up (from) [ˌlʊk_ˈʌp]

Hockey hockey [ˈhɒki]
Hockeyplatz, -feld hockey pitch [pɪtʃ]
Hockeyschuhe hockey shoes [ʃuːz]
Hof yard [jɑːd] • **auf dem Hof** in the yard
hoffen hope [həʊp]
holen (besorgen) get [get]
Holz wood [wʊd]
hören hear [hɪə] • **Na hör mal!** Come on. [ˌkʌm_ˈɒn]
Hose trousers (pl) [ˈtraʊzəz]
▶ S.147 Plural words
Hotel hotel [həʊˈtel]
Hotline hotline [ˈhɒtlaɪn]
hübsch pretty [ˈprɪti]
Hubschrauber helicopter [ˈhelɪkɒptə]
Hügel hill [hɪl]
Huhn chicken [ˈtʃɪkɪn]
Hülle cover [ˈkʌvə]
Hund dog [dɒg]
hundert hundred [ˈhʌndrəd]
Hunger haben, hungrig sein be hungry [ˈhʌŋgri]
Hurra! Hooray! [huˈreɪ]
Hut hat [hæt]

I

ich I [aɪ] • **Ich auch.** Me too. [ˌmiː ˈtuː] • **Das bin ich.** That's me. **Warum ich?** Why me?
Idee idea [aɪˈdɪə]
Igel hedgehog [ˈhedʒhɒg]
ihm him; (bei Dingen, Tieren) it
ihn him; (bei Dingen, Tieren) it
ihnen them [ðəm, ðem]
Ihnen (höfliche Anrede) you [juː]
ihr (Plural von „du") you [juː]
ihr: Hilf ihr. Help her. [hə, hɜː]
ihr(e) ... (besitzanzeigend) (zu „she") her ... [hə, hɜː]; (zu „they") their ... [ðeə]
Ihr(e) ... (höfliche Anrede) your ... [jɔː]
ihrer, ihre, ihrs (zu „she") hers [hɜːz]; (zu „they") theirs [ðeəz]
▶ S.147 Possessive pronouns
Ihrer, Ihre, Ihrs (höfliche Anrede) yours [jɔːz]
▶ S.147 Possessive pronouns
im: im Alter von 16 Jahren at 16 **im Ausland** abroad [əˈbrɔːd] • **im Fernsehen** on TV • **im Flugzeug** on the plane • **im Haus der Shaws** at the Shaws' house • **im hinteren Teil (des Zimmers)** at the back (of the room) [bæk] • **im Internet surfen** surf the internet • **im Jahr 1948** in 1948 • **im Mai** in May **im Moment** at the moment • **im Radio** on the radio • **im Zug** on the train

Dictionary (German – English)

Imbiss snack [snæk]
immer always ['ɔːlweɪz] • **immer noch** still [stɪl]
in in • **in … (hinein)** into … ['ɪntə, 'ɪntʊ] • **in den Zug/Bus einsteigen** get on the train/bus • **in der …straße** in … Street • **in der Hamiltonstraße 7** at 7 Hamilton Street • **in der Nacht** at night **in der Nähe von** near • **in der Pause** *(zwischen Schulstunden)* at break • **in der Schule** at school **in die falsche Richtung** the wrong way • **in die Sauna gehen** have a sauna • **in Eile sein** be in a hurry **ins Bett gehen** go to bed • **ins Kino gehen** go to the cinema • **in Schwierigkeiten sein** be in trouble ['trʌbl] • **in Urlaub fahren** go on holiday • **in Urlaub sein** be on holiday • **in welche Richtung?** which way? • **Ich bin noch nie in Bath gewesen.** I've never been to Bath.
indirekte Frage indirect question [ˌɪndərekt 'kwestʃən]
▶ S.164 Höflich um Auskunft bitten
Infinitiv infinitive [ɪn'fɪnətɪv]
Information(en) (über) information (about/on) *(no pl)* [ˌɪnfə'meɪʃn]
Informationstechnologie (IT) information technology (IT) [tek'nɒlədʒi], [ˌaɪ 'tiː]
Ingenieur/in engineer [ˌendʒɪ'nɪə]
Inliner skates [skeɪts] • **Inliner fahren** skate
innen (drin) inside [ˌɪn'saɪd]
Innenstadt city centre [ˌsɪti 'sentə]
Insel island ['aɪlənd]
Installation installation [ˌɪnstə'leɪʃn]
installieren install [ɪn'stɔːl]
Instrument instrument ['ɪnstrəmənt]
interessant interesting ['ɪntrəstɪŋ]
Internet internet ['ɪntənet] • **im Internet surfen** surf the internet
Interview interview ['ɪntəvjuː]
interviewen interview ['ɪntəvjuː]
irgendetwas anything ['eniθɪŋ]
▶ S.160 something – anything
irgendjemand anybody ['enibɒdi]
▶ S.160 somebody – anybody
irgendwelche any ['eni]
irgendwo(hin) somewhere ['sʌmweə]; anywhere ['eniweə]
▶ S.160 somewhere – anywhere
irren: sich irren be wrong [rɒŋ]
IT (Informationstechnologie) IT (information technology) [ˌaɪ 'tiː], [tek'nɒlədʒi]

J

ja yes [jes]
Jacke, Jackett jacket ['dʒækɪt]
Jahr year [jɪə]
Jahrgangsstufe year [jɪə]
Jahrhundert century ['sentʃəri]
Januar January ['dʒænjuəri]
Jazz jazz [dʒæz]
je? *(jemals?)* ever? ['evə]
▶ S.157 The present perfect: questions
Jeans jeans *(pl)* [dʒiːnz]
▶ S.147 Plural words
jede(r, s) … *(Begleiter)* **1.** every … ['evri] **2.** *(jeder einzelne)* each … [iːtʃ]
jeder *(alle)* everybody ['evribɒdi]
jemals? ever? ['evə]
▶ S.157 The present perfect: questions
jemand somebody ['sʌmbədi]; *(irgendjemand)* anybody ['enibɒdi]
▶ S.160 somebody – anybody
jene(r, s) *(Singular)* that [ðət, ðæt]; *(Plural)* those [ðəʊz]
jetzt now [naʊ] • **jetzt gerade, jetzt sofort** right now
Job job [dʒɒb]
jubeln cheer [tʃɪə]
Judo judo ['dʒuːdəʊ] • **Judo machen** do judo
Jugend- junior ['dʒuːnɪə]
Jugendliche(r) kid [kɪd]; teenager ['tiːneɪdʒə]
Juli July [dʒu'laɪ]
jung young [jʌŋ]
Junge boy [bɔɪ]
Juni June [dʒuːn]
Junioren- junior ['dʒuːnɪə]

K

Käfig cage [keɪdʒ]
Kalender calendar ['kælɪndə]
kalt cold [kəʊld]
Kamel camel ['kæml]
Kamera camera ['kæmərə]
Kanal *(Fernseh-, Radiosender)* channel ['tʃænl]
Känguru kangaroo [ˌkæŋgə'ruː]
Kaninchen rabbit ['ræbɪt]
Kappe cap [kæp]
kaputt broken ['brəʊkən]
Karotte carrot ['kærət]
Karte *(Post-, Spielkarte)* card [kɑːd]
Kartoffel potato [pə'teɪtəʊ], *pl* -toes
Kartoffelchips crisps *(pl)* [krɪsps]
Käse cheese [tʃiːz]
Kästchen, Kasten box [bɒks]
Katze cat [kæt]
kaufen buy [baɪ]
Kaufhaus department store [dɪ'pɑːtmənt stɔː]

Kehle throat [θrəʊt]
kein(e) no; not a; not (…) any • **Ich habe keinen Stuhl.** I haven't got a chair. • **Ich mag kein(e) …** I don't like … • **keine Musik mehr** no more music
Keks biscuit ['bɪskɪt]
Kellner waiter ['weɪtə]
Kellnerin waitress ['weɪtrəs]
kennen know [nəʊ]
kennenlernen meet [miːt]
kennzeichnen mark up [ˌmɑːk_'ʌp]
Kind child [tʃaɪld], *pl* children ['tʃɪldrən]; kid [kɪd]
Kino cinema ['sɪnəmə] • **ins Kino gehen** go to the cinema
Kirche church [tʃɜːtʃ]
Kiste box [bɒks]
Klang sound [saʊnd]
klar clear [klɪə]
Klasse class [klɑːs]; form [fɔːm] **Klassenkamerad/in** classmate ['klɑːsmeɪt] • **Klassenlehrer/in** class teacher; form teacher • **Klassenzimmer** classroom ['klɑːsruːm]
klatschen: Beifall klatschen cheer [tʃɪə]
Klavier piano [pi'ænəʊ] • **Klavier spielen** play the piano
kleben: (auf-, ein)kleben glue [gluː]
Klebestift glue stick ['gluː stɪk]
Klebstoff glue [gluː]
Kleid dress [dres]
Kleider *(Kleidungsstücke)* clothes *(pl)* [kləʊðz, kləʊz]
Kleiderschrank wardrobe ['wɔːdrəʊb]
Kleidung(sstücke) clothes *(pl)* [kləʊðz, kləʊz]
klein little ['lɪtl]; small [smɔːl]
Kleinstadt town [taʊn]
klettern climb [klaɪm] • **Klettere auf einen Baum.** Climb a tree.
Klingel bell [bel]
klingeln ring [rɪŋ]
klingen sound [saʊnd]
Klinik clinic ['klɪnɪk]
klopfen (an) knock (on) [nɒk]
Klub club [klʌb]
klug clever ['klevə]
knapp: Das war knapp. That was close. [kləʊs]
Kneipe pub [pʌb]
Knie knee [niː]
kochen cook [kʊk]
Koffer suitcase ['suːtkeɪs]
Koje *(Etagenbett)* bunk (bed) [bʌŋk]
komisch *(witzig)* funny ['fʌni]
kommen come [kʌm]; *(hinkommen)* get [get] • **Ich komme aus …** I'm from … • **Wo kommst du her?** Where are you from? • **nach Hause kommen** come home; get

Dictionary (German – English) **197**

home • **zu spät kommen** be late
Kommt nicht in Frage! No way!
Ach komm! Come on. [ˌkʌm_ˈɒn]
Na los, komm. Come on.
König king [kɪŋ]
können can [kən, kæn] • **ich kann
nicht ...** I can't ... [kɑːnt]
konnte(n): ich/er konnte ... I/he
could ... [kəd, kʊd]
kontrollieren *(prüfen)* check [tʃek]
Kopf head [hed]
Kopfschmerzen headache [ˈhedeɪk]
▶ S.157 What's wrong with you?
kopieren copy [ˈkɒpi]
Korb basket [ˈbɑːskɪt] • **ein Korb
Äpfel** a basket of apples
Körper body [ˈbɒdi]
korrigieren correct [kəˈrekt]
kosten *(Essen probieren)* try [traɪ]
kosten: Er/Sie/Es kostet 1 Pfund. It's
£1. • **Sie kosten 35 Pence.** They
are 35p. • **Wie viel kostet/kosten
...?** How much is/are ...?
kostenlos free [friː]
köstlich delicious [dɪˈlɪʃəs]
Kraft *(Energie)* energy [ˈenədʒi]
Kram stuff [stʌf]
krank ill [ɪl]
▶ S.157 What's wrong with you?
Krankenhaus hospital [ˈhɒspɪtl]
kreuzen; sich kreuzen cross [krɒs]
kriegen get [get]
Krokodil crocodile [ˈkrɒkədaɪl]
Krug jug [dʒʌg] • **ein Krug
Orangensaft** a jug of orange juice
Küche kitchen [ˈkɪtʃɪn]
Kuchen cake [keɪk]
Küchenschrank cupboard [ˈkʌbəd]
Kugelschreiber pen [pen]
Kuh cow [kaʊ]
kühl cool [kuːl]
Kühlschrank fridge [frɪdʒ]
Kummer worry [ˈwʌri]
**kümmern 1. sich um etwas/jn.
kümmern** look after sth./sb.
[ˌlʊk_ˈɑːftə]
**2. Kümmere dich um deine
eigenen Angelegenheiten!** Mind
your own business. [ˌmaɪnd jər_ˌəʊn
ˈbɪznəs]
Kunde, Kundin customer [ˈkʌstəmə]
Kunst art [ɑːt]
kurz short [ʃɔːt] • **kurze Hose**
shorts *(pl)* [ʃɔːts]
▶ S.147 Plural words

L

lächeln smile [smaɪl]
lachen laugh [lɑːf] • **laut lachen**
laugh out loud

Laden *(Geschäft)* shop [ʃɒp]
Lampe lamp [læmp]
Land *(auch als Gegensatz zur Stadt)*
country [ˈkʌntri]; *(Grund und Boden)*
land [lænd] • **auf dem Land** in the
country
landen land [lænd]
Landkarte map [mæp]
lang long [lɒŋ] • **drei Tage lang** for
three days
langsam slow [sləʊ]
langweilig boring [ˈbɔːrɪŋ]
Lärm noise [nɔɪz]
lärmend noisy [ˈnɔɪzi]
Lasagne lasagne [ləˈzænjə]
lassen let [let] • **Lass uns ... / Lasst
uns ...** Let's ... • **Lass das!** Stop
that!
Lauf run [rʌn]
laufen run [rʌn]
Läufer/in runner [ˈrʌnə]
laut loud [laʊd]; *(lärmend)* noisy
[ˈnɔɪzi] • **laut lachen** laugh out
loud
Laut sound [saʊnd]
läuten ring [rɪŋ]
leben live [lɪv]
Leben life [laɪf], *pl* lives [laɪvz]
Lebensmittel food [fuːd]
lecker delicious [dɪˈlɪʃəs]
ledig single [ˈsɪŋgl]
leer empty [ˈempti]
legen *(hin-, ablegen)* put [pʊt]
lehren teach [tiːtʃ]
Lehrer/in teacher [ˈtiːtʃə]
leicht *(nicht schwierig)* easy [ˈiːzi]
leider I'm afraid [əˈfreɪd]
leidtun: Tut mir leid. I'm sorry. [ˈsɒri]
leise quiet [ˈkwaɪət]
Lektion *(im Schulbuch)* unit [ˈjuːnɪt]
lernen learn [lɜːn]
Lern- und Arbeitstechniken study
skills [ˈstʌdi skɪlz]
lesen read [riːd]
Leser/in reader [ˈriːdə]
letzte(r, s) last [lɑːst]
leuchtend bright [braɪt]
Leute people [ˈpiːpl]
Liebe love [lʌv]
Liebe Grüße, ... *(Briefschluss)* Love ...
[lʌv]
lieben love [lʌv]
Lieber Jay, ... Dear Jay ... [dɪə]
lieber: etwas lieber mögen like sth.
better
Liebling dear [dɪə]; sweetheart
[ˈswiːthɑːt]
Lieblings-: meine Lieblingsfarbe my
favourite colour [ˈfeɪvərɪt]
Lied song [sɒŋ]
lila purple [ˈpɜːpl]
Limonade lemonade [ˌleməˈneɪd]

Lineal ruler [ˈruːlə]
linke(r, s) left [left] • **links, auf der
linken Seite** on the left • **(nach)
links abbiegen** turn left • **nach
links schauen** look left
▶ S.143 left – right
▶ S.165 (to) turn
Liste list [lɪst]
Livemusik live music [laɪv]
Loch hole [həʊl]
Lokal *(Kneipe)* pub [pʌb]
Löwe lion [ˈlaɪən]

M

machen do [duː]; make [meɪk] • **die
Hausaufgabe(n) machen** do
homework • **einen Ausflug
machen** go on a trip • **einen
Spaziergang machen** go for a walk
• **eine Übung machen** do an
exercise • **Ferien machen** be on
holiday • **Fotos machen** take
photos • **Judo machen** do judo
sich Notizen machen take notes
sich Sorgen machen (wegen, um)
worry (about) [ˈwʌri] • **(Zauber-)
Kunststücke machen** do tricks
Reiten macht Spaß. Riding is fun.
Mädchen girl [gɜːl]
Magazin *(Zeitschrift)* magazine
[ˌmægəˈziːn]
Magen stomach [ˈstʌmək]
Magenschmerzen stomach ache
[ˈstʌmək_eɪk]
▶ S.157 What's wrong with you?
Magst du ...? Do you like ...?
Mai May [meɪ]
Make-up make-up [ˈmeɪkʌp]
Mal(e); -mal time(s) [taɪm(z)]
malen paint [peɪnt]
Maler/in painter [ˈpeɪntə]
Mama mum [mʌm]
manchmal sometimes [ˈsʌmtaɪmz]
Mann man [mæn], *pl* men [men]
Mannschaft team [tiːm]
Mappe *(des Sprachenportfolios)*
dossier [ˈdɒsieɪ]
markieren mark up [ˌmɑːk_ˈʌp]
Markt market [ˈmɑːkɪt]
Marmelade *(Orangenmarmelade)*
marmalade [ˈmɑːməleɪd]
März March [mɑːtʃ]
Mathematik maths [mæθs]
Mauer wall [wɔːl]
Maulwurf mole [məʊl]
Maus mouse [maʊs], *pl* mice [maɪs]
Mediation *(Sprachmittlung)*
mediation [ˌmiːdiˈeɪʃn]
Meer sea [siː]

Meerschweinchen guinea pig ['gɪni pɪg]
mehr more [mɔː] • **mehr als** more than • **mehr als ich** more than me • **nicht mehr** not (...) any more • **viel mehr** lots more **keine Musik mehr** no more music
Meile *(= ca. 1,6 km)* mile [maɪl]
meilenweit for miles [maɪlz]
mein(e) ... my ... [maɪ] • **meine neuen** my new ones [wʌnz]
meinen *(glauben)* think [θɪŋk]; *(sagen wollen)* mean [miːn] **Meinst du wirklich?** Do you really think so?
meiner, meine, meins mine [maɪn]
▶ S.147 Possessive pronouns
meist: (der/die/das) meiste ...; am meisten most [məʊst] • **die meisten Leute** most people
meistens usually ['juːʒuəli]
Meister/in *(Champion)* champion ['tʃæmpiən]
Menge: eine Menge *(viel, viele)* a lot (of) [lɒt]; lots (of) [lɒts]
Menschen people ['piːpl]
merken: sich etwas merken remember sth. [rɪ'membə]
Meter metre ['miːtə]
mich me [miː]
Milch milk [mɪlk]
Mindmap mind map ['maɪnd mæp]
Mini- mini- ['mɪni]
Minute minute ['mɪnɪt]
mir me [miː]
mit with [wɪð] • **mit 16 (Jahren)** at 16 • **mit dem Auto/Zug/Rad/... fahren** go by car/train/bike/...
mitbringen bring [brɪŋ]
mitmachen: bei etwas/jm. mitmachen join sth./sb. [dʒɔɪn]
Mitschüler/in classmate ['klɑːsmeɪt]
Mittagessen lunch [lʌntʃ] • **zum Mittagessen** for lunch
Mittagspause lunch break ['lʌntʃ breɪk]
Mitte centre ['sentə]; middle ['mɪdl]
Mitteilung *(Notiz)* note [nəʊt]
mittel(groß) medium ['miːdiəm]
Mittelteil middle ['mɪdl]
Mittwoch Wednesday ['wenzdeɪ, 'wenzdi] *(siehe auch unter „Freitag")*
Mobiltelefon mobile phone [,məʊbaɪl 'fəʊn]; mobile ['məʊbaɪl]
möchte: Ich möchte gern ... (haben) I'd like ... (= I would like ...) [laɪk] **Ich möchte gehen** I'd like to go **Ich möchte nicht gehen** I wouldn't like to go • **Möchtest du / Möchten Sie ...?** Would you like ...?
Mode fashion ['fæʃn]

Modell *(-auto, -schiff; Fotomodell)* model ['mɒdl]
Moderator/in presenter [prɪ'zentə]
mögen like [laɪk]; *(sehr mögen)* love [lʌv] • **etwas lieber mögen** like sth. better
möglich possible ['pɒsəbl]
Möglichkeit *(Gelegenheit, Chance)* chance [tʃɑːns]
Möhre carrot ['kærət]
Moment moment ['məʊmənt] • **im Moment** at the moment • **genau in dem Moment** just then • **Moment mal!** Wait a minute. ['mɪnɪt]
Monat month [mʌnθ]
Mond moon [muːn]
Montag Monday ['mʌndeɪ, 'mʌndi] *(siehe auch unter „Freitag")*
morgen tomorrow [tə'mɒrəʊ] • **das Wetter von morgen** tomorrow's weather
▶ S.150 tonight's programme – Zeitangaben mit s-Genitiv
Morgen morning ['mɔːnɪŋ] • **am Morgen, morgens** in the morning
MP3-Spieler MP3 player [,empiː'θriː ,pleɪə]
müde tired ['taɪəd]
Müll rubbish ['rʌbɪʃ]
Mülltonne bin [bɪn]; dustbin ['dʌstbɪn]
Multiple-Choice multiple choice [,mʌltɪpl 'tʃɔɪs]
Mund mouth [maʊθ] • **Halt den Mund!** Shut up. [,ʃʌt '_ʌp]
murren grumble ['grʌmbl]
Museum museum [mju'ziːəm]
Musical musical ['mjuːzɪkl]
Musik music ['mjuːzɪk]
müssen have to; must [mʌst] **nicht müssen** needn't ['niːdnt]
▶ S.166 must – needn't – mustn't
Mutter mother ['mʌðə]
Mutti mum [mʌm]
Mütze cap [kæp]

N

Na ja ... / Na gut ... Oh well ... [əʊ 'wel]
Na und? So? [səʊ]
nach **1.** *(örtlich)* to [tə, tu] • **nach draußen** outside • **nach drinnen** inside • **nach Hause gehen** go home • **nach Hause kommen** come home; get home • **nach oben** up; *(im Haus)* upstairs [,ʌp'steəz] • **nach unten** down; *(im Haus)* downstairs [,daʊn'steəz] **nach vorn** to the front [frʌnt] **2.** *(zeitlich)* after • **Viertel nach 11** quarter past 11 [pɑːst] **3. nach etwas fragen** ask about sth.

[ə'baʊt] • **jn. nach dem Weg fragen** ask sb. the way
Nachbar/in neighbour ['neɪbə]
nachdem after ['ɑːftə]
nachdenken über think about [θɪŋk]
▶ S.159 (to) think
Nachmittag afternoon [,ɑːftə'nuːn] **am Nachmittag, nachmittags** in the afternoon
Nachrichten news *(no pl)* [njuːz]
nächste(r, s): am nächsten Tag the next day [nekst] • **der Nächste sein** be next • **Was haben wir als Nächstes?** What have we got next?
Nacht night [naɪt] • **heute Nacht** tonight [tə'naɪt] • **in der Nacht, nachts** at night
nahe (bei) near [nɪə]
Nähe: in der Nähe von near [nɪə]
Name name [neɪm]
Nase nose [nəʊz] • **die Nase voll haben (von etwas)** be fed up (with sth.) [,fed_'ʌp]
Nashorn rhino ['raɪnəʊ]
natürlich of course [əv 'kɔːs]
Naturwissenschaft science ['saɪəns]
Nebel fog [fɒg]
neben next to ['nekst tə]
neblig foggy ['fɒgi]
nehmen take [teɪk] • **Ich nehme es.** *(beim Einkaufen)* I'll take it.
nein no [nəʊ]
nennen *(rufen, bezeichnen)* call [kɔːl]; *(benennen)* name [neɪm]
nervös nervous ['nɜːvəs]
nett nice [naɪs]
neu new [njuː]
nicht not [nɒt] • **nicht mehr** not (...) any more • **Das glaube ich nicht. / Ich glaube nicht.** I don't think so. • **..., nicht wahr?** ..., right? **Du machst Witze, nicht wahr? / Das ist nicht dein Ernst, oder?** You're joking, aren't you? • **noch nicht** not (...) yet [jet]
▶ S.156 The present perfect: statements
nichts nothing ['nʌθɪŋ]; not (...) anything ['eniθɪŋ] • **Nichts zu danken.** You're welcome. ['welkəm]
▶ S.160 something – anything
nicken (mit) nod [nɒd]
nie, niemals never ['nevə]
▶ S.156 The present perfect: statements
niemand nobody ['nəʊbədi]; not (...) anybody ['enibɒdi]
▶ S.160 somebody – anybody
nirgendwo(hin) not (...) anywhere ['eniweə]
▶ S.160 somewhere – anywhere
noch: noch ein(e) ... another ... [ə'nʌðə]; one more ... [mɔː] • **noch 45 Pence** another 45p • **noch**

Dictionary (German – English)   199

einmal again [əˈgen] • **noch nicht** not (...) yet [jet] • **(immer) noch** still [stɪl]
▶ S.156 The present perfect: statements
nörgeln grumble [ˈgrʌmbl]
normalerweise usually [ˈjuːʒəli]
Notiz note [nəʊt] • **sich Notizen machen** take notes
November November [nəʊˈvembə]
null o [əʊ]; zero [ˈzɪərəʊ]
Nummer number [ˈnʌmbə]
nun now [naʊ] • **Nun, ...** Well, ... [wel]
nur only [ˈəʊnli]; just [dʒʌst] • **nur zum Spaß** just for fun

O

ob if [ɪf]
oben *(an der Spitze)* at the top (of) [tɒp]; *(im Haus)* upstairs [ˌʌpˈsteəz]
nach oben up; *(im Haus)* upstairs
Oberbegriff group word [ˈgruːp wɜːd]
oberhalb von over [ˈəʊvə]
Oberteil top [tɒp]
Obst fruit [fruːt]
Obstkuchen pie [paɪ]
Obstsalat fruit salad [ˈfruːt ˌsæləd]
oder or [ɔː] • **Das ist nicht dein Ernst, oder?** You're joking, aren't you?
offen open [ˈəʊpən]
öffnen; sich öffnen open [ˈəʊpən]
oft often [ˈɒfn]
ohne without [wɪˈðaʊt]
Ohr ear [ɪə]
Ohrenschmerzen earache [ˈɪəreɪk]
▶ S.157 What's wrong with you?
Ohrring earring [ˈɪərɪŋ]
Oje! Oh dear! [əʊ ˈdɪə]
okay OK [əʊˈkeɪ]
Oktober October [ɒkˈtəʊbə]
Oma grandma [ˈgrænmɑː]; granny [ˈgræni]
Onkel uncle [ˈʌŋkl]
Opa grandpa [ˈgrænpɑː]
Orange orange [ˈɒrɪndʒ]
orange(farben) orange [ˈɒrɪndʒ]
Orangenmarmelade marmalade [ˈmɑːməleɪd]
Orangensaft orange juice [ˈɒrɪndʒ dʒuːs]
ordentlich tidy [ˈtaɪdi]
Ordnung: in Ordnung all right [ɔːl ˈraɪt]
Orgel organ [ˈɔːgən]
Ort place [pleɪs]
Outfit *(Kleidung; Ausrüstung)* outfit [ˈaʊtfɪt]

P

paar: ein paar some [səm, sʌm]; *(einige wenige)* a few [fjuː]
Paar: ein Paar a pair (of) [peə]
Päckchen packet [ˈpækɪt] • **ein Päckchen Pfefferminzbonbons** a packet of mints
packen pack [pæk]
Packung packet [ˈpækɪt] • **eine Packung Pfefferminzbonbons** a packet of mints
Paket parcel [ˈpɑːsl]
pantomimisch darstellen mime [maɪm]
Papa dad [dæd]
Papagei parrot [ˈpærət]
Papier paper [ˈpeɪpə]
Park park [pɑːk]
Partner/in partner [ˈpɑːtnə]
Partnerstadt twin town [ˌtwɪn ˈtaʊn]
Party party [ˈpɑːti] • **eine Party feiern/veranstalten** have a party
passen fit [fɪt]
passieren (mit) happen (to) [ˈhæpən]
Pause break [breɪk] • **in der Pause** *(zwischen Schulstunden)* at break
Pence pence (p) [pens]
Person person [ˈpɜːsn]
Pfad path [pɑːθ]
Pfefferminzbonbons mints [mɪnts]
pfeifen whistle [ˈwɪsl]
Pferd horse [hɔːs]
Pfund *(britische Währung)* pound (£) [paʊnd] • **Es kostet 1 Pfund.** It's £1.
Piano piano [piˈænəʊ]
Picknick picnic [ˈpɪknɪk]
piepsen bleep [bliːp]
Piepton bleep [bliːp]
pink(farben) pink [pɪŋk]
Pirat/in pirate [ˈpaɪrət]
Pizza pizza [ˈpiːtsə]
Plan plan [plæn]
planen plan [plæn]
Planet planet [ˈplænɪt]
Platz *(Ort, Stelle)* place [pleɪs]; *(in der Stadt)* square [skweə]
Plätzchen biscuit [ˈbɪskɪt]
plaudern chat [tʃæt]
plötzlich suddenly [ˈsʌdnli]
Polizei police *(pl)* [pəˈliːs]
Polizeiwache, Polizeirevier police station [pəˈliːs steɪʃn]
Polizist/in policeman [pəˈliːsmən]/ policewoman [pəˈliːswʊmən]
Poltergeist poltergeist [ˈpəʊltəgaɪst]
Pommes frites chips *(pl)* [tʃɪps]
Popcorn popcorn [ˈpɒpkɔːn]
Postamt post office [ˈpəʊst ˌɒfɪs]
Poster poster [ˈpəʊstə]
Postkarte postcard [ˈpəʊstkɑːd]

Präsentation presentation [ˌpreznˈteɪʃn]
präsentieren: (jm.) etwas präsentieren present sth. (to sb.) [prɪˈzent]
Preis *(Kaufpreis)* price [praɪs]; *(Gewinn)* prize [praɪz]
Probe *(am Theater)* rehearsal [rɪˈhɜːsl]
proben *(am Theater)* rehearse [rɪˈhɜːs]
probieren try [traɪ]
Problem problem [ˈprɒbləm]
Programm programme [ˈprəʊgræm]
Projekt (über, zu) project (on, about) [ˈprɒdʒekt] • **ein Projekt machen, durchführen** do a project
prüfen *(überprüfen)* check [tʃek]
Publikum audience [ˈɔːdɪəns]
Pullover pullover [ˈpʊləʊvə]
Punkt *(bei Test, Quiz)* point [pɔɪnt]
putzen clean [kliːn] • **Ich putze mir die Zähne.** I clean my teeth.
Putzfrau, -mann cleaner [ˈkliːnə]

Q

Quiz quiz [kwɪz], *pl* quizzes [ˈkwɪzɪz]

R

Rad fahren cycle [ˈsaɪkl]; ride a bike [ˌraɪd ə ˈbaɪk]
Radfahrt bike ride [ˈbaɪk raɪd]
Radiergummi rubber [ˈrʌbə]
Radio radio [ˈreɪdɪəʊ] • **im Radio** on the radio
Radweg cycle path [ˈsaɪkl pɑːθ]
Rap rap [ræp]
raten guess [ges]
Ratespiel quiz [kwɪz], *pl* quizzes [ˈkwɪzɪz]
Rätsel *(Geheimnis)* mystery [ˈmɪstri]
Rauch smoke [sməʊk]
rauchen smoke [sməʊk]
Raum room [ruːm]
Recht haben be right [raɪt]
rechte(r, s) right [raɪt] • **rechts, auf der rechten Seite** on the right **(nach) rechts abbiegen** turn right **nach rechts schauen** look right
▶ S.143 left – right
▶ S.165 (to) turn
rechtzeitig in time [ɪn ˈtaɪm]
recycelt recycled [ˌriːˈsaɪkld]
Recycling recycling [ˌriːˈsaɪklɪŋ]
reden (mit, über) talk (to, about) [tɔːk]; speak (to, about) [spiːk] **Wovon redest du?** What are you talking about?
Regal(brett) shelf [ʃelf], *pl* shelves [ʃelvz]
Regen rain [reɪn]

regnen rain [reɪn]
regnerisch rainy ['reɪni]
Reh deer, *pl* deer [dɪə]
reich rich [rɪtʃ]
reichen *(weitergeben)* pass [pɑːs]
Reihe **1. Du bist an der Reihe.** It's your turn. [tɜːn] • **Wer ist an der Reihe?** Whose turn is it? [huːz]
2. *(Sendereihe, Serie)* series, *pl* series ['sɪəriːz]
Reise trip [trɪp]; *(Fahrt)* journey ['dʒɜːni]
reisen travel ['trævl]
reiten ride [raɪd] • **reiten gehen** go riding
Religion *(Religionsunterricht)* RE [ˌɑːr'iː], Religious Education [rɪˌlɪdʒəs_edʒu'keɪʃn]
rennen run [rʌn]
Reportage (über) report (on) [rɪ'pɔːt]
Rest rest [rest]
Restaurant restaurant ['restrɒnt]; *(Imbissstube, Café)* café ['kæfeɪ]
Resultat result [rɪ'zʌlt]
retten save [seɪv]
richtig right [raɪt]
Richtung way [weɪ] • **in diese Richtung** this way • **in die falsche Richtung** the wrong way • **in welche Richtung?** which way?
▶ S.165 way
riechen smell [smel]
Ring ring [rɪŋ]
Rock skirt [skɜːt]
Rollenspiel role play ['rəʊl pleɪ]
Rollstuhl wheelchair ['wiːltʃeə]
römisch; Römer, Römerin Roman ['rəʊmən]
rosa pink [pɪŋk]
rot red [red]
Rückfahrkarte return ticket [rɪ'tɜːn ˌtɪkɪt]
rufen call [kɔːl]; shout [ʃaʊt] • **die Polizei rufen** call the police
ruhig quiet ['kwaɪət]
rund round [raʊnd]
Rundgang (durch das Haus) tour (of the house) [tʊə]
runterladen download [ˌdaʊn'ləʊd]

S

Sache thing [θɪŋ]
Saft juice [dʒuːs]
sagen say [seɪ] • **Sagt mir eure Namen.** Tell me your names. [tel] **jm. sagen, dass er/sie etwas tun soll** tell sb. to do sth.
Salat **1.** *(Kopfsalat)* lettuce ['letɪs]
2. *(Gericht, Beilage)* salad ['sæləd]
sammeln collect [kə'lekt]

Sammler/in collector [kə'lektə]
Samstag Saturday ['sætədeɪ, 'sætədi] *(siehe auch unter „Freitag")*
Sandale sandal ['sændl]
Sandwich sandwich ['sænwɪtʃ]
Sänger/in singer ['sɪŋə]
Sanitäter/in paramedic [ˌpærə'medɪk]
Satz sentence ['sentəns]
sauber clean [kliːn] • **sauber machen** clean
Sauna sauna ['sɔːnə] • **in die Sauna gehen** have a sauna
Schachtel packet ['pækɪt]
Schaf sheep, *pl* sheep [ʃiːp]
Schale bowl [bəʊl] • **eine Schale Cornflakes** a bowl of cornflakes
Schatz dear [dɪə]; sweetheart ['swiːthɑːt]
schätzen *(erraten)* guess [ges]
schauen look [lʊk] • **nach links/ rechts schauen** look left/right
Schaufenster shop window [ˌʃɒp 'wɪndəʊ]
Schauspiel drama ['drɑːmə]
Schauspieler/in actor ['æktə]
scheinen *(Sonne)* shine [ʃaɪn]
scherzen joke [dʒəʊk]
scheu shy [ʃaɪ]
scheußlich horrible ['hɒrəbl]
schicken (an) *(Post, E-Mail)* send (to) [send]; mail (to) [meɪl]
schieben push [pʊʃ]
Schiff boat [bəʊt]; ship [ʃɪp]
Schildkröte tortoise ['tɔːtəs]
Schlafanzug pyjamas *(pl)* [pə'dʒɑːməz]
schlafen sleep [sliːp]; *(nicht wach sein)* be asleep [ə'sliːp]
Schlafzimmer bedroom ['bedruːm]
schlagen hit [hɪt]
Schlange snake [sneɪk]
schlau clever ['klevə]
schlecht bad [bæd] • **schlechter** worse [wɜːs] • **am schlechtesten; der/die/das schlechteste** (the) worst [wɜːst]
▶ S.149 bad – worse – worst
schließen *(zumachen)* close [kləʊz]
schließlich at last [ət 'lɑːst]
schlimm bad [bæd] • **schlimmer** worse [wɜːs] • **am schlimmsten; der/die/das schlimmste** (the) worst [wɜːst]
▶ S.149 bad – worse – worst
Schlittschuh laufen skate [skeɪt]
Schlittschuhbahn ice rink ['aɪs rɪŋk]
Schloss castle ['kɑːsl]
Schluss end
Schlüssel key [kiː]
Schlüsselwort key word ['kiː wɜːd]
Schmuck jewellery ['dʒuːəlri]
schmutzig dirty ['dɜːti]

Schnee snow [snəʊ]
schnell quick [kwɪk]; fast [fɑːst]
Schokolade chocolate ['tʃɒklət]
schon already [ɔːl'redi] • **schon? yet?** [jet] • **schon mal?** ever? ['evə] **(vorher) schon mal** before [bɪ'fɔː]
▶ S.156 The present perfect: statements
▶ S.157 The present perfect: questions
schön beautiful ['bjuːtɪfl]; *(nett)* nice [naɪs] • **schön ordentlich** neat and tidy
Schrank cupboard ['kʌbəd]; *(Kleiderschrank)* wardrobe ['wɔːdrəʊb]
schrecklich terrible ['terəbl]; awful ['ɔːfl]
schreiben (an) write (to) [raɪt]
Schreiber/in writer ['raɪtə]
Schreibtisch desk [desk]
schreien shout [ʃaʊt]
Schriftsteller/in writer ['raɪtə]
Schritt step [step]
schüchtern shy [ʃaɪ]
Schuh shoe [ʃuː]
Schule school [skuːl] • **in der Schule** at school
Schüler/in student ['stjuːdənt]
Schulfach (school) subject ['sʌbdʒɪkt]
Schulheft exercise book ['eksəsaɪz bʊk]
Schulklasse class [klɑːs]; form [fɔːm]
Schultasche school bag ['skuːl bæg]
Schulter shoulder ['ʃəʊldə]
Schüssel bowl [bəʊl]
Schusswaffe gun [gʌn]
schwach weak [wiːk]
schwarz black [blæk]
schwer *(schwierig)* difficult ['dɪfɪkəlt]; hard [hɑːd]
Schwester sister ['sɪstə]
schwierig difficult ['dɪfɪkəlt]; hard [hɑːd]
Schwierigkeiten trouble ['trʌbl] • **in Schwierigkeiten sein** be in trouble
Schwimmbad, -becken swimming pool ['swɪmɪŋ puːl]
schwimmen swim [swɪm] **schwimmen gehen** go swimming
Schwimmer/in swimmer ['swɪmə]
See **1.** *(Binnensee)* lake [leɪk]
2. *(die See, das Meer)* sea [siː]
segeln sail [seɪl]
sehen see [siː] • **Siehst du?** See?
sehr very ['veri] • **Danke sehr!** Thanks very much! • **Er mag sie sehr.** He likes her a lot. [ə 'lɒt] **etwas sehr mögen/sehr lieben** like/love sth. very much
Seife soap [səʊp]
sein *(Verb)* be [biː]
sein(e) ... *(besitzanzeigend)* *(zu „he")* his ...; *(zu „it")* its ...
seiner, seine, seins his [hɪz]
▶ S.147 Possessive pronouns

Dictionary (German – English) 201

Seite 1. side [saɪd] • **auf der linken Seite** on the left • **auf der rechten Seite** on the right
2. *(Buch-, Heftseite)* page [peɪdʒ]
Auf welcher Seite sind wir? What page are we on?
selbstverständlich of course [əv ˈkɔːs]
senden (an) *(Post, E-Mail)* send (to) [send]; mail (to) [meɪl]
Sender *(Fernseh-, Radiokanal)* channel [ˈtʃænl]
Sendereihe series, *pl* series [ˈsɪəriːz]
September September [sepˈtembə]
Serie *(Sendereihe)* series, *pl* series [ˈsɪəriːz]
Sessel armchair [ˈɑːmtʃeə]
setzen: sich setzen sit [sɪt] • **Setz dich/Setzt euch zu mir.** Sit with me.
Shorts shorts *(pl)* [ʃɔːts]
▶ S.147 Plural words
Show show [ʃəʊ]
sicher 1. *(in Sicherheit)* safe (from) [seɪf]
2. sicher sein *(nicht zweifeln)* be sure [ʃʊə, ʃɔː]
Sicherheit: in Sicherheit (vor) safe (from) [seɪf]
Sicht: aus meiner Sicht from my point of view [ˌpɔɪnt_əv ˈvjuː]
sie 1. *(weibliche Person)* she [ʃiː]
Frag sie. Ask her. [hə, hɜː]
2. *(Ding, Tier)* it [ɪt]
3. *(Plural)* they [ðeɪ] • **Frag sie.** Ask them. [ðəm, ðem]
4. Sie *(höfliche Anrede)* you [juː]
Sieger/in winner [ˈwɪnə]
Silbe syllable [ˈsɪləbl]
singen sing [sɪŋ]
sitzen sit [sɪt]
Skateboard skateboard [ˈskeɪtbɔːd]
Skateboard fahren skate [skeɪt]
Sketch sketch [sketʃ]
Sklave, Sklavin slave [sleɪv]
Snack snack [snæk]
so: so süß so sweet [səʊ] • **so groß/ aufregend wie** as big/exciting as
sobald as soon as [əz ˈsuːn_əz]
Socke sock [sɒk]
soeben just [dʒʌst]
▶ S.156 The present perfect: statements
Sofa sofa [ˈsəʊfə]
Software software [ˈsɒftweə]
sogar even [ˈiːvn]
Sohn son [sʌn]
Sommer summer [ˈsʌmə]
Song song [sɒŋ]
Sonnabend Saturday [ˈsætədeɪ, ˈsætədi] *(siehe auch unter „Freitag")*
Sonne sun [sʌn]

Sonnenbrille: (eine) Sonnenbrille sunglasses *(pl)* [ˈsʌŋglɑːsɪz]
▶ S.147 Plural words
sonnig sunny [ˈsʌni]
Sonntag Sunday [ˈsʌndeɪ, ˈsʌndi] *(siehe auch unter „Freitag")*
sonst: Was weißt du sonst noch über ...? What else do you know about ...? [els]
Sorge worry [ˈwʌri] • **sich Sorgen machen (wegen, um)** worry (about) • **Mach dir keine Sorgen.** Don't worry.
sorgfältig careful [ˈkeəfl]
sowie *(sobald)* as soon as [əz ˈsuːn_əz]
sowieso anyway [ˈeniweɪ]
Spaghetti spaghetti [spəˈɡeti]
spannend exciting [ɪkˈsaɪtɪŋ]
sparen save [seɪv]
Spaß fun [fʌn] • **Spaß haben** have fun • **nur zum Spaß** just for fun **Reiten macht Spaß.** Riding is fun. **Viel Spaß!** Have fun!
spät late [leɪt] • **Wie spät ist es?** What's the time? • **zu spät sein/ kommen** be late
später later [ˈleɪtə]
spazieren gehen go for a walk [wɔːk]
Spaziergang walk [wɔːk] • **einen Spaziergang machen** go for a walk
Specht woodpecker [ˈwʊdpekə]
Spiegel mirror [ˈmɪrə]
Spiel game [ɡeɪm]; *(Wettkampf)* match [mætʃ]
spielen play [pleɪ]; *(Szene, Dialog)* act [ækt] • **Fußball spielen** play football • **Gitarre/Klavier spielen** play the guitar/the piano • **jm. einen Streich spielen** play a trick on sb.
Spieler/in player [ˈpleɪə]
Spielstein *(für Brettspiele)* counter [ˈkaʊntə]
Spion/in spy [spaɪ]
Spitze *(oberes Ende)* top [tɒp] • **an der Spitze (von)** at the top (of)
Sport; Sportart sport [spɔːt] • **Sport treiben** do sport
Sportausrüstung, Sportsachen sports gear *(no pl)* [ˈspɔːts ɡɪə]
Sportunterricht PE [ˌpiː_ˈiː], Physical Education [ˌfɪzɪkəl_edʒʊˈkeɪʃn]
Sprache language [ˈlæŋɡwɪdʒ]
Sprachmittlung *(Mediation)* mediation [ˌmiːdiˈeɪʃn]
sprechen (mit) speak (to) [spiːk]
Hier spricht Isabel. *(am Telefon)* This is Isabel.
springen jump [dʒʌmp]
Spülbecken, Spüle sink [sɪŋk]
Stadt *(Großstadt)* city [ˈsɪti]; *(Kleinstadt)* town [taʊn]

Stadtplan map [mæp]
Stadtzentrum city centre [ˌsɪti ˈsentə]
Stall *(für Kaninchen)* hutch [hʌtʃ]
Stammbaum family tree [ˈfæməli triː]
Standpunkt point of view [ˌpɔɪnt_əv ˈvjuː] • **von meinem Standpunkt aus gesehen** from my point of view
Star *(Film-, Popstar)* star [stɑː]
stark strong [strɒŋ]
Start start [stɑːt]
starten start [stɑːt]
Statue statue [ˈstætʃuː]
stehen stand [stænd] • **Hier steht: ...** *(im Text)* It says here: ...
▶ S.157 The text says ...
stehlen steal [stiːl]
Steigerung comparison [kəmˈpærɪsn]
Stein stone [stəʊn]
stellen *(hin-, abstellen)* put [pʊt] **Fragen stellen** ask questions • **(jm.) eine Falle stellen** set a trap (for sb.) [set] • **sich (hin)stellen** stand [stænd] • **Stell dir vor! / Stellt euch vor!** Guess what! [ˌges ˈwɒt]
sterben (an) die (of) [daɪ]
Stern star [stɑː]
Stichwort *(Schlüsselwort)* key word [ˈkiː wɜːd]
Stiefel boot [buːt]
still quiet [ˈkwaɪət]
Stimme voice [vɔɪs]
stimmen: Das stimmt. That's right. [raɪt] • **..., stimmt's?** ..., right?
stolz (auf jn./etwas) proud (of sb./sth.) [praʊd]
stoßen push [pʊʃ]
Strand beach [biːtʃ] • **am Strand** on the beach
Straße road [rəʊd]; street [striːt]
Streich trick [trɪk] • **jm. einen Streich spielen** play a trick on sb.
streiten: sich streiten argue [ˈɑːɡjuː]
strukturieren structure [ˈstrʌktʃə]
Strumpf sock [sɒk]
Stück piece [piːs] • **ein Stück Papier** a piece of paper
Student/in student [ˈstjuːdənt]
Studio studio [ˈstjuːdiəʊ]
Stuhl chair [tʃeə]
stumm: „stummer" Buchstabe *(nicht gesprochener Buchstabe)* silent letter [ˌsaɪlənt ˈletə]
Stunde hour [ˈaʊə]; *(Schulstunde)* lesson [ˈlesn]
Stundenplan timetable [ˈtaɪmteɪbl]
Sturm storm [stɔːm]
stürmisch stormy [ˈstɔːmi]
stürzen *(hinfallen)* fall [fɔːl]
suchen look for [ˈlʊk fɔː]; search (for) [sɜːtʃ]

Dictionary (German – English)

Supermarkt supermarket ['su:pəmɑːkɪt]
Suppe soup [su:p]
Surfbrett surfboard ['sɜːfbɔːd]
surfen gehen go surfing ['sɜːfɪŋ]
　im Internet surfen surf the internet [sɜːf]
süß sweet [swiːt]
Süßigkeiten sweets (pl) [swiːts]
Sweatshirt sweatshirt ['swetʃɜːt]
Szene scene [siːn]

T

Tabak tobacco [tə'bækəʊ]
Tafel (Wandtafel) board [bɔːd] • **an der/die Tafel** on the board
Tag day [deɪ] • **drei Tage (lang)** for three days • **eines Tages** one day
　Guten Tag. Hello.; (nachmittags) Good afternoon. [ɡʊd ˌɑːftə'nuːn]
Tagebuch diary ['daɪəri]
Tal valley ['væli]
Talboden valley floor [ˌvæli 'flɔː]
Tante aunt [ɑːnt]; auntie ['ɑːnti]
Tanz dance [dɑːns]
tanzen dance [dɑːns]
Tanzen dancing ['dɑːnsɪŋ]
Tänzer/in dancer ['dɑːnsə]
Tanzstunden, Tanzunterricht
　dancing lessons ['dɑːnsɪŋ ˌlesnz]
Tasche (Tragetasche, Beutel) bag [bæɡ]; (Hosentasche, Jackentasche) pocket ['pɒkɪt]
Taschengeld pocket money ['pɒkɪt ˌmʌni]
Tätigkeit activity [æk'tɪvəti]
tausend thousand ['θaʊznd]
Team team [tiːm]
Tee tea [tiː]
Teenager teenager ['tiːneɪdʒə]
Teil part [pɑːt]
teilen: sich etwas teilen (mit jm.)
　share sth. (with sb.) [ʃeə]
Telefon (tele)phone ['telɪfəʊn] • **am Telefon** on the phone
Telefongespräch: ein Telefongespräch führen make a call ['kɔːl]
Telefonnummer (tele)phone number ['telɪfəʊn ˌnʌmbə]
Teller plate [pleɪt] • **ein Teller Pommes frites** a plate of chips
Temperatur temperature ['temprətʃə]
Tennis tennis ['tenɪs]
Termin appointment [ə'pɔɪntmənt]
Terminkalender diary ['daɪəri]
teuer expensive [ɪk'spensɪv]
Text text [tekst]
Theater theatre ['θɪətə]
Theaterstück play [pleɪ]
Thema, Themenbereich topic ['tɒpɪk]

Thermometer thermometer [θə'mɒmɪtə]
Tier animal ['ænɪml]; (Haustier) pet [pet]
Tierhandlung pet shop ['pet ʃɒp]
Tiger tiger ['taɪɡə]
Tisch table ['teɪbl]
Tischtennis table tennis ['teɪbl tenɪs]
Titel title ['taɪtl]
Toast(brot) toast [təʊst]
Tochter daughter ['dɔːtə]
Toilette toilet ['tɔɪlət]
toll fantastic [fæn'tæstɪk]; great [ɡreɪt]
Tomate tomato [tə'mɑːtəʊ], pl tomatoes
Top (Oberteil) top [tɒp]
Tornado tornado [tɔː'neɪdəʊ]
Torte cake [keɪk]
tot dead [ded]
töten kill [kɪl]
Tour (durch das Haus) tour (of the house) [tʊə]
Tourist/in tourist ['tʊərɪst]
tragen (Kleidung) wear [weə]
trainieren practise ['præktɪs]
Traum dream [driːm]
Traumhaus dream house
traurig sad [sæd]
treffen; sich treffen meet [miːt]
Treppe(nstufen) stairs (pl) [steəz]
Trick (Zauberkunststück) trick [trɪk]
Trimester term [tɜːm]
trinken drink [drɪŋk] • **Milch zum Frühstück trinken** have milk for breakfast
trotzdem anyway ['eniweɪ]
Tschüs. Bye. [baɪ]; See you. ['siː juː]
T-Shirt T-shirt ['tiːʃɜːt]
tun do [duː] • **tun müssen** have to do • **tun wollen** want to do [wɒnt]
　Tut mir leid. I'm sorry. ['sɒri]
Tunnel tunnel ['tʌnl]
Tür door [dɔː]
Türklingel doorbell ['dɔːbel]
Turm tower ['taʊə]
Turnen (Sportunterricht) PE [ˌpiː'iː], Physical Education [ˌfɪzɪkəl ˌedʒu'keɪʃn]
Turnschuhe trainers (pl) ['treɪnəz]
Tut mir leid. I'm sorry. ['sɒri]
Tüte bag [bæɡ]
tyrannisieren bully ['bʊli]

U

U-Bahn: die U-Bahn the underground ['ʌndəɡraʊnd] (BE); the subway ['sʌbweɪ] (AE)
üben practise ['præktɪs]
über about [ə'baʊt]; (räumlich) over ['əʊvə]

überall everywhere ['evriweə]
übereinstimmen: mit jm./etwas übereinstimmen agree with sb./sth. [ə'ɡriː]
überleben survive [sə'vaɪv]
Überleben survival [sə'vaɪvl]
übernachten (über Nacht bleiben) stay [steɪ]
überprüfen check [tʃek]
überqueren cross [krɒs]
Überraschung surprise [sə'praɪz]
Überschrift title ['taɪtl]
Übung (Schulbuch) exercise ['eksəsaɪz]
　eine Übung machen do an exercise
Übungsheft exercise book ['eksəsaɪz bʊk]
Uhr 1. (Armbanduhr) watch [wɒtʃ]; (Wand-, Stand-, Turmuhr) clock [klɒk]
　2. elf Uhr eleven o'clock • **7 Uhr morgens/vormittags** 7 am [ˌeɪ 'em] **7 Uhr nachmittags/abends** 7 pm [ˌpiː 'em] • **um 8 Uhr 45** at 8.45
Uhrzeit time [taɪm]
um 1. (örtlich) **um … (herum)** round [raʊnd] • **ganz um die Burg herum** all around the castle ['ɔːl ˌə'raʊnd]
　2. (zeitlich) **um 8.45** at 8.45
　3. Es geht um Mr Green. This is about Mr Green.
　4. um zu to
umdrehen: sich umdrehen turn [tɜːn]
　▶ S.165 (to) turn
Umfrage (über) survey (on) ['sɜːveɪ]
umher: in … umher round [raʊnd]
umsehen: sich umsehen look round [ˌlʊk 'raʊnd]
umziehen (nach, in) (die Wohnung wechseln) move (to) [muːv]
und and [ənd, ænd] • **Und? / Na und?** So? [səʊ]
Unfall accident ['æksɪdənt]
ungefähr about [ə'baʊt]
unglaublich amazing [ə'meɪzɪŋ]
unheimlich scary ['skeəri]
unhöflich rude [ruːd]
Uniform uniform ['juːnɪfɔːm]
unmöglich impossible [ɪm'pɒsəbl]
unordentlich: sehr unordentlich sein (Zimmer) be a mess [mes]
Unordnung: alles in Unordnung bringen make a mess [ˌmeɪk ə 'mes]
Unrecht haben be wrong [rɒŋ]
uns us [əs, ʌs]
unser(e) … our … ['aʊə] • **unser eigenes Schwimmbad** our own pool [əʊn]
unserer, unsere, unseres ours ['aʊəz]
　▶ S.147 Possessive pronouns
unten (im Haus) downstairs [ˌdaʊn'steəz] • **am unteren Ende**

Dictionary (German – English) 203

(von) at the bottom (of) ['bɒtəm]
dort unten down there • **nach unten** down [daʊn]; *(im Haus)* downstairs
unter under ['ʌndə]
untere(r, s): am unteren Ende (von) at the bottom (of) ['bɒtəm]
unterhalten: sich unterhalten (mit, über) talk (to, about) [tɔːk]
Unterricht lessons *(pl)* ['lesnz]
unterrichten teach [tiːtʃ]
unterschiedlich different ['dɪfrənt]
Untersuchung (über) *(Umfrage)* survey (on) ['sɜːveɪ]
unverschämt rude [ruːd]
Urlaub holiday ['hɒlədeɪ] • **in Urlaub fahren** go on holiday • **in Urlaub sein** be on holiday

V

Vater father ['fɑːðə]
Vati dad [dæd]
Verabredung appointment [ə'pɔɪntmənt]
verabschieden: sich verabschieden say goodbye [ˌseɪ gʊd'baɪ]
verängstigt scared [skeəd]
verbinden *(einander zuordnen)* link [lɪŋk]
verbringen: Zeit verbringen (mit etwas) spend time (on sth.) [spend]
Verein club [klʌb]
verfolgen follow ['fɒləʊ]
Vergangenheit past [pɑːst]
Vergleich comparison [kəm'pærɪsn]
verheiratet (mit) married (to) ['mærɪd]
verkaufen sell [sel]
Verkäufer/in shop assistant ['ʃɒp əˌsɪstənt]
Verkehr traffic ['træfɪk]
verkehrt *(falsch)* wrong [rɒŋ]
verknüpfen *(einander zuordnen)* link [lɪŋk]
verlassen leave [liːv]
verletzen hurt [hɜːt]
verletzt hurt [hɜːt]
verlieren lose [luːz]
vermissen miss [mɪs]
Vermittlung *(Sprachmittlung, Mediation)* mediation [ˌmiːdi'eɪʃn]
vermuten suppose [sə'pəʊz]
verpassen miss [mɪs]
verrückt mad [mæd]
verschieden different ['dɪfrənt]
verschwinden disappear [ˌdɪsə'pɪə]
versprechen promise ['prɒmɪs]
verstecken; sich verstecken hide [haɪd]
verstehen understand [ˌʌndə'stænd]

versuchen try [traɪ]
verwenden use [juːz]
verwirrt puzzled ['pʌzld]
viel a lot (of) [lɒt]; lots (of) [lɒts]; much [mʌtʃ] • **viele** a lot (of); lots (of); many ['meni] • **Viel Glück (bei/ mit ...)!** Good luck (with ...)! • **viel mehr** lots more • **Viel Spaß!** Have fun! • **wie viel?** how much? **wie viele?** how many? • **Vielen Dank!** Thanks a lot!
vielleicht maybe ['meɪbi]
Viertel: Viertel nach 11 quarter past 11 ['kwɔːtə] • **Viertel vor 12** quarter to 12
violett purple ['pɜːpl]
Virus virus ['vaɪrəs]
Vogel bird [bɜːd]
Vokabelverzeichnis vocabulary [və'kæbjələri]
Vokallaut vowel sound ['vaʊəl saʊnd]
voll full [fʊl] • **die Nase voll haben (von etwas)** be fed up (with sth.) [ˌfed_'ʌp]
Volleyball volleyball ['vɒlibɔːl]
von of [əv, ɒv]; from [frəm, frɒm] • **ein Aufsatz von ...** an essay by ... [baɪ]
vor **1.** *(räumlich)* in front of [ɪn 'frʌnt_ əv]
2. *(zeitlich)* **vor dem Abendessen** before dinner [bɪ'fɔː] • **vor einer Minute** a minute ago [ə'gəʊ] • **Viertel vor 12** quarter to 12
vorbei (an) *(vorüber)* past [pɑːst]
vorbei sein be over ['əʊvə]
vorbereiten prepare [prɪ'peə] • **sich vorbereiten (auf)** prepare (for); get ready (for) ['redi] • **Dinge vorbereiten** get things ready
Vordergrund foreground ['fɔːgraʊnd]
Vormittag morning ['mɔːnɪŋ]
vorsichtig careful ['keəfl]
vorspielen *(pantomimisch darstellen)* mime [maɪm]
vorstellen: (jm.) etwas vorstellen *(präsentieren)* present sth. (to sb.) [prɪ'zent] • **Stell dir vor! / Stellt euch vor!** Guess what! [ˌges 'wɒt]
Vorstellung *(Präsentation)* presentation [ˌprezn'teɪʃn]; *(Show)* show [ʃəʊ]
vorüber (an) *(vorbei)* past [pɑːst]

W

wachsen grow [grəʊ]
Waffe: (Schuss-)Waffe gun [gʌn]
wählen *(auswählen)* choose [tʃuːz]
wahr true [truː]
während *(als)* as [əz, æz]
wahrscheinlich probably ['prɒbəbli]

Wald forest ['fɒrɪst]; woods *(pl)* [wʊdz]
walisisch; Walisisch Welsh [welʃ]
Wand wall [wɔːl]
wann when [wen]
warm warm [wɔːm]
Wärmflasche hot-water bottle [ˌhɒt 'wɔːtə bɒtl]
warten (auf) wait (for) [weɪt] • **Warte mal!** Wait a minute. ['mɪnɪt]
warum why [waɪ]
was what [wɒt] • **Was fehlt dir?** *(bei Krankheit)* What's wrong with you? • **Was haben wir als Hausaufgabe auf?** What's for homework? • **Was ist los? / Was ist denn?** What's the matter? ['mætə] **Was ist mit ...?** What about ...? • **Was kostet/kosten ...?** How much is/are ...? • **Was war das Beste an ...?** What was the best thing about ...? • **Was weißt du sonst noch über ...?** What else do you know about ...? [els] • **alles, was wir jetzt (noch) tun müssen, ...** all we have to do now ...
waschen wash [wɒʃ] • **Ich wasche mir das Gesicht.** I wash my face.
Wasser water ['wɔːtə]
Webcam webcam ['webkæm]
Website website ['websaɪt]
Wechselgeld change [tʃeɪndʒ]
weg away [ə'weɪ] • **weg sein** *(nicht zu Hause sein)* be out [aʊt]
Weg way [weɪ]; *(Pfad)* path [pɑːθ] **auf dem Weg (zu/nach)** on the way (to) • **jm. den Weg beschreiben** tell sb. the way • **jn. nach dem Weg fragen** ask sb. the way
▶ S.165 way
Wegbeschreibung(en) directions *(pl)* [də'rekʃnz]
weggehen leave [liːv]; *(raus-, ausgehen)* go out
wehtun hurt [hɜːt]; be sore [sɔː]
▶ S.157 What's wrong with you?
Weide field [fiːld]
weil because [bɪ'kɒz]
weiß white [waɪt]
weit (entfernt) far [fɑː]
weiter: geradeaus weiter straight on [streɪt_'ɒn]
weitere(r, s): ein(e) weitere(r, s) one more [mɔː] • **weitere 45 Pence** another 45p [ə'nʌðə]
weitergeben pass [pɑːs]
weitermachen go on [ˌgəʊ_'ɒn]
welche(r, s) which [wɪtʃ] • **Auf welcher Seite sind wir?** What page are we on? [wɒt] • **Welche Farbe hat ...?** What colour is ...?
wellenreiten gehen go surfing ['sɜːfɪŋ]

Wellensittich budgie [ˈbʌdʒi]
Welt world [wɜːld]
wem? who? [huː] • **Wem gehören diese?** Whose are these? [huːz]
► S.162 who?
wen? who? [huː]
► S.162 who?
wenden: sich an jn. wenden turn to sb. [tɜːn]
► S.165 (to) turn
wenigstens at least [ət ˈliːst]
wenn 1. *(zeitlich)* when [wen]
2. *(falls)* if [ɪf]
wer? who? [huː] • **Wer ist dran / an der Reihe?** Whose turn is it? [huːz]
► S.162 who?
werden become [bɪˈkʌm] • **wütend/heiß/... werden** get angry/ hot/... • **du wirst frieren; ihr werdet frieren** you'll be cold (= you will be cold) [wɪl] • **du wirst nicht frieren; ihr werdet nicht frieren** you won't be cold (= you will not be cold) [wəʊnt]
werfen throw [θrəʊ]
wessen? whose? [huːz]
Wetter weather [ˈweðə]
Whisky whisky [ˈwɪski]
wichtig important [ɪmˈpɔːtnt]
wie 1. *(Fragewort)* how [haʊ] • **Wie bitte?** Sorry? [ˈsɒri] • **Wie geht es dir/Ihnen/euch?** How are you? [ˌhaʊ_ˈɑː jə] • **Wie heißt du?** What's your name? • **Wie spät ist es?** What's the time? • **wie viel?** how much? • **wie viele?** how many? • **Wie war ...?** How was ...? **Wie war das Wetter?** What was the weather like? • **Wie wär's mit ...?** What about ...?
2. so groß/aufregend wie as big/ exciting as • **wie du sehen kannst** as you can see
3. wie ein Filmstar like a film star [laɪk] • **genau wie du** just like you
wieder again [əˈɡen]
Wiederholung *(des Lernstoffs)* revision [rɪˈvɪʒn]
Wiedersehen: Auf Wiedersehen. Goodbye. [ˌɡʊdˈbaɪ]
wiederverwendet/-verwertet recycled [ˌriːˈsaɪkld]
Wiederverwertung recycling [ˌriːˈsaɪklɪŋ]
wild wild [waɪld]
willkommen: Willkommen (in ...). Welcome (to ...). [ˈwelkəm] • **Sie heißen dich in ... willkommen** They welcome you to ...
Wind wind [wɪnd]
windig windy [ˈwɪndi]

winken wave [weɪv]
Winter winter [ˈwɪntə]
wir we [wiː]
Wirbelsturm tornado [tɔːˈneɪdəʊ]
wirklich 1. *(tatsächlich)* really [ˈrɪəli] **Meinst du wirklich?/Glaubst du das wirklich?** Do you really think so?
2. *(echt)* real [rɪəl]
wischen *(Fußboden)* wash [wɒʃ]
wissen know [nəʊ] • **Ich weiß es nicht.** I don't know. • **von etwas wissen; über etwas Bescheid wissen** know about sth. • **..., wissen Sie. / ..., weißt du.** ..., you know. **Weißt du was, Sophie?** You know what, Sophie? • **Woher weißt du ...?** How do you know ...?
wissen wollen wonder [ˈwʌndə]
Witz joke [dʒəʊk] • **Witze machen** joke
witzig funny [ˈfʌni]
wo where [weə] • **Wo kommst du her?** Where are you from?
Woche week [wiːk]
Wochenende weekend [ˌwiːkˈend] **am Wochenende** at the weekend
Wochentage days of the week
Wofür? What for? [ˌwɒt ˈfɔː]
Woher weißt du ...? How do you know ...? [nəʊ]
wohin where [weə]; *(in welche Richtung)* which way
Wohlfahrtsorganisation charity [ˈtʃærəti]
Wohltätigkeitsbasar jumble sale [ˈdʒʌmbl seɪl]
wohnen live [lɪv]
Wohnung flat [flæt]
Wohnungstür front door [ˌfrʌnt ˈdɔː]
Wohnwagen caravan [ˈkærəvæn]
Wohnzimmer living room [ˈlɪvɪŋ ruːm]
Wolf wolf, *pl* wolves [wʊlf, wʊlvz]
Wolke cloud [klaʊd]
wollen *(haben wollen)* want [wɒnt] **tun wollen** want to do
Wort word [wɜːd]
Wortbildung word building [ˈwɜːd ˌbɪldɪŋ]
Wörterbuch dictionary [ˈdɪkʃənri]
Wörterverzeichnis vocabulary [vəˈkæbjələri]; *(alphabetisches)* dictionary [ˈdɪkʃənri]
Wovon redest du? What are you talking about?
wund sein be sore [sɔː]
► S.157 What's wrong with you?
Würfel dice, *pl* dice [daɪs]
Wurst, Würstchen sausage [ˈsɒsɪdʒ]
wütend sein (über etwas/auf jn.) be angry (about sth./with sb.) [ˈæŋgri]

Y

Yoga yoga [ˈjəʊgə]

Z

Zahl number [ˈnʌmbə]
zählen count [kaʊnt]
Zahn tooth [tuːθ], *pl* teeth [tiːθ] • **Ich putze mir die Zähne.** I clean my teeth.
Zahnschmerzen toothache [ˈtuːθeɪk]
► S.157 What's wrong with you?
zanken: sich zanken argue [ˈɑːɡjuː]
Zauberkunststück trick [trɪk] • **Zauberkunststücke machen** do tricks
Zebra zebra [ˈzebrə]
Zeh toe [təʊ]
zeigen show [ʃəʊ] • **auf etwas zeigen** point at/to sth. [pɔɪnt]
Zeile line [laɪn]
Zeit time [taɪm] • **Zeit verbringen (mit)** spend time (on) [spend]
Zeitschrift magazine [ˌmægəˈziːn]
Zeitung newspaper [ˈnjuːspeɪpə]; paper [ˈpeɪpə]
Zentrum centre [ˈsentə]
zerbrochen broken [ˈbrəʊkən]
Zeug *(Kram)* stuff [stʌf]
ziehen pull [pʊl]
ziemlich gut pretty good [ˈprɪti]; quite good [kwaɪt]
Ziffer number [ˈnʌmbə]
Zimmer room [ruːm]
zittern shiver [ˈʃɪvə]
zu 1. *(örtlich)* to [tə, tu] • **zu Jenny** to Jenny's • **zu Hause** at home **Setz dich zu mir.** Sit with me. **auf jn./etwas zu** towards sb./sth. [təˈwɔːdz]
2. zum Beispiel for example [ɪgˈzɑːmpl] • **zum Frühstück/ Mittagessen/Abendbrot** for breakfast/lunch/dinner
3. zu viel too much [tuː] • **zu spät sein/kommen** be late
4. versuchen zu tun try and do / try to do
5. um zu to
zubereiten *(kochen)* cook [kʊk]
Zucker sugar [ˈʃʊɡə]
zuerst first [fɜːst]
Zug train [treɪn] • **im Zug** on the train
Zuhause home [həʊm]
zuhören listen (to) [ˈlɪsn]
Zuhörer/in listener [ˈlɪsnə] • **Zuhörer/innen** *(Publikum)* audience [ˈɔːdɪəns]
Zukunft future [ˈfjuːtʃə]
zumachen close [kləʊz]

Dictionary (German – English) / English sounds / The English alphabet

zumindest at least [ət 'liːst]
zurück (nach) back (to) [bæk]
zurücklassen leave [liːv]
zusammen together [təˈgeðə]
zusätzlich extra [ˈekstrə]
Zuschauer/innen *(Publikum)*
  audience [ˈɔːdiəns]

zusehen watch [wɒtʃ]
zustimmen: jm./etwas zustimmen
  agree with sb./sth. [əˈgriː]
zuwenden: sich jm. zuwenden turn
  to sb. [tɜːn]
  ▶ S.165 (to) turn
zweite(r, s) second [ˈsekənd]

Zwillinge twins *(pl)* [twɪnz]
Zwillingsbruder twin brother [ˈtwɪn
  ˌbrʌðə]
zwischen between [bɪˈtwiːn]

English sounds (Englische Laute)

Die Lautschrift in den eckigen Klammern zeigt dir, wie ein Wort ausgesprochen wird.
In der folgenden Übersicht findest du alle Lautzeichen.

Vokale (Selbstlaute)

[iː]	green	[eɪ]	skate
[i]	happy	[aɪ]	time
[ɪ]	in	[ɔɪ]	boy
[e]	yes	[əʊ]	old
[æ]	black	[aʊ]	now
[ɑː]	park	[ɪə]	here
[ɒ]	song	[eə]	where
[ɔː]	morning	[ʊə]	tour
[uː]	blue		
[ʊ]	book		
[ʌ]	mum		
[ɜː]	T-shirt		
[ə]	a partner		

Konsonanten (Mitlaute)

[b]	box	[f]	full
[p]	play	[v]	very
[d]	dad	[s]	sister
[t]	ten	[z]	please
[g]	good	[ʃ]	shop
[k]	cat	[ʒ]	television
[m]	mum	[tʃ]	teacher
[n]	no	[dʒ]	Germany
[ŋ]	sing	[θ]	thanks
[l]	hello	[ð]	this
[r]	red	[h]	he
[w]	we		
[j]	you		

The English alphabet (Das englische Alphabet)

a [eɪ]	**h** [eɪtʃ]	**o** [əʊ]	**v** [viː]
b [biː]	**i** [aɪ]	**p** [piː]	**w** [ˈdʌbljuː]
c [siː]	**j** [dʒeɪ]	**q** [kjuː]	**x** [eks]
d [diː]	**k** [keɪ]	**r** [ɑː]	**y** [waɪ]
e [iː]	**l** [el]	**s** [es]	**z** [zed]
f [ef]	**m** [em]	**t** [tiː]	
g [dʒiː]	**n** [en]	**u** [juː]	

List of names

First names (Vornamen)

Adam ['ædəm]
Alan ['ælən]
Alexander [ˌælɪg'zɑːndə]
Amit ['æmɪt]
Ananda [ə'nændə]
Angus ['æŋgəs]
Anna ['ænə]
Ashton ['æʃtən]
Barnabas ['bɑːnəbəs]
Barry ['bæri]
Bart [bɑːt]
Becky ['beki]
Ben [ben]
Beth [beθ]
Binta ['bɪntə]
Bob [bɒb]
Bobby ['bɒbi]
Bryn [brɪn]
Carol ['kærəl]
Caroline ['kærəlaɪn]
Caspar ['kæspə]
Catherine ['kæθrɪn]
Christine ['krɪstiːn]
Cid [sɪd]
Dan [dæn]
Daniel ['dænjəl]
David ['deɪvɪd]
Derek ['derɪk]
Dilip ['dɪlɪp]
Donald ['dɒnld]
Drew [druː]
Elaine [ɪ'leɪn]
Emily ['eməli]
Emma ['emə]
Eva ['iːvə]
Fiona [fi'əʊnə]
Graham ['greɪəm]
Greg [greg]
Griselda [grɪ'zeldə]
Guy [gaɪ]
Gwyneth ['gwɪnəθ]
Harry ['hæri]
Henry ['henri]
Ilo ['aɪləʊ]
Isabel ['ɪzəbel]
Isambard ['ɪzəmbɑːd]
Jack [dʒæk]
Jay [dʒeɪ]
Jo [dʒəʊ]
Jody ['dʒəʊdi]
Jonah ['dʒəʊnə]
Josh [dʒɒʃ]
Judy ['dʒuːdi]
Laura ['lɔːrə]
Lesley ['lezli]
Linda ['lɪndə]
Lucy ['luːsi]
Maggie ['mægi]
Maria [mə'riːə]
Mary ['meəri]
Max [mæks]
Meera ['mɪərə]
Mel [mel]

Merlin ['mɜːlɪn]
Micky ['mɪki]
Mike [maɪk]
Milly ['mɪli]
Minnie ['mɪni]
Molly ['mɒli]
Natale ['nætəli]
Nathaniel [nə'θæniəl]
Nick [nɪk]
Nicola ['nɪkələ]
Oliver ['ɒlɪvə]
Paul [pɔːl]
Peter ['piːtə]
Philip ['fɪlɪp]
Prunella [pru'nelə]
Queenie ['kwiːni]
Rachel ['reɪtʃəl]
Rebecca [rɪ'bekə]
Richard ['rɪtʃəd]
Robinson ['rɒbɪnsən]
Ronnie ['rɒni]
Rosie ['rəʊzi]
Sally ['sæli]
Sandhya ['sændʒə]
Sandra ['sɑːndrə]
Simon ['saɪmən]
Sophie ['səʊfi]
Stephen ['stiːvn]
Steve [stiːv]
Susan ['suːzn]
Thomas ['tɒməs]
Tim [tɪm]
Toby ['təʊbi]
Tom [tɒm]
Tracy ['treɪsi]
Trixie ['trɪksi]
Val [væl]
Vinny ['vɪni]
Vortigern ['vɔːtɪgɜːn]
Wallace ['wɒlɪs]
Will [wɪl]
William ['wɪljəm]
Willy ['wɪli]

Family names (Familiennamen)

Bader ['beɪdə]
Baxter ['bækstə]
Bean [biːn]
Brooks [brʊks]
Brunel [bru'nel]
Carter-Brown [ˌkɑːtə 'braʊn]
Crusoe ['kruːsəʊ]
Defoe [dɪ'fəʊ]
Duck [dʌk]
Edwards ['edwədz]
Evans ['evnz]
Fawkes [fɔːks]
Ghent [gent]
Grumble ['grʌmbl]
Gupta ['gʊptə]
Hanson ['hænsn]
Harper ['hɑːpə]
Herschel ['hɜːʃl]

Kapoor [kə'pɔː, kə'pʊə]
King [kɪŋ]
Kingdom ['kɪŋdəm]
Kingsley ['kɪŋzli]
Kutcher ['kʊtʃə]
Miller ['mɪlə]
Muddles ['mʌdlz]
O'Grady [əʊ'greɪdi]
Orleans ['ɔːliːnz]
Park [pɑːk]
Pinney ['pɪni]
Pitt [pɪt]
Potter ['pɒtə]
Selkirk ['selkɜːk]
Shaw [ʃɔː]
Simpson ['sɪmpsn]
Smith [smɪθ]
Thompson ['tɒmpsən]
Walter ['wɒltə]
Wu [wuː]

Place names (Ortsnamen)

Aardman Studios
[ˌɑːdmən 'stjuːdiəʊz]
Alfred Street ['ælfrəd striːt]
Bartlett Street ['bɑːtlət striːt]
Bath [bɑːθ]
Battersea ['bætəsi]
Beauford Square
[ˌbəʊfəd 'skweə]
The **Brecon Beacons**
[ˌbrekən 'biːkənz]
Bristol ['brɪstl]
Cabot Tower [ˌkæbət 'taʊə]
Caerphilly Castle
[keəˌfɪli 'kɑːsl]
Cardiff ['kɑːdɪf]
Cardozo High School
[kɑːˌdəʊzəʊ 'haɪ skuːl]
Charlotte Street ['ʃɑːlət striːt]
Cheap Street [tʃiːp striːt]
Chester ['tʃestə]
Christchurch ['kraɪsttʃɜːtʃ]
Clifton ['klɪftən]
Cornwall ['kɔːnwɔːl]
Cotham ['kɒtəm]
Crickhowell [krɪk'haʊəl]
Dinas Emrys [ˌdiːnʌs 'emrɪs]
Dover ['dəʊvə]
The **Downs** [daʊnz]
Duckpool Beach
[ˌdʌkpuːl 'biːtʃ]
The **Empire State Building**
[ˌempaɪə 'steɪt ˌbɪldɪŋ]
Exeter ['eksɪtə]
Fiordland ['fjɔːdlænd]
George Street ['dʒɔːdʒ striːt]
Georgian House
[ˌdʒɔːdʒən 'haʊs]
Hamilton Street
['hæməltən striːt]
Hayle Beach [ˌheɪl 'biːtʃ]
Heidelberg ['haɪdlbɜːg]
Jupiter ['dʒuːpɪtə]

Leeds [liːdz]
Llandoger Trow
[hlænˌdɒgə 'trəʊ]
Llanfoist [hlæn'vɔɪst]
London ['lʌndən]
Longleat Safari Park
[ˌlɒnliːt sə'fɑːri pɑːk]
Majorca [mə'jɔːkə]
Manchester ['mæntʃɪstə]
Manhattan [mæn'hætn]
Manvers Street
['mænvəs striːt]
Mars [mɑːz]
Milsom Street ['mɪlsəm striːt]
Newbridge ['njuːbrɪdʒ]
New York [ˌnjuː 'jɔːk]
Oslo ['ɒzləʊ]
Paddington Station
[ˌpædɪŋtən 'steɪʃn]
Portsmouth ['pɔːtsməθ]
Queens [kwiːnz]
Queenstown ['kwiːnztaʊn]
The **River Avon** [ˌrɪvər 'eɪvn]
Rome [rəʊm]
Saturn ['sætɜːn]
St Ives [sənt 'aɪvz]
St Nicholas Market
[sənt ˌnɪkələs 'mɑːkɪt]
Statue of Liberty
[ˌstætʃuː_əv 'lɪbəti]
Stockholm ['stɒkhəʊm]
Temple Meads Station
[ˌtempl ˌmiːdz 'steɪʃn]
Theatre Royal [ˌθɪətə 'rɔɪəl]
Tredegar [trɪ'diːgə]
Union Street ['juːniən striːt]
Upper Borough Walls
[ˌʌpə ˌbʌrə 'wɔːls]
Uranus ['jʊərənəs]
Valencia [və'lenʃiə]
Venus ['viːnəs]
Warmley ['wɔːmli]
Waterloo [ˌwɔːtə'luː]
West Wallaby Street
[ˌwest 'wɒləbi striːt]
Wigan ['wɪgən]
York Street ['jɔːk striːt]

Other names (Andere Namen)

Anansi [ə'nænsi]
Batman ['bætmæn]
Blackbeard ['blækbɪəd]
Cawl mamgu [kaʊl 'mæmgi]
Dogwarts University
[ˌdɒgwɔːts juːni'vɜːsəti]
Fifi ['fiːfiː]
Gromit ['grɒmɪt]
Hogwarts ['hɒgwɔːts]
Holi ['həʊli]
Polly ['pɒli]
Scruffy ['skrʌfi]
Smokey ['sməʊki]
Travelot ['trævəlɒt]

Countries and continents

Country/Continent	Adjective	Person	People
Africa ['æfrɪkə] *Afrika*	African ['æfrɪkən]	an African	the Africans
America [ə'merɪkə] *Amerika*	American [ə'merɪkən]	an American	the Americans
Asia ['eɪʃə, 'eɪʒə] *Asien*	Asian ['eɪʃn, 'eɪʒn]	an Asian	the Asians
Australia [ɒ'streɪliə] *Australien*	Australian [ɒ'streɪliən]	an Australian	the Australians
Austria ['ɒstriə] *Österreich*	Austrian ['ɒstriən]	an Austrian	the Austrians
Belgium ['beldʒəm] *Belgien*	Belgian ['beldʒən]	a Belgian	the Belgians
Brazil [brə'zɪl] *Brasilien*	Brazilian [brə'zɪliən]	a Brazilian	the Brazilians
Chile ['tʃɪli] *Chile*	Chilean ['tʃɪliən]	a Chilean	the Chileans
(Great) Britain ['brɪtn] *Großbritannien*	British ['brɪtɪʃ]	a Briton ['brɪtn]	the British
the Caribbean [ˌkærə'biːən] *die Karibik*	Caribbean [ˌkærə'biːən]	a Caribbean	the Caribbeans
China ['tʃaɪnə] *China*	Chinese [ˌtʃaɪ'niːz]	a Chinese	the Chinese
Croatia [krəʊ'eɪʃə] *Kroatien*	Croatian [krəʊ'eɪʃn]	a Croatian	the Croatians
the Czech Republic [ˌtʃek rɪ'pʌblɪk] *Tschechien, die Tschechische Republik*	Czech [tʃek]	a Czech	the Czechs
Denmark ['denmɑːk] *Dänemark*	Danish ['deɪnɪʃ]	a Dane [deɪn]	the Danes
England ['ɪŋglənd] *England*	English ['ɪŋglɪʃ]	an Englishman/-woman	the English
Europe ['jʊərəp] *Europa*	European [ˌjʊərə'piːən]	a European	the Europeans
Finland ['fɪnlənd] *Finnland*	Finnish ['fɪnɪʃ]	a Finn [fɪn]	the Finns
France [frɑːns] *Frankreich*	French [frentʃ]	a Frenchman/-woman	the French
Germany ['dʒɜːməni] *Deutschland*	German ['dʒɜːmən]	a German	the Germans
Greece [griːs] *Griechenland*	Greek [griːk]	a Greek	the Greeks
Holland ['hɒlənd] *Holland, die Niederlande*	Dutch [dʌtʃ]	a Dutchman/-woman	the Dutch
Hungary ['hʌŋgəri] *Ungarn*	Hungarian [hʌŋ'geəriən]	a Hungarian	the Hungarians
India ['ɪndiə] *Indien*	Indian ['ɪndiən]	an Indian	the Indians
Ireland ['aɪələnd] *Irland*	Irish ['aɪrɪʃ]	an Irishman/-woman	the Irish
Italy ['ɪtəli] *Italien*	Italian [ɪ'tæliən]	an Italian	the Italians
Jamaica [dʒə'meɪkə] *Jamaika*	Jamaican [dʒə'meɪkən]	a Jamaican	the Jamaicans
Japan [dʒə'pæn] *Japan*	Japanese [ˌdʒæpə'niːz]	a Japanese	the Japanese
the Netherlands ['neðələndz] *die Niederlande, Holland*	Dutch [dʌtʃ]	a Dutchman/-woman	the Dutch
New Zealand [ˌnjuː'ziːlənd] *Neuseeland*	New Zealand [ˌnjuː'ziːlənd]	a New Zealander	the New Zealanders
Norway ['nɔːweɪ] *Norwegen*	Norwegian [nɔː'wiːdʒən]	a Norwegian	the Norwegians
Poland ['pəʊlənd] *Polen*	Polish ['pəʊlɪʃ]	a Pole [pəʊl]	the Poles
Portugal ['pɔːtʃʊgl] *Portugal*	Portuguese [ˌpɔːtʃʊ'giːz]	a Portuguese	the Portuguese
Russia ['rʌʃə] *Russland*	Russian ['rʌʃn]	a Russian	the Russians
Scotland ['skɒtlənd] *Schottland*	Scottish ['skɒtɪʃ]	a Scotsman/-woman, a Scot [skɒt]	the Scots, the Scottish
Slovakia [sləʊ'vɑːkiə, sləʊ'vækiə] *die Slowakei*	Slovak ['sləʊvæk]	a Slovak	the Slovaks
Slovenia [sləʊ'viːniə] *Slowenien*	Slovenian [sləʊ'viːniən], Slovene ['sləʊviːn]	a Slovene, a Slovenian	the Slovenes, the Slovenians
Spain [speɪn] *Spanien*	Spanish ['spænɪʃ]	a Spaniard ['spænɪəd]	the Spaniards
Sweden ['swiːdn] *Schweden*	Swedish ['swiːdɪʃ]	a Swede [swiːd]	the Swedes
Switzerland ['swɪtsələnd] *die Schweiz*	Swiss [swɪs]	a Swiss	the Swiss
Taiwan [taɪ'wɒn, taɪ'wɑːn] *Taiwan*	Taiwanese [ˌtaɪwə'niːz]	a Taiwanese	the Taiwanese
Thailand ['taɪlænd] *Thailand*	Thai [taɪ]	a Thai	the Thais
Turkey ['tɜːki] *die Türkei*	Turkish ['tɜːkɪʃ]	a Turk [tɜːk]	the Turks
Ukraine [juː'kreɪn] *die Ukraine*	Ukrainian [juː'kreɪniən]	a Ukrainian	the Ukrainians
the United Kingdom (the UK) [juˌnaɪtɪd 'kɪŋdəm, juː'keɪ] *das Vereinigte Königreich (Großbritannien und Nordirland)*	British ['brɪtɪʃ]	a Briton ['brɪtn]	the British
the United States of America (the USA) [juˌnaɪtɪd ˌsteɪts_əv_ə'merɪkə, juːˌes_'eɪ] *die Vereinigten Staaten von Amerika*	American [ə'merɪkən]	an American	the Americans
Wales [weɪlz] *Wales*	Welsh [welʃ]	a Welshman/-woman	the Welsh

Irregular verbs

Infinitive	Simple past form	Past participle	
(to) **be**	**was/were**	**been**	sein
(to) **become**	**became**	**become**	werden
(to) **bring**	**brought**	**brought**	(mit-, her)bringen
(to) **build**	**built**	**built**	bauen
(to) **buy**	**bought**	**bought**	kaufen
(to) **catch**	**caught**	**caught**	fangen; erwischen
(to) **choose** [uː]	**chose** [əʊ]	**chosen** [əʊ]	(aus)wählen; (sich) aussuchen
(to) **come**	**came**	**come**	kommen
(to) **do**	**did**	**done** [ʌ]	tun, machen
(to) **drink**	**drank**	**drunk**	trinken
(to) **drive** [aɪ]	**drove**	**driven** [ɪ]	*(ein Auto)* fahren
(to) **eat**	**ate** [et, eɪt]	**eaten**	essen
(to) **fall**	**fell**	**fallen**	(hin)fallen, stürzen
(to) **feed**	**fed**	**fed**	füttern
(to) **feel**	**felt**	**felt**	(sich) fühlen; sich anfühlen
(to) **find**	**found**	**found**	finden
(to) **fly**	**flew**	**flown**	fliegen
(to) **get**	**got**	**got**	bekommen; holen; werden; (hin)kommen
(to) **give**	**gave**	**given**	geben
(to) **go**	**went**	**gone** [ɒ]	gehen, fahren
(to) **grow**	**grew**	**grown**	wachsen; anbauen, anpflanzen
(to) **have (have got)**	**had**	**had**	haben, besitzen
(to) **hear** [ɪə]	**heard** [ɜː]	**heard** [ɜː]	hören
(to) **hide** [aɪ]	**hid** [ɪ]	**hidden** [ɪ]	(sich) verstecken
(to) **hit**	**hit**	**hit**	schlagen
(to) **hold**	**held**	**held**	halten
(to) **hurt**	**hurt**	**hurt**	wehtun; verletzen
(to) **keep**	**kept**	**kept**	*(warm/offen/...)* halten
(to) **know** [nəʊ]	**knew** [njuː]	**known** [nəʊn]	wissen; kennen
(to) **lay** the table	**laid**	**laid**	den Tisch decken
(to) **leave**	**left**	**left**	(weg)gehen; abfahren; verlassen; zurücklassen
(to) **let**	**let**	**let**	lassen
(to) **lose** [uː]	**lost** [ɒ]	**lost** [ɒ]	verlieren
(to) **make**	**made**	**made**	machen; bauen; bilden
(to) **mean** [iː]	**meant** [e]	**meant** [e]	bedeuten; meinen
(to) **meet**	**met**	**met**	(sich) treffen
(to) **pay**	**paid**	**paid**	bezahlen
(to) **put**	**put**	**put**	legen, stellen, *(wohin)* tun
(to) **read** [iː]	**read** [e]	**read** [e]	lesen

Irregular verbs   209

Infinitive	Simple past form	Past participle	
(to) ride [aɪ]	rode	ridden [ɪ]	reiten; *(Rad)* fahren
(to) ring	rang	rung	klingeln, läuten
(to) run	ran	run	rennen, laufen
(to) say [eɪ]	said [e]	said [e]	sagen
(to) see	saw	seen	sehen; besuchen, aufsuchen
(to) sell	sold	sold	verkaufen
(to) send	sent	sent	schicken, senden
(to) set a trap	set	set	eine Falle stellen
(to) shine	shone [ɒ]	shone [ɒ]	scheinen *(Sonne)*
(to) show	showed	shown	zeigen
(to) shut up	shut	shut	den Mund halten
(to) sing	sang	sung	singen
(to) sit	sat	sat	sitzen; sich setzen
(to) sleep	slept	slept	schlafen
(to) speak	spoke	spoken	sprechen
(to) spend	spent	spent	*(Zeit)* verbringen; *(Geld)* ausgeben
(to) stand	stood	stood	stehen; sich (hin)stellen
(to) steal	stole	stolen	stehlen
(to) swim	swam	swum	schwimmen
(to) take	took	taken	nehmen; (weg-, hin)bringen
(to) teach	taught	taught	unterrichten, lehren
(to) tell	told	told	erzählen, berichten
(to) think	thought	thought	denken, glauben, meinen
(to) throw	threw	thrown	werfen
(to) understand	understood	understood	verstehen
(to) wear [eə]	wore [ɔː]	worn [ɔː]	tragen *(Kleidung)*
(to) win	won [ʌ]	won [ʌ]	gewinnen
(to) write	wrote	written	schreiben

Classroom English

Was *du* im Klassenzimmer sagen kannst

What *you* can say in the classroom

Du brauchst Hilfe

Können Sie mir bitte helfen?
Auf welcher Seite sind wir, bitte?
Was heißt ... auf Englisch/Deutsch?
Wie spricht man das erste Wort in Zeile 2 aus?
Können Sie bitte ... buchstabieren?
Können Sie es bitte an die Tafel schreiben?
Kann ich es auf Deutsch sagen?
Können Sie/Kannst du bitte lauter sprechen?
Können Sie/Kannst du das bitte noch mal sagen?

You need help

Can you help me, please?
What page are we on, please?
What's ... in English/German?
How do you say the first word in line 2?
Can you spell ..., please?
Can you write it on the board, please?
Can I say it in German?
Can you speak louder, please?
Can you say that again, please?

Beim Zuhören und beim Lesen

Ich kann die CD nicht hören.
Ich finde die Geschichte ...
schön/interessant/langweilig/schrecklich/....
Es war lustig/gruselig/langweilig/..., als ...
Ich fand es gut/nicht gut, als ...
Ich finde Tom hat recht/nicht recht, weil ...
Ich bin mir nicht sicher. Vielleicht ...

Listening and reading

I can't hear the CD.
I think the story is ...
nice/interesting/boring/terrible/...
It was funny/scary/boring/... when ...
I liked it/didn't like it when ...
I think Tom is right/wrong because ...
I'm not sure. Maybe ...

Hausaufgaben und Übungen

Tut mir leid, ich habe mein Schulheft nicht dabei, Herr ...
Ich habe meine Hausaufgaben vergessen, Frau ...
Ich verstehe diese Übung nicht.
Ich kann Nummer 3 nicht lösen.
Entschuldigung, ich bin noch nicht fertig.
Ich habe ... Ist das auch richtig?
Tut mir leid, das weiß ich nicht.
Was haben wir (als Hausaufgabe) auf?

Homework and exercises

Sorry, I haven't got my exercise book, Mr ...
I've forgotten my homework, Mrs/Ms/Miss ...
I don't understand this exercise.
I can't do number 3.
Sorry, I haven't finished yet.
I've got ... Is that right too?
Sorry, I don't know.
What's for homework?

Bei der Partnerarbeit

Kann ich mit Julian arbeiten?
Kann ich bitte dein Lineal/deinen Filzstift/... haben?
Ich bin Lisas Meinung. / Ich bin anderer Meinung.
Du bist dran.

Work with a partner

Can I work with Julian?
Can I have your ruler/felt tip/..., please?
I agree with Lisa. / I don't agree (with Lisa).
It's your turn.

What your *teacher* says

Open your books at page 24, please.
Look at the picture/line 8/... on page 24.
Copy/Complete the chart/network/...
Correct the mistakes.
Fill/Put in the right words.
Put the words in the right order.
Take notes.
Do exercise 3 for homework, please.
Bring some photos/... to school.
Have you finished?
Switch off your mobile phones.
Don't send text messages in class.
Walk around the class and ask other pupils.

Was dein/e *Lehrer/in* sagt

Schlagt bitte Seite 24 auf.
Seht euch das Bild/Zeile 8/... auf Seite 24 an.
Übertragt/Vervollständigt die Tabelle/das Wörternetz/...
Verbessert die Fehler.
Setzt die richtigen Wörter ein.
Bringt die Wörter in die richtige Reihenfolge.
Macht euch Notizen.
Macht bitte Übung 3 als Hausaufgabe.
Bringt ein paar Fotos/... mit in die Schule.
Seid ihr fertig? / Bist du fertig?
Schaltet eure Handys aus.
Verschickt keine SMS während des Unterrichts.
Geht durch die Klasse und fragt andere Schüler/innen.

Arbeitsanweisungen | **211**

Diese Arbeitsanweisungen findest du häufig im Schülerbuch

Act out your dialogue for the class.	Spielt der Klasse euren Dialog vor.
Agree on one place.	Einigt euch auf einen Ort.
Answer the questions.	Beantworte die Fragen.
Ask your partner questions.	Stelle deiner Partnerin/deinem Partner Fragen.
Check with a partner.	Überprüfe das Ergebnis mit deiner Partnerin/deinem Partner.
Check your answers.	Überprüfe deine Antworten.
Collect ideas.	Sammle Ideen.
Compare with a partner.	Vergleiche mit einer Partnerin/einem Partner.
Complete the sentences.	Vervollständige die Sätze.
Copy the chart.	Schreib die Tabelle ab.
Correct your answers.	Verbessere deine Antworten.
Draw a picture.	Zeichne ein Bild.
Fill in the answers.	Trage die Antworten ein.
Find the missing words.	Finde die fehlenden Wörter.
Listen. / Listen again.	Hör zu. / Hör noch einmal zu.
Look at page ...	Sieh auf Seite ... nach.
Make a chart.	Lege eine Tabelle an.
Make appointments.	Verabrede dich.
Match the letters and numbers.	Ordne die Buchstaben den Nummern zu.
Prepare a dialogue.	Bereitet einen Dialog vor.
Put the sentences in the right order.	Bring die Sätze in die richtige Reihenfolge.
Read the sentences.	Lies die Sätze.
Report to the class.	Berichte der Klasse.
Right or wrong?	Richtig oder falsch?
Scan the text for ...	Überfliege den Text und suche nach ...
Swap after three questions.	Wechselt euch nach drei Fragen ab.
Take notes.	Mach dir Notizen.
Talk to your partner.	Sprich mit deiner Partnerin/deinem Partner.
Tell your partner about your picture.	Erzähle deiner Partnerin/deinem Partner etwas über dein Bild.
Use ideas from the box.	Verwende Ideen aus dem Kasten.
What's different?	Was ist anders?
Work in groups of four.	Arbeitet in Vierergruppen.
Write down five questions.	Schreib fünf Fragen auf.

Illustrationen

Graham-Cameron Illustration, UK; **Fliss Cary**, Grafikerin (wenn nicht anders angegeben); **Roland Beier**, Berlin (Vignetten vordere Umschlaginnenseite; S. 14–15 oben; 18; 31–33; 35 unten; 47; 50; 52; 56–57; 62; 69; 72 unten; 75 unten; 101; 109; 112–113 oben; 114–167); **Carlos Borrell**, Berlin (Karten und Stadtpläne: vordere und hintere Umschlaginnen-seite; S. 8; 24; 65; 80; 92 unten li.; 95; 99 u. 111; **Julie Colthorpe**, Berlin (S. 6; 17 unten; 68 re.; 81 unten; 108; 113 Mitte); **Linda Rogers Associates**, London: Gary Rees (S. 89–91); **Michael Teßmer**, Hamburg (S. 92/93 The Roman Baths); **Katherine Wells**, Hamburg (S. 73); **Korinna Wilkes**, Berlin (S. 58/59).

Fotos

Rob Cousins, Bristol (wenn im Bildquellenverzeichnis nicht anders angegeben)

Bildquellen

AA Guides Ltd, Glenfield (S. 106 map); **AJ Hackett Bungy**, Queenstown (S. 106/107 unten); **Alamy**, Abingdon (S. 6 Bild A: Paul Broadbent; S. 7 Bild D: David Noton Photography; S. 12 oben: Ambient Images Inc./Peter Bennett (M); S. 26 knee elbow guards: Photolibrary; S. 27 oben: Design Pics, Mitte: BananaStock; S. 37 bus: Stockdisc Classic, cup: Eddie Gerald); S. 43 deer: Vic Pigula; S. 75 unten li.: Rolf Richardson; S. 79 unten: North Wind Picture Archives); **Alpine Recreation Ltd**, Lake Tekapo/www.alpinerecreation.com (S. 107 oben re.); **Avenue Images**, Hamburg (S. 26 hat: Stockbyte); **Bank of England**, London (S. 26/27 banknotes, reproduced with kind permission); **Camillo Beretta**, Berlin (S. 26 magazine, comic, ticket, book); **British Empire and Commonwealth Museum**, Bristol (S. 75 oben); **Celtic Scene**, Cornwall (S. 6 Bild B: Claire Sellick); **Corbis**, Düsseldorf (S. 7 Bild C: Chris Rogers; S. 10 colourful ball (M): RF; S. 21; S. 24 unten li.: George D. Lepp, unten re.: Reuters/Daniel Aguilar; S. 41 unten: Kevin R. Morris; S. 43 hedgehog: Herbert Spichtinger/zefa; S. 83 unten: Bureau L.A. Collection); **Corel Library** (S. 6/7 seagulls; S. 12 oben clouds (M); S. 26 coke; S. 36; S. 48 woodland; S. 52 giraffe, tiger; S. 61 re. u. 73); **Cornelsen Verlag**, Berlin (S. 26 Genius); **Cotham School**, Bristol (S. 10/11 Website-Frame, Logo); **Destination Bristol**, Bristol (S. 74/75 map; S. 85: Michaela Norris); **Gareth Evans**, Berlin (S. 8; S. 29 game); **Simon Evans**, Berlin (S. 45 li.); **Explore-at-Bristol**, Bristol (S. 74 Mitte li. u. S. 84: Martin Chainey); **Explore Franz Josef**/ www.explorefranzjosef.com (S. 106 unten li.) **FAN travelstock**, Hamburg (S. 24 Mitte re.); **Fiordland Wilderness Experiences – Sea Kayak Fiordland**, Te Anau/www.fiordlandseakayak.co.nz, info@fiordlandseakayak.co.nz (S. 107 Mitte u. unten re.); **Fotosearch**, Waukesha (S. 29 ice cream); **Georgian House**, Bristol/Bristol Museums & Art Gallery (S. 75); **Getty Images**, München (S. 49 cover photo: Stuart McClymont; S. 61 li.: Ryan McVay); **Glacier Helicopters Ltd**, Franz Josef Glacier (S. 107 unten Mitte); **Bonnie Glänzer**, Berlin (S. 48 li., S. 51 oben); **Hassle-free Tours**, Christchurch, New Zealand (S. 106/107 Mitte); The Helicopter Line Ltd, Mt. Cook (S. 106 oben li.); **Herschel House**, Bristol (S. 97 oben re.); **Ingram Publishing**, UK (S. 27: gift box); **Keystone**, Hamburg (S. 40 oben: TopFoto/Arena Images/Keith Saunders); **Look**, München (S. 40 unten: Karl Johaentges;) **Marketing for Education**, Nelson (S. 10/11 Bild 2–6); **Mauritius**, Hamburg (S. 10/11 boules (M): Image Source; S. 26 bottle of water: photolibrary rf; S. 37 snow globe: Image Source); **Photolibrary Wales**, Cardiff (S. 59 oben; S. 60 unten li.; S. 65 oben u. Mitte); **Picture-Alliance**, Frankfurt/Main (S. 41 oben: dpa; S. 43 woodpecker, mole (u. S. 118): Okapia/Manfred Danegger, frog: Okapia/Markus Essler; S. 52 monkey: Godong; S. 75 u. S. 83 oben Wallace and Gromit: obs; S. 107 Legolas: KPA Honorar & Belege; S.

121: dpa-Report); **Queenstown Adventure Group**, Queenstown (S. 106 Mitte re.); **Real Journeys, Queenstown**/www.realjourneys.co.nz (S. 107 oben Mitte); **RSPCA Photolibrary**, Horsham (S. 45 re.); **Rosco's Milford Sound Sea Kayaks**, Te Anau Fiordland (S. 107 Mitte re.); **Shutterstock**, New York (S. 29 DVDs: Jostein Hauge; S. 42: Mark Simms; S. 43 grey squirrel: John L. Richbourg, small squirrel: Joe Gough; S. 118 baby moles: Devin Koob); **Somerfield Stores Ltd**, Bristol (S. 29 juice); **Stills-Online**, Hamburg (S. 26 sweets in bag, pile of sweets, shirt, top, dress, jumper, jacket, trousers, skirt, trainers, CDs; S. 27 unten: mobile, pens, pencils, lipstick, rouge); **Stockfood**, München (S. 26 bottle and glass of orange juice: Christina Peters, chips: Foodcollection, crisps: Kröger/Gross, chocolate: FoodPhotography Eising); **Techniquest Science Discovery Centre**, Cardiff (S. 65 unten); **Christine Thomas**, Crickhowell (S. 59 sign); **ullstein bild**, Berlin (S. 9 CARO/Sorge); **Visum**, Hamburg (S. 24 oben: Markus Hanke); **Wales Tourist Board**, Cardiff (S. 60 unten re.); **Walker Books Ltd.**, London (S. 49: Cover photo © 2005 by Stuart McClymont/Getty Images from NO SMALL THING by Natale Ghent. Reproduced by permission of Walker Books Ltd, London SE11 5HJ). **Wanaka Sightseeing**, Christchurch (S. 106/107 oben).

Titelbild

Rob Cousins, Bristol; **IFA-Bilderteam**, Ottobrunn (Hintergrund Union Jack: Jon Arnold Images); **Mpixel/Achim Meissner**, Krefeld (Himmel).

Textquellen

S. 31: *Why is it?* by Shel Silverstein from "Falling up 10th Anniversary Edition". © Harper Collins Publishers, New York 2006; S. 57: *The frog on the log* by Ilo Orleans from: "Prepositions" by Ann Heinrichs, published by The Child's World, Chanhassen 2004; *The song of a mole* by Richard Edwards from: "The Word Party", published by Lutterworth Press, Cambridge 1986.

Liedquellen

S. 56: *I know an old lady.* K. & T.: Rosemary Bedeau, Alan Mills © Peermusic (Germany) GmbH, Hamburg; S. 105 *Summer Holiday.* K. & T.: Bruce Welch, Brian Bennett © Edition Accord Musikverlag GmbH & Co. KG c/o EMI Music Publishing Germany GmbH & KG.

Nicht alle Copyrightinhaber konnten ermittelt werden; deren Urheberrechte werden hiermit vorsorglich und ausdrücklich anerkannt.